SMIDGEN PRESS

Happily Owned By:

AN ESSAY TOWARDS A Philosophy of Education

CHARLOTTE MASON

Smidgen Press

An Essay Towards a Philosophy of Education
Centenary Expanded Edition

"Two Educational Ideals" chapter text courtesy of the Charlotte Mason Poetry transcription team.

"Some Impressions of the Ambleside Method" chapter text courtesy of the Charlotte Mason Institute.

Photos licensed from The Armitt Trust and used with permission.
ALM Box 36; 1958.871; Charlotte Mason c. 1920
CMC Box 29a; 2017.785.76; House of Education postcard

1st Foreword © 2022 by Deani Van Pelt
2nd Foreword © 2022 by Art Middlekauff
Cover design by Terri Shown
Book design by Skinner Book Services

Library of Congress Control Number: 2023900360

ISBNs: 978-1-950536-44-3 (paperback)
　　　　978-1-950536-45-0 (hardcover)
　　　　978-1-950536-46-7 (dust jacket hardcover)
　　　　978-1-950536-47-4 (Barnes & Noble paperback)
　　　　978-1-950536-48-1 (Barnes & Noble hardcover)
　　　　978-1-950536-49-8 (epub)

Special edition hardcover available exclusively at SmidgenPress.com

"All knowledge for all men."
—*Comenius.*

"Books, we know,
Are a substantial world, both pure and good,
Round which, with tendrils strong as flesh and blood,
Our pastime and our happiness will grow."
—*Wordsworth.*

HOUSE OF EDUCATION, AMBLESIDE.

This building, called Scale How, became the headquarters of Charlotte Mason's House of Education in 1894. It still stands as a listed historic building in Ambleside, Cumbria, England. Photo is property of The Armitt Trust and used with permission.

Some readers may find the original descriptive Contents pages to be helpful. Readers may download an enlarged printable copy, along with the original index, at SmidgenPress.com/centenary-extras.

Contents

Book I

Publisher's Note

Jody E. Skinner

When I set up Smidgen Press and put out my first book reprint in 2020, I did so with vague, hand-wave-y ideas about "preserving old books." The impetus was a treasure adopted in my teen years (an 1894 book found for fifty cents at a yard sale) and a wish that there was a non-fragile edition of it to share with friends.

With recognition decades after that book find—as I was then working as a proofreader, typesetter, and ebook formatter for indie authors—that there was a noticeable lack of quality in digital books, I knew I had something to contribute. I didn't really have an audience in mind other than . . . well, the people who liked old books, good old books, and who wanted these for their e-reader or their bookshelf.

In the process of looking for the readers who were in turn looking for good literature, I discovered an entire community of individuals and families who used the term "living books." As I got to know them and listened to what they were saying, I discovered that, yes, they were some of the readers and learners I wanted Smidgen Press to serve. And the more I heard about a woman called Charlotte Mason, the more I wanted to know even more about her and how she came to the concepts that feel right now like such revolutionary common sense: *letting* children learn, not making them, seeing them as a whole person and not only as information regurgitators.

The encounters that have paved the path and built the team for this project still amaze me.

A casual meeting in 2020 with a graphic designer who is a Charlotte Mason homeschooler gave me the courage to reach out to the University of Cumbria in 2021, as their grounds are where Mason's House of Education was headquartered. From them I was connected with The Armitt Museum and Library where Mason's artefacts are housed, and we started a conversation about a project honoring her.

Further connections with the Charlotte Mason Institute in 2022 led to me being informed that Mason intended this book you're reading not to be merely a series-ender but as a standalone. So then, *An Essay towards a Philosophy of Education* became *the project*: a more complete edition of Mason's final work, adding an appendix she had planned to include but which had been omitted prior to its posthumous publication. Then a timely article from Charlotte Mason Poetry supplied yet another missing link in the project's original design, a chapter omitted from "Supplementary"—now "Book III" to honor Mason's notes. The following forewords provide those details, and you can also read more at SmidgenPress.com/legacy-of-charlotte-mason.

I'm thrilled. And honored. What a humbling experience to bring an author's vision to life so many years later, and even more especially in the hundredth-year remembrance of her life so well lived.

What a joy that education—that learning—truly can be a delight.

—**Jody E. Skinner**
Founder, Smidgen Press

Foreword

Deani Van Pelt

In our twenty-first-century days, when parents and educators across the world are searching for an approach to education for their children and students that respects their personhood, that recognizes their physical, spiritual, and intellectual capacities, and that offers a vitalizing joy and fulness of life, many are encountering Charlotte Mason.

For those eager to become more deeply acquainted with Mason's design for education, *An Essay Towards a Philosophy of Education: A Liberal Education for All* offers a rich resource and a coherent philosophy of education, one to which the thoughtful educator will return often.

Charlotte Mason's first biographer, Essex Cholmondeley, in *The Story of Charlotte Mason* (1960), characterizes the last years of Mason's life as a time of focused occupation and productivity. "Despite frail health" she:

was finishing [this] her last book. Into it she gathered the experience and joy brought to her by the ten years' activity of the 'liberal education for all' movement. The book was an essay, a trial step towards the discovery of a philosophy of education ... Now during her last years she wrote for the men and women of the teaching world she had recently come to know so well ... No one can live without a philosophy which points out the means and end of effort ... Her last book makes such a philosophy available in education. (p. 176-177)

Mason begins this work with her view of the infinite possibilities of the child, that they are born persons with a hunger for knowledge and a need for the sustenance of great ideas. Along the way she encouragingly explains that education is an atmosphere, a discipline, and a life, and she reviews the scope of the curriculum of a liberal education—knowledge of God, of humans, and of the universe, a curriculum characterized by a literary voice and experienced acquaintance with the natural world. In the second part of the volume Mason includes her more recently published works (in *The Times* or in booklet form), all of which address the application of her theory in the education of *all* students—in elementary, secondary, and continuation schools. Throughout she makes the passionate plea that the education she proposed is for *all*.

One gets the sense that this volume is hardly a "trial step towards the discovery of philosophy of education," as

Cholmondeley claims, but rather that it is the distillation of a lifetime of work by a deeply thoughtful and vastly experienced education leader.

It was a life marked by humble beginnings and difficulty as Mason was orphaned by age sixteen. After she attended one of the few institutions of the day where teacher certification might be obtained (Home and Colonial School Society), Mason taught in a large infants' school, which took in over 200 children between four and seven years of age, and then taught in a teacher training institution (Bishop Otter College). Her life pivoted the year she gave a series of captivating talks on education—shortly thereafter published as "Home Education: A Course of Lectures to Ladies Delivered in Bradford, in the winter of 1885-1886". Within a few short years she then founded a Parents' National Educational Union (the P.N.E.U.), a monthly journal for parents (the *Parents' Review*), a teacher training college (the House of Education, later Charlotte Mason College and today a campus of the University of Cumbria), a network of schools, and a curriculum. Mason wrote extensively, including five geography books, six education volumes, at least six volumes on the gospels, and built lasting professional and personal friendships. Her death was marked by a valuable memorial book, *In Memoriam Charlotte M. Mason* (1923), and by a service at St. Martin-in-the-Fields in London several months later wherein many testified that her presence was an inspiration and her quiet charm remarkable.

Mason's six volumes on education have been frequently republished over the years. What makes this Centenary Edition unique?

It is unique in several ways—one in particular stands out. If you've ever held a first edition (1925) of *An Essay Towards a Philosophy of Education* you might have noticed these words just below the table of contents on page xxii:

> The Trustees have, at the request of the Publishers, been obliged to reduce the original volume. Two important sections on the practical work have been omitted,—(A)—Children's examination answers and, **(B)—Some discussions of the method by Educational Authorities and teachers. A pamphlet will be issued from the P.N.E.U. Office, 26, Victoria Street, S.W., covering section B** [bold added]. Sets of children's answers (A) can be seen at the P.N.E.U. Office, 26, Victoria Street, S.W.

When I first saw those words, I was curious about the last two sentences as they had been omitted in subsequent editions, not appearing in the second edition (1931), the third edition (1954), or in anything up to the 1989 reprints. I began wondering if I'd ever seen the P.N.E.U. pamphlet referred to in this note as **"Some discussions of the method by Educational Authorities and teachers"**.

Some years prior, through funding by the Social Sciences

and Humanities Research Council of Canada, support of Redeemer University and others, a small team of us had the opportunity to digitize some of the Charlotte Mason Collection (CMC) at the Armitt Museum in Ambleside, UK. Indeed, there had been such a booklet in the CMC, although with a slightly different title, "***Some Impressions of the Ambleside Method: Arranged by Charlotte M. Mason to accompany her last book, 'An Essay towards a Philosophy of Education.'***" It was the first part of the title that caught my attention at that time because it called Mason's approach to education "The Ambleside Method", a label I'd not seen used elsewhere in her writings. It was only later that I realized, this pamphlet, "***Some Impressions of the Ambleside Method***", was indeed the missing section B.

Thus, in this Centenary Edition of Mason's last volume, we have chosen to reprint the first edition from 1925 and we have decided to include the omitted section B as well. This, to our knowledge, is the first time "Some Discussions" (or shall we call it "Some Impressions"?) will appear with the volume. We think Mason would approve.

You can find the P.N.E.U. pamphlet "Some Impressions of the Ambleside Method" in several other places. It can be located in original booklet form in the Charlotte Mason Collection at the Armitt*.

---

* CMC Box 51 File 432, Modes 2017.1019, or in the Charlotte Mason Digital Collection at Internet Archive, via SmidgenPress.com/some-impressions.

Within its pages we find numerous testimonials of the benefits and pleasures of "The Ambleside Method." Consider, for example, from page 53, the words of Willingham F. Rawnsley, a founder of England's heritage preservation society the National Trust:

> Such then is the education by humanities ... Books have a tremendous influence on character, and to bring children up amongst good books is an education in itself. ... By means of well-selected books on various subjects many doors are opened to the children leading by pleasant paths to knowledge of birds and flowers and the nature of the earth and wonders of the starry heavens; and by the pictures they study and by the classic stories and modern fairy tales their emotions are stirred, and the realms of art and beauty opened to them. All this and not less than this is aimed at and certainly attained in considerable measure, whilst the life of the teacher is made easier and more joyful, to match the delights of the children in helping themselves to knowledge and power.

Mason has impacted many lives—thousands during her life and many thousands more in the century since. I count myself among those she has influenced both professionally and personally. While living within the context of a changing and evolving world, her courageous decades-long journeying within valued circles of friends and colleagues around key ideas and insights—which she carefully and attentively embodied institutionally—serve as a model to me of what it is to lead and learn and live life in all its fullness.

—**Deani Van Pelt, PhD**
Hamilton, Ontario, Canada
Board Chair, Charlotte Mason Institute,
Roanoke, Virginia, USA; November 2022

The Trustees have, at the request of the Publishers, been obliged to reduce the original volume. Two important sections on the practical work have been omitted,—(A)—Children's examination answers and, (B)—Some discussions of the method by Educational Authorities and teachers. A pamphlet will be issued from the P.N.E.U. Office, 26, Victoria Street, S.W., covering section B. Sets of children's answers (A) can be seen at the P.N.E.U. Office, 26, Victoria Street, S.W.

Excerpt from *Philosophy of Education*'s 1st edition contents, noting the removal of the material added in this edition as the Appendix.

Foreword

Art Middlekauff

The Fourteenth Annual P.N.E.U. Conference was held in July 1910 in London. Charlotte Mason was not present, but the conference opened with a reading of her new paper, presented by her friend Ella Glover. It was a unique essay entitled "Two Differing Ideals and a Danger." In it, Mason offered a close analysis of the work of Jean-Jacques Rousseau, much more thorough than the brief references in *Parents and Children*. As a contrast, she also interacted with the ideals of John Milton. Her paper was then published in *The Parents' Review* in November of the same year.*

Twelve years later, Mason was preparing the draft for her sixth volume, *Towards a Philosophy of Education*. She was racing against the clock to complete it before her passage to eternity. The volume was eventually published in three sections: Book I, Book II, and Supplementary. Mason's

---

* *The Parents' Review*, vol. 21, pp. 801–820.

handwritten notes*, however, clearly reveal that she intended for the third section to be entitled "Book III," not Supplementary. The "Supplementary" has only one chapter, the final chapter of the book, entitled "Too Wide a Mesh." But Mason planned for a second chapter. The title was to be "Two Educational Ideals."

Mason cut out her article from the 1910 *Parents' Review* and added handwritten notations for how she wanted it to be revised for her final book. Most notably, she changed the title from "Two Differing Ideals and a Danger" to "Two Educational Ideals." She also added a stirring pair of sentences about the heroism of British soldiers in the Great War, a war which she never failed to portray in salutary terms.

Sadly, the trustees ignored Mason's directions and summarily shortened "Book III" to a single chapter. The dropped chapter was not forgotten, however. The ever-faithful Elsie Kitching became the editor of *The Parents' Review*. In 1928, she (who else would it have been?) took Mason's annotations and had them typeset for publication at last. In the January issue, the article was published with this footnote: "A paper written for the P.N.E.U. Conference, 1910, and revised 1922."†

Later that year, the article was republished as a stand-alone booklet. Although I have never seen that booklet, several lists of "books and pamphlets" by Charlotte Mason

---

* See these notes in the Charlotte Mason Digital Collection by visiting SmidgenPress.com/handwritten-notes.
† *The Parents' Review*, vol. 39, p. 1.

from 1928 onwards begin with her sixth volume and end with "Two Educational Ideals." The existence of this pamphlet reflects a partial fulfilment of Mason's vision to have her paper widely disseminated and read. The excised chapter was reprinted again in the June 1940 *Parents' Review*, this time with the footnote "A paper written for the P.N.E.U. Conference, 1910, and revised 1922. The reader will add illustrations from his own reading of modern thinkers and movements since 1922."* An additional note at the end of the article reiterated that the text was available as a separate pamphlet.

This edition of *An Essay Towards a Philosophy of Education* is the first ever to restore the second chapter of Book III to its originally intended place. Using the text from the 1928 *Parents' Review*, the Smidgen Press edition fulfills Mason's vision and includes her description of two educational ideals, one progressive and one classical. A description that shows that she is not beholden to either, but to an authority that is higher than both.

—Art Middlekauff
Founder, Charlotte Mason Poetry
Canton, Michigan, USA
October 2022

---

* *The Parents' Review*, vol. 51, p. 314.

For Readers New to Charlotte Mason

If you are seeking an overview of Charlotte Mason's work and educational philosophy—this volume is a worthy pursuit. However, you'll quickly find Mason expects readers to be familiar with her previous writings and her then-currently-active organizations.

Here are some notes and perspectives that may be helpful.

Home Education

"Home Education" refers both to a single book and to a series named for it. In the 1880s, Mason gave a series of lectures, and in 1886 these were compiled into a book and given the title *Home Education*.

This was followed with more volumes over the next nineteen years, which you may see referenced in footnotes throughout this edition you're reading: *Parents and Children*; *School Education*; *Ourselves, Our Souls and Bodies* (sometimes printed in two volumes); and *Some Studies in the Formation of Character*.

As mentioned previously in this edition, *An Essay towards a Philosophy of Education* is now marketed as "Book 6" in the series but was not written specifically with the series in mind.

And regarding home education in general: Mason's writing does assume some parents would be teaching their own children, as we think of "homeschooling" today. But many households would have had tutors or governesses to help teach, or had other help in the home. We think it's worth mentioning that today's families may be relieved to realize not every family will do everything without help somewhere or finding some happy medium to their life and routine.

The P.N.E.U.

The Parents' National Educational Union (P.N.E.U.) was a British educational organization, founded first as a local group in 1887 called the P.E.U. (Parents' Educational Union), and renamed in 1890 with the "National" element added. In 1891 the organization was moved from Yorkshire to the town of Ambleside in the county of Cumbria (hence our Appendix's title "Some Impressions of the *Ambleside* Method").

The P.N.E.U. was established to promote the principles of character education, seeking to develop the whole person of each child and promoting a broad, well-rounded educational experience for all children. The organization worked to provide support and guidance for parents, teachers, tutors, governesses, anyone who wanted to implement Mason's thoughts on learning.

The P.U.S.

The first Parents' Union School (P.U.S.) was first called the Parents' Review School and was run by the P.N.E.U. It was intended to be a model for other schools, providing a high-quality education to students from a wide range of economic and social backgrounds. The idea that proper education should not only be for those who could afford it was revolutionary for its time, as was Mason's insistence that children from less privileged backgrounds could learn just as well as those from well-to-do families.

"The P.U.S." then became the label for the network of all schools and homes following the P.N.E.U. programmes each term. You can see case studies in the Appendix to this edition.

AN ESSAY TOWARDS

A Philosophy of Education

Reprints produced first by the Charlotte Mason Research Company, then Simply Charlotte Mason, Living Book Press, and the online editions at Ambleside Online and Charlotte Mason Poetry all share the same page numbering.

To facilitate referencing while allowing our edition's larger font to have its own pagination, we have preserved those original page numbers faintly in the margins, as you can see on the opposite page. These numbers fall near the original page breaks but are imprecise. For any citations using the original page numbers, we encourage you to seek out a previous edition for greatest accuracy.

Overleaf: Photograph of Charlotte Mason c. 1920; other pictured individuals unknown. Photo is property of The Armitt Trust and is used by permission.

Foreword

from the 1925 publication

Our forefathers trusted of yore to the rod and to coercion for the evoking in children of a love of learning. For the last fifty years we have rested our hopes on the enthusiasm of the teachers. But that enthusiasm, when not fictitious, often acts prejudicially by diverting the child's love of knowledge and new ideas into admiration for his teacher: and when that fails, as it frequently does, nothing is left, except extraneous and baneful appeals to self-interest.

Miss Mason saw and in this volume has explained that the natural and only quite wholesome way of teaching is to let the child's desire for knowledge operate in the schoolboy and guide the teacher. This means that without foregoing discipline, nor cutting ourselves off from tradition, we must continue experiments already being started in our elementary schools. These are based on the chastening fact that children learn best before we adults begin to teach them at all: and hence that however uncongenial the task may be, we must conform our teaching methods to those of Nature. The attempt has often been made before. But in this volume there is a rare combination of intuitive insight and practical sagacity. The author refused to believe that the collapse of the desire for knowledge between seven and seventeen years of age is inevitable. So must we.

—Edward Lyttelton, D.D.

Preface

It would seem a far cry from *Undine* to a 'liberal education' but there is a point of contact between the two;
a soul awoke within a water-sprite at the touch of love;
so, I have to tell of the awakening of a 'general soul' at the
touch of knowledge. Eight years ago* the 'soul' of a class of
children in a mining village school awoke simultaneously
at this magic touch and has remained awake. We know
that religion can awaken souls, that love makes a new man,
that the call of a vocation may do it, and in the age of the
Renaissance, men's souls, the general soul, awoke to knowledge: but this appeal rarely reaches the modern soul; and,
notwithstanding the pleasantness attending lessons and
marks in all our schools, I believe the ardour for knowledge
in the children of this mining village is a phenomenon that
indicates new possibilities. Already many thousands of the
children of the Empire had experienced this intellectual

---

* Now ten.

conversion, but they were the children of educated persons. To find that the children of a mining population were equally responsive seemed to open a new hope for the world. It may be that the souls of all children are waiting for the call of knowledge to awaken them to delightful living.

This is how the late Mrs. Francis Steinthal, who was the happy instigator of the movement in Council Schools, wrote,—"Think of the meaning of this in the lives of the children,—disciplined lives, and no lawless strikes, justice, an end to class warfare, developed intellects, and no market for trashy and corrupt literature! We shall, or rather they will, live in a redeemed world." This was written in a moment of enthusiasm on hearing that a certain County Council had accepted a scheme of work for this pioneer school; enthusiasm sees in advance the fields white to the harvest, but indeed the event is likely to justify high expectations. Though less than nine years have passed since that pioneer school made the bold attempt, already many thousands of children working under numerous County Councils are finding that "Studies serve for delight."

No doubt children are well taught and happy in their lessons as things are, and this was specially true of the school in question; yet both teachers and children find an immeasurable difference between the casual interest roused by marks, pleasing oral lessons and other school devices, and the sort of steady avidity for knowledge that comes with the awakened soul. The children have converted the school inspectors: "And the English!" said one of these in astonishment as he listened to their long, graphic, dramatic narrations of what they had heard. During the last thirty years we (including many fellow workers) have had thousands of children, in our schoolrooms, home and other, working on the lines of Dean Colet's prayer for St. Paul's School,—"Pray for the children to prosper in good life and good literature;" probably all children so taught grow up with such principles and pursuits as make for happy and useful citizenship.

I should like to add that we have no axe to grind. The public good is our aim; and the methods proposed are applicable in any school. My object in offering this volume to the public is to urge upon all who are concerned with education a few salient principles which are generally either unknown or disregarded; and a few methods which, like that bathing in Jordan, are too simple to commend them- selves to the 'general.' Yet these principles and methods make education entirely effectual.

I should like to add that no statement that I have advanced in the following volume rests upon opinion only. Every point has been proved in thousands of instances, and the method may be seen at work in many schools, large and small, Elementary and Secondary.

I have to beg the patience of the reader who is asked to approach the one terminus by various avenues, and I cannot do so better than in the words of old Fuller:—"Good Reader. I suspect I may have written some things twice; if not in the same words yet in sense, which I desire you to pass by favourably, forasmuch as you may well think, it was difficult and a dull thing for me in so great a number of independent sentences to find out the repetitions. . . . Besides the pains, such a search would cost me more time than I can afford it; for my glass of life running now low, I must not suffer one sand to fall in waste nor suffer one minute in picking of straws. . . . But to conclude this, since in matters of advice, Precept must be upon Precept, Line upon Line, I apologise in the words of St. Paul, 'To write the same things to you to me indeed is not grievous, but for you it is safe.'"

I am unwilling to close what is probably the last preface I shall be called upon to write without a very grateful recognition of the co-operation of those friends who are working with me in what seems to us a great cause. The Parents' National Educational Union has fulfilled its mission, as declared in its first prospectus, nobly and generously. "The Union exists for the benefit of parents and teachers of *all classes*;" and, for the last eight years[*] it has undertaken the labour and expense of an energetic propaganda on behalf of xxviii Elementary Schools, of which about 150[†] are now working on the programmes of the Parents' Union School. During the last year a pleasing and hopeful development has taken place under the auspices of the Hon. Mrs. Franklin. It was suggested to the Head of a London County Council School to form an association of the parents of the children in that

[*] Now ten.
[†] Now over 300 in 1924.

school, offering them certain advantages and requiring a small payment to cover expenses. At the first meeting one of the fathers present got up and said that he was greatly disappointed. He had expected to see some three hundred parents and there were only about sixty present! The promoters of the meeting were, however, well pleased to see the sixty, most of whom became members of the Parents' Association, and the work goes on with spirit.

We are deeply indebted to many fellow-workers, but not even that very courteous gentleman who once wrote a letter to the Romans could make suitable acknowledgments to all of those to whom we owe the success of a movement the *rationale* of which I attempt to make clear in the following pages.

CHARLOTTE M. MASON.
House of Education,
Ambleside.
1922

A Short Synopsis

"No sooner doth the truth . . . come into the soul's sight, but the soul knows her to be her first and old acquaintance."

"The consequence of truth is great; therefore the judgment of it must not be negligent." (Whichcote).

1. Children are born *persons*.

2. They are not born either good or bad, but with possibilities for good and for evil.

3. The principles of authority on the one hand, and of obedience on the other, are natural, necessary and fundamental; but—

4. These principles are limited by the respect due to the personality of children, which must not be encroached upon, whether by the direct use of fear or love, suggestion or influence, or by undue play upon any one natural desire.

5. Therefore, we are limited to three educational instruments—the atmosphere of environment, the discipline of habit, and the presentation of living ideas. The P.N.E.U. Motto is: "Education is an atmosphere, a discipline, and a life."

9

6. When we say that "*education is an atmosphere*," we do not mean that a child should be isolated in what may be called a 'child-environment' especially adapted and prepared, but that we should take into account the educational value of his natural home atmosphere, both as regards persons and things, and should let him live freely among his proper conditions. It stultifies a child to bring down his world to the 'child's' level.

7. By "*education is a discipline*," we mean the discipline of habits, formed definitely and thoughtfully, whether habits of mind or body. Physiologists tell us of the adaptation of brain structures to habitual lines of thought, *i.e.*, to our habits.

8. In saying that "*education is a life*," the need of intellectual and moral as well as of physical sustenance is implied. The mind feeds on ideas, and therefore children should have a generous curriculum.

9. We hold that the child's mind is no mere *sac* to hold ideas; but is rather, if the figure may be allowed, a spiritual *organism*, with an appetite for all knowledge. This is its proper diet, with which it is prepared to deal; and which it can digest and assimilate as the body does foodstuffs.

10. Such a doctrine as *e.g.* the Herbartian, that the mind is a receptacle, lays the stress of Education (the preparation of knowledge in enticing morsels duly ordered) upon the teacher. Children taught on this principle are in danger of receiving much teaching with little knowledge; and the teacher's axiom is "what a child learns matters less than how he learns it."

11. But we, believing that the normal child has powers of mind which fit him to deal with all knowledge proper to him, give him a full and generous curriculum; taking care only that all knowledge offered him is vital, that is, that facts are not presented without their informing ideas. Out of this conception comes our principle that,—

12. "*Education is the Science of Relations*"; that is, that a child has natural relations with a vast number of things and thoughts: so we train him upon physical exercises, nature lore, handicrafts, science and art, and upon *many living* books, for we know that our business is not to teach him all about anything, but to help him to make valid as many as may be of—

"Those first-born affinities
That fit our new existence to existing things."

13. In devising a Syllabus for a normal child, of whatever social class, three points must be considered:—

(*a*) He requires *much* knowledge, for the mind needs sufficient food as much as does the body.

(*b*) The knowledge should be various, for sameness in mental diet does not create appetite (*i.e.*, curiosity).

(*c*) Knowledge should be communicated in well-chosen language, because his attention responds naturally to what is conveyed in literary form.

14. As knowledge is not assimilated until it is reproduced, children should 'tell back' after a single reading or hearing: or should write on some part of what they have read.

15. A *single reading* is insisted on, because children have naturally great power of attention; but this force is dissipated by the re-reading of passages, and also, by questioning, summarising, and the like.

Acting upon these and some other points in the behaviour of mind, we find that *the educability of children is enormously greater than has hitherto been supposed*, and is but little dependent on such circumstances as heredity and environment.

Nor is the accuracy of this statement limited to clever children or to children of the educated classes: thousands of children in Elementary Schools respond freely to this method, which is based on the *behaviour of mind*.

16. There are two guides to moral and intellectual self-management to offer to children, which we may call 'the way of the will' and 'the way of the reason.'

17. *The way of the will*: Children should be taught, (*a*) to distinguish between 'I want' and 'I will.' (*b*) That the way to will effectively is to turn our thoughts from that which we desire but do not will. (*c*) That the best way to turn our thoughts is to think of or do some quite different thing, entertaining or interesting. (*d*) That after a little rest in this way, the will returns to its work with new vigour. (This adjunct of the will is familiar to us as *diversion*, whose

office it is to ease us for a time from will effort, that we may 'will' again with added power. The use of *suggestion* as an aid to the will *is to be deprecated*, as tending to stultify and stereotype character. It would seem that spontaneity is a condition of development, and that human nature needs the discipline of failure as well as of success.)

18. *The way of reason*: We teach children, too, not to 'lean (too confidently) to their own understanding'; because the function of reason is to give logical demonstration (*a*) of mathematical truth, (*b*) of an initial idea, accepted by the will. In the former case, reason is, practically, an infallible guide, but in the latter, it is not always a safe one; for, whether that idea be right or wrong, reason will confirm it by irrefragable proofs.

19. Therefore, children should be taught, as they become mature enough to understand such teaching, that the chief responsibility which rests on them as *persons* is the acceptance or rejection of ideas. To help them in this choice we give them principles of conduct, and a wide range of the knowledge fitted to them. These principles should save children from some of the loose thinking and heedless action which cause most of us to live at a lower level than we need.

20. We allow no separation to grow up between the intellectual and 'spiritual' life of children, but teach them that the Divine Spirit has constant access to their spirits, and is their continual Helper in all the interests, duties and joys of life.

Introduction

These are anxious days for all who are engaged in education. We rejoiced in the fortitude, valour and devotion shown by our men in the War and recognize that these things are due to the Schools as well as to the fact that England still breeds "very valiant creatures." It is good to know that "the whole army was illustrious." The heroism of our officers derives an added impulse from that tincture of 'letters' that every Public schoolboy gets, and those "playing fields" where boys acquire habits of obedience and command. But what about the abysmal ignorance shown in the wrong thinking of many of the men who stayed at home? Are we to blame? I suppose most of us feel that we are: for these men are educated as we choose to understand education, that is, they can read and write, think perversely, and follow an argument, though they are unable to detect a fallacy. If we ask in perplexity, why do so

15

many men and women seem incapable of generous impulse, of reasoned patriotism, of seeing beyond the circle of their own interests, is not the answer, that men are enabled for such things by education? These are the marks of educated persons; and when millions of men who should be the backbone of the country seem to be dead to public claims, we have to ask,—Why then are not these persons educated, and what have we given them in lieu of education?

Our errors in education, so far as we have erred, turn upon the conception we form of 'mind,' and the theory which has filtered through to most teachers implies the out-of-date notion of the development of 'faculties,' a notion which itself rests on the axiom that thought is no more than a function of the brain. Here we find the sole justification of the scanty curricula provided in most of our schools, for the tortuous processes of our teaching, for the mischievous assertion that "it does not matter what a child learns but only how he learns it." If we teach much and children learn little we comfort ourselves with the idea that we are 'developing' this or the other 'faculty.' A great future lies before the nation which shall perceive that knowledge is the sole concern of education proper, as distinguished from training, and that knowledge is the necessary daily food of the mind.

Teachers are looking out for the support of a sound theory, and such a theory must recognize with conviction the part mind plays in education and the conditions under which this prime agent acts. We want a philosophy of education which, admitting that thought alone appeals to mind, that thought begets thought, shall relegate to their proper subsidiary places all those sensory and muscular activities which are supposed to afford intellectual as well as physical training. The latter is so important in and for itself that it needs not to be bolstered up by the notion that it includes the whole, or the practically important part, of education. The same remark holds good of vocational training. Our journals ask with scorn,—"Is there no education but what is got out of books at school? Is not the lad who works in the fields getting education?" and the public lacks the courage to say definitely, "No, he is not," because there is no clear notion current as to what education means, and how it is to be distinguished from vocational training. But the people themselves begin to understand and to clamour for an education which shall qualify their children for life rather than for earning a living. As a matter of fact, it is the man who has read and thought on many subjects who is, with the necessary training, the most capable whether in handling tools, drawing plans, or keeping books. The more of a person we succeed in making a child, the better will he both fulfil his own life and serve society.

Much thoughtful care has been spent in ascertaining the causes of the German breakdown in character and conduct; the war scourge was symptomatic and the symptoms have been duly traced to their cause in the thoughts the people have been taught to think during three or four generations. We have heard much about Nietszche, Treitschke,

Bernhardi and the rest; but Professor Muirhead did us good service in carrying the investigation further back. Darwin's theories of natural selection, the survival of the fittest, the struggle for existence, struck root in Germany in fitting soil; and the ideas of the superman, the super state, the right of might—to repudiate treaties, to eliminate feebler powers, to recognize no law but expediency—all this appears to come as naturally out of Darwinism as a chicken comes out of an egg. No doubt the same *dicta* have struck us in the *Commentaries* of Frederick the Great; "they shall take who have the power, and they shall keep who can," is ages older than Darwin, but possibly this is what our English philosopher did for Germany:—There is a tendency in human nature to elect the obligations of natural law in preference to those of spiritual law; to take its code of ethics from science, and, following this tendency, the Germans found in their reading of Darwin sanction for manifestations of brutality.

4   Here are a few examples of how German philosophers amplify the Darwinian text:—"In matter dwell all natural and spiritual potencies. Matter is the foundation of all being." "What we call spirit, thought, the faculty of knowledge, consists of natural though peculiarly combined forces." Darwin himself protests against the struggle for existence being the most potent agency where the higher part of man's nature is concerned, and he no more thought of giving a materialistic tendency to modern education than Locke thought of teaching principles which should bring about the French Revolution; but men's thoughts are more

potent than they know, and these two Englishmen may be credited with influencing powerfully two world-wide movements. In Germany, "prepared by a quarter of a century of materialistic thought," the teaching of Darwin was accepted as offering emancipation from various moral restraints. Ernst Haeckel, his distinguished follower, finds in the law of natural selection sanction for Germany's lawless action, and also, that pregnant doctrine of the superman. "This principle of selection is nothing less than democratic; on the contrary it is aristocratic in the strictest sense of the word." We know how Büchner, again, simplified and popularised these new theories,—"All the faculties which we include under the name of psychical activities are only functions of the brain substance. Thought stands in the same relation to the brain as the gall to the liver."

What use, or misuse, Germany has made of the teaching of Darwin would not (save for the War) be of immediate concern to us, were it not that she has given us back our own in the form of that "mythology of faculty psychology" which is all we possess in the way of educational thought. English psychology proper has advanced if not to firm ground, at any rate to the point of repudiating the 'faculty' basis. "However much assailed, the concept of a 'mind' is," we are told, "to be found in all psychological writers."* But there are but mind and matter, and when we are told again

---

* I quote from the article on Psychology in the *Encyclopaedia Britannica* as being the most likely to exhibit the authoritative position.

that "psychology rests on feeling," where are we? Is there a middle region?

II

We fail to recognise that as the body requires wholesome food and cannot nourish itself upon *any* substance so the mind too requires meat after its kind. If the War taught nothing else it taught us that men are spirits, that the spirit, mind, of a man is more than his flesh, that his spirit *is* the man, that for the thoughts of his heart he gives the breath of his body. As a consequence of this recognition of our spiritual nature, the lesson for us at the moment is that the great thoughts, great events, great considerations, which form the background of our national thought, shall be the content of the education we pass on.

The educational thought we hear most about is, as I have said, based on sundry Darwinian axioms out of which we get the notion that nothing matters but physical fitness and vocational training. However important these are, they are not the chief thing. A century ago when Prussia was shipwrecked in the Napoleonic wars it was discovered that not Napoleon but Ignorance was the formidable national enemy; a few philosophers took the matter in hand, and history, poetry, philosophy, proved the salvation of a ruined nation, because such studies make for the development of personality, public spirit, initiative, the qualities of which the State was in need, and which most advance individual happiness and success. On the other hand, the period when Germany made her school curriculum utilitarian marks 6 the beginning of her moral downfall. History repeats itself. There are interesting rumours afloat of how the students at Bonn, for example, went in solemn procession to make a bonfire of French novels, certain prints, articles of luxury and the like; things like these had brought about the ruin of Germany and it was the part of the youth to save her now as before. Are they to have another Tugendbund?

We want an education which shall nourish the mind while not neglecting either physical or vocational training; in short, we want a working philosophy of education. I think that we of the P.N.E.U. have arrived at such a body of theory, tested and corrected by some thirty years of successful practice with thousands of children. This theory has already been set forth in volumes* published at intervals during the last thirty-five years; so I shall indicate here only a few salient points which seem to me to differ from general theory and practice,—

(*a*) The children, not the teachers, are the responsible persons; they do the work by self-effort.
(*b*) The teachers give sympathy and occasionally elucidate, sum up or enlarge, but the actual work is done by the scholars.
(*c*) These read in a term one, or two, or three thousand pages, according to their age, school and Form, in

* *The Home Education Series.*

a large number of set books. The quantity set for each lesson allows of only a single reading; but the reading is tested by narration, or by writing on a test passage. When the terminal examination is at hand so much ground has been covered that revision is out of the question; what the children have read they know, and write on any part of it with ease and fluency, in vigorous English; they usually spell well.

7   Much is said from time to time to show that 'mere book-learning' is rather contemptible, and that "Things are in the saddle and ride mankind." May I point out that whatever discredit is due to the use of books does not apply to this method, which so far as I can discover has not hitherto been employed. Has an attempt been made before on a wide scale to secure that scholars should know their books, many pages in many books, at a single reading, in such a way that months later they can write freely and accurately on any part of the term's reading?

(*d*) There is no selection of studies, or of passages or of episodes, on the ground of interest. The best available book is chosen and is read through perhaps in the course of two or three years.

(*e*) The children study many books on many subjects, but exhibit no confusion of thought, and 'howlers' are almost unknown.

(*f*) They find that, in Bacon's phrase, "Studies serve for

delight"; this delight being not in the lessons or the personality of the teacher, but purely in their 'lovely books,' 'glorious books.'

(*g*) The books used are, whenever possible, literary in style.

(*h*) Marks, prizes, places, rewards, punishments, praise, blame, or other inducements are not necessary to secure attention, which is voluntary, immediate and surprisingly perfect.

(*i*) The success of the scholars in what may be called disciplinary subjects, such as Mathematics and Grammar, depends largely on the power of the teacher, though the pupils' habit of attention is of use in these too.

(*j*) No stray lessons are given on interesting subjects; the knowledge the children get is consecutive.

The unusual interest children show in their work, their power of concentration, their wide, and as far as it goes, accurate knowledge of historical, literary and some scientific subjects, has challenged attention and the general conclusion is that these are the children of educated and cultivated parents. It was vain to urge that the home schoolroom does not usually produce remarkable educational results; but the way is opening to prove that the power these children show is common to *all* children; at last there is hope that the offspring of working-class parents may be led into the wide pastures of a liberal education. 8

Are we not justified in concluding that singular effects must have commensurate causes, and that we have chanced to light on unknown tracts in the region of educational thought. At any rate that GOLDEN RULE of which Comenius was in search has discovered itself, the Rule,—"WHEREBY TEACHERS SHALL TEACH LESS AND SCHOLARS SHALL LEARN MORE."

Let me now outline a few of the educational principles which account for unusual results.

III

PRINCIPLES HITHERTO UNRECOGNIZED
OR DISREGARDED

I have enumerated some of the points in which our work is exceptional in the hope of convincing the reader that unusual work carried on successfully in hundreds of school-rooms—home and other—is based on principles hitherto unrecognized. The recognition of these principles should put our national education on an intelligent basis and should make for general stability, joy in living, and personal initiative.

May I add one or two more arguments in support of my plea,—

9   The appeal is not to the clever child only, but to the average and even to the 'backward' child.

This scheme is carried out in less time than ordinary school work on the same subjects.

There are no revisions, no evening lessons, no cramming or 'getting up' of subjects; therefore there is much time whether for vocational work or interests or hobbies.

All intellectual work is done in the hours of morning school, and the afternoons are given to field nature studies, drawing, handicrafts, etc. Notwithstanding these limitations the children produce a surprising amount of good intellectual work.

No home-work is required.

It is not that 'we' (of the P.N.E.U.) are persons of peculiar genius; it is that, like Paley's man who found the watch, "we have chanced on a good thing."

> "No gain
> That I experience must remain unshared."

We feel that the country and indeed the world should have the benefit of educational discoveries which act powerfully as a moral lever, for we are experiencing anew the joy of the Renaissance, but without its pagan lawlessness.

Let me trace as far as I can recall them the steps by which I arrived at some of the conclusions upon which we are acting. While still a young woman I saw a great deal of a family of Anglo-Indian children who had come 'home' to their grandfather's house and were being brought up by an aunt who was my intimate friend. The children were astonishing to me; they were persons of generous impulses and sound judgment, of great intellectual aptitude, of imagination and moral insight. These last two points were, I recollect, illustrated one day by a little maiden of five who came home from her walk silent and sad; some letting alone, and some wise openings brought out at last between sobs,—"a poor man—no home—nothing to eat—no bed to lie upon,"—and then the child was relieved by tears. Such incidents are common enough in families, but they were new to me. I was reading a good deal of philosophy and 'Education' at the time for I thought with the enthusiasm of a young teacher that Education should regenerate the world. I had an Elementary School and a pioneer Church High School at this same time so that I was enabled to study children in large groups; but at school children are not so self-revealing as at home. I began under the guidance of these Anglo-Indian children to take the measure of a *person* and soon to suspect that children are *more* than we, their elders, except that their ignorance is illimitable.

One limitation I did discover in the minds of these little people; my friend insisted that they could not understand English Grammar; I maintained that they could and wrote a little Grammar (still waiting to be prepared for publication!) for the two of seven and eight; but she was right; I was allowed to give the lessons myself with what lucidity and freshness I could command; in vain; the Nominative 'Case' baffled them; their minds rejected the abstract conception just as children reject the notion of writing an "Essay on Happiness." But I was beginning to make discoveries; the second being, that the mind of a child takes or rejects according to its needs.

From this point it was not difficult to go on to the perception that, whether in taking or rejecting, the mind was functioning for its own nourishment; that the mind, in fact, requires sustenance as does the body, in order that it increase and be strong; but because the mind is not to be measured or weighed but is spiritual, so its sustenance must be spiritual too, must, in fact, be ideas (in the Platonic sense of images). I soon perceived that children were well equipped to deal with ideas, and that 11 explanations, questionings, amplifications, are unnecessary and wearisome. Children have a natural appetite for knowledge which is informed with thought. They bring imagination, judgment, and the various so-called 'faculties,' to bear upon a new idea pretty much as the gastric juices act upon a food ration. This was illuminating but rather startling; the whole intellectual apparatus of the teacher, his power of vivid presentation, apt illustration, able summing up, subtle questioning, all these were hindrances and intervened between children and the right nutriment duly served; this, on the other hand, they received with the sort of avidity and simplicity with which a healthy child eats his dinner.

The Scottish school of philosophers came to my aid here with what may be called their doctrine of the desires, which, I perceived, stimulate the action of mind and so cater for spiritual (not necessarily religious) sustenance as the appetites do for that of the body and for the continuance of the race. This was helpful; I inferred that one of these, the Desire of Knowledge (Curiosity) was the chief instrument of education; that this desire might be paralysed or made powerless like an unused limb by encouraging other desires to intervene between a child and the knowledge proper for him; the desire for place,—emulation; for prizes,—avarice; for power,—ambition; for praise,—vanity, might each be a stumbling block to him. It seemed to me that we teachers had unconsciously elaborated a system which should secure the discipline of the schools and the eagerness of the scholars,—by means of marks, prizes, and the like,—and yet eliminate that knowledge-hunger, itself the quite sufficient incentive to education.

Then arose the question,—Cannot people get on with little knowledge? Is it really necessary after all? My child-friends supplied the answer: their insatiable curiosity shewed me that the wide world and its history was barely enough to satisfy a child who had not been made apathetic by spiritual malnutrition. What, then, is knowledge?—was the next question that occurred; a question which the intellectual labour of ages has not settled; but perhaps this is enough to go on with;—that only becomes knowledge to a person which he has assimilated, which his mind has acted upon.

Children's aptitude for knowledge and their eagerness for it made for the conclusion that the field of a child's knowledge may not be artificially restricted, that he has a right to and necessity for as much and as varied knowledge as he is able to receive; and that the limitations in his curriculum should depend only upon the age at which he must leave school; in a word, a *common* curriculum (up to the age of say, fourteen or fifteen) appears to be due to all children.

We have left behind the feudal notion that intellect is a class prerogative, that intelligence is a matter of inheritance and environment; inheritance, no doubt, means much but everyone has a very mixed inheritance; environment makes for satisfaction or uneasiness, but education is of the spirit and is not to be taken in by the eye or effected by the hand; mind appeals to mind and thought begets thought and that is how we become educated. For this reason we owe it to every child to put him in communication with great minds that he may get at great thoughts; with the minds, that is, of those who have left us great works; and the only vital method of education appears to be that children should read worthy books, many worthy books.

It will be said on the one hand that many schools have their own libraries or the scholars have the free use of a public library and that children do read; and on the other that the literary language of first-rate books offers an impassable barrier to working-men's children. In the first place we all know that desultory reading is delightful and incidentally profitable but is not *education* whose concern is *knowledge*. That is, the mind of the desultory reader only rarely makes the act of appropriation which is necessary before the matter we read becomes personal knowledge. We must read in order to know or we do not know by reading.

As for the question of literary form, many circumstances and considerations which it would take too long to describe brought me to perceive that delight in literary form is native to us all until we are 'educated' out of it.

It is difficult to explain how I came to a solution of a puzzling problem,—how to secure attention. Much observation of children, various incidents from one's general reading, the recollection of my own childhood and the consideration of my present habits of mind brought me to the recognition of certain laws of the mind, by working in accordance with which the steady attention of children of any age and any class in society is insured, week in, week out,—attention, not affected by distracting circumstances. It is not a matter of 'personal magnetism,' for hundreds of teachers of very varying quality, working in home schoolrooms and in Elementary and Secondary Schools on this method*, secure it without effort; neither does it rest upon the 'doctrine of interest'; no doubt the scholars are interested, sometimes delighted; but they are interested in a great variety of matters and their attention does not flag in the 'dull parts.'

It is not easy to sum up in a few short sentences those principles upon which the mind naturally acts and which I have tried to bring to bear upon a school curriculum. The fundamental idea is, that children are *persons* and are therefore moved by the same springs of conduct as their elders. Among these is the Desire of Knowledge, knowledge-hunger being natural to everybody. History, Geography, the

14

---

* In connection with the *Parents' Union School.*

thoughts of other people, roughly, the humanities, are proper for us all, and are the objects of the natural desire of knowledge. So too, are Science, for we all live in the world; and Art, for we all require beauty, and are eager to know how to discriminate; social science, Ethics, for we are aware of the need to learn about the conduct of life; and Religion, for, like those men we heard of at the Front, we all 'want God.'

In the nature of things then the unspoken demand of children is for a wide and very varied curriculum; it is necessary that they should have some knowledge of the wide range of interests proper to them as human beings, and for no reasons of convenience or time limitations may we curtail their proper curriculum.

Perceiving the range of knowledge to which children as persons are entitled the questions are, how shall they be induced to take that knowledge, and what can the children of the people learn in the short time they are at school? We have discovered a working answer to these two conundrums. I say discovered, and not invented, for there is only one way of learning, and the intelligent persons who can talk well on many subjects and the expert in one learn in the one way, that is, *they read to know*. What I have found out is, that this method is available for every child, whether in the dilatory and desultory home schoolroom or in the large classes of Elementary Schools.

Children no more come into the world without provision for dealing with knowledge than without provision for dealing with food. They bring with them not only that intellectual appetite, the desire of knowledge, but also an enormous, an unlimited power of attention to which the power of retention (memory) seems to be attached, as one digestive process succeeds another, until the final assimilation. "Yes," it will be said, "they are capable of much curiosity and consequent attention but they can only occasionally be beguiled into attending to their lessons." Is not that the fault of the lessons, and must not these be regulated as carefully with regard to the behaviour of mind as the children's meals are with regard to physical considerations?

Let us consider this behaviour in a few aspects. The mind concerns itself only with thoughts, imaginations, reasoned arguments; it declines to assimilate the facts unless in combination with its proper pabulum; it, being active, is wearied in the passive attitude of a listener, it is as much bored in the case of a child by the discursive twaddle of the talking teacher as in that of a grown-up by conversational twaddle; it has a natural preference for literary form; given a more or less literary presentation, the curiosity of the mind is enormous and embraces a vast variety of subjects.

I predicate these things of 'the mind' because they seem true of all persons' minds. Having observed these, and some other points in the behaviour of mind, it remained to apply the conclusions to which I had come to a test curriculum for schools and families. Oral teaching was to a great extent ruled out; a large number of books on many subjects were set for reading in morning school-hours; so much work was set that there was only time for a single reading; all reading was tested by a narration of the whole or a given passage, whether orally or in writing. Children working on these lines know months after that which they have read and are remarkable for their power of concentration (attention); they have little trouble with spelling or composition and become well-informed, intelligent persons.*

But, it will be said, reading or hearing various books read, chapter by chapter, and then narrating or writing what has been read or some part of it,—all this is mere memory work. The value of this criticism may be readily tested; will the critic read before turning off his light a leading article from a newspaper, say, or a chapter from Boswell or Jane Austen, or one of Lamb's Essays; then, will he put himself to sleep by narrating silently what he has read. He will not be satisfied with the result but he will find that in the act of narrating every power of his mind comes into play, that points and bearings which he had not observed are brought out; that the whole is visualized and brought into relief in an extraordinary way; in fact, that scene or argument has become a part of his personal experience; he *knows*, he has assimilated what he has read. *This is not memory work.* In

16

---

* The small Practising School attached to the House of Education (ages of scholars from six to eighteen) affords opportunities for testing the programmes of work sent out term by term, and the examinations set at the end of each term. The work in each Form is easily done in the hours of morning-school.

order to memorise, we repeat over and over a passage or a series of points or names with the aid of such clues as we can invent; we do memorise a string of facts or words, and the new possession serves its purpose for a time, but it is not assimilated; its purpose being served, we know it no more. This is memory work by means of which examinations are passed with credit. I will not try to explain (or understand!) this power to memorise; it has its subsidiary use in education, no doubt, but it must not be put in the place of the prime agent which is *attention*.

Long ago, I was in the habit of hearing this axiom quoted by a philosophical old friend:—"The mind can know nothing save what it can produce in the form of an answer to a question put to the mind by itself." I have failed to trace the saying to its source, but a conviction of its importance has been growing upon me during the last forty years. It tacitly prohibits questioning from without; (this does not, of course, affect the Socratic use of questioning for purposes of *moral* conviction); and it is necessary to intellectual certainty, to the act of knowing. For example, to secure a conversation or an incident, we 'go over it in our minds'; that is, the mind puts itself through the process of self-questioning which I have indicated. This is what happens in the narrating of a passage read: each new consecutive incident or statement arrives because the mind asks itself,—"What next?" For this reason it is important that only one reading should be allowed; efforts to memorise weaken the power of attention, the proper activity of the mind; if it is desirable

17

to ask questions in order to emphasize certain points, these should be asked after and not before, or during, the act of narration.

Our more advanced psychologists come to our support here; they, too, predicate "instead of a congerie of faculties, a single subjective activity, attention;" and again, there is "one common factor in all psychical activity, that is attention."* My personal addition is that attention is unfailing, prompt and steady when matter is presented suitable to a child's intellectual requirements, *if* the presentation be made with the conciseness, directness, and simplicity proper to literature.

Another point should be borne in mind; the intellect requires a moral impulse, and we all stir our minds into action the better if there is an implied 'must' in the background; for children in class the 'must' acts through the *certainty* that they will be required to narrate or write from what they have read with no opportunity of 'looking up,' or other devices of the idle. Children find the act of narrating so pleasurable in itself that urgency on the part of the teacher is seldom necessary.

Here is a complete chain of the educational philosophy I 18
have endeavoured to work out, which has, at least, the merit that it is successful in practice. Some few hints I have, as I have said, adopted and applied, but I hope I have succeeded in methodising the whole and making education what it

---

* I again quote from the article on Psychology in the *Encyclopaedia Brittanica*.

should be, a system of applied philosophy; I have, however, carefully abstained from the use of philosophical terms.

This is, briefly, how it works:—

A child is a *person* with the spiritual requirements and capabilities of a person.

Knowledge 'nourishes' the mind as food nourishes the body.

A child requires knowledge as much as he requires food.

He is furnished with the desire for Knowledge, i.e., Curiosity;

> with the power to apprehend Knowledge, that is, attention;
>
> with powers of mind to deal with Knowledge without aid from without—such as imagination, reflection, judgment;
>
> with innate interest in all Knowledge that he needs as a human being;
>
> with power to retain and communicate such Knowledge; and to assimilate all that is necessary to him.

He requires that in most cases Knowledge be communicated to him in literary form;

> and reproduces such Knowledge touched by his own personality; thus his reproduction becomes original.

The natural provision for the appropriation and assimilation of Knowledge is adequate and no stimulus is required; but some moral control is necessary to secure the act of attention;

> a child receives this in the certainty that he will　19
> be required to recount what he has read.

Children have a right to the best we possess; therefore their lesson books should be, as far as possible, our best books.

They weary of talk, and questions bore them, so that they should be allowed to use their books for themselves; they will ask for such help as they wish for.

They require a great variety of knowledge,—about religion, the humanities, science, art;

> therefore, they should have a wide curriculum, with a definite amount of reading set for each short period of study.

The teacher affords direction, sympathy in studies, a vivifying word here and there, help in the making of experiments, etc., as well as the usual teaching in languages, experimental science and mathematics.

Pursued under these conditions, "Studies serve for delight," and the consciousness of daily progress is exhilarating to both teacher and children.

The reader will say with truth,—"I knew all this before and have always acted more or less on these principles"; and

I can only point to the unusual results we obtain through adhering not 'more or less,' but strictly to the principles and practices I have indicated. I suppose the difficulties are of the sort that Lister had to contend with; every surgeon knew that his instruments and appurtenances should be kept clean, but the saving of millions of lives has resulted from the adoption of the great surgeon's antiseptic treatment; that is from the substitution of exact principles scrupulously applied for the rather casual 'more or less' methods of earlier days.

20   Whether the way I have sketched out is the right and the only way remains to be tested still more widely than in the thousands of cases in which it has been successful; but assuredly education is slack and uncertain for the lack of sound principles *exactly* applied. The moment has come for a decision; we have placed our faith in 'civilisation,' have been proud of our progress; and of the pangs that the War has brought us, perhaps none is keener than that caused by the utter breakdown of the civilisation which we have held to be synonymous with education. We know better now, and are thrown back on our healthy human instincts and the Divine sanctions. The educable part of a person is his mind. The training of the senses and muscles is, strictly speaking, training and not education. The mind, like the body, requires quantity, variety and regularity in the sustenance offered to it. Like the body, the mind has its appetite, the desire for knowledge. Again, like the body,

the mind is able to receive and assimilate by its powers of attention and reflection. Like the body, again, the mind rejects insipid, dry, and unsavoury food, that is to say, its pabulum should be presented in a literary form. The mind is restricted to pabulum of one kind: it is nourished upon ideas and absorbs facts only as these are connected with the living ideas upon which they hang. Children educated upon some such lines as these respond in a surprising way, developing capacity, character, countenance, initiative and a sense of responsibility. They are, in fact, even as children, good and thoughtful citizens.

I have in this volume attempted to show the principles and methods upon which education of this sort is being successfully carried out, and have added chapters which illustrate the history of a movement the aim of which is, in the phrase of Comenius,—"All knowledge for all men." As well as these I have been permitted to use the criticisms* of various teachers and Directors of education and others 21 upon the practical working of the scheme.

It is a matter of rejoicing that the way is open to give to all classes a basis of common thought and common knowledge, including a common store of literary and historic allusions, a possession which has a curious power of cementing bodies of men, and, in the next place, it is an enormous gain that we are within sight of giving to the

---

* See *Some Discussions of the Method*. (P.N.E.U. Office, 1/–). [Now the Appendix to this edition, p. 501.]

working-classes, notwithstanding their limited opportunities, that stability of mind and magnanimity of character which are the proper outcome and the unfailing test of A LIBERAL EDUCATION.

I shall confine myself in this volume to the amplification and illustration of some of the points I have endeavoured to make in this introductory statement.

Book 1

Chapter 1

Self-Education

The title of this chapter may awaken some undeserved sympathy; gratifying visions of rhythmic
movements, independent action, self-expression
in various interesting ways, occur to the mind—for surely
these things constitute 'self-education'? Most of these modern panacea are desirable and by no means to be neglected;
limbs trained to grace and agility, a hand, to dexterity and
precision, an eye made to see and an ear to hear, a voice
taught to interpret,—we know to-day that all these possibilities of joy in living should be open to every child, and we
look forward even too hopefully to the manner of citizen
who shall be the outcome of our educational zeal.

Now, although we, of the Parents' Union, have initiated
some of these educational outworks and have gladly and
gratefully adopted others, yet is our point of view different;
we are profoundly sceptical as to the effect of all or any of

these activities upon character and conduct. A person is not built up from without but from within, that is, he is *living*, and all external educational appliances and activities which are intended to mould his character are decorative and not vital.

This sounds like a stale truism; but, let us consider a few corollaries of the notion that 'a child is a person,' and that a person is, primarily, living. Now no external application is capable of nourishing life or promoting growth; baths of wine, wrappings of velvet have no effect upon physical life except as they may hinder it; life is sustained on that which is taken in by the organism, not by that which is applied from without.

Perhaps the only allowable analogy with the human mind is the animal body, especially the human body, for it is that which we know most about; the well-worn plant and garden analogy is misleading, especially as regards that tiresome busybody, the gardener, who *will* direct the inclination of every twig, the position of every leaf; but, even then apart from the gardener, the child-garden is an intolerable idea as failing to recognize the essential property of a child, his personality, a property all but absent in a plant. Now, let us consider for a moment the parallel behaviour of body and mind. The body lives by air, grows on food, demands rest, flourishes on a diet wisely various. So, of the mind,—(by which I mean the entire spiritual nature, all that which is not body),—it breathes in air, calls for both activity and rest and flourishes on a wisely varied dietary.

We go round the house and round the house, but rarely go into the House of Mind; we offer mental gymnastics, but these do not take the place of food, and of that we serve the most meagre rations, no more than that bean a day! Diet for the body is abundantly considered, but no one pauses to say, "I wonder does the mind need food, too, and regular meals, and what is its proper diet?"

I have asked myself this question and have laboured for fifty years to find the answer, and am anxious to impart what I think I know, but the answer cannot be given in the form of 'Do' this and that, but rather as an invitation to 'Consider' this and that; action follows when we have thought duly.

The life of the mind is sustained upon ideas; there is 25 no intellectual vitality in the mind to which ideas are not presented several times, say, every day. But 'surely, surely,' as 'Mrs. Proudie' would say, scientific experiments, natural beauty, nature study, rhythmic movements, sensory exercises, are all fertile in ideas? Quite commonly, they are so, as regards ideas of invention and discovery; and even in ideas of art; but for the moment it may be well to consider the ideas that influence life, that is, character and conduct; these, it would seem, pass directly from mind to mind, and are neither helped nor hindered by educational outworks. Every child gets many of these ideas by word of mouth, by way of family traditions, proverbial philosophy,—in fact, by what we might call a kind of oral literature. But, when we compare the mind with the body, we perceive that three 'square' meals a day are generally necessary to health, and that a casual diet of ideas is poor and meagre. Our schools turn out a good many clever young persons, wanting in nothing but initiative, the power of reflection and the sort of moral imagination which enables you to 'put yourself in his place.' These qualities flourish upon a proper diet; and this is not afforded by the ordinary school book, or, in sufficient quantity by the ordinary lesson. I should like to emphasize *quantity*, which is as important for the mind as for the body; both require their 'square meals.'

It is no easy matter to give its proper sustenance to the mind; hard things are said of children, that they have 'no brains,' 'a low order of intellect,' and so on; but many of us are able to vouch for the fine intelligence shewn by children who are fed with the proper mind-stuff; but teachers do not usually take the trouble to find out what this is. We come dangerously near to what Plato condemns as "that lie of the soul," that corruption of the highest truth, of which Protagoras is guilty in the saying that, "Knowledge is sensation." What else are we saying when we run after educational methods which are purely sensory? Knowledge is not sensation, nor is it to be derived through sensation; we feed upon the thoughts of other minds; and thought applied to thought generates thought and we become more thoughtful. No one need invite us to reason, compare, imagine; the mind, like the body, digests its proper food, and it must have the labour of digestion or it ceases to function.

But the children ask for bread and we give them a stone; we give information about objects and events which mind does not attempt to digest but casts out bodily (upon an examination paper?). But let information hang upon a principle, be inspired by an idea, and it is taken with avidity and used in making whatsoever in the spiritual nature stands for tissue in the physical.

"Education," said Lord Haldane, some time ago, "is a matter of the spirit,"—no wiser word has been said on the subject, and yet we persist in applying education from without as a bodily activity or emollient. We begin to see light. No one knoweth the things of a man but the spirit of a man which is in him; therefore, there is no education but self-education, and as soon as a young child begins his education he does so as a student. Our business is to give him mind-stuff, and both quality and quantity are essential. Naturally, each of us possesses this mind-stuff only in limited measure, but we know where to procure it; for the best thought the world possesses is stored in books; we must open books to children, the best books; our own concern is abundant provision and orderly serving.

I am jealous for the children; every modern educational movement tends to belittle them intellectually; and none more so than a late ingenious attempt to feed normal children with the pap-meat which may (?) be good for the mentally sick: but, "To all wildly popular things comes suddenly and inexorably death, without hope of resurrection." If Mr. Bernard Shaw is right, I need not discuss a certain 27 popular form of 'New Education.' It has been ably said that education should profit by the divorce which is now in progress from psychology on the one hand and sociology on the other; but what if education should use her recovered liberty to make a monstrous alliance with pathology?

Various considerations urge upon me a rather distasteful task. It is time I showed my hand and gave some account of work, the principles and practices of which should, I think, be of general use. Like those lepers who feasted at the gates of a famished city, I begin to take shame to myself! I have attempted to unfold (in various volumes*) a system of educational theory which seems to me able to meet any rational demand, even that severest criterion set up by Plato; it is able to "run the gauntlet of objections, and is ready to disprove them, not by appeals to opinion, but to absolute truth." Some of it is new, much of it is old. Like the quality of mercy, it is not strained; certainly it is twice blessed, it blesses him that gives and him that takes, and a sort of radiancy of look distinguishes both scholar and teacher engaged in this manner of education; but there are no startling results to challenge attention.

Professor Bompas Smith remarked in an inaugural address at the University of Manchester that,—"If we can guide our practice by the light of a comprehensive theory we shall widen our experience by attempting tasks which would not otherwise have occurred to us." It is possible to offer the light of such a comprehensive theory, and the

---

* The Home Education Series.

result is precisely what the Professor indicates,—a large number of teachers attempt tasks which would not otherwise have occurred to them. One discovers a thing because it is there, and no sane person takes credit to himself for such discovery. On the contrary, he recognizes with King Arthur,—"These jewels, whereupon I chanced Divinely, are for public use." For many years we have had access to a sort of Aladdin's cave which I long to throw open 'for public use.' 28

Let me try to indicate some of the advantages of the theory I am urging:—It fits all ages, even the seven ages of man! It satisfies brilliant children and discovers intelligence in the dull. It secures attention, interest, concentration, without effort on the part of teacher or taught.

Children, I think, all children, so taught express themselves in forcible and fluent English and use a copious vocabulary. An unusual degree of nervous stability is attained; also, intellectual occupation seems to make for chastity in thought and life. Parents become interested in the schoolroom work, and find their children 'delightful companions.' Children shew delight in books (other than story books) and manifest a genuine love of knowledge. Teachers are relieved from much of the labour of corrections. Children taught according to this method do exceptionally well at any school. It is unnecessary to stimulate these young scholars by marks, prizes, etc.

After all, it is not a quack medicine I am writing about, though the reader might think so, and there is no 1s./1½d. a bottle in question!

Over thirty years ago I published a volume about the home education of children and people wrote asking how those counsels of perfection could be carried out with the aid of the private governess as she then existed; it occurred to me that a series of curricula might be devised embodying sound principles and securing that children should be in a position of less dependence on their teacher than they then were; in other words, that their education should be largely self-education. A sort of correspondence school was set up, the motto of which,—"I am, I can, I ought, I will," has had much effect in throwing children upon the possibilities, capabilities, duties and determining power belonging to them as persons.

"Children are born persons," is the first article of the educational *credo* in question. The response made by children (ranging in age from six to eighteen) astonished me; though they only shewed the power of attention, the avidity for knowledge, the clearness of thought, the nice discrimination in books, and the ability to deal with many subjects, for which I had given them credit in advance. I need not repeat what I have urged elsewhere on the subject of 'Knowledge' and will only add that anyone may apply a test; let him read to a child of any age from six to ten an account of an incident, graphically and tersely told, and the child will relate what he has heard point by point, though not word for word, and will add delightful original touches; what is more, he will relate the passage months later because he has visualised the scene and appropriated that bit of knowledge. A rhetorical passage, written in 'journalese,' makes no impression on him; if a passage be read more than once, he may become letter-perfect, but the spirit, the individuality has gone out of the exercise. An older boy or girl will read one of Bacon's Essays, say, or a passage from De Quincey, and will write or tell it forcibly and with some style, either at the moment or months later. We know how Fox recited a whole pamphlet of Burke's at a College supper though he had probably read it no more than once. Here on the very surface is the key to that attention, interest, literary style, wide vocabulary, love of books and readiness in speaking, which we all feel should belong to an education that is only begun at school and continued throughout life; these are the things that we all desire, and how to obtain them is some part of the open 30 secret I am labouring to disclose 'for public use.'

I am anxious to bring a quite successful educational experiment before the public at a moment when we are told on authority that "Education must be . . . an appeal to the spirit if it is to be made interesting." Here is Education which is as interesting and fascinating as a fine art to parents, children and teachers.

During the last thirty years thousands of children educated on these lines have grown up in love with Knowledge and manifesting a 'right judgment in all things' so far as a pretty wide curriculum gives them data.

I would have children taught *to read* before they learn the mechanical arts of reading and writing; and they learn delightfully; they give perfect attention to paragraph or page read to them and are able to relate the matter point by point, *in their own words*; but they demand classical English and cannot learn to read in this sense upon anything less. They begin their 'schooling' in 'letters' at six, and begin at the same time to learn mechanical reading and writing. A child does not lose by spending a couple of years in acquiring these because he is meanwhile 'reading' the Bible, history, geography, tales, with close attention and a remarkable power of reproduction, or rather, of translation into his own language; he is acquiring a copious vocabulary and the habit of consecutive speech. In a word, he is an educated child from the first, and his power of dealing with books, with several books in the course of a morning's 'school,' increases with his age.

But children are not all alike; there is as much difference between them as between men or women; two or three months ago, a small boy, not quite six, came to school (by post); and his record was that he could read anything in five languages, and was now teaching himself the Greek characters, could find his way about the Continental Bradshaw, and was a chubby, vigorous little person. All this the boy brings with him when he comes to school; he is exceptional, of course, just as a man with such accomplishments is exceptional; but I believe that all children bring with them much capacity which is not recognized by their teachers, chiefly intellectual capacity, (always in advance of motor power), which we are apt to drown in deluges of explanation, or dissipate in futile labours in which there is no advance.

People are naturally divided into those who read and think and those who do not read or think; and the business of schools is to see that all their scholars shall belong to the former class; it is worth while to remember that thinking is inseparable from reading which is concerned with the content of a passage and not merely with the printed matter.

I am afraid that some knowledge of the theory we advance is necessary to the open-minded teacher who would give our practices a trial, because every detail of schoolroom work is the outcome of certain principles. For instance, it would be quite easy, without much thought to experiment 32 with our use of books; but in education, as in religion, it is the motive that counts, and the boy who reads his lesson for a 'good mark' becomes word-perfect, but does not know. But these principles are obvious and simple enough, and, when we consider that at present education is chaotic for want of a unifying theory, and that there happens to be no other comprehensive theory in the field which is in line with modern thought and fits every occasion, might it not be well to try one which is immediately practicable and always pleasant and has proved itself by producing many capable, serviceable, dutiful men and women of sound judgment and willing mind?

In urging a method of self-education for children in lieu of the vicarious education which prevails, I should like to dwell on the enormous relief to teachers, a self-sacrificing and greatly overburdened class; the difference is just that between driving a horse that is light and a horse that is heavy in hand; the former covers the ground of his own gay will and the driver goes merrily. The teacher who allows his scholars the freedom of the city of books is at liberty to be their guide, philosopher and friend; and is no longer the mere instrument of forcible intellectual feeding.

Chapter 2

Children are Born Persons

"No sooner doth the truth . . . come into the soul's sight, but the soul knows her to be her first and old acquaintance."

"The consequence of truth is great, therefore the judgment of it must not be negligent."

I.—THE MIND OF A CHILD

It should not surprise the reader that a chapter, de-³³ signed to set forth a startling truth, should open with the weighty words of an old Divine (Whichcote). But truths get flat and wonders stale upon us. We do not care much about the starry firmament, the budding trees, the cunning architecture of the birds; and to all except young parents and young brothers and sisters a baby is no longer a marvel. The completeness of the new baby brother is what children admire most, his toes and his fingers, his ears and all the small perfections of him. His guardians have some understanding of the baby; they know that his chief business is to grow and they feed him with food convenient for him. If they are wise they give free play to all the wrigglings and stretchings which give power to his feeble muscles. His parents know what he will come to, and feel that here is a new chance for the world. In the meantime, he needs food, sleep and shelter and a great deal of love. So much we all know. But is the baby more than a 'huge oyster'? That is the problem before us and hitherto educators have been inclined to answer it in the negative. Their notion is that by means of a pull here, a push there, a compression elsewhere a person is at last turned out according to the pattern the educator has in his mind.

34

The other view is that the beautiful infant frame is but the setting of a jewel of such astonishing worth that, put the whole world in one scale and this jewel in the other, and the scale which holds the world flies up outbalanced. A poet looks back on the glimmering haze of his own infancy and this is the sort of thing he sees,—

> "I was entertained "I was entertained like an angel with the works of God in their splendour and glory. . . . Is it not strange that an infant should be heir of the whole world and see those mysteries which the books of the learned never unfold? . . . The corn was orient and immortal wheat which never should be reaped nor was ever sown. I thought it had stood from everlasting to everlasting. The dust and stones of the street were as precious gold. The green trees transported and ravished me. Their sweetness and unusual beauty made my heart

to leap. . . . Boys and girls tumbling in the streets were moving jewels. I knew not that they were born or should die. . . . The streets were mine, the people were mine, their clothes and gold and silver were mine as much as their sparkling eyes, fair skins and ruddy faces. The skies were mine and so were the sun and moon and stars, and all the world was mine and I the only spectator and enjoyer of it."

It takes a poet like Traherne to retain and produce such vivid memories, though perhaps we can all recall the sense that we were spectators at the show of life, and we can recollect a sunny time before we were able to speak or tell what we knew. *Punch* amused us at one time with a baby's views of his nurse and his surroundings and especially of the unwarranted pulls and pushes to which he was subject; but probably an infant is no critic. His business is to perceive and receive and these he does day in and day out.

We have an idea that poets say more than they know, express more than they see, and that their version of life must be taken *cum grano*, but perhaps the fact is that no labour of the mind enables them to catch and put into words the full realities of which they are cognisant, and therefore we may take Wordsworth, Coleridge, Vaughan and the rest as witnesses who only hint at the glory which might be revealed. We are not poets and are disposed to discount the sayings of the poets, but the most prosaic of us comes across evidence of mind in children, and of mind astonishingly alert. Let

35

us consider, in the first two years of life they manage to get through more intellectual effort than any following two years can show. Supposing that much-discussed Martian were at last able to make his way to our planet, think of how much he must learn before he could accommodate himself to our conditions! Our notions of hard and soft, wet and dry, hot and cold, stable and unstable, far and near, would be as foreign to him as they are to an infant who holds out his pinafore for the moon. We do not know what the Martian means of locomotion are but we can realise that to run and jump and climb stairs, even to sit and stand at will must require fully as much reasoned endeavour as it takes in after years to accomplish skating, dancing, ski-ing, fencing, whatever athletic exercises people spend years in perfecting; and all these the infant accomplishes in his first two years. He learns the properties of matter, knows colours and has first notions of size, solid, liquid; has learned in his third year to articulate with surprising clearness. What is more, he has learned a language, two languages, if he has had the opportunity, and the writer has known of three languages being mastered by a child of three, and one of them was Arabic; mastered, that is, so far that a child can say all that he needs to say in any one of the three—the sort of mastery most of us wish for when we are travelling in foreign countries.

36   Lady Mary Wortley Montagu tells us that in her time the little children of Constantinople prattled in five tongues with a good knowledge of each. If we have not proved that

a child is born a person with a mind as complete and as beautiful as his beautiful little body, we can at least show that he always has all the mind he requires for his occasions; that is, that his mind is the instrument of his education and that *his education does not produce his mind.*

Who shall measure the range of a child's thoughts? His continual questions about God, his speculations about 'Jesus,' are they no more than idle curiosity, or are they symptoms of a God-hunger with which we are all born, and is a child able to comprehend as much of the infinite and the unseen as are his self-complacent elders? Is he 'cabined, cribbed, confined,' in our ways and does the fairy tale afford a joyful escape to regions where all things are possible? We are told that children have no imagination, that they must needs see and touch, taste and handle, in order to know. While a child's age is still counted by months, he devotes himself to learning the properties of things by touching, pulling, tearing, throwing, tasting, but as months pass into years a *coup d'oeil* suffices for all but new things of complicated structure. Life is a continual progress to a child. He does not go over old things in old ways; his joy is to go on. The immensity of his powers brings its own terrors. Let me again quote Traherne,—

> "Another time in a lowering and sad evening being alone in the field when all things were dead and quiet a certain wanton horror fell upon me beyond imagination. The unprofitableness and silence of the place dissatisfied me:

its wildness terrified me. From the utmost ends of the earth fear surrounded me.... I was a weak and little child and had forgotten there was a man alive on the earth. Yet also something of hope and expectation comforted me from every border."

37   Traherne never loses the lessons that come to him and he goes on,—

"This taught me that I was concerned in all the world ... that the beauties of the earth were made to entertain me ... that the presence of cities, temples and kingdoms, ought to sustain me and that to be alone in the world was to be desolate and miserable."

Reason is present in the infant as truly as imagination. As soon as he can speak he lets us know that he has pondered the 'cause why' of things and perplexes us with a thousand questions. His 'why?' is ceaseless. Nor are his reasonings always disinterested. How soon the little urchin learns to manage his nurse or mother, to calculate her moods and play upon her feelings! It is in him to be a little tyrant; "he has a will of his own," says his nurse, but she is mistaken in supposing that his stormy manifestations of greed, wilfulness, temper, are signs of will. It is when the little boy is able to stop all these and restrain himself with quivering lip that his will comes into play; for he has a conscience too. Before he begins to toddle he knows the difference between right and wrong; even a baby in arms will blush at the 'naughty baby!' of his nurse; and that strong will of his acts in proportion as he learns the difficult art of obedience; for no one can make a child obey unless he wills to do so, and we all know how small a rebel may make confusion in house or schoolroom.

2.—THE MIND OF A SCHOOL-CHILD

But we must leave the quite young child, fascinating as he is, and take him up again when he is ready for lessons. I have made some attempt elsewhere* to show what his parents and teachers owe to him in those years in which he is engaged in self-education, taking his lessons from everything he sees and hears, and strengthening his powers by everything he does. Here, in a volume which is chiefly concerned with education in the sense of schooling, I am anxious to bring before teachers the fact that a child comes into their hands with a mind of amazing potentialities: he has a brain too, no doubt, the organ and instrument of that same mind, as a piano is not music but the instrument of music. Probably we need not concern ourselves about the brain which is subject to the same conditions as the rest of the material body, is fed with the body's food, rests, as the body rests, requires fresh air and wholesome exercise to keep it in health, but depends upon the mind for its proper activities.

38

---

* *Home Education*, by the Writer.

The world has concerned itself of late so much with psychology, whose province is what has been called 'the unconscious mind,' a region under the sway of nerves and blood (which it is best perhaps to let alone) that in our educational efforts we tend to ignore the *mind* and address ourselves to this region of symptoms. Now mind, being spiritual, knows no fatigue; brain, too, duly nourished with the food proper for the body, allowed due conditions of fresh air and rest, should not know fatigue; given these two conditions, we have a glorious field of educational possibilities; but it rests with us to evolve a theory and practice which afford due recognition to mind. An authoritative saying which we are apt to associate with the religious life only is equally applicable to education. That which is born of the flesh, is flesh, we are told; but we have forgotten this great principle in our efforts at schooling children. We give them a 'play way' and play is altogether necessary and desirable but is not the avenue which leads to mind. We give them a fitting environment, which is again altogether desirable and, again, is not the way to mind. We teach them beautiful motion and we do well, for the body too must have its education; but we are not safe if we take these by-paths as approaches to mind. It is still true that that which is born of the spirit, is spirit. The way to mind is a quite direct way. Mind must come into contact with mind through the medium of ideas. "What is mind?" says the old conundrum, and the answer still is "No matter." It is necessary for us who teach to realize that things material have little effect upon mind, because there are still among us schools in which the work is altogether material and technical, whether the teaching is given by means of bars of wood or more scientific apparatus. The mistress of an Elementary School writes,--"The father of one of my girls said to me yesterday, 'You have given me some work to do. E. has let me have no rest until I promised to set up my microscope and get pond water to look for monads and other wonders.'" Here we have the right order. That which was born of the spirit, the idea, came first and demanded to confirm and illustrate. "How can these things be?" we ask, and the answer is not *evident*.

Education, like faith, is the evidence of things not seen. We must begin with the notion that the business of the body is to grow; and it grows upon food, which food is composed of living cells, each a perfect life in itself. In like manner, though all analogies are misleading and inadequate, the only fit sustenance for the mind is ideas, and an idea too, like the single cell of cellular tissue, appears to go through the stages and functions of a life. We receive it with appetite and some stir of interest. It appears to feed in a curious way. We hear of a new patent cure for the mind or the body, of the new thought of some poet, the new notion of a school of painters; we take in, accept, the idea and for days after every book we read, every person we talk with brings food to the newly entertained notion. 'Not proven,' will be the verdict of the casual reader; but if he watch the behaviour of his own mind towards any of 40 the ideas 'in the air,' he will find that some such process as I have described takes place; and this process must be considered carefully in the education of children. We may not take things casually as we have done. Our business is to give children the great ideas of life, of religion, history, science; but it is the *ideas* we must give, clothed upon with facts as they occur, and must leave the child to deal with these as he chooses.

This is how he deals with Geography, for example,—

"When I heard of any new kingdom beyond the seas the light and glory of it entered into me. It rose up within me and I was enlarged by the whole. I entered into it, I saw its commodities, springs, meadows, inhabitants and became possessor of that new room as if it had been prepared for me so much was I magnified and delighted in it. When the Bible was read my spirit was present in other ages. I saw the light and splendour of them, the land of Canaan, the Israelites entering into it, the ancient glory of the Amorites, their peace and riches, their cities, houses, vines and fig trees. . . . I saw and felt all in such a lively manner as if there had been no other way to those places but in spirit only. . . . Anything when it was proposed though it was a thousand years ago being always present before me."

I venture again to quote Traherne because I know of no writer who retains so clear a memory of his infancy;

but Goethe gives as full and convincing an account of his experience of the Bible;* I say 'experience' advisedly, for the word denotes the process by which children get to know. They *experience* all the things they hear and read of; these enter into them and are their life; and thus it is that ideas feed the mind in the most literal sense of the word 'feed.'

Do our Geography lessons take the children *there*? Do, they experience, live in, our story of the call of Abraham?— or of the healing of the blind man on the way to Jericho? If they do not, it is not for lack of earnestness and intention on the part of the teacher; his error is rather want of confidence in children. He has not formed a just measure of a child's mind and bores his scholars with much talk about matters which they are able to understand for themselves much better than he does. How many teachers know that children require no pictures excepting the pictures of great artists, which have quite another function than that of illustration? They see for themselves in their own minds a far more glorious, and indeed more accurate, presentation than we can afford in our miserable daubs. They read between the lines and put in all the author has left out. A child of nine, who had been reading Lang's *Tales of Troy and Greece*, drew Ulysses on the Isle of Calypso cutting down trees to make a raft; a child of ten, revelling in *A Midsummer Night's Dream*, drew that Indian Princess bringing her lovely boy to Titania. We others are content to know that Ulysses built a raft, that

---

* See *Some Studies in the Formation of Character*, by the Writer.

the boy was the child of an Indian Princess. This is how any child's mind works, and our concern is not to starve these fertile intelligences. They must have food in great abundance and variety. They know what to do with it well enough and we need not disturb ourselves to provide for the separate exercise of each so-called 'faculty'; for the mind is one and works all together; reason, imagination, reflection, judgment, what you please, are like 'all hands' summoned by the 'heave-ho!' of the boatswain. All swarm on deck for the lading of cargo, that rich and odorous cargo of ideas which the fair vessel of a child's mind is waiting to receive. Do we wish every child in a class to say,—or, if he does not say, to feel,--"I was enlarged wonderfully" by a Geography lesson? Let him see the place with the eyes of those who have seen or conceived it; your barographs, thermographs, contour lines, relief models, sections, profiles and the like, will not do it. A map of the world must be a panorama to a child of pictures so entrancing that he would rather ponder them than go out to play; and nothing is more easy than to give him this *joie de vivre*. Let him see the world as we ourselves choose to see it when we travel; its cities and peoples, its mountains and rivers, and he will go away from his lesson with the piece of the world he has read about, be it county or country, sea or shore, as that of "a new room prepared for him, so much will he be magnified and delighted in it." All the world is in truth the child's possession, prepared for him, and if we keep him out of his rights by our technical, commercial, even historical, geography, any sort of geography,

42

in fact, made to illustrate our theories, we are guilty of fraudulent practices. What he wants is the world and every bit, piece by piece, each bit a key to the rest. He reads of the tidal Bore of the Severn and is on speaking terms with a 'Bore' wherever it occurs. He need not see a mountain to know a mountain. He sees all that is described to him with a vividness of which we know nothing just as if there had been "no other way to those places but in spirit only." Who can take the measure of a child? The Genie of the Arabian tale is nothing to him. He, too, may be let out of his bottle and fill the world. But woe to us if we keep him corked up.

Enough, that the children have minds, and every man's mind is his means of living; but it is a great deal more. Working men will have leisure in the future and how this leisure is to be employed is a question much discussed. Now, no one can employ leisure fitly whose mind is not brought into active play every day; the small affairs of a man's own life supply no intellectual food and but small and monotonous intellectual exercise. Science, history, philosophy, literature, must no longer be the luxuries of the 'educated' 43 classes; all classes must be educated and sit down to these things of the mind as they do to their daily bread. History must afford its pageants, science its wonders, literature its intimacies, philosophy its speculations, religion its assurances to every man, and his education must have prepared him for wanderings in these realms of gold.

How do we prepare a child, again, to use the aesthetic sense with which he appears to come provided? His education should furnish him with whole galleries of mental pictures, pictures by great artists old and new;—Israels' *Pancake Woman*, his *Children by the Sea*; Millet's *Feeding the Birds, First Steps, Angelus*; Rembrandt's *Night Watch, The Supper at Emmaus*; Velaszuez's *Surrender of Breda*,— in fact, every child should leave school with at least a couple of hundred pictures by great masters hanging permanently in the halls of his imagination, to say nothing of great buildings, sculpture, beauty of form and colour in things he see. Perhaps we might secure at least a hundred lovely landscapes too,—sunsets, cloudscapes, star-light nights. At any rate he should go forth well furnished because imagination has the property of magical expansion, the more it holds the more it will hold.

It is not only a child's intellect but his heart that comes to us thoroughly furnished. Can any of us love like a little child? Father and mother, sisters and brothers, neighbours and friends, "our" cat and "our" dog, the wretchedest old stump of a broken toy, all come in for his lavish tenderness. How generous and grateful he is, how kind and simple, how pitiful and how full of benevolence in the strict sense of goodwill, how loyal and humble, how fair and just! His conscience is on the alert. Is a tale true? Is a person good?— these are the important questions. His *conscience* chides him when he is naughty, and by degrees as he is trained, his will comes to his aid and he learns to order his life. He is taught to say his prayers, and we elders hardly realize how real his prayers are to a child.

3.—MOTIVES FOR LEARNING

Now place a teacher before a class of persons the beauty and immensity of each one of whom I have tried to indicate and he will say, "What have I to offer them?" His dull routine lessons crumble into the dust they are when he faces children as they are. He cannot go on offering them his stale commonplaces; he feels that he may not bore them; that he may not prick the minds he has dulled by unworthy motives of greed or emulation; he would not invite a parcel of children to a Timon feast of smoke and lukewarm water. He knows that children's minds hunger at regular intervals as do their bodies; that they hunger for knowledge, not for information, and that his own poor stock of knowledge is not enough, his own desultory talk has not substance enough; that his irrelevant remarks interrupt a child's train of thought; that, in a word, he is not sufficient for these things.

On the other hand, the children, the children of the slums especially, have no vocabulary to speak of, no background of thought derived from a cultured environment. They are like goodly pitchers, capable of holding much but with necks so narrow that only the thinnest stream can trickle in. So we have thought hitherto, and our teaching has been diluted to dishwater and the pitchers have gone empty away.

But we have changed all that. Just as in the War the magnanimous, patriotic citizen was manifested in every man so in our schools every child has been discovered to be a person of infinite possibilities. I say every child, for

45   so-called 'backward' children are no exception. I shall venture to bring before the reader some experiences of the *Parents' Union School* as being ground with which I am familiar. Examination papers representing tens of thousands of children working in Elementary Schools, Secondary Schools and home schoolrooms have just passed under my eye. How the children have revelled in knowledge! and how good and interesting all their answers are! How well they spell on the whole and how well they write! We do not need the testimony of their teachers that the work of the term has been joyous; the verve with which the children tell what they know proves the fact. Every one of these children knows that there are hundreds of pleasant places for the mind to roam in. They are good and happy because some little care has been taken to know what they are and what they require; a care very amply rewarded by results which alter the whole outlook on education. In our Training College, the students are not taught how to stimulate attention, how to keep order, how to give marks, how to punish or even how to reward, how to manage a large class or a small school with children in different classes. All these things come by nature in a school where the teachers know something of the capacities and requirements of children. To hear children of the slums 'telling' *King Lear* or *Woodstock*, by the hour if you will let them, or describing with minutest details Van Eyck's *Adoration of the Lamb* or Botticelli's *Spring*, is a surprise, a revelation. We take off our shoes from off our feet; we 'did not know it

was in them,' whether we be their parents, their teachers or mere lookers-on. And with some feeling of awe upon us we shall be the better prepared to consider how and upon what children should be educated. I will only add that I make no claims for them which cannot be justified by hundreds, thousands, of instances within our experience.

Chapter 3

The Good and Evil Nature of a Child
*Children are not born bad but with possibilities
for good and for evil.*

I.—WELL-BEING OF BODY

A well-known educationalist has brought heavy 46 charges against us all on the score that we bring up children as 'children of wrath.' He probably exaggerates the effect of any such teaching, and the 'little angel' theory is fully as mischievous. The fact seems to be that children are like ourselves, not because they have become so, but because they are born so; that is, with tendencies, dispositions, towards good and towards evil, and also with a curious intuitive knowledge as to which is good and which is evil. Here we have the work of education indicated. There are good and evil tendencies in body and mind, heart and soul; and the hope set before us is that we can foster the good so as to attenuate the evil; that is, on condition that we put Education in her true place as the handmaid of Religion. The community, the nation, the race, are now taking their due place in our religious thought. We are no longer solely occupied in what an Irish woman called 'saving yer dirty sowl.' Our religion is becoming more magnanimous and more responsible and it is time that a like change should take place in our educational thought.

47   We find ourselves in open places breathing fresher air when we consider, not the education of an individual child or of a social class or even of a given country, but of the race, of the human nature common to every class and country, every individual child. The prospect is exhilarating and the recognition of the potentialities in any child should bring about such an educational renaissance as may send our weary old world rejoicing on its way.

Physicians and physiologists tell us that new-born children start fair. A child is not born with tuberculosis, for example, if with a tendency which it is our business to counteract. In the same way all possibilities for good are contained in his moral and intellectual outfit, hindered it may be by a corresponding tendency to evil for every such potentiality. We begin to see our way. It is our business to know of what parts and passions a child is made up, to discern the dangers that present themselves, and still more the possibilities of free-going in delightful paths. However disappointing, even forbidding, the failings of a child, we may be quite sure that in every case the opposite tendency is there and we must bring the wit to give it play.

Parents have this sort of mother-wit more commonly than we outsiders, teachers and the like. Of course, we know of the mothers and fathers who can't do anything with Tom and hope the schoolmaster will lick him into shape. But how often on the other hand are we surprised to see how much more of persons Bob and Polly are in their own homes than at school! Perhaps this is because parents know their children better than do others and for that reason believe in them more; for our faith in the divine and the human keeps pace with our knowledge. For this reason it behoves us teachers to get a bird's eye view of the human nature which is present in every child. Everybody knows that hunger, thirst, rest, chastity are those natural endowments of the body by means of which it grows and functions; but in every child there are tendencies to greediness, restlessness, sloth, impurity, any one of which by allowance may ruin the child and the man that he will be. Again, our old friends, the five senses, require direction and practice. Smell, especially, might be made a source of delicate pleasure by the habit of discriminating the good smells of field and garden, flower and fruit, for their own sakes, not as ministering to taste, which, unduly pampered, becomes a man's master. But there is little that is new to be learned about the body and those various body-servants with which it is equipped. Education already does her part in training the muscles, cultivating the senses, ordering the nerves, of all children, rich and poor; for in these days we perceive that the development which is due to one child is due to all. If we make a mistake in regard to physical education it is perhaps in the matter of ordering the nerves of a child. We do not consider enough that the nourishment, rest, fresh air and natural exercise, proper for the body as a whole, meet the requirements of the nervous system and that the undue nervous tension which a small child suffers in carrying a cup of tea, an older boy or girl in cramming for an examination, may be the cause later of a distressing nervous breakdown. We are becoming a nervous, overstrained nation and though golf and cricket may do something for us, a watchful education, alert to arrest every symptom of nervous over-pressure, would do much to secure for every child a fine physique and a high degree of staying power.

A snare which attends the really brilliant teacher is the exhausting effect upon children of an overpowering personality. They are such ardent and responsive little souls that the teacher who gives them nods and becks and
49 wreathéd smiles may play the Pied Piper with them. But he or she should beware. The undue play of the personality of the teacher is likely to suppress and subdue that of his scholars; and, not only so, children are so eager to live up to the demands made upon them that they may be brought to a state of continual nervous over-pressure under the influence of a 'charming personality.' This sort of subjection, the *Schwarmerei* of the Germans, was powerfully set forth in a recent novel in which an unprincipled and fascinating mistress 'ran' her personality with disastrous results. But the danger does not lie in extreme cases. The girl who kisses

the chamber door of her class mistress will forget this lady by and by; but the parasitic habit has been formed and she must always have some person or some cause on which to hang her body and soul. I speak of 'she' and 'her' perhaps unfairly, because ever since the Greek youth hung about their masters in the walks of the Academy there have been teachers who have undermined the stability of the boys to whom they devoted themselves. Were his countrymen entirely wrong about Socrates? A tendency to this manner of betrayal is the infirmity of noble minds, of those who have the most to give; and for this reason, again, it is important that we should have before us a bird's eye view, let us call it, of human nature.

2.—WELL-BEING OF MIND

There is a common notion that it is our inalienable right not only to say what we please but to think as we please, that is, we believe that while body is subject to physical laws, while the affections, love and justice, are subject to moral laws, the mind is a chartered libertine. Probably this notion has much to do with our neglect of intellect. We do not perceive that the mind, too, has its tendencies both good and evil and that every inclination towards good is hindered and may be thwarted by a corresponding incli- 50 nation towards evil; I am not speaking of moral evil but of those intellectual evils which we are slow to define and are careless in dealing with. Does the teacher of a large class always perceive that intellect is enthroned before him in every child, however dull and inattentive may be his outer show ? Every child in such a class is open to the wonders that science reveals, is interested in the wheeling worlds of the winter firmament. "Child after child," said a schoolmistress, "writes to say how much they have enjoyed reading about the stars." "As we are walking sometimes and the stars are shining," says a girl of eleven in an Elementary School, "I tell mother about the stars and planets and comets. She said she should think astronomy very interesting."

But we teach astronomy, no, we teach 'light and heat' by means of dessicated text-books, diagrams and experiments, which last are no more to children than the tricks of white magic. The infinitely little is as attractive to them as the infinitely great and the behaviour of an atom, an ion, is a fairy tale they delight in, that is, if no semblance to a fairy tale be suggested. The pageant of history with its interplay of characters is as delightful as any tale because every child uses his own film to show the scenes and exhibit the persons. We fuss a good deal about the dress, implements and other small details of each historic period but we forget that, give the child a few fit and exact words on the subject and he has the picture in his mind's eye, nay, a series, miles long of really glorious films; for a child's amazing, vivifying imagination is part and parcel of his intellect.

The way children make their own the examples offered to them is amazing. No child would forget the characterisation of Charles IX as 'feeble and violent,' nor fail to take to himself a lesson in self-control. We may not point the moral; that is the work proper for children themselves and they do it without fail. The comparative difficulty of the subject does not affect them. A teacher writes (of children of eleven),—"They cannot have enough of Publicola and there are always groans when the lesson comes to an end."

I have said much of history and science, but mathematics, a mountainous land which pays the climber, makes its appeal to mind, and good teachers know that they may not drown their teaching in verbiage. As for literature—to introduce children to literature is to instal them in a very rich and glorious kingdom, to bring a continual holiday to their doors, to lay before them a feast exquisitely served. But they must learn to know literature by being familiar with it from the very first. A child's intercourse must always be with good books, the best that we can find. Of course, we have always known that this is the right thing for children in cultivated homes, but what about those in whose dwellings books are little known? One of the wise teachers in Gloucestershire* notes that a recognition of two things is necessary in dealing with this problem. First, that,—

> "To explain the meaning of words destroys interest in
> the story and annoys the child. Second, that in many
> instances it is unnecessary. Although a child's dictionary
> knowledge of words is lacking it does not follow that

---

* See *Some Impressions of the Ambleside Method*. (P.N.E.U. Office, price 9d.) [Now the Appendix to this edition.]

the meaning of a sentence or paragraph is unknown to him.... Neither is the correct employment of the words beyond him in writing or narrating. Two examples of this power to sense the meaning were observed last term. There is a particular boy in Form IIB who has not hitherto been looked upon as possessing high intelligence. Classified by age he ought to be two Forms higher. Last term in taking the story of Romulus and Remus, I found that in power of narrating and degree of understanding (that is, of 'sensing' a paragraph and either translating it into his vocabulary or in using the words read to him) he stood above the others and also above the majority in the next higher Form."

52   "What has surprised us most," said the Headmaster of A., "is the ready way in which boys absorb information and become interested in literature, literature which we have hitherto considered outside the scope of primary school teaching. A year ago I could not have believed that boys would have read Lytton's *Harold*, Kingsley's *Hereward*, and Scott's *Talisman* with real pleasure and zest or would study with understanding and delight Shakespeare's *Macbeth*, *King John* and *Richard II*; but experience has shown us we have underrated the abilities and tastes of the lads we should have known better."

That is the capital charge against most schools. The teachers underrate the tastes and abilities of their pupils. In things intellectual, children, even backward children, have extraordinary 'possibilities for good'—possibilities so great that if we had the wit to give them their head they would carry us along like a stream in spate.

But what about intellectual tendencies, or 'possibilities for evil'? One such tendency dominates many schools notwithstanding prodigious efforts on the part of the teachers to rouse slumbering minds. Indeed, the more the teacher works, the greater the *incuria* of the children, so the class is prodded with marks, the boys take places, the bogie of an oncoming examination is held before them. Some spasmodic effort is the result but no vital response and, though boys and girls love school, like their teachers and even their lessons, they care not at all for knowledge, for which the school should create enthusiasm. I can touch here on no more than two potent means of creating *incuria* in a class. One is the talky-talky of the teacher. We all know how we are bored by the person in private life who explains and expounds. What reason have we to suppose that children are not equally bored? They try to tell us that they are by wandering eyes, inanimate features, fidgetting hands and feet, by every means at their disposal; and the kindly souls among us think that they want to play or to be out of doors. But they have no use for play except at proper intervals. 53 What they want is knowledge conveyed in literary form and the talk of the facile teacher leaves them cold.

Another soothing potion is little suspected of producing mental lethargy. We pride ourselves upon going over and over the same ground 'until the children know it'; the monotony is deadly. A child writes,— "Before we had these (books) we had to read the same old lot again and again." Is it not true? In the home schoolroom books used by the grandmother are fit for the grandchildren, books used in boys' schools may be picked up at second-hand stalls with the obliterated names of half-a-dozen successive owners. And what of the compilations, neither books nor textbooks, which do duty in Elementary Schools? No wonder Mr. Fisher said, in opening a public library, that he had been "surprised and pained when visiting Elementary Schools to find that there was nothing in them which could be called a book, nothing that would charm and enlighten and expand the imagination." And yet, as he went on to say, the country is "full of artistic and literary ability and always has been so." If this ability is to be brought into play we must recognise that children are not ruminants intellectually any more than physically. They cannot go over the same ground repeatedly without deadening, even paralysing results, for progress, continual progress is the law of intellectual life.

In matters of the mind again *Habit* is a good servant but a bad master. Specialisation, the fetish of the end of the last century, is to be deprecated because it is at our peril that we remain too long in any one field of thought. We may not, for example, allow the affairs and interests of daily life to deprive the mind of its proper range of interests and occupations. It is even possible for a person to go into any one of the great fields of thought and to work therein with delight until he become incapable of finding his way into any other such field. We know how Darwin lost himself in science until he could not read poetry, find pleasure in pictures, think upon things divine; he was unable to turn his mind out of the course in which it had run for most of his life. In the great (and ungoverned) age of the Renaissance, the time when great things were done, great pictures painted, great buildings raised, great discoveries made, the same man was a painter, an architect, a goldsmith and a master of much knowledge besides; and all that he did he did well, all that he knew was part of his daily thought and enjoyment. Let us hear Vasari on Leonardo,—

> "Possessed of a divine and marvellous intellect and being an excellent geometrician, he not only worked at sculpture . . . but also prepared many architectural plans and buildings. . . . He made designs for mills and other engines to go by water; and, as painting was to be his profession, he studied drawing from life."

Leonardo knew nothing about Art for Art's sake, that shibboleth of yesterday, nor did our own Christopher Wren, also a great mathematician and master of much and various knowledge, to whom architecture was rather a by-the-way interest, and yet he built St. Paul's. What an irreparable loss we had when that plan of his for a beautiful and spacious London was flung aside because it would cost too much to carry it out! Just so of our parsimony do we fling aside the minds of the children of our country, also capable of being wrought into pleasaunces of delight, structures of utility and beauty, at a pitifully trifling cost. It is well we should recognise that the business of education is with us all our lives, that we must always go on increasing our knowledge.

Of the means we employ to hinder the growth of mind perhaps none is more subtle than the *questionnaire*. It is as though one required a child to produce for inspection at its various stages of assimilation the food he consumed for his dinner; we see at once how the digestive processes would be hindered, how, in a word, the child would cease to be fed. But the mind also requires its food and leave to carry on those quiet processes of digestion and assimilation which it must accomplish for itself. The child with capacity, which implies depth, is stupified by a long rigmarole on the lines of,—"If John's father is Tom's son, what relation is Tom to John?" The shallow child guesses the riddle and scores; and it is by the use of tests of this kind that we turn out young people sharp as needles but with no power of reflection, no intelligent interests, nothing but the aptness of the city *gamin*.

Imagination may become like that cave Ezekiel tells of wherein were all manner of unseemly and evil things; it may be a temple wherein self is glorified; it may be a chamber of horrors and dangers; but it may also be a House Beautiful. It is enough for us to remember that imagination is stored with those images supplied day by day whether by the cinema, the penny dreadful, by Homer or Shakespeare, by the great picture or the flaming 'shocker.' We have heard of the imaginative man who conceived a passion for the Sphinx!

In these days when *Reason* is deified by the unlearned and plays the part of the Lord of Misrule it is necessary that every child should be trained to recognize fallacious reasoning and above all to know that a man's reason is his servant and not his master; that there is no notion a man chooses to receive which his reason will not justify, whether it be mistrust of his neighbour, jealousy of his wife, doubts about his religion, or contempt for his country.

Realising this, we 'see reason' in the fact that thousands of men go on strike because two of their body have been denied permission to attend a certain meeting. We see 56 reason in this but the men themselves confound reason with right and consider that such a strike is a righteous protest. The only safeguard against fallacies which undermine the strength of the nation morally and economically is a liberal education which affords a wide field for reflection and comparison and abundant data upon which to found sound judgments.

As for that *aesthetic* 'appetency' (to use Coleridge's word) upon which so many of the gentle pleasures of life depend, it is open to many disasters: it dies of inanition when beauty is not duly presented to it, beauty in words, in pictures and music, in tree and flower and sky. The function of the sense of beauty is to open a paradise of pleasure for us; but what if we grow up admiring the wrong things, or, what is morally worse, arrogant in the belief that it is only we and our kind who are able to appreciate and distinguish beauty? It is no small part of education to have seen much beauty, to recognize it when we see it, and to keep ourselves humble in its presence.

3.—INTELLECTUAL APPETITE

As the body is provided with its appetites, by undue indulgence of any one of which a man may make shipwreck, but which duly ordered should result in a robust and vigorous frame; so, too, the spiritual part of us is provided with certain caterers whose business it is to secure that kind of nourishment which promotes spiritual or intellectual growth in one or another direction. Perhaps in no part of our educational service do we make more serious blunders than in our use of those *desires* which act as do the appetites for the body's service. Every child wants to be approved, even baby in his new red shoes; to be first in what is going on; to get what is going; to be admired; to lead and manage the rest; to have the companionship of children and grown people; and last, but not least, every child wants *to know*. There they are, those desires, ready to act on occasion and our business is to make due use of this natural provision for the work of education. We do make use of the desires, not wisely, but too well. We run our schools upon *emulation*, the desire of every child to be first; and not the ablest, but the most pushing, comes to the front. We quicken emulation by the common desire to get and to have, that is, by the impulse of avarice. So we offer prizes, exhibitions, scholarships, every incentive that can be proposed. We cause him to work for our *approbation*, we play upon his vanity, and the boy does more than he can. What is the harm, we say, when all those springs of action are in the child already? The athlete is beginning to discover that he suffers elsewhere from the undue development of any set of muscles; and the boy whose ambition, or emulation, has been unduly stimulated becomes a flaccid person. But there is a worse evil. We all want knowledge just as much as we want bread. We know it is possible to cure the latter appetite by giving more stimulating food; and the worst of using other spurs to learning is that a natural love of knowledge which should carry us through eager school-days, and give a spice of adventure to the duller days of mature life, is effectually choked; and boys and girls 'Cram to pass but not to know; they do pass but they don't know.' The divine curiosity which should have been an equipment for life hardly survives early schooldays.

Now it has been demonstrated very fully indeed that the delightfulness of knowledge is sufficient to carry a pupil joyfully and eagerly through his school life and that prizes and places, praise, blame and punishment, are unnecessary in so far as they are used to secure ardent interest and eager work. The love of knowledge is sufficient. Each of those other stimuli should no doubt have its natural action, 58 but one or two springs of action seem to be played upon excessively in our schools. Conduct gives opportunity for 'virtue emulously rapid in the race' and especially that part of conduct known as 'play' in which most of the natural desires come into action; but even in play we must beware of the excess of zeal which risks the elimination of the primary feelings of love and justice. In the schoolroom, without doubt, the titillation of knowledge itself affords sufficient stimulus to close attention and steady labour; and the desire of acquisition has due play in a boy who is constantly increasing his acquirements.

4.—MISDIRECTED AFFECTIONS

We are aware of more than mind and body in our dealings with children. We appeal to their 'feelings'; whether 'mind' or 'feelings' be more than names we choose to give to manifestations of that spiritual entity which is each one of us. Probably we have not even taken the trouble to analyse and name the feelings and to discover that they all fall under the names of love and justice, that it is the glory of the human being to be endowed with such a wealth of these two as is sufficient for every occasion of life. More, the occasions come and he is ready to meet them with the ease and triumph of the solvent debtor.

But this rich endowment of the moral nature is also a matter with which the educator should concern himself. Alas, he does so. He points the moral with a thousand tedious platitudes, directs, instructs, illustrates and bores exceedingly the nimble and subtle minds of his scholars.

This, of the feelings and their manifestations, is certainly the field for the spare and guarded praise and blame of parent and teacher; but this praise or blame is apt to be either scrapped by children, or, taken as the sole motive for conduct, they go forth unused to do a thing 'for it is right' 59 but only because somebody's approbation is to be won.

This education of the feelings, moral education, is too delicate and personal a matter for a teacher to undertake trusting to his own resources. Children are not to be fed morally like young pigeons with predigested food. They must pick and eat for themselves and they do so from the conduct of others which they hear of or perceive. But they want a great quantity of the sort of food whose issue is conduct, and that is why poetry, history, romance, geography, travel, biography, science and sums must all be pressed into service. No one can tell what particular morsel a child will select for his sustenance. One small boy of eight may come down late because—"I was meditating upon Plato and couldn't fasten my buttons," and another may find his meat in 'Peter Pan'! But all children must read widely, and know what they have read, for the nourishment of their complex nature.

As for moral lessons, they are worse than useless; children want a great deal of fine and various moral feeding, from which they draw the 'lessons' they require. It is a wonderful thing that every child, even the rudest, is endowed with *Love* and is able for all its manifestations,—kindness, benevolence, generosity, gratitude, pity, sympathy, loyalty, humility, gladness; we older persons are amazed at the lavish display of any one of these to which the most ignorant child may treat us. But these aptitudes are so much coin of the realm with which a child is provided that he may be able to pay his way through life; and, alas, we are aware of certain vulgar commonplace tendencies in ourselves which make us walk delicately and trust, not to our own teaching, but to the best that we have in art and literature and above all to that storehouse of example and precept, the Bible, to 60   enable us to touch these delicate spirits to fine issues. St. Francis, Collingwood, Father Damien, one of the V.C.'s among us, will do more for children than years of talk.

Then there is that other wonderful provision for right living without which no neglected or savage man-soul exists. Everyone has *Justice* in his heart; a cry for 'fair play' reaches the most lawless mob, and we all know how children torment us with their 'It's not fair.' It is much to know that as regards justice as well as love there exists in everyone an adequate provision for the conduct of life: general unrest, which has its rise in wrong thinking and wrong judging far more than in faulty conditions, is the misguided outcome of that sense of justice with which, thank God, we are all endued.

Here, on the face of it, we get one office of education. This, of justice, is another spiritual provision which we fail to employ duly in our schools; and so wonderful is this principle that we cannot kill, paralyse, or even benumb it, but, choked in its natural course, it spreads havoc and devastation where it should have made the soil fertile for the fruits of good living.

Few of the offices of education are more important than that of preparing men to distinguish between their rights and their duties. We each have our rights and other persons have their duties towards us as we towards them; but it is not easy to learn that we have precisely the same rights as other people and no more; that other people owe to us just such duties as we owe to them. This fine art of self-adjustment is possible to everyone because of the ineradicable principle which abides in us. But our eyes must be taught to see, and hence the need for all the processes of education, futile in proportion as they do not serve this end. To think fairly requires, we know, knowledge as well as consideration.

Young people should leave school knowing that their thoughts are not their own;* that what we think of other people is a matter of justice or injustice; that a certain manner of words is due from them to all manner of persons with whom they have to deal; and that not to speak those words is to be unjust to their neighbours. They should know that truth, that is, justice in word, is their due and that of all other persons; there are few better equipments for a citizen than a mind capable of discerning the truth, and this just mind can be preserved only by those who take heed what they think. "Yet truth," says Bacon, "which only

---

* See *Ourselves, our Souls and Bodies*. By the Writer. (P.N.E.U. Office.)

doth judge itself, teacheth that the enquiry of truth, which is the lovemaking, or wooing of it, the knowledge of truth, which is the presence of it, and the belief of truth, which is the enjoying of it, is the sovereign good of human nature."

If justice in word is to be duly learned by all scholars still more is integrity, justice in action; integrity in work, which disallows ca'canny methods, whether those of the artisan who does as little as he can in the time, or of the schoolboy who receives payment in kind—in his support, the cost of his education and the trust imposed in him by parents and teachers. Therefore he may not scamp, dawdle over, postpone, crib, or otherwise shirk his work. He learns that "my duty towards my neighbour" is "to keep my hands from picking and stealing," and, whether a man be a workman, a servant, or a prosperous citizen, he must know that justice requires from him the integrity in material which we call honesty; not the common honesty which hates to be found out, but that refined and delicate sense of values which George Eliot exhibits for us in 'Caleb Garth.'

There is another form in which the magnanimous citizen of the future must be taught the sense of justice. Our opinions show our integrity of thought. Every person has many opinions whether his own honestly thought out, or notions picked up from his pet newspaper or his companions. The person who thinks out his opinions modestly and carefully is doing his duty as truly as if he saved a life because there is no more or less about duty.

If a schoolboy is to be guided into the justice of thought

from which sound opinions emanate, how much more does he need guidance in arriving at that justice in motive which we call sound principles. For what, after all, are principles but those motives of first importance which govern us, move us in thought and action? We appear to pick up these in a casual way and are seldom able to render an account of them and yet our lives are ordered by our principles, good or bad. Here, again, we have a reason for wide and wisely ordered reading; for there are always catch-words floating in the air, as,—'What's the good?' 'It's all rot,' and the like, which the vacant mind catches up for use as the basis of thought and conduct, as, in fact, paltry principles for the guidance of a life.

Here we have one more reason why there is nothing in all those spiritual stores in the world's treasury too good for the education of *all* children. Every lovely tale, illuminating poem, instructive history, every unfolding of travel and revelation of science exists for children. "*La terre appartient à l'enfant, toujours à l'enfant,*" was well said by Maxim Gorky, and we should do well to remember the fact.

The service that some of us (of the P.N.E U.) believe we have done in the cause of education is to discover that all children, even backward children, are aware of their needs and pathetically eager for the food they require; that no preparation whatever is necessary for this sort of diet; that a limited vocabulary, sordid surroundings, the absence of a literary background to thought are not hindrances; indeed they may turn out to be incentives to learning, just as the more hungry the child, the readier he is for his dinner.

63 This statement is no mere pious opinion; it has been amply proved in thousands of instances. Children of a poor school in the slums are eager to tell the whole story of *Waverley*, falling continually into the beautiful language and style of the author. They talk about the Rosetta Stone and about treasures in their local museum; they discuss Coriolanus and conclude that 'his mother must have spoiled him.' They know by heart every detail of a picture by La Hooch, Rembrandt, Botticelli, and not only is no evolution of history or drama, no subtle sweetness, no inspiration of a poet, beyond them, but they decline to know that which does not reach them in literary form.

What they receive under this condition they absorb immediately and show that they *know* by that test of knowledge which applies to us all, that is, they can tell it with power, clearness, vivacity and charm. These are the children to whom we have been doling out the 'three R's' for generations! Small wonder that juvenile crime increases; the intellectually starved boy must needs find food for his imagination, scope for his intellectual power; and crime, like the cinema, offers it must be admitted, brave adventures.

5.—THE WELL-BEING OF THE SOUL

If we leave the outer courts of mind and body, the holy places of the affections and the will (we shall consider this last later) and enter that holy of holies where man performs his priestly functions, we may well ask with diffidence and humility what may education do for the Soul of a child? "What is there that outwits the understanding of a man or that is out of the range of his thoughts, the reach of his aspirations? He is, it is true, baffled on all hands by his ignorance, the illimitable ignorance of even the wisest, but ignorance is not incapacity and the wings of a man's soul beat with impatience against the bars of his ignorance. He would out, out into the universe of infinite thought and infinite possibilities. How is the soul of a man to be satisfied? Crowned kings have thrown up dominion because they want that which is greater than kingdoms; profound scholars fret under limitations which keep them playing upon the margin of the unsounded ocean of knowledge; no great love can satisfy itself with loving; there is no satisfaction save one for the soul of a man, because the things about him are finite, measurable, incomplete and his reach is beyond his grasp. He has an urgent, incessant, irrepressible need of the infinite."* "I want, am made for, and must have a God;"—not a mere serviceable religion,—because we have in us an infinite capacity for love, loyalty and service which we cannot expend upon any other.

But what sort of approaches do we prepare for children towards the God whom they need, the Saviour in Whom is all help, the King Who affords all delight, commands all adoration and loyalty? Any words or thoughts of ours are poor and insufficient, but we have a treasury of divine

64

---

* *Ourselves, our Souls and Bodies.* By the Writer

words which they read and know with satisfying pleasure and tell with singular beauty and fitness. "The Bible is the most interesting book I know," said a young person of ten who had read a good many books and knew her Bible. By degrees children get that knowledge of God which is the object of the final daily prayer in our beautiful liturgy—the prayer of St. Chrysostom—"Grant us in this world knowledge of Thy truth," and all other knowledge which they obtain gathers round and illuminates this.

Here is an example of how such knowledge grows. I heard a class of girls aged about thirteen read an essay on George Herbert. Three or four of his poems were included, and none of the girls had read either essay or poems before. They 'narrated' what they had read and in the course of their narration gave a full paraphrase of *The Elixir*, *The Pulley*, and one or two other poems. No point made by the poet was omitted and his exact words were used pretty freely. The teacher made comments upon one or two unusual words and that was all; to explain or enforce (otherwise than by a reverently sympathetic manner, the glance and words that showed that she too, cared), would have been impertinent. It is an interesting thing that hundreds of children of this age in Secondary and Elementary Schools and in families scattered over the world read and narrated the same essay and no doubt paraphrased the verses with equal ease. I felt humbled before the children knowing myself incapable of such immediate and rapid apprehension of several pages of new matter including poems whose intention is by no means obvious. In such ways the great thoughts of great thinkers illuminate children and they grow in knowledge, chiefly the knowledge of God.

And yet this, the chief part of education, is drowned in torrents of talk, in tedious repetition, in objurgation and recrimination, in every sort of way in which the mind may be bored and the affections deadened.

I have endeavoured to sketch some of the possibilities for good and the corresponding possibilities for evil present in all children; they are waiting for direction and control, certainly, but still more for the formative influence of knowledge. I have avoided philosophical terms, using only names in common use,—body and soul, body and mind, body, soul and spirit,—because these represent ideas that we cannot elude and that convey certain definite notions; and these ideas must needs form the basis of our educational thought.

We must know something about the material we are to work upon if the education we offer is not to be scrappy and superficial. We must have some measure of a child's requirements not based upon his uses to society, nor upon the standard of the world he lives in, but upon his own capacity and needs. We would not willingly educate him towards what is called 'self-expression'; he has little to express except what he has received as knowledge, whether by way of record or impression; what he can do is to assimilate and give this forth in a form which is original because it is modified, re-created, by the action of his own mind; and this originality is produced by the common bread and milk which is food for everyone, acting upon the mind which is peculiar to each individual child.

Education implies a continuous going forth of the mind; but whatever induces introspection or any form of self-consciousness holds up as it were the intellectual powers and brings progress to a standstill. The reader may have noticed with some disappointment that I have not invited him to the study of psychology as it is understood to-day. No doubt there exists a certain dim region described as the unconscious mind, a sort of half-way house between mind and matter, a place where the intellect is subdued to the action of nerves and blood. Mind is of its nature infinitely and always conscious and to speak of the unconscious mind is a contradiction in terms; but what is meant is that the mind thinks in ways of which we are unconscious; and that our business is to make ourselves aware by much introspection, much self-occupation, of the nature and tendencies of this 'unconscious' region. The results of this study, so far as they have been arrived at, are not encouraging. The best that is in us would appear to find its origin in 'complexes,' sensual, erotic, greedy. Granting that such possibilities are in us safety, lies in so nourishing the mind that seed of baseness may bear fruit of beauty. Researches in this region are deeply interesting no doubt, to the psychologist, and may eventually bear fruit if only as contributing a quota to the classification of knowledge; but no authority on the subject is willing to offer at present his researches as a contribution to educational lore. It may be that the mind as well as the body has its regions where *noli me tangere* is a counsel of expedience; and, by the time we have dealt with those functions of the mind which we know, we may find ourselves in a position to formulate that which we certainly do not possess, a Science, should it not be a Philosophy, of Education?

Chapter 4

Authority and Docility
The principles of Authority on the one hand and Docility on the other are natural, necessary and fundamental.

The War has made surprises stale but in those remote pre-war days we were enormously startled by the discovery of wireless telegraphy. That communications should pass through almost infinite space without sign or sound or obvious channel and arrive instantly at their destination took away our breath. We had the grace to value the discovery for something more than its utility; we were awed in the presence of a law which had always been there but was only now perceived. In something the same way we have been electrified by the discovery in the fields of France of heroism in the breast of every common soldier. Now, just such discoveries wait us in the field of education and any miner in this field may strike a vein of ore which shall enrich the world. The citizens of an ancient city on the shores of Gennesaret made one of those startling discoveries and knew how to give it a name; they found out that Christ 'spake with authority' and not as their scribes.

It is not ours to speak with authority; the 'verily, verily I say unto you' is a divine word not for us. Nevertheless deputed authority is among us and in us. 'He is an authority' on such and such a subject, is a correct expression because by much study he has made it his own and has a right to speak. This deputed authority appears to be lodged in everyone, ready for occasion. Mr. Benjamin Kidd has told us how the London policeman is the very embodiment of authority, implicitly obeyed in a way surprising to strangers. Every king and commander, every mother, elder sister, school prefect, every foreman of works and captain of games, finds that within himself which secures faithful obedience, not for the sake of his merits but because authority is proper to his office. Without this principle, society would cease to cohere. Practically there is no such thing as anarchy; what is so-called is a mere transference of authority, even if in the last resort the anarchist find authority in himself alone. There is an idea abroad that authority makes for tyranny, and that obedience, voluntary or involuntary, is of the nature of slavishness; but authority is, on the contrary, the condition without which liberty does not exist and, except it be abused, is entirely congenial to those on whom it is exercised: we are so made that we like to be ordered even if the ordering be only that of circumstances. Servants take pride in the orders they receive;

that our badge of honour is an 'Order' is a significant use of words. It is still true that 'Order is heaven's first law' and order is the outcome of authority.

That principle in us which brings us into subjection to authority is docility, teachableness, and that also is universal. If a man in the pride of his heart decline other authority, he will submit himself slavishly to his 'star' or his 'destiny.' It would seem that the exercise of docility is as natural and necessary as that of reason or imagination; and the two principles of authority and docility act in every life precisely as do those two elemental principles which enable the earth to maintain its orbit, the one drawing it towards the sun, the other as constantly driving it into space; between the two, the earth maintains a more or less middle course and the days go on.

The same two principles work in every child, the one 70 producing ordered life, the other making for rebellion, and the crux in bringing up children is to find the mean which shall keep a child true to his elliptical orbit. The solution offered to-day is freedom in our schools; children may be governed but they must not be aware that they are governed, and, 'Go as you please,' must be the apparent rule of their lives, while, 'Do as you're bid,' is the moving force. The result of an ordered freedom is obtained, that ordered freedom which rules the lives of 999 in 1000 of the citizens of the world; but the drawback to an indirect method of securing this result is that when, 'Do as you please,' is substituted for, 'Do as you're bid,' there is dissimulation in the air and children fail to learn that habit of 'proud subjection and dignified obedience' which distinguishes great men and noble citizens. No doubt it is pleasing that children should behave naturally, should get up and wander about, should sit still or frolic as they have a mind to, but they too, must 'learn obedience'; and it is no small element in their happiness and ours that obedience is both delightful and reposeful.

It is the part of the teacher to secure willing obedience, not so much to himself as to the laws of the school and the claims of the matter in hand. If a boy have a passage to read, he obeys the call of that immediate duty, reads the passage with attention and is happy in doing so. We all know with what a sense of added importance we say,—"I must be at Mrs. Jones's by eleven." "It is necessary that I should see Brown.' The life that does not obey such conditions has got out of its orbit and is not of use to society. It is necessary that we should all follow an ordered course, and children, even infant children, must begin in the way in which they will have to go on. Happily they come to us with the two inherent forces, centripetal and centrifugal, which secure to them freedom, *i.e.*, self-authority, on the one hand, and 'proud subjection' on the other.

But parents and those who stand *in loco parentis* have a delicate task. There must be subjection, but it must be proud, worn as a distinction, an order of merit. Probably the way to secure this is to avoid standing between children and those laws of life and conduct by which we are all ultimately ruled. The higher the authority, the greater distinction in obedience, and children are quick to discriminate between the mere will and pleasure of the arbitrary teacher or parent and the chastened authority of him who is himself under rule. That subservience should take the place of docility is the last calamity for nation, family or school. Docility implies equality; there is no great gulf fixed between teacher and taught; both are pursuing the same ends, engaged on the same theme, enriched by mutual interests; and probably the quite delightful pursuit of knowledge affords the only intrinsic liberty for both teacher and taught. "He is the freeman whom the truth makes free," and this freedom the steady pursuit and delightful acquirement of knowledge afford to us day by day. "The mind is its own place," we are told, "and in itself can make a heaven of hell, a hell of heaven"; and that heaven of the mind, is it not continual expansion in ordered freedom? And that restless, burning, inflammatory hell, does it not come of continual chafing against natural and righteous order?

As for the superficial freedom of sitting or standing, going or coming, that is a matter which settles itself, as do all the relations between teacher and taught, once children are allowed a due share in their own education, not a benefit for us to confer but rather a provision for them to take. Our chief concern for the mind or for the body is to supply a well-ordered table with abundant, appetising, nourishing and very varied food, which children deal with in their own 72 way and for themselves. This food must be served *au naturel*, without the predigestion which deprives it of stimulating and nourishing properties and no sort of forcible feeding or spoon feeding may be practised. Hungry minds sit down to such a diet with the charming greediness of little children; they absorb it, assimilate it and grow thereby in a manner astonishing to those accustomed to the dull profitless ruminating so often practised in schools. When the teacher avoids hortatory methods, his scholars change position when they have a mind to; but their mind is commonly to sit still during a lesson time because they are so intent on their work that they have no desire for small divagations; while, on the other hand, the teacher makes it his business to see that the body gets its share, and an abundant share, of gymnastics whether by way of games or drill. But this is a subject well understood in modern schools and it is only necessary to say that though mental activity promotes bodily functions in a surprising way—has not an American physiologist discovered that people may live to 160 or 1000 years(!) if they continue to use their minds?—athleticism, on the other hand, if unduly pursued, by no means promotes mental activity.

In days when the concern of educators seems to be to provide an easy option for that mental activity, the sole condition of education, it must be *urged* that manual dexterity, gardening, folk-dancing, and the like, while they fulfil their proper function in training nerve and muscle to ready responsiveness, *do not sustain mind*. Not, again, can we educate children upon the drama, even the

Shakespearean drama, nor upon poetry, even the most musical and emotional. These things children must have; but they come into the world with many relations waiting to be established; relations with places far and near, with the wide universe, with the past of history, with the social economics of the present, with the earth they live on and all its delightful progeny of beast and bird, plant and tree; with the sweet human affinities they entered into at birth; with their own country and other countries, and, above all, with that most sublime of human relationships—their relation to God. With such a programme before his pupils only the uninstructed teacher will put undue emphasis upon and give undue time to arithmetic and handicrafts, singing or acting, or any of the hundred specifics which are passed off as education in its entirety.

The sense of *must* should be present with children; our mistake is to act in such a way that they, only, seem to be law-compelled while their elders do as they please. The parent or teacher who is pestered for 'leave' to do this or that, contrary to the discipline of the house or school, has only himself to thank; he has posed as a person *in* authority, not *under* authority, and therefore free to allow the breach of rules whose only *raison d'être* is that they minister to the well-being of the children. Two conditions are necessary to secure all proper docility and obedience and, given these two, there is seldom a conflict of wills between teacher and pupils. The conditions are,—the teacher, or other head, may not be arbitrary but must act so evidently as one under authority* that the children, quick to discern, see that he too must do the things he ought; and therefore that regulations are not made for his convenience. (I am assuming that everyone entrusted with the bringing up of children recognises the supreme Authority to Whom we are subject; without this recognition I do not see how it is possible to establish the nice relation which should exist between teacher and taught.) The other condition is that children should have a fine sense of the freedom which comes of 74 knowledge which they are allowed to appropriate as they choose, freely given with little intervention from the teacher. They do choose and are happy in their work, so there is little opportunity for coercion or for deadening, hortatory talk.

But the principle of authority, as well as that of docility, is inherent in children and it is only as the tact and judgment of the teacher make opportunity for its free play that they are prepared for the duties of life as citizens and members of a family. The movement in favour of prefects, as in Public Schools, is a recognition of this fact and it is well that children should become familiar with the idea of representative authority, that is, that they are governed by chosen members of their own body, a form of self-government. To give effect to the idea, the prefect should be elected and children shew extraordinary insight in choosing the right officers. But that is not enough because only a few are set in authority; certain small offices should be held in rotation by every member of a class. The office makes the

* *Parents and Children.* By the Writer.

man as much as the man makes the office and it is surprising how well rather incompetent children will perform duties laid on them.

All school work should be conducted in such a manner that children are aware of the responsibility of learning; it is *their business* to know that which has been taught. To this end the subject matter should not be repeated. We ourselves do not attend to the matters in our daily paper which we know we shall meet with again in a weekly review, nor to that if there is a monthly review in prospect; these repeated aids result in our being persons of wandering attention and feeble memory. To allow repetition of a lesson is to shift the responsibility for it from the shoulders of the pupil to those of the teacher who says, in effect,—"I'll see that you know it," so his pupils make no effort of attention. Thus the same stale stuff is repeated again and again and the children get bored and restive, ready for pranks by way of a change.

Teachers are apt to slight their high office and hinder the processes of education because they cherish two or three fallacies. They regard children as inferior, themselves as superior, beings;—why else their office? But if they recognized that the potency of children's minds is as great or greater than that of their own, they would not conceive that spoon-feeding was their mission, or that they must masticate a morsel of knowledge to make it proper for the feeble digestion of the scholar.

We depreciate children in another way. We are convinced that they cannot understand a literary vocabulary so we explain and paraphrase to our own heart's content but not to theirs. Educated mothers know that their children can read anything and do not offer explanations unless they are asked for them; and we have taken it for granted that this quickness of apprehension comes only to the children of educated parents.

Another misapprehension which makes for disorder is our way of regarding attention. We believe that it is to be cultivated, nursed, coddled, wooed by persuasion, by dramatic presentation, by pictures and illustrative objects: in fact, the teacher, the success of whose work depends upon his 'personality,' is an actor of no mean power whose performance would adorn any stage. Attention, we know, is not a 'faculty' nor a definable power of mind but is the ability to turn on every such power, to concentrate, as we say. We throw away labour in attempting to produce or to train this necessary function. There it is in every child in full measure, a very Niagara of force, ready to be turned on in obedience to the child's own authority and capable of infinite resistance to authority imposed from without. Our part is to regard attention, too, as an appetite and to feed it with the best we have in books and in all knowledge. But children do it 'on their own'; we may not play Sir Oracle any more; our knowledge is too circumscribed, our diction too poor, vague, desultory, to cope with the ability of young creatures who thirst for knowledge. We must put into their hands the sources which we must needs use for ourselves, the best books of the best writers.

I will mention only one more disability which hinders us in our work as teachers; I mean that depreciation of knowledge which is just now characteristic of Englishmen. A well-known educationalist lately nailed up the thesis that what children want in the way of knowledge is just two things,—How to do the work by which they must earn their living and how to behave as citizens. This writer does not see that work is done and duties performed in the ratio of the person who works: the more the man is as a person, the more valuable will be his work and the more dependable his conduct: yet we omit from popular education that tincture of humane letters which makes for efficiency! One hears, for instance, of an adolescent school with some nine thousand pupils who come in batches of a few hundreds, each batch to learn one or other of a score or so of admirable crafts and accomplishments; but not one hour is spent in a three or four years' course in this people's university on any sort of humane knowledge, in any reading or thinking which should make the pupils better men and women and better citizens.

To return to our method of employing attention; it is not a casual matter, a convenient, almost miraculous way of covering the ground, of getting children to know certainly and lastingly a surprising amount; all this is to the good, but it is something more, a root principle vital to education. In this way of learning the child comes to his own; he makes use of the authority which is in him in its highest function as a self-commanding, self-compelling, power. It is delightful to use any power that is in us if only that of keeping up in cup and ball a hundred times as (to the delight of small nephews and nieces), Jane Austen did. But to make yourself attend, make yourself know, this indeed is to come into a kingdom, all the more satisfying to children because they are so made that they revel in knowledge.

Here is some notice of a day or two spent in London by a child of eleven which reaches me as I write:—

"Mother took her to Westminster Abbey one afternoon and while I was seeing her to bed she told me all the things she had noticed there which they had been hearing about in 'architecture' this term. She loves 'architecture.' She also expressed her anxiety to make acquaintance with the British Museum and see the things there that they had been 'having' in their term's work. So the next morning we went there and studied the Parthenon Room in great detail. She was a most interesting companion and taught me ever so much! We also went to St. Paul's and Madame Tussaud's where she was delighted to see so many people out of 'history.' The modern people did not interest her so much except Jack Cornwell and Nurse Cavell."

It will be noticed that the child is educating herself; her friends merely take her to see the things she knows about and she tells what she has read, a quite different matter from the act of pouring information down the throats of the unhappy children who are taken to visit our national treasure houses.

A short time ago when the King and Queen paid a private visit to the British Museum, in the next hall, also, no doubt, examining the Parthenon Room, were a group of children from a London County Council School, as full of information and interest as the child above mentioned because they had been doing the same work. It was not a small thing for those children to know that their interests and delights were common to them and their Sovereigns. Of such strands are formed the cord which binds society; and one of the main purposes of a 'liberal education for 78 all' is to form links between high and low, rich and poor, the classes and the masses, in the strong sympathy of common knowledge. The Public Schools have arrived at this through the medium of the classics; an occasional 'tag' from Horace moves and unites the House of Commons, not only through the urbane thought of the poet but because it is a key to a hundred associations. If this has been effected through the medium of a dead language, what may we not hope for in the way of common thought, universal springs of action, conveyed through our own rich and inspiring literature?

Consider what this power of perfect attention and absolute recollection should be to every employer and chief, what an asset to the nation! I heard this week of a Colonel who said that his best subaltern was an old "P.U.S." (Parents' Union School) boy; and this sort of evidence reaches us continually. There are few who do not know the mischievous and baffling effects of inattention and forgetfulness on the part of subordinates; and we visualize a world of surprising achievement when children shall have been trained to quick apprehension and retention of instructions.

We may not pose before children, nor pride ourselves on dutiful getting up of knowledge in order to deliver it as emanating from ourselves. There are those who have a right to lecture, those who have devoted a lifetime to some one subject about which they have perhaps written their book. Lectures from such persons are, no doubt, as full of insight, imagination and power as are their written works; but we cannot have a score of such lecturers in every school, each to elucidate his own subject, nor, if we could, would it be good for the children. The personality of the teacher would influence them to distraction from the delight in knowledge which is itself a sufficient and compelling force to secure perfect attention, and seemly discipline.

I am not figuring an 'Erewhon,' some Utopia of our dreams; we of the P.N.E.U. seem to have let loose a force capable of sending forth young people firm with the resolve—

> "I will not cease from mental strife
> Nor shall my sword sleep in my hand
> Till we have built Jerusalem
> In England's green and pleasant land."

Practically all schools are doing wonders. The school-master is abroad in the land and we are educating 'our masters' with immense zeal and self-devotion. What we have reason to deplore is that after some eight or twelve years' brilliant teaching in school, the cinema show and the football field, polo or golf, satisfy the needs of our former pupils to whatever class they belong. We are filled with compassion when we detect the lifeless hand or leg, the artificial nose or jaw, that many a man has brought home as a consequence of the War. But many of our young men and women go about more seriously maimed than these. They are devoid of intellectual interests, history and poetry are without charm for them, the scientific work of the day is only slightly interesting, their 'job' and the social amenities they can secure are all that their life has for them.

The maimed existence in which a man goes on from day to day without either nourishing or using his intellect, is causing anxiety to those interested in education, who know that after religion it is our chief concern, is, indeed, the necessary handmaid of religion.

Chapter 5

The Sacredness of Personality

These principles (i.e., authority and docility) are limited by the respect due to the personality of children which may not be encroached upon whether by the direct use of fear or love, suggestion or influence, or by undue play upon any one natural desire.

People are too apt to use children as counters in a game, to be moved hither and thither according to the whim of the moment. Our crying need to-day is less for a better method of education than for an adequate conception of children,—children, merely as human beings, whether brilliant or dull, precocious or backward. Exceptional qualities take care of themselves and so does the 'wanting' intelligence, and both of these share with the rest in all that is claimed for them in the previous chapters. Our business is to find out how great a mystery a person is *quâ* person. All action comes out of the ideas we hold and if we ponder duly upon personality we shall come to

80

perceive that we cannot commit a greater offence than to maim or crush, or subvert any part of a person.

We have many ingenious, not to say affectionate, ways of doing this, all of them more or less based upon that egoism which persuades us that in proportion to a child's dependence is our superiority, that all we do for him is of our grace and favour, and that we have a right, whether as parents or teachers, to do what we will with our own. Have we considered that in the Divine estimate the child's estate is higher than ours; that it is ours to "become as little children," rather than theirs to become as grown men and women; that the rules we receive for the bringing up of children are for the most part negative? We may not despise them, or hinder them, ("suffer little children"), or offend them by our brutish clumsiness of action and want of serious thought; while the one positive precept afforded to us is "feed" (which should be rendered 'pasture') "my lambs," place them in the midst of abundant food. A teacher in a Yorkshire Council School renders this precept as,—"I had left them in the pasture and came back and found them feeding," that is, she had left a big class reading a given lesson and found them on her return still reading with eagerness and satisfaction. *Maxima reverentia debetur pueris* has a wider meaning than it generally receives. We take it as meaning that we should not do or say anything unseemly before the young, but does it not also include a profound and reverent study of the properties and possibilities present in a child?

Nor need we be alarmed at so wide a programme. The vice which hinders us in the bringing up of children is that so heavily censured in the Gospel. We are not simple; we act our parts and play in an unlawful way upon motives. Perhaps after all the least reprehensible pedagogic motive is that which is most condemned and the terrorism of 'Mr. Creakle' may produce a grey record in comparison with the blackness of more subtle methods of undermining personality. We can only touch upon a few of these, but a part may stand for the whole. For the action of fear as a governing motive we cannot do better than read again our *David Copperfield* (a great educational treatise) and study 'Mr. Creakle' in detail for terrorism in the schoolroom and 'Mr. Murdstone' for the same vice in the home. But, —is it through the influence of Dickens?—fear is no longer the acknowledged basis of school discipline; we have methods more subtle than the mere terrors of the law. Love is one of these. The person of winning personality attracts his pupils (or hers) who will do anything for his sake and are fond and eager in all their ways, docile to that point where personality is submerged, and they live on the smiles, perish on the averted looks, of the adored teacher. Parents look on with a smile and think that all is well; but Bob or Mary is losing that growing time which should make a self-dependent, self-ordered person, and is day by day becoming a parasite who can go only as he is carried, the easy prey of fanatic or demagogue. This sort of encroachment upon the love of children offers as a motive, 'do this for my sake';

82

wrong is to be avoided lest it grieve the teacher, good is to be done to pleasure him; for this end a boy learns his lessons, behaves properly, shows good will, produces a whole catalogue of schoolboy virtues and yet his character is being undermined.

'Suggestion' goes to work more subtly. The teacher has mastered the gamut of motives which play upon human nature and every suggestion is aimed at one or other of these. He may not use the nursery suggestions of lollipops or bogies but he does in reality employ these if expressed in more spiritual values, suggestions subtly applied to the idiosyncracies of a given child. 'Suggestion' is too subtle to be illustrated with advantage: Dr. Stephen Paget holds that it should be used only as a surgeon uses an anaesthetic; but it is an instrument easy to handle, and unconsidered suggestion plays on a child's mind as the winds on a weathercock. "Unstable as water, thou shalt not excel" is the unfortunate child's doom; for how is it possible for stability of mind and character to evolve under a continual play of changing suggestions? But this it will be said is true of the unconsidered suggestion. What of a carefully laid train, all leading in the same direction, to produce perseverance, frankness, courage, any other excellent virtue? The child is even worse off in such a case. That particular virtue becomes detestable; no other virtue is inviting; and he is acquiring no strength to stand alone but waits in all his doings for promptings from without. Perhaps the gravest danger attending this practice is that every suggestion received lays the person open to the next and the next. A due respect for the personality of children and a dread of making them incompetent to conduct their own lives will make us chary of employing a means so dangerous, no matter how good the immediate end.

Akin to suggestion is influence, which acts not so much by well-directed word or inciting action as by a sort of atmosphere proceeding from the teacher and enveloping the taught. Late in the last century goody-goody books were written about the beauty of influence, the duty of influence, the study of the means of influence, and children were brought up with the notion that to influence other persons consciously was a moral duty. No doubt such influence is inevitable; we must needs affect one another, not so much by what we do or say as by that which we are, and so far influence is natural and wholesome. We imbibe it from persons real and imaginary and we are kept strong and upright by currents and counter-currents of unstudied influence. Supineness before a single, steady, persistent influence is a different matter, and the schoolgirl who idolises her mistress, the boy who worships his master, is deprived of the chance of free and independent living. His personality fails to develop and he goes into the world as a parasitic plant, clinging ever to the support of some stronger character.

So far we have considered incidental ways of trespassing upon those rights of personality proper to children, but we have more pervasive, if less injurious, ways of stultifying intellectual and moral growth. Our school ethic rests 84 upon, our school discipline is supported by, undue play upon certain natural desires. It is worth while to reflect that the mind also has its appetites, better known as desires. It is as necessary that Mind should be fed, should grow and should produce, as that these things should happen to Body, and just as Body would not take the trouble to feed itself if it never became hungry, so Mind also would not take in that which it needs if it were not that certain Desires require to be satisfied. Therefore schoolmasters do not amiss in basing their practice upon the Desires whose very function appears to be to bring nourishment to Mind. Where we teachers err is in stimulating the wrong Desires to accomplish our end. There is the desire of approbation which even an infant shows, he is not happy unless mother or nurse approve of him. Later this same desire helps him to conquer a sum, climb a hill, bring home a good report from school, and all this is grist to the mill, knowledge to the mind; because the persons whose approbation is worth having care that he should learn and know, conquer idleness, and get habits of steady work, so that his mind may be as duly nourished every day as is his body. Alas for the vanity that attends this desire of approbation, that makes the boy more solicitous for the grin of the stable-boy than for the approval of his master! Nay, this desire for approval may get such possession of him that he thinks of nothing else; he must have approval whether from the worthless or the virtuous. It is supposed that outbreaks of violence, robbery, assassinations, occur at times for the mere sake of infamy, just as deeds of heroism are done for the sake of fame. Both infamy and fame mean being thought about and talked about by a large number of people; and we know how this natural desire is worked by the daily press; how we get, now a film actress, now a burglar, a spy, a hero, or a scientist set 85 before us to be our admiration and our praise.

Emulation, the desire of excelling, works wonders in the hands of the schoolmaster; and, indeed, this natural desire is an amazing spur to effort, both intellectual and moral. When in pursuit of virtue two or a score are 'emulously rapid in the race,' a school acquires a 'good tone' and parents are justified in thinking it the right place for their boy. In the intellectual field, however, there is danger; and nothing worse could have happened to our schools than the system of marks, prizes, place-taking, by which many of them are practically governed. A boy is so taken up with the desire to forge ahead that there is no time to think of anything else. What he learns is not interesting to him; he works to get his remove.

But emulation does not stand alone as Vicegerent in our schools; another natural desire whose unvarnished name is avarice labours for good government and so-called progress cheek by jowl with emulation. "He must get a scholarship,"—is the duty of a small boy even before he goes to school, and indeed for good and sufficient reasons. Sometimes the sons of rich parents carry off these prizes but as a rule they fall to those for whom they are intended, the sons of educated parents in rather straitened circumstances, sons of the clergy, for example. The scholarship system is no more than a means of distributing the vast wealth left by benefactors in the past for this particular purpose. Every Grammar School has its own scholarships; the Universities have open scholarships and bursaries often of considerable value; and a free, or partially free, education is open to the majority of the youth of the upper middle class on one condition, that of brains. It is small wonder that every Grammar and Public School bases its curriculum upon these conditions, knows exactly what standard of merit will secure the 'Hastings,' knows the boys who have a chance, and orders their very strenuous work towards the end in view. It is hard to say what better could be done and yet this deliberate cult of cupidity is disastrous; for there is no doubt that here and there we come upon impoverishment of personality due to enfeebled intellectual life; the boy did not learn to delight in knowledge in his schooldays and the man is shallow in mind and whimsical in judgment.

It is hopeless to make war from without on a system which affords very effectual help in the education of boys who are likely later to become of service to the country; but Britain must make the most of her sons and many of these men are capable of being more than they are. It is from within the schools that help must come and the way is fairly obvious. Most schools give from eleven in the lowest to eight hours in the highest Forms to 'English' that is, from twenty to sixteen consecutive readings a week might be afforded in a wide selection of books,—literature, history, economics, etc.,—books read with the concentrated attention which makes a single reading suffice. The act of narrating what has been read might well be useful to boys who should be prepared for public speaking. By a slight alteration of this kind, in procedure rather than in curriculum or time-table, it is probable that our schools would turn out many more well-read, well-informed men and convincing speakers than they do at present. Such a method, even if applied to 'English' only, would tend to correct any tendency in schools to become mere cramming places for examinations, would infect boys with a love of knowledge and should divert the natural desire for acquisition into a new channel, for few things are more delightful than the acquisition of knowledge.

We need not delay over that desire of power, ambition, which plays its part in every life; but the educator must see that it plays no more than its part. Power is good in proportion as it gives opportunities for serving; but it is mischievous in boy or man when the pleasure of ruling, managing, becomes a definite spring of action. Like each of the other natural desires, that for power may ruin a life that it is allowed to master; ambition is the cause of half the disasters under which mankind suffers. The ambitious boy or man would as soon lead his fellows in riot and disorder as in noble effort in a good cause; and who can say how far the labour unrest under which we suffer is inspired and inflamed by ambitious men who want to rule if only for the immediate intoxication of rousing and leading men? It is a fine thing to say of a multitude of men,—"I can wind them round my little finger"; and the much-burdened Head of a school must needs beware! If the able, ambitious fellow be allowed to manage the rest, he cheats them out of their fair share of managing their own lives; no boy should be allowed to wax feeble to make another great; the harm to the ambitious boy himself must be considered too, lest he become an ignoble, manoeuvring person. It is within a teacher's scope to offer wholesome ambitions to a boy, to make him keen to master knowledge rather than manage men; and here he has a wide field without encroaching on another's preserve.

Another desire which may well be made to play into the schoolmaster's hands is that of society, a desire which has much to do with the making of the naughty boys, idle youths and silly women of our acquaintance. It is sheer delight to mix with our fellows, but much depends on whom we take for our fellows and why; and here young people may be helped by finger-posts. If they are so taught that knowledge delights them, they will choose companions who share that pleasure. In this way princes are trained; they must know something of botany to talk with botanists, of history to meet with historians; they cannot afford to be in the company of scientists, adventurers, poets, painters, philanthropists or economists, and themselves be able to do no more than 'change the weather and pass the time of day'; they must know modern languages to be at home with men of other countries, and ancient tongues to be familiar with classical allusions. Such considerations rule the education of princes, and every boy has a princely right to be brought up so that he may hold his own in good society, that is, the society of those who 'know.'

We hear complaints of the cast-iron system of British society; but how much of it is due to the ignorance which makes it only possible to men and women to talk to those of their own clique, soldiers with soldiers, schoolmasters and schoolboys with their kind? The boy who wants to be able to talk to people who 'know' has no unworthy motive for working.

We have considered the several desires whose function is to stimulate the mind and save us from that *vis inertiae* which is our besetting danger. Each such desire has its place but the results are disastrous if any one should dominate. It so happens that the last desire we have to consider, the desire of knowledge, is commonly deprived of its proper function in our schools by the predominance of other springs of action, especially of emulation, the desire of place, and avarice, the desire of wealth, tangible profit. This divine curiosity is recognised in ordinary life chiefly as a desire to know trivial things. What did it cost? What did she say? Who was with him? Where are they going? How many postage stamps in a line would go round the world? And curiosity is satisfied by incoherent, scrappy information which serves no purpose, assuredly not the purpose of knowledge whose function is to nourish the mind as food nourishes the body. But so besotted is our educational thought that we believe children regard knowledge rather 89 as repulsive medicine than as inviting food. Hence our dependence on marks and prizes, athletics, alluring presentation, any jam we can devise to disguise the powder. The man who wilfully goes on crutches has feeble incompetent legs; he who chooses to go blindfold has eyes that cannot bear the sun; he who lives on pap-meat has weak digestive powers, and he whose mind is sustained by the crutches of emulation and avarice loses that one stimulating power which is sufficient for his intellectual needs. This atrophy of the desire of knowledge is the penalty our scholars pay because we have chosen to make them work for inferior ends. Our young men and maidens do not read unless with the stimulus of a forthcoming examination. They are good-natured and pleasant but have no wide range of thought, lofty purpose, little of the magnanimity which is proper for a citizen. Great thoughts and great actions are strange to them, though the possibility is still there and they may yet shew in peace such action as we have seen and wondered at during the War. But we cannot always educate by means of a great war; the penalties are too heavy for human nature to endure for long. Therefore the *stimuli* to greatness, magnanimity, which the war afforded we must produce in the ordinary course of education.

But knowledge is delectable. We have all the 'satiable curtiosity' of Mr. Kipling's Elephant even when we content ourselves with the broken meats flung by the daily press. Knowledge is to us as our mother's milk, we grow thereby and in the act of sucking are admirably content.

The work of education is greatly simplified when we
realize that children, apparently all children, want to know
all human knowledge; they have an appetite for what is
put before them, and, knowing this, our teaching becomes   90
buoyant with the courage of our convictions. We know how
Richelieu shut up colleges throughout France, both Jesuit
and secular, "in order to prevent the mania of the poor for
educating their children which distracts them from the
pursuits of trade and war." This mania exists with us, not
only in the parents but in the children, the mania of hungry
souls clamouring for meat, and we choke them off, not by
shutting up schools and colleges, but by offering matter
which no living soul can digest. The complaints made by
teachers and children of the monotony of the work in our
schools is full of pathos and all credit to those teachers who
cheer the weary path by entertaining devices. But mind
does not live and grow upon entertainment; it requires its
solid meals.

The Gloucestershire teachers, under Mr. Household's
direction, have entered so fully into the principles implied in the method, that I am tempted to illustrate largely
from their experience.* But they by no means stand alone.
Hundreds of other teachers have the same experiences and
describe them as opportunity offers. The finding of this
power which is described as 'sensing a passage,' is as the
striking of a vein of gold in that fabulously rich country,

---

* See *Some Impressions of the Ambleside Method*. (P.N.E.U.
Office, price 9d.) [Now the Appendix to this edition.]

human nature. Our 'find' is that children have a natural aptitude for literary expression which they enjoy in hearing or reading and employ in telling or writing. We might have guessed this long ago. All those speeches and sayings of untamed warriors and savage potentates which the historians have preserved for us, critics have declined as showing too much cultivated rhetoric to have been possible for any but highly educated persons. But the time is coming when we shall perceive that only minds like those of children are capable of producing thoughts so fresh and so finely expressed. This natural aptitude for literature, or, shall we say, rhetoric, which overcomes the disabilities of a poor vocabulary without effort, should direct the manner of instruction we give, ruling out the talky-talky of the oral lesson and the lecture; ruling out, equally, compilations and text-books; and placing books in the hands of children and only those which are more or less literary in character that is, which have the terseness and vividness proper to literary work. The natural desire for knowledge does the rest and the children feed and grow.

It must be borne in mind that in proportion as other desires are stimulated that of knowledge is suppressed. The teacher who proposes marks and places as worthy aims will get work certainly but he will get no healthy love of knowledge for its own sake and no provision against the *ennui* of later days. The monotony I have spoken of attends all work prompted by the *stimuli* of marks and places; such work becomes mechanical, and there is hardly enough of it prepared to last through the course of a boy's school life. The master of a Preparatory School remarks,—"It must be a well-known fact (I am not speaking of the exceptional but of the average boy) that new boys are placed too low. We find—it is a common experience—that if we send up a boy whether he be a good mathematician, a good classic, a good English scholar or a good linguist, a couple of years will pass by before he is doing at the Public School the work he was doing when he left us." The Public Schoolmaster makes the same sort of complaint; he says, that "At twenty the boy is climbing the same pear-tree that he climbed at twelve," that is to say, work which is done in view of examinations must be of the rather narrow mechanical kind upon which it is possible to set questions and mark answers with absolute fairness. Now, definite progress, continual advance from day to day with no treading of old ground, is a condition of education.

There is an uneasy dread in some minds lest a liberal   92
education for all, the possibility which is now before us, should cause a social *bouleversement*, such an upheaval as obtained in the French Revolution. But this fear arises from an erroneous conception. The doctrine of equal opportunities for all is no doubt dangerous. It is the intellectual rendering of the 'survival of the fittest' and we have had a terrible object lesson as to how that doctrine works. The uneasy, ambitious spirit comes to the front, gets all the chances, dominates his fellows, and thinks no upheaval too great a price for the advancement of himself and his notions.

Men of this type come to the top through the avenue of examinations. Ambition and possibly greed are seconded by dogged perseverance. As was said of Louis XIV, such men elevate their practice into a theory and arrogate to their habits the character of principles of government. And these pseudo-principles inflame the populace because they promise place and power to every man in the state, with no sense of the proportion he bears to the rest. Probably the 'labour unrest' of to-day is not without connexion with the habit of working in our schools for prizes and places. The boy who works to be first and to get something out of it does not always become the quiet, well-ordered citizen who helps to cement society and carries on the work of the State.

Knowledge pursued for its own sake is sedative in so far as it is satisfying; and the splendid consciousness that every boy in your Form has your own delight in knowing, your own pleasure in expressing that which he knows, shares your intimacy with this and the other sage and hero, makes for good fellowship and magnanimity and should deliver the citizen from a restless desire to come to the front. It is possible that a conscientious and intelligent teacher may be a little overwhelmed when he considers all that goes to 93 a man, all that goes to each of the boys under his care. It is true that,—

> "There lives
> No faculty within us which the Soul
> Can spare: and humblest earthly weal demands

For dignity not placed beyond her reach
Zealous co-operation of all means
Given or required to raise us from the mire
And liberate our hearts from low pursuits
By gross utilities enslaved; we need
More of ennobling impulse from the past
If for the future aught of good must come."

Wordsworth is no doubt right. There is no faculty within the soul which can be spared in the great work of education; but then every faculty, or rather power, works to the one end if we make the pursuit of knowledge for its own sake the object of our educational efforts. We find children ready and eager for this labour and their accomplishment is surprising.

Chapter 6

Three Instruments of Education

I.—EDUCATION IS AN ATMOSPHERE

Seeing that we are limited by the respect due to the personality of children we can allow ourselves but three educational instruments—the atmosphere of environment, the discipline of habit and the presentation of living ideas. Our motto is,—'Education is an atmosphere, a discipline, a life.' When we say that education is an atmosphere we do not mean that a child should be isolated in what may be called a 'child environment' specially adapted and prepared, but that we should take into account the educational value of his natural home atmosphere both as regards persons and things and should let him live freely among his proper conditions. It stultifies a child to bring down his world to the 'child's' level.

Having cut out the direct use of fear or love, sug- 94 gestion or influence, undue play upon any one natural desire, emulation, for example, we are no longer free to use all means in the education of children.

135

There are but three left for our use and to each of these we must give careful study or we shall not realise how great a scope is left to us. To consider the first of these educational instruments; for a decade or two we have pinned our faith on environment as a great part of education; as, say, nine-tenths rather than a third part of the whole. The theory has been,—put a child in the right environment and so subtle is its influence, so permanent its effects that he is to all intents and purposes educated thereby. Schools may add Latin and sums and whatever else their curriculum contains, but the actual education is, as it were, performed upon a child by means of colour schemes, harmonious sounds, beautiful forms, gracious persons. He grows up aesthetically educated into sweet reasonableness and harmony with his surroundings.

95

"Peter's nursery was a perfect dream in which to hatch the soul of a little boy. Its walls were done in warm, cream-coloured paint and upon them Peter's father had put the most lovely patterns of trotting and jumping horses and dancing cats and dogs and leaping lambs, a carnival of beasts. . . . There was a big brass fire-guard in Peter's nursery . . . and all the tables had smoothly rounded corners against the days when Peter would run about. The floor was of cork carpet on which Peter would put his toys and there was a crimson hearthrug on which Peter was destined to crawl. . . . There were scales in Peter's nursery to weigh Peter every week and tables to show how much he ought to weigh and when one should begin to feel anxious. There was nothing casual about the early years of Peter."

So, Mr. Wells, in that inconclusive educational treatise of his, *Joan and Peter*. It is an accurate picture of the preparation for 'high-souled' little persons all over the world. Parents make tremendous sacrifices to that goddess who presides over Education. We hear of a pair investing more than their capital in a statue to adorn the staircase in order that 'Tommy' should make his soul by the contemplation of beauty. This sort of thing has been going on since the 'eighties at any rate and, as usual, Germany erected a high altar for the cult which she passed on to the rest of us. Perhaps it is safe to say that the young Intelligenzia of Europe have been reared after this manner. And is the result that Neo-Georgian youth *Punch* presents to us with his air of weariness, condescension and self-complacency? Let us hear Professor Sir Jagadis Chandra Bose, the Indian scientist, on one of his conclusions concerning the nervous impulse in plants,—

"A plant carefully protected under glass from outside shocks looks sleek and flourishing but its higher nervous function is then found to be atrophied. But when a succession of blows" (electric shocks) "is rained on this effete and bloated specimen, the shocks themselves create nervous channels and arouse anew the deteriorated

96

nature. Is it not the shocks of adversity and not cotton wool protection that evolve true manhood?"

We had thought that the terrible succession of blows inflicted by the War had changed all that; but, no; the errors of education still hold sway and we still have amongst us the better-than-my-neighbour folk, whose function, let us hope, is to administer the benefits of adversity to most of us. What if parents and teachers in their zeal misread the schedule of their duties, magnified their office unduly and encroached upon the personality of children? It is not an environment that these want, a set of artificial relations carefully constructed, but an *atmosphere* which nobody has been at pains to constitute. It is there, about the child, his natural element, precisely as the atmosphere of the earth is about us. It is thrown off, as it were, from persons and things, stirred by events, sweetened by love, ventilated, kept in motion, by the regulated action of common sense. We all know the natural conditions under which a child should live; how he shares household ways with his mother, romps with his father, is teased by his brothers and petted by his sisters; is taught by his tumbles; learns self-denial by the baby's needs, the delightfulness of furniture by playing at battle and siege with sofa and table; learns veneration for the old by the visits of his great-grandmother; how to live with his equals by the chums he gathers round him; learns intimacy with animals from his dog and cat; delight in the fields where the buttercups grow and greater delight in the blackberry hedges. And, what tempered 'fusion of classes' is so effective as a child's intimacy with his betters, and also with cook and housemaid, blacksmith and joiner, with everybody who comes in his way? Children have a genius for this sort of general intimacy, a valuable part of their education; care and guidance are needed, of course, 97 lest admiring friends should make fools of them, but no compounded 'environment' could make up for this fresh air, this wholesome wind blowing now from one point, now from another.

We certainly may use atmosphere as an instrument of education, but there are prohibitions, for ourselves rather than for children. Perhaps the chief of these is, that no artificial element be introduced, no sprinkling with rose-water, softening with cushions. Children must face life as it is; if their parents are anxious and perturbed children feel it in the air. "Mummie, Mummie, you aren't going to cry this time, are you?" and a child's hug tries to take away the trouble. By these things children live and we may not keep them in glass cases; if we do, they develop in succulence and softness and will not become plants of renown. But due relations must be maintained; the parents are in authority, the children in obedience; and again, the strong may not lay their burdens on the weak; nor must we expect from children that effort of decision, the most fatiguing in our lives, of which the young should generally be relieved.

School, perhaps, offers fewer opportunities for vitiating the atmosphere than does home life. But teaching may be so watered down and sweetened, teachers may be so suave and condescending, as to bring about a condition of intellectual feebleness and moral softness which it is not easy for a child to overcome. The bracing atmosphere of truth and sincerity should be perceived in every school; and here again the common pursuit of knowledge by teacher and class comes to our aid and creates a current of fresh air perceptible even to the chance visitor, who sees the glow of intellectual life and moral health on the faces of teachers and children alike. But a school may be working hard, not for love of knowledge, but for love of marks, our old enemy; and then young faces are not serene and joyous but eager, restless, apt to look anxious and worried. The children do not sleep well and are cross; are sullen or in tears if anything goes wrong, and are, generally, difficult to manage. When this is the case there is too much oxygen in the air; they are breathing a too stimulating atmosphere, and the nervous strain to which they are subjected must needs be followed by reaction. Then teachers think that lessons have been too hard, that children should be relieved of this and that study; the doctors probably advise that so-and-so should 'run wild' for a year. Poor little soul, at the very moment when he is most in need of knowledge for his sustenance he is left to prey upon himself! No wonder the nervous symptoms become worse, and the boy or girl suffers under the stigma of 'nervous strain.' The fault has been in the atmosphere and not in the work; the teacher, perhaps, is over anxious that her children should do well and her nervous excitation is catching. "I am afraid X— cannot do his examination;

he loves his work but he bursts into tears when he is asked an examination question. Perhaps it is that I have insisted too much that he must never be satisfied with anything but his best." Poor little chap (of seven) pricked into over exertion by the spur of moral stimulus! We foresee happy days for children when all teachers know that no other exciting motive whatever is necessary to produce good work in each individual of however big a class than that love of knowledge which is natural to every child. The serenity and sweetness of schools conducted on this principle is surprising to the outsider who has not reflected upon the contentment of a baby with his bottle!

There are two courses open to us in this matter. One, to create by all manner of modified conditions a hot-house atmosphere, fragrant but emasculating, in which children grow apace but are feeble and dependent; the other to leave them open to all the "airts that blow," but with care lest they be unduly battered; lest, for example, a miasma come their way in the shape of a vicious companion.

99

2.—EDUCATION IS A DISCIPLINE

By this formula we mean the discipline of habits formed definitely and thoughtfully whether habits of mind or of body. Physiologists tell us of the adaptation of brain structure to habitual lines of thought, i.e., to our habits.

Education is not after all to either teacher or child the fine careless rapture we appear to have figured it. We who teach and they who learn are alike constrained; there is always effort to be made in certain directions; yet we face our tasks from a new point of view. We need not labour to get children to learn their lessons; that, if we would believe it, is a matter which nature takes care of. Let the lessons be of the right sort and children will learn them with delight. The call for strenuousness comes with the necessity of forming habits; but here again we are relieved. The intellectual habits of the good life form themselves in the following out of the due curriculum in the right way. As we have already urged, there is but one right way, that is, children must do the work for themselves. They must read the given pages and tell what they have read, they must perform, that is, what we may call the *act of knowing*. We are all aware, alas, what a monstrous quantity of printed matter has gone into the dustbin of our memories, because we have failed to perform that quite natural and spontaneous 'act of knowing,' as easy to a child as breathing and, if we would believe it, comparatively easy to ourselves. The reward is two-fold: no intellectual habit is so valuable as that of attention; it is a mere habit but it is also the hall-mark of an educated person. Use is second nature, we are told; it is not too much to say that 'habit is ten natures,' and we can all imagine how our work would be eased if our subordinates listened to instructions with the full attention which implies recollection. Attention is not the only habit that follows due self-education. The habits of fitting and ready expression, of obedience, of good-will, and of an impersonal outlook are spontaneous bye-products of education in this sort.

So, too, are the habits of right thinking and right judging; while physical habits of neatness and order attend upon the self-respect which follows an education which respects the personality of children.

Physiologists tell us that thoughts which have become habitual make somehow a mark upon the brain substance, but we are bold in calling it a mark for there is no discernible effect to be quoted. Whether or no the mind be served by the brain in this matter, we are empirically certain that a chief function of education is the establishment of such ways of thinking in children as shall issue in good and useful living, clear thinking, aesthetic enjoyment, and, above all, in the religious life. How it is possible that spirit should act upon matter is a mystery to us, but that such act takes place we perceive every time we note a scowling brow, or, on the other hand,—

> "A sweet attractive kind of grace,
> A full assurance given by looks;
> Continual comfort in a face.
> The lineaments of gospel books."

We all know how the physical effort of smiling affects ourselves in our sour moods,—

> "Nor soul helps flesh more now, than flesh
> helps soul."

Both are at our service in laying down the rails, so to speak, upon which the good life must needs run.

In the past we have, no doubt, gone through an age of infant slavery, an age of good habits enforced by vigorous penalties, conscientiously by the over scrupulous eighteenth century parent, and infamously by the schoolmasters, the 'Creakles' and the 'Squeers' who laboured only for their own ease and profit. Now, the pendulum swings the other way. We have lost sight of the fact that habit is to life what rails are to transport cars. It follows that lines of habit must be laid down towards given ends and after careful survey, or the joltings and delays of life become insupportable. More, habit is inevitable. If we fail to ease life by laying down habits of right thinking and right acting, habits of wrong thinking and wrong acting fix themselves of their own accord. We avoid decision and indecision brings its own delays, "and days are lost lamenting o'er lost days." Almost every child is brought up by his parents in certain habits of decency and order without which he would be a social outcast. Think from another point of view how the labour of life would be increased if every act of the bath, toilet, table, every lifting of the fork and use of spoon were a matter of consideration and required an effort of decision! No; habit is like fire, a bad master but an indispensable servant; and probably one reason for the nervous scrupulosity, hesitation, indecision of our day, is that life was not duly eased for us in the first place by those whose business it was to lay down lines of habit upon which our behaviour might run easily.

It is unnecessary to enumerate those habits which we should aim at forming, for everyone knows more about these than anyone practises. We admire the easy carriage of the soldier but shrink from the discipline which is able to produce it. We admire the lady who can sit upright through a long dinner, who in her old age prefers a straight chair because she has arrived at due muscular balance and has done so by a course of discipline. There is no other way of forming any good habit, though the discipline is usually that of the internal government which the person exercises upon himself; but a certain strenuousness in the formation of good habits is necessary because every such habit is the result of conflict. The bad habit of the easy life is always pleasant and persuasive and to be resisted with pain and effort, but with hope and certainty of success, because in our very structure is the preparation for forming such habits of muscle and mind as we deliberately propose to ourselves. We entertain the idea which gives birth to the act and the act repeated again and again becomes the habit; 'Sow an act,' we are told, 'reap a habit.' 'Sow a habit, reap a character.' But we must go a step further back, we must sow the idea or notion which makes the act worth while. The lazy boy who hears of the Great Duke's narrow camp bed, preferred by him because when he wanted to turn over it was time to get up, receives the idea of prompt rising. But his nurse or his mother knows how often and how ingeniously the tale must be brought to his mind before the habit of prompt rising is formed; she knows too how the idea of self-conquest

102

must be made at home in the boy's mind until it become a chivalric impulse which he cannot resist. It is possible to sow a great idea lightly and casually and perhaps this sort of sowing should be rare and casual because if a child detect a definite purpose in his mentor he is apt to stiffen himself against it. When parent or teacher supposes that a good habit is a matter of obedience to his authority, he relaxes a little. A boy is late who has been making evident efforts to be punctual; the teacher good-naturedly foregoes rebuke or penalty, and the boy says to himself,—"It doesn't matter," and begins to form the unpunctual habit. The mistake the teacher makes is to suppose that to be punctual is troublesome to the boy, so he will let him off; whereas the office of the habits of an ordered life is to make such life easy and

103   spontaneous; the effort is confined to the first half dozen or score of occasions for doing the thing.

Consider how laborious life would be were its wheels not greased by habits of cleanliness, neatness, order, courtesy; had we to make the effort of decision about every detail of dressing and eating, coming and going, life would not be worth living. Every cottage mother knows that she must train her child in habits of decency, and a whole code of habits of propriety get themselves formed just because a breach in any such habit causes a shock to others which few children have courage to face. Physical fitness, morals and manners, are very largely the outcome of habit; and not only so, but the habits of the religious life also become fixed and delightful and give us due support in the effort to live a godly, righteous and sober life. We need not be deterred by the fear that religious habits in a child are mechanical, uninformed by the ideas which should give them value. Let us hear what the young De Quincey felt about going to church:—

"On Sunday mornings I went with the rest of my family to church: it was a church on the ancient model of England having aisles, galleries, organ, all things ancient and venerable, and the proportions were majestic. Here, whilst the congregation knelt through the long litany, as often as we came to that passage so beautiful amongst many that are so where God is supplicated on behalf of 'all sick persons and young children' and 'that He would show His pity upon all prisoners and captives,' I wept in secret, and raising my streaming eyes to the upper windows saw, on days when the sun was shining, a spectacle as affecting as ever prophet can have beheld. ... *There* were the Apostles that had trampled upon earth and the glories upon earth, *there* were the martyrs who had borne witness to the truth through flames. . . . And all the time I saw through the wide central field of the window where the glass was uncoloured white fleecy clouds sailing over the azure depths of the sky."

And then the little boy had visions of sick children upon whom God would have pity.—

104

"These visions were self-sustained, the hint from the Litany, the fragment from the clouds, those and the storied windows were sufficient. . . . God speaks to children also in dreams and by the oracles that lurk in darkness; but in solitude, above all things when made vocal to the meditative heart by the truths and services of a national church, God holds with children 'communion undisturbed.'"

With such a testimony before us, supported by gleams of recollection on our own part, we may take courage to believe that what we rightly call Divine Service is particularly appropriate to children; and will become more so as the habit of reading beautifully written books quickens their sense of style and their unconscious appreciation of the surpassingly beautiful diction of our liturgy.

We have seen the value of habit in mind and morals, religion and physical development. It is as we have seen disastrous when child or man learns to think in a groove, and shivers like an unaccustomed bather on the steps of a new notion. This danger is perhaps averted by giving children as their daily diet the wise thoughts of great minds, and of many great minds; so that they may gradually and unconsciously get the courage of their opinions. If we fail in this duty, so soon as the young people get their 'liberty' they will run after the first fad that presents itself; try it for a while and then take up another to be discarded in its turn, and remain uncertain and ill-guided for the rest of their days.

3.—EDUCATION IS A LIFE

We have left until the last that instrument of education implied in the phrase 'Education is a life'; 'implied' because life is no more self-existing than it is self-supporting; it requires sustenance, regular, ordered and fitting. This is fully recognised as regards bodily life and, possibly, the great discovery of the twentieth century will be that mind too requires its ordered rations and perishes when these fail. We know that food is to the body what fuel is to the steam-engine, the sole source of energy; once we realise that the mind too works only as it is fed education will appear to us in a new light. The body pines and develops humours upon tabloids and other food substitutes; and a glance at a 'gate' crowd watching a football match makes us wonder what sort of mind-food those men and boys are sustained on, whether they are not suffering from depletion, inanition, notwithstanding big and burly bodies. For the mind is capable of dealing with only one kind of food; it lives, grows and is nourished upon ideas only; mere information is to it as a meal of sawdust to the body; there are no organs for the assimilation of the one more than of the other.

105

What is an idea? we ask, and find ourselves plunged beyond our depth. A live thing of the mind, seems to be the conclusion of our greatest thinkers from Plato to Bacon, from Bacon to Coleridge. We all know how an idea '*strikes*,' '*seizes*,' '*catches hold of*,' '*impresses*' us and at last, if it be big enough, '*possesses*' us; in a word, behaves like an entity.

If we enquire into any person's habits of life, mental

preoccupation, devotion to a cause or pursuit, he will usually tell us that such and such an idea struck him. This potency of an idea is matter of common recognition. No phrase is more common and more promising than, 'I have an idea'; we rise to such an opening as trout to a well-chosen fly. There is but one sphere in which the word idea never occurs, in which the conception of an idea is curiously absent, and that sphere is education! Look at any publisher's list of school books and you shall find that the books recommended are carefully dessicated, drained of the least suspicion of an idea, reduced to the driest statements of fact. Here perhaps the Public Schools have a little pull over the rest of us; the diet they afford may be meagre, meagre almost to starvation point for the average boy, but it is not destitute of ideas; for, however sparsely, boys are nourished on the best thoughts of the best minds.

106

Coleridge has done more than other thinkers to bring the conception of an idea within the sphere of the scientific thought of to-day; not as that thought is expressed in *psychology*, a term which he himself launched upon the world with an apology for it as *insolens verbum* ("we beg pardon for the use of this *insolens verbum* but it is one of which our language stands in great need." *Method*, S. T. Coleridge) but as shewing the re-action of mind to an idea. This is how in his *Method* Coleridge illustrates the rise and progress of such an idea:—

"We can recall no incident of human history that impresses the imagination more deeply than the moment when Columbus on an unknown ocean first perceived that baffling fact, the change of the magnetic needle. How many instances occur in history when the ideas of nature (presented to chosen minds by a Higher Power than Nature herself) suddenly unfold as it were in prophetic succession systematic views destined to produce the most important revolutions in the state of man! The clear spirit of Columbus was doubtless eminently methodical. He saw distinctly that great leading idea which authorised the poor pilot to become a 'promiser of kingdoms.'"

Here we get such a genesis of an idea as fits in curiously with what we know of the history of great inventions and discoveries "presented to chosen minds by a higher Power than Nature herself." It corresponds too, not only with the ideas that rule our own lives, but with the origin of practical ideas which is unfolded to us by the prophet Isaiah:—

> "Doth the ploughman plough continually to ... open and break the clods of his ground? When he hath made plain the face thereof, doth he not cast abroad the fitches and scatter the cummin and put the wheat in rows ... for his God doth instruct him aright and doth teach him. . . . Bread corn is ground for he will not ever be threshing it. . . . This also cometh from the Lord of Hosts which is wonderful in counsel and excellent in working."*

107

---

* Isaiah xxviii.

Let us hear Coleridge further on the subject of those ideas which may invest us as an atmosphere rather than strike as a weapon:—

> "The idea may exist in a clear and definite form as that of a circle in that of the mind of a geometrician or it may be a mere instinct, a vague appetency towards something... like the impulse which fills a young poet's eyes with tears."

These indefinite ideas which express themselves in an 'appetency' towards something and which should draw a child towards things honest, lovely and of good report, are not to be offered of set purpose or at set times: they are held in that thought-atmosphere which surrounds him, breathed as his breath of life.

It is distressing to think that our poor words and ways should be thus *inspired* by children; but to recognise the fact will make us careful not to admit sordid or unworthy thoughts and motives into our dealings with them.

Coleridge treats in more detail those definite ideas which are not inhaled as air but are conveyed as meat to the mind:—

> "From the first or initiative idea, as from a seed, successive ideas germinate." "Events and images, the lively and spirit-stirring machinery of the external world, are like light and air and moisture to the seed of the mind which would else rot and perish." "The paths in which

we may pursue a methodical course are manifold and at the head of each stands its peculiar and guiding idea. Those ideas are as regularly subordinate in dignity as the paths to which they point are various and eccentric in direction. The world has suffered much in modern times from a subversive and necessary natural order of science ... from summoning reason and faith to the bar of that limited physical experience to which by the true laws of method they owe no obedience. Progress follows the path of the idea from which it sets out requiring however a constant wakefulness of mind to keep it within the due limits of its course. Hence the orbits of thought, so to speak, must differ from among themselves as the initiative ideas differ." (*Method*, S. T. C.).

Is it not a fact that the new light which biology is throwing upon the laws of mind is bringing us back to the Platonic doctrine that "An idea is a distinguishable power, self-affirmed and seen in unity with the Eternal Essence"?

I have ventured to repeat from an earlier volume* this slight exposition of Coleridge's teaching, because his doctrine corresponds with common experience and should reverse our ordinary educational practice. The whole subject is profound, but as practical as it is profound. We must disabuse our minds of the theory that the functions of education are in the main gymnastic, a continual drawing

---

* *Parents and Children*, by the Writer.

out without a corresponding act of putting in. The modern emphasis upon 'self-expression' has given new currency to this idea; we who know how little there is in us that we have not received, that the most we can do is to give an original twist, a new application, to an idea that has been passed on to us; who recognise, humbly enough, that we are but torch-bearers, passing on our light to the next as we have received it from the last, even we invite children to 'express themselves' about a tank, a Norman castle, the Man in the Moon, not recognising that the quaint things children say on unfamiliar subjects are no more than a patchwork of notions picked up here and there. One is not sure that so-called original composition is wholesome for children, because their consciences are alert and they are quite aware of their borrowings; it may be better that they should read on a theme before they write upon it, using then as much latitude as they like.

109 In the early days of a child's life it makes little apparent difference whether we educate with a notion of filling a receptacle, inscribing a tablet, moulding plastic matter, or nourishing a life, but as a child grows we shall perceive that only those *ideas* which have fed his life are taken into his being; all the rest is cast away or is, like sawdust in the system, an impediment and an injury.

Education is a life. That life is sustained on ideas. Ideas are of spiritual origin, and God has made us so that we get them chiefly as we convey them to one another, whether by word of mouth, written page, Scripture word, musical symphony; but we must sustain a child's inner life with ideas as we sustain his body with food. Probably he will reject nine-tenths of the ideas we offer, as he makes use of only a small proportion of his bodily food, rejecting the rest. He is an eclectic; he may choose this or that; our business is to supply him with due abundance and variety and his to take what he needs. Urgency on our part annoys him. He resists forcible feeding and loathes predigested food. What suits him best is pabulum presented in the indirect literary form which Our Lord adopts in those wonderful parables whose quality is that they cannot be forgotten though, while every detail of the story is remembered, its application may pass and leave no trace. We, too, must take this risk. We may offer children as their sustenance the Lysander of Plutarch, an object lesson, we think, shewing what a statesman or a citizen should avoid: but, who knows, the child may take to Lysander and think his 'cute' ways estimable! Again, we take the risk, as did our Lord in that puzzling parable of the Unjust Steward. One other caution; it seems to be necessary to present ideas with a great deal of padding, as they reach us in a novel or poem or history book written with literary power. A child cannot in mind or body live upon tabloids however scientifically prepared; out of a whole big book he may not get more than half a dozen of those ideas upon which his spirit thrives; and they come in unexpected places and unrecognised forms, so that no grown person is capable of making such extracts from Scott or Dickens or Milton, as will certainly give him nourishment. It is a

110

case of,—"In the morning sow thy seed and in the evening withhold not thine hand for thou knowest not whether shall prosper, either this or that."

One of our presumptuous sins in this connection is that we venture to offer opinions to children (and to older persons) instead of ideas. We believe that an opinion expresses thought and therefore embodies an idea. Even if it did so once the very act of crystallization into opinion destroys any vitality it may have had; *pace* Ruskin, a crystal is not a living body and does not feed men. We think to feed children on the dogmas of a church, the theorems of Euclid, mere abstracts of history, and we wonder that their education does not seem to take hold of them. Let us hear M. Fouillée* on this subject, for to him the idea is all in all both in philosophy and education. But there is a function of education upon which M. Fouillée hardly touches, that of the formation of habits, physical, intellectual, moral.

"'Scientific truths,' said Descartes, 'are battles won.' Describe to the young the principal and most heroic of these battles; you will thus interest them in the results of science and you will develop in them a scientific spirit by means of the enthusiasm for the conquest of truth. ... How interesting Arithmetic and Geometry might be if we gave a short history of their principal theorems, if the child were meant to be present at the labours of a Pythagoras, a Plato, a Euclid, or in modern times, of a

* *Education from a National Standpoint.*

Descartes, a Pascal, or a Leibnitz. Great theories instead of being lifeless and anonymous abstractions would become living human truths each with its own history like a statue by Michael Angelo or like a painting by Raphael."

Here we have an application of Coleridge's 'captain-idea' of every train of thought; that is, not a naked generalisation, (neither children nor grown persons find aliment in these), but an idea clothed upon with fact, history and story, so that the mind may perform the acts of selection and inception from a mass of illustrative details. Thus Dickens makes 'David Copperfield' tell us that,—"I was a very observant child," and that "all children are very observant," not as a dry abstraction, but as an inference from a number of charming natural incidents.

All roads lead to Rome, and all I have said is meant to enforce the fact that much and varied humane reading, as well as human thought expressed in the forms of art, is, not a luxury, a tit-bit, to be given to children now and then, but their very bread of life, which they must have in abundant portions and at regular periods. This and more is implied in the phrase, "The mind feeds on ideas and therefore children should have a generous curriculum."

Chapter 7

How We Make Use of Mind

"We hold that the child's mind is no mere sac to hold ideas but is rather, if the figure may be allowed, a 'spiritual organism' with an appetite for all knowledge. This is its proper diet with which it is prepared to deal and what it is able to digest and assimilate as the body does food-stuffs.

"Such a doctrine as the Herbartian, that the mind is a receptacle, lays the stress of education, the preparation of food in enticing morsels, duly ordered, upon the teacher. Children taught on this principle are in danger of receiving much teaching but little knowledge; the teacher's axiom being 'what a child learns matters less than how he learns it.'"

I cannot resist presenting the Herbartian Psychology in the dry light of Scottish humour.* 112

"We have failed to explain ideas by the mind, how about explaining the mind by ideas? You are not to suppose

---

* *The Herbartian Psychology applied to Education*, by John Adams.

159

that this is exactly how Herbart puts it, Herbart is a philosopher, a German philosopher. It is true that he starts with the mind or, as he prefers to call it, a soul: but do not fear that the sport of the hunt is to be spoiled for that. . . . The 'given' soul is no more a real soul than it is a real crater of a volcano. It has absolutely no content: it is not even an idea trap. Ideas can slip in and out of it as they please, or, rather, as other ideas please but the soul has no power either to call, make, keep, or recall, an idea. The ideas arrange all these matters among themselves. The mind can make no objection."

"'The soul has no capacity nor faculty whatever either to receive or produce anything: it is therefore no *tabula rasa* in the sense that impressions, foreign to its nature, may be made on it. Also it is no substance in Leibnitz's sense, which includes original self-activity. It has originally neither ideas, nor feelings, nor desires. Further, within it lie no forms of intuition and thought, no laws of willing and acting, nor any sort of predisposition however remote towards these. The simple nature of the soul is totally unknown and for ever remains so. It is as little a subject for speculative as for empirical psychology.' (*Lehrbuch zur Psychologie*, by Herbart: Part III: pp. 153, 153.) Thus, a vigorous *vis inertiae* is the only power of the mind. Still it is subject to the action of certain forces. Nothing but ideas (*Vorstellung*) can attack the soul so that the ideas really make up the mind."

We are familiar with the struggle of ideas on the threshold, with the good luck of those that get in and especially of those that get in first and mount to high places; with the behaviour of ideas, very much like that of persons who fall into groups in an anarchical state. This behaviour is described as the formation of 'apperception masses' and the mass that is sufficiently strong has it all its own way and dominates the mind. Our business is not to examine the psychology of Herbart, a very serious and suggestive contribution to our knowledge of educational principles, but rather to consider how it works out practically in education. But before we examine how Herbartian psychology bears this test of experiment, let us consider what Professor William James has to say of psychology in general.

"When we talk of psychology as a natural science," he tells us, "we must not assume that that means a sort of psychology that stands at last on solid ground. It means just the reverse. It means a psychology particularly fragile and into which the waters of metaphysical criticism leak at every joint, a psychology all of whose elementary assumptions and data must be reconsidered in wider connections and translated into other terms. It is, in short, a phrase of diffidence and not of arrogance; and it is indeed strange to hear people talk triumphantly of the 'New Psychology' and write Histories of Psychology when into the real elements and forces which the word covers not the first glimpse of clear insight exists.

114   A string of raw facts, a little gossip and wrangle about
        opinions, a little classification and generalisation on the
        mere descriptive level . . . but not a single law . . . not a
        single proposition from which any consequence can
        casually be deduced."

But Professor James went on and wrote his extraordinarily interesting book on psychology, and we must do the same though our basis is no more than the common experience of mankind so far as one mind can express the experience common to us all.

Herbart's psychology is extraordinarily gratifying and attractive to teachers who are, like other people, eager to magnify their office; and here is a scheme which shows how every child is a new creation as he comes forth from the hands of his teacher. The teacher learns how to do it; he has but to draw together a mass of those ideas which themselves will combine in the mind into which they effect an entrance, and, behold, the thing is done: the teacher has done it; he has selected the ideas, shewn the correlation of each with the other and the work is complete! The ideas establish themselves, the most potent rule and gather force, and if these be good, the man is made.

Here, for example, is a single week's 'Correlation of Subjects' worked out by a highly qualified teacher. "*Arithmetic (Decimal Fractions), Mathematics (Simple Equations, Parallelograms), Science (Latent Heat), Housecraft (Nerves, Thought, Habits), Geography (Scotland, General Industries);*

or, again, for another week,—under the same headings,—
*Metric problems, Symbols (four rules), Triangles (sum angles),
Machinery, Circulation, Sculpture of the British Isles.*" The
ideas, no doubt, have an agility and ability which we do not
possess and know how to jump at each other and form the
desired 'apperception masses.'

A successful and able modern educationalist gives us a
valuable introduction to Herbartian Principles, and by way   115
of example, "*A Robinson Crusoe Concentration Scheme*," a
series of lessons given to children in Standard I in an Elementary School. First we have nine lessons in literature
and language, the subjects being such as '*Robinson climbs
a hill and finds he is on an island.*' Then, ten object lessons
of which the first is,—*The Sea*, the second, *A Ship from
Foreign Parts*, the sixth, *A Life-Boat*, the seventh, *Shell-Fish*,
the tenth, *A Cave*. How these 'objects' are to be produced
one does not see. The third series are drawing lessons, probably as many, a boat, a ship, an oar, an anchor and so on.
Then follows a series on manual training, still built upon
'Robinson'; the first, a model of the sea-shore; then, models
of Robinson's island, of Robinson's house and Robinson's
pottery. The next course consists of reading, an indefinite
number of lessons,—'passages from *The Child's Robinson
Crusoe* and from a general Reader on the matters discussed
in object lessons.' Then follows a series of writing lessons,
"simple composition on the subject of the lessons. . . . The
children framed the sentences which the teacher wrote on
the blackboard and the class copied afterwards." Here is

one composition,—"Robinson spent his first night in a tree. In the morning he was hungry but he saw nothing round him but grass and trees without fruit. On the sea-shore he found some shell-fish which he ate." Compare this with the voluminous output of children of six or seven working on the P.U.S. scheme upon any subject that they know; with, indeed, the pages they will dictate after a single reading of a chapter of Robinson Crusoe, not a 'child's edition.'

Arithmetic follows with, no doubt, as many lessons, "many mental examples and simple problems dealt with Robinson"; the eighth and last course was in singing and recitation,—'I am monarch of all I survey,' etc. "The lessons lasted about forty-five minutes each. . . . Under ordinary conditions the story of 'Robinson Crusoe' would be the leading feature in the work of a whole year. . . . In comparing the English classes with the German classes I have seen studying 'Robinson Crusoe' I was convinced that the eagerness and interest was as keen among the children here as in the German schools. . . . One easily sees what a wealth of material there is in the further development of the story." One does indeed! The whole thing must be highly amusing to the teacher, as ingenious amplifications self-produced always are: that the children too were entertained, one does not doubt. The teacher was probably at her best in getting by sheer force much out of little: she was, in fact, acting a part and the children were entertained as at a show, cinema or other; but of one thing we may be sure, an utter distaste, a loathing, on the part of the children ever after, not only for 'Robinson Crusoe' but for every one of the subjects lugged in to illustrate his adventures. We read elsewhere of an apple affording a text for a hundred lessons, including the making of a ladder, (in paper), to gather the apples; but, alas, the eating of the worn-out apple is not suggested! The author whom we quote for 'Robinson Crusoe' and whom we refrain from naming because, as a Greek Chorus might say, 'we cannot praise,' follows the 'Robinson' series with another interminable series on the Armada.

The conscientious, ingenious and laborious teachers who produce these 'concentration series' are little aware that each such lesson is an act of *lèse majesté*. The children who are capable of and eager for a wide range of knowledge and literary expression are reduced to inanities; a lifelong *ennui* is set up; every approach to knowledge suggests avenues for boredom, and the children's minds sicken and perish long before their school-days come to an end. I have pursued this subject at some length because we, too, believe in ideas as the proper and only diet upon which children's minds grow. 117 We are more in the dark about Mind than about Mars! We can but judge by effects, and these appear to point to the conclusion that mind is a 'spiritual organism.' (I need not apologise for speaking of that which has no substance as an 'organism,'—no greater a contradiction in terms than Herbart's 'apperception masses.') By an analogy with Body we conclude that Mind requires regular and sufficient sustenance; and that this sustenance is afforded by ideas we may gather from the insatiable eagerness with which these are appropriated, and the evident growth and development manifested under such pabulum. That children like feeble and tedious oral lessons, feeble and tedious story books, does not at all prove that these are wholesome food; they like lollipops but cannot live upon them; yet there is a serious attempt in certain schools to supply the intellectual, moral, and religious needs of children by appropriate 'sweetmeats.'

As I have said elsewhere, the ideas required for the sustenance of children are to be found mainly in books of literary quality; given these the mind does for itself the sorting, arranging, selecting, rejecting, classifying, which Herbart leaves to the struggle of the promiscuous ideas which manage to cross the threshold. Nor is this merely a nominal distinction; Herbart was a philosopher and therefore his thought embraced the universal. Probably few schools of the day are consciously following the theories of this philosopher; but in most schools, in England and elsewhere, so far as any intelligent rationale is followed it is that of Herbart. There are many reasons for this fact. A scheme which throws the whole burden of education on the teacher, which exalts the personality of the teacher as the chief agent in education, which affords ingenious, interesting, and more or less creative work to a vast number of highly intelligent and devoted persons, whose passionate hope is to leave the world a little better than they found it by means of those children whom they have raised to a higher level, must needs make a wide and successful appeal.

It appeals equally to Education Committees and school managers. Consider the saving involved in the notion that teachers are compendiums of all knowledge, that they have but, as it were, to turn on the tap and the necessary knowledge flows forth. All responsibility is shifted, and the relief is very great. Not only so but lessons are delightful to watch and to hear; the success of jig-saw puzzles illustrates a tendency in human nature to delight in the ingenious putting together of unlikely things, as, for example, a lifebuoy and Robinson Crusoe. There is a series of small triumphs to be observed any day of the week, and these same triumphs are brought about by dramatic display,—so ingenious, pleasing, fascinating, are the ways in which the teacher chooses to arrive at her point. I say 'her' point because women excel in this kind of teaching, but men do not come far short. What of the children themselves? They, too, are amused and entertained, they enjoy the puzzle-element and greatly enjoy the teacher who lays herself out to attract them. There is no flaw in the practical working of the method while it is being carried out. Later, it gives rise to dismay and anxiety among thoughtful people.

Much water has run under the bridge since several years ago Mr. A. Paterson startled us out of self-complacency with his *Across the Bridges*. We as a nation were well pleased at the time with the result of our efforts; nothing could be more intelligent, alert, brighter, than the seventh standard boy about to leave school and take up his life work. Conditions were unpropitious. We know the old story of inviting blind alleys, present success and then unemployment, with resulting depreciation in character. What is to be done? The question of after conditions is now being taken up seriously.

119 We have Continuation Classes which even if a boy be out of work will help him to the Chinese art of 'saving his face.' But Mr. Paterson condemns the schools for the rapidity with which their best boys run to seed. He does not quote the case of the boy who gets work, earns fair wages, conducts himself respectably, goes to a 'Polytechnic,' the sort of boy with whom Mr. Pett Ridge makes us familiar, who is so much less than he might be, so crude in his notions, so unmoral in his principles, so poor in interests, so meagre if not coarse in his choice of pleasures and after all such a good fellow at bottom. He might have been taught in school to utilise his powers, to come into the enjoyment of the fine mind that is in him; but in schools,—

> "There is too much learning and too little work. The teacher ready to use the powers that his training and experience have given him works too hard while the boy's share in the struggle is too light. It is possible to make education too easy for children and to rob learning of the mental discipline which often wearies but in the end produces concentration and the capacity to work alone. ... He is rarely left to himself with the book in his hands, forced to concentrate all his mind on the dull words before him with no one at hand to explain or make the memory work easier by little tricks of repetition

and association. . . . The boy who reaches the seventh standard with every promise and enters the service of a railway company is first required to sit down by himself and master the symbols of the telegraphic code. This he finds extremely irksome for the only work he has ever done alone before is the learning of racy poetry which is the very mildest form of mental discipline." "'Silent reading' is occasionally allowed in odd half-hours. . . . It might well be a regular subject for reading aloud is but a poor gift compared with the practice of reading in private."*

What does his curriculum do for the boy? Let us again hear Mr. Paterson:—[†]

"What is the educational ideal set before the average boy whose school-days are to end at fourteen? What type is it that the authorities seek to produce? A glance at the syllabus will reassure the ordinary cynic who still labours under the quaint delusion that French and Algebra and violin-playing are taught in every London Elementary School at the expense of the ratepayer. . . . The syllabus was designed to leave a boy at fourteen with a thoroughly sound and practical knowledge of reading, writing and arithmetic and with such grounding in English, geography and history, as may enable him to read a newspaper

120

---

* *Across the Bridges*, by A. Paterson.
† *Across the Bridges*, by A. Paterson.

or give a vote with some idea of what he is doing. . . . But these are all subsidiary to teaching the three 'R's' which between them occupy more than half the twenty-four hours of teaching in the week. . . . It is certain that the present object in view is dispiriting to master and boy alike for a knowledge of reading, writing and arithmetic is no education and no training but merely the elementary condition of further knowledge. In many schools the boy is labouring on with these mere rudiments for two or more years after all reasonable requirements have been satisfied. The intelligent visitor looking at the note-books of an average class will be amazed at the high standard of the neatness and accuracy but he will find the excellence of a very visible order. The handwriting is admirable, sixteen boys out of thirty can write compositions without a flaw in grammar or spelling. Yet it will occur to him that the powers of voluntary thought and reason, of spontaneous enquiry and imagination, have not been stirred. This very perfection of form makes him suspicious as to the fundamental principles of our State curriculum. In Public Schools boys are not trained to be lawyers, or parsons, or doctors, but to be men. If they have learned to work systematically and think independently they are then fit to be trained for such life and profession as taste or necessity may dictate. But at our Elementary Schools we seem to aim at producing a nation of clerks for it is only to a clerk that this perfection of writing and spelling is a necessary training."

The very faults of his qualities nullify the work of the teacher. His failing is that he does too much. Once more we quote our authority:—

"With the average boy there is a marked waste of mental capital between the ages of ten and thirteen and the aggregate of this loss to the country is heavy indeed. Ten years at school conquer many of the drawbacks of home and discover a quick, receptive mind in the normal child. . . . Many opportunities have been lost in these years of school but after fourteen there is a more disastrous relapse. The brain is not taxed again and shrivels into a mere centre of limited formulae acting automatically in response to appetite or sensation. The boy's general education fails utterly. Asia is but a name that it is difficult to spell though at school he spoke of its rivers and ports. . . . It is probable that the vocabulary of a working man at forty is actually smaller than it was at fourteen so shrunk is the power of the mind to feed upon the growing experience of life. . . . Of the majority of boys it is true to say that only half their ability is ever used in the work they find to do on leaving school, the other half curls up and sleeps for ever."

121

Here we have a depressing prospect of grievous waste in the future. We all applaud the Education Act of 1918, are convinced that every boy and girl will receive education until the end of his sixteenth, possibly eighteenth, year. A wave of generous feeling passed over the nation and employers were willing to support the law; and if the eight hours conceded be spent in making the young people more reliable, intelligent and responsible persons no doubt the employers will be rewarded for their generosity.

But there are rocks ahead. The only way to take advantage of this provision is to make this an eight hours' University course. Now as Mr. Paterson happily remarks the Universities do not undertake to prepare barristers, parsons, stockbrokers, bankers, or even soldiers and sailors, with a specialised knowledge proper for each profession. Their implicit contention is, given a well-educated man with cultivated imagination, trained judgment, wide interests, and he is prepared to master the intricacies of any profession; while he knows at the same time how to make use of himself, of the powers with which nature and education have endowed him for his own happiness; the delightful employment of his leisure; for the increased happiness of his neighbours and the well-being of the community; that is, such a man is able, not only to earn his living, but to *live*. The Universities fulfil this claim; the various professions abound with men who, in newspaper phrase, are 'ornaments to their professions,' and who gave up leisure and means to serve their fellow-citizens as magistrates, churchwardens, members of committees, special constables when needed, until lately, members of Parliament, holding service as an honour, and as proud as was 'Godfrey Bertram,' that unhappy laird in *Guy Mannering*, to write

'J.P.' after their names. The enormous amount of voluntary service rendered in such ways throughout the Empire as well as that of insufficiently, or duly, paid service justifies the Universities in their reading of their peculiar function. But not only so, generous disinterested work can never be paid for, and our great statesmen, churchmen, soldiers and civil servants, as well as the members of County, Municipal, and Urban District Councils, have done their *devoir* over and above the bond.

To secure this same splendidly devoted voluntary service from all classes is the task set before us as a nation, a task the more easy because we have all seen it fulfilled in the War when every man was a potential hero. Now is it not the fact that the Army proved itself an unequalled University for our men, offering them increased knowledge, broad views, lofty aims, duty and discipline, along with the finest physical culture? So much so, that instead of going on from where the War left off, we have to be on the watch against retrograde movements, physical, moral, intellectual. The downward grade is always at hand and we know how easy it is. We cannot afford another great war for the education of our people but we must in some way supply the 'University' element and Mr. Fisher's great Act points out such a way. The young people are for four years (a proper academic period) to be under influences that make for 'sweetness and light.' But we must keep to the academic ideal: all preparation for specialised industries should be taboo. Special teaching towards engineering, 123 cotton-spinning, and the rest, is quite unnecessary for every manufacturer knows that given a 'likely' lad he will soon be turned into a good workman in the works themselves. The splendid record of women workers in the war supports our contention. The efforts of Technical Schools and the like are not greatly prized by the heads of firms so far as the technical knowledge they afford goes. Boys from them are employed rather on the off chance that they may turn out intelligent and apt than for what they know beforehand of the business. Here is one more reason for treating the Continuation School as the People's University and absolutely eschewing all money-making arts and crafts. Denmark and Scandinavia have tried this generous policy of educating young people, not according to the requirements of their trade but according to their natural capacity to know and their natural desire for knowledge, that desire to know history, poetry, science, art, which is natural to every man; and the success of the experiment now a century old is an object lesson for the rest of the world.

Germany has pursued a different ideal. Her efforts, too, have been great, unified by the idea of utility; and, if we will only remember the lesson, the war has shown us how futile is an education which affords no moral or intellectual uplift, no motive higher than the learner's peculiar advantage and that of the State. Germany became morally bankrupt (for a season only, let us hope) not solely because of the war but as the result of an education which ignored the things of the spirit or gave these a nominal place and a poor rendering in a utilitarian syllabus. We are encouraged to face the fact boldly that it is a People's University we should aim at, a University with its thousands of Colleges up and down the land, each of them the Continuation School (the name is not inviting) for some one neighbourhood.

But, it will be argued, the subject matter of a University education is conveyed for the most part through the channel of dead languages, Latin and Greek. Our contention is that, however ennobling the literature in these tongues, we cannot honestly allow our English literature to take a second place to any other, and that therefore whatever Sophocles, Thucydides, Virgil, have it in them to do towards a higher education, may be effected more readily by Milton, Gibbon, Shakespeare, Bacon, and a multitude of great thinkers who are therefore great writers. Learning conveyed in our common speech is easier come by than that secreted in a dead language and this fact will help us to deal with the inadequacy of the period allowed. Given absolute attention, and we can do much with four hundred hours a year (1,600 hours in our four years' course) but only if we go to work with a certainty that the young students crave knowledge of what we call the 'humanities,' that they read with absolute attention and that, having read, they *know*. They will welcome the preparation for public speaking, an effort for which everyone must qualify in these days, which the act of narration offers.

The alternative is some such concentration scheme as that indicated in *Robinson Crusoe*,—a year's work on soap,

124

its manufacture, ingredients, the Soap Trade, Soap Transport, the Uses of Soap, how to make out a Soap invoice, the Sorts of Soap, and so on *ad infinitum*. Each process in the iron, cotton, nail, pin, engine, button,—each process in our thousand and one manufactures—will offer its own ingenious Concentration Scheme. The advocates of utilitarian education will be delighted, the young students will be kept busy and will to some extent use their wits all the time. With what result? Some two centuries ago when a movement for adolescent education agitated Europe, devastated by the Napoleonic wars, we English took our part.

125　The current early divided into two streams, the material and the spiritual, the useful and the educative, and England, already great in manufactures, was carried along by the first of these streams, followed by Germany, France, Switzerland; while the Scandinavian group of countries learned at the lips of that 'Father of the People's High Schools' that "spirit is might, spirit reveals itself in spirit, spirit works only in freedom." We see the apotheosis of utilitarian education in the Munich schools on the one hand and in the *morale* of the German army on the other. But we are slow to learn because we have set up a little tin god of efficiency in that niche within our private pantheon which should be occupied by personality. We trouble ourselves about the uses of the young person to society. As for his own use, what he should be in and for himself, why, what matter? Because, say we, if we fit him to earn his living we fit him also to be of service to the world and what better can we do for him personally? We forget that it is written, Man shall not live by bread alone, but by every word that proceedeth out of the mouth of God shall man live,—whether it be spoken in the way of some truth of religion, poem, picture, scientific discovery, or literary expression; by these things men live and in all such is the life of the spirit. The spiritual life requires the food of ideas for its daily bread. We shall find, in the words of a well-known Swedish professor, that, "just as enrichment of the soil gives the best conditions for the seed sown in it so a well-grounded humanistic training provides the surest basis for a business capacity, and not the least so in the case of the coming farmer." But we need not go so far afield, we have a prophet of our own, and I will close this part of my subject by quoting certain of Mr. Fisher's words of wisdom:—

"Now let me say something about the content of education, about the things which should be actually taught in the schools, and I am only going to talk in the very broadest possible way. In my afternoon's reading I came upon another very apposite remark in the letters of John Stuart Mill. Let me read it to you:—

126

'What the poor, as well as the rich, require is not to be taught other people's opinions, but to be induced and enabled to think for themselves. It is not physical science that will do this, even if they could learn it much more thoroughly than they are able to do.'

"The young people of this country are not to be regenerated by economic doctrine or economic history or physical science; they can only be elevated by ideas which act upon the imagination and act upon the character and influence the soul, and it is the function of all good teachers to bring those ideas before them.

"I have sometimes heard it said that you should not teach patriotism in the school. I dissent from that doctrine. I think that patriotism should be taught in the schools. I will tell you what I mean by patriotism. By patriotism I do not mean Jingoism, but what I mean by patriotism is an intelligent appreciation of all things noble in the romances, in the literature and in the history of one's own country. Young people should be taught to admire what is great while they are at school. And remember that for the poor of this country the school is a far more important factor than it is for the rich people of this country. . . .

"I say that I want patriotism in the larger sense of the term taught in the schools. Of course there is a great deal to criticise in any country, and I should be the last person to suggest that the critical faculty should not be exercised and trained at school. But before we teach children to criticise the institutions of their country, before we teach them to be critical of what is bad, let us teach them to recognize and admire what is good. After all life is very short; we all of us have only one life to live, and during that life let us get into ourselves as much love, as much admiration, as much elevating pleasure as we can, and if we view education merely as discipline in critical bitterness, then we shall lose all the sweets of life and we shall make ourselves unnecessarily miserable. There is quite enough sorrow and hardship in this world as it is without introducing it prematurely to young people.". . .

N.B.—Probably some educational authorities may decide to give one hour or two weekly to physical training and handicrafts, in which case the time-table must allow for so much the less reading. But I should like to urge that, with the long evening leisure of which there is promise, Club life will become an important feature in every village and district. Classes will certainly be arranged for military and other drills, gymnastics, dancing, singing, swimming, carpentry, cooking, nursing, dress-making, weaving, pottery, acting,—in fact, whatever the quickened intelligence of the community demands. No compulsion would be necessary to enforce attendance at classes, for which the machinery is already in existence in most places, and which, associated with Club life, would have certain social attractions in the way of public displays, prize givings and so on. The intellectual life of the Continuation School should give zest to these evening occupations as well as to the Saturday Field Club which no neighbourhood should be without.

I have put the case for Continuation Schools as strongly as may be, but there is a more excellent way. In these days

127

of high wages it may well happen that parents will be willing to let their children remain at school until the end of their seventeenth year, in which case they will be able to go on with the 'secondary education' which they have begun at the age of six and we shall see a new thing in the world. Every man and woman will have received a liberal education; life will no longer discount the ideas and aims of the schoolroom, and, if according to the Platonic saying, "Knowledge is virtue," knowledge informed by religion, we shall see even in our own day how righteousness exalteth a nation.

Chapter 8

1.—The Way of the Will

We may offer to children two guides to moral and intellectual self-management which we may call 'the Way of the Will' and 'the Way of the Reason.'

The Way of the Will: Children should be taught (a) to distinguish between 'I want' and 'I will.' (b) That the way to will effectively is to turn our thoughts away from that which we desire but do not will. (c) That the best way to turn our thoughts is to think of, or do some quite different thing, entertaining or interesting. (d) That after a little rest in this way, the will returns to its work with new vigour. (This adjunct of the will is familiar to us as diversion, whose office it is to ease us for a time from will effort that we may 'will' again with added power. The use of suggestion as an aid to the will is to be deprecated, as lending to stultify and stereotype character. It would seem that spontaneity is a condition of development, and that human nature needs the discipline of failure as well as of success.)

The great things of life, life itself, are not easy of definition. The Will, we are told, is 'the sole practical faculty of man.' But who is to define the Will? We are told again that 'the Will is the man'; and yet most men go through life without a single definite act of willing. Habit, convention, the customs of the world have done so much for us that we get up, dress, breakfast, follow our morning's occupations, our later relaxations, without an act of choice. For this much at any rate we know about the will. Its function is to *choose*, to decide, and there seems to be no doubt that the greater becomes the effort of decision the weaker grows the general will. Opinions are provided for us, we take our principles at second or third hand, our habits are suitable, and convenient, and what more is necessary for a decent and orderly life? But the one achievement possible and necessary for every man is character; and character is as finely wrought metal beaten into shape and beauty by the repeated and accustomed action of will. We who teach should make it clear to ourselves that our aim in education is less conduct than character; conduct may be arrived at, as we have seen, by indirect routes, but it is of value to the world only as it has its source in character.

129

Every assault upon the flesh and spirit of man is an attack however insidious upon his personality, his will; but a new Armageddon is upon us in so far as that the attack is no longer indirect but is aimed consciously and directly at the will, which is the man; and we shall escape becoming a nation of imbeciles only because there will always be persons of good will amongst us who will resist the general trend. The office of parents and teachers is to turn out such persons of good will; that they should deliberately weaken the moral fibre of their children by suggestion is a very grave offence and a thoughtful examination of the subject should act as a sufficient deterrent. For, let us consider. What we do *with the will* we describe as voluntary. What we do *without the* conscious action of *will* is involuntary. The will has only one mode of action, its function is to 'choose,' and with every choice we make we grow in force of character.

From the cradle to the grave suggestions crowd upon us, and such suggestions become part of our education because we must choose between them. But a suggestion given by intent and supported by an outside personality has an added strength which few are able to resist, just because the 130 choice has been made by another and not by ourselves, and our tendency is to accept this vicarious choice and follow the path of least resistance. No doubt much of this vicarious choosing is done for our good, whether for our health of body or amenableness of mind; but those who propose suggestion as a means of education do not consider that with every such attempt upon a child they weaken that which should make a man of him, his own power of choice. The parasitic creatures who live upon the habits, principles and opinions of others may easily become criminal. They only wait the occasion of some popular outburst to be carried into such a fury of crime as the Gordon Riots presented: a mad fury of which we have had terrible examples in our own day, though we have failed to ascribe them to their proper cause, the undermining of the will of the people, who have not been instructed in that ordering of the will which is their chief function as men and women. His will is the safeguard of a man against the unlawful intrusion of other persons. We are taught that there are offences against the bodies of others which may not be committed, but who teaches us that we may not intrude upon the minds and overrule the wills of others; that it is indecent to let another probe the thoughts of the 'unconscious mind' whether of child or man? Now the thought that we choose is commonly the thought that we ought to think and the part of the teacher is to afford to each child a full reservoir of the right thought of the world to draw from. For right thinking is by no means a matter of *self*-expression. Right thought flows upon the stimulus of an idea, and ideas are stored as we have seen in books and pictures and the lives of men and nations; these instruct the conscience and stimulate the will, and man or child 'chooses.' An accomplished statesman* exhibited to us lately how the disintegration of a great empire was brought about by the weakness of its rulers who allowed their will-power to be tampered with, their judgment suggested, their actions directed, by those who gained access to them.

There is no occasion for panic, but it is time that we realised that to *fortify the will* is one of the great purposes of education, and probably some study of the map of the

131

---

* *Memoirs of Count Witte.*

City of Mansoul would afford us guidance: at least a bird's eye view of the riches of the City should be spread before children. They should themselves know of the wonderful capacities to enter upon the world as a great inheritance which exist in every human being. All its beauty and all its thought are open to everyone. Everyone may take service for the world's use, everyone may climb those delectable mountains from whence he gets the vision of the City of God. He must know something of his body with its senses and its appetites: of his intellect, imagination and aesthetic sense: of his moral nature, ordered by love and justice. Realising how much is possible to Mansoul and the perils that assail it, he should know that the duty of self-direction belongs to him; and that powers for this direction are lodged in him, as are intellect and imagination, hunger and thirst. These governing powers are the conscience and the will. The whole ordering of education with its history, poetry, arithmetic, pictures, is based on the assumption that conscience is incapable of ordering life without regular and progressive instruction. We need instruction also concerning the will. Persons commonly suppose that the action of the will is automatic, but no power of Mansoul acts by itself and of itself, and some little study of the 'way of the will'—which has the ordering of every other power—may help us to understand the functions of this Premier in the kingdom of Mansoul.

Early in his teens we should at least put clearly before the child the possibility of a drifting, easy life led by appetite 132 or desire in which will plays no part; and the other possibility of using the power and responsibility proper to him as a person and *willing* as he goes. He must be safeguarded from some fallacies. No doubt he has heard at home that Baby has a strong will because he cries for a knife and insists on pulling down the tablecloth. In his history lessons and his readings of tale and poem, he comes across persons each of whom carries his point by strong wilfulness. He laughs at that rash boy Phaëton, measures Esau with a considering eye, finds him more attractive than Jacob who yet wins higher approval; perceives that Esau is wilful but that Jacob has a strong will, and through this and many other examples, recognises that a strong will is not synonymous with 'being good,' nor with a determination to have your own way. He learns to distribute the characters he comes across in his reading on either side of a line, those who are wilful and those who are governed by will; and this line by no means separates between the bad and the good.

It does divide, however, between the impulsive, self-pleasing, self-seeking, and the persons who have an aim beyond and outside of themselves, even though it be an aim appalling as that of Milton's Satan. It follows for him that he must not only *will*, but will with a view to an object outside himself. He will learn to recognise in Louis XI a mean man and a great king, because France and not himself was the object of his crooked policy. The will, too, is of slow growth, nourished upon the ideas proposed to it, and so all things work together for good to the child

who is duly educated. It is well that children should know
that while the turbulent person is not ruled by will at all
but by impulse, the movement of his passions or desires,
yet it is possible to have a constant will with unworthy or
evil ends, or, even to have a steady will towards a good end
and to compass that end by unworthy means. The simple
rectified will, what our Lord calls 'the single eye,' would
appear to be the one thing needful for straight living and
serviceableness. But always the first condition of will, good
or ill, is an object outside of self. The boy or girl who sees
this will understand that self-culture is not to be accepted
as an ideal, will not wonder why *Bushido* is mighty in Japan,
will enter into the problem which Browning raises in *The
Statue and the Bust*. By degrees the scholar will perceive that
just as to *reign* is the distinctive function of a king, so to
will is the function of a man. A king is not a king unless he
reigns and a man is less than a man unless he wills. Another
thing to be observed is that even the constant will has its
times of rise and fall, and one of the secrets of living is how
to tide over the times of fall in will power.

The boy must learn too that the will is subject to solic-
itations all round, from the lust of the flesh and the lust of
the eye and the pride of life; that will does not act alone; it
takes the whole man to will and a man wills wisely, justly
and strongly, in proportion as all his powers are in training
and under instruction. We must understand in order to
will. "How is that ye *will* not understand?" said our Lord
to the Jews; and that is the way with most of us, we *will* not

understand. We look out for great occasions which do not come and do not see that the sphere for the action of our wills is in ourselves. Our concern with life is to be fit, and according to our fitness come our occasions and the uses we shall be put to.

Unlike every other power in the kingdom of Mansoul, the will is able to do what it likes, is a free agent, and the one thing the will has to do is to prefer. "Choose ye this day," is the command that comes to each of us in every affair and on every day of our lives, and the business of the will

134   is to choose. But, choice, the effort of decision, is a heavy labour, whether it be between two lovers or two gowns. So, many people minimise this labour by following the fashion in their clothes, rooms, reading, amusements, the pictures they admire and the friends they select. We are zealous in choosing for others but shirk the responsibility of decisions for ourselves.

What is to be said about obedience, to the heads of the house first, to the State, to the Church, and always to the laws of God? Obedience is the test, the sustainer of personality, but it must be the obedience of choice; because choice is laborious, little children must be trained in the obedience of habit; but every gallant boy and girl has learned to *choose* to obey all who are set in authority.

Such obedience is of the essence of chivalry and chivalry is that temper of mind opposed to self-seeking. The chivalrous person is a person of constant will for, as we have seen, will cannot be exercised steadily for ends of personal gain.

It is well to know what it is we choose between. Things are only signs which represent ideas and several times a day we shall find two ideas presented to our minds and must make our choice upon right and reasonable grounds. We shall thus be on our guard against the weak allowance which we cause to do duty for choice and against such dishonest fallacies as, that it is our business to get the best that is to be had at the lowest price; and it is not only in matters of dress and ornament, household use and decoration, that we run after the cheapest and newest. We chase opinions and ideas with the same restlessness and uncertainty; any fad, any notion in the newspapers, we pick up with eagerness. Once again, the will is the man. The business of the will is to choose. There are many ways to get out of the task of choosing but it is always,—"Choose you this day whom ye will serve." There are two services open to us all, the service of God, (including that of man) and the service of self. If our aim is just to get on, 'to do ourselves well,' to get all possible ease, luxury and pleasure out of our lives, we are serving self and for the service of self no act of will is required. Our appetites and desires are always at hand to spur us into the necessary exertions. But if we serve God and our neighbour, we have to be always on the watch to choose between the ideas that present themselves. What the spring is to the year, school days are to our life. You meet a man whose business in the world appears to be to eat and drink, play golf and motor; he may have another and deeper life that we know nothing about, but, so far as

135

we can see, he has enlisted in the service of self. You meet another, a man of position, doing important work, and his ideas are those he received from the great men who taught him at school and College. The Greek Plays are his hobby. He is open to great thoughts and ready for service, because that which we get in our youth we keep through our lives.

Though the will affects all our actions and all our thoughts, its direct action is confined to a very little place, to that postern at either side of which stand conscience and reason, and at which ideas must needs present themselves. Shall we take an idea in or reject it? Conscience and reason have their say, but *will* is supreme and the behaviour of will is determined by all the principles we have gathered, all the opinions we have formed. We accept the notion, ponder it. At first we vaguely intend to act upon it; then we form a definite purpose, then a resolution and then comes an act or general temper of mind. We are told of Rudyard Kipling that his great ambition and desire at one time was to keep a tobacconist's shop. Why? Because in this way he could get into human touch with the men who came to buy their weekly allowance of tobacco. Happily for the world he did not become a tobacconist but the idea which moved him in the first place has acted throughout his life. Always he has men, young men, about him and who knows how many he has moved to become 'Captains Courageous' by his talk as well as by his books!

But suppose an unworthy idea present itself at the postern, supported by public opinion, by reason, for which

even conscience finds pleas? The will soon wearies of opposition, and what is to be done? Fight it out? That is what
the medieval Church did with those ideas which it rightly
regarded as temptations; the lash, the hair shirt, the stone
couch, the emaciated frame told of these not too successful
Armageddons.

When the overstrained will asks for repose, it may not
relax to yielding point but may and must seek recreation,
diversion,—Latin thought has afforded us beautiful and
appropriate names for that which we require. A change
of physical or mental occupation is very good, but if no
other change is convenient, let us *think* of something else,
no matter how trifling. A new tie, or our next new hat, a
story book we are reading, a friend we hope to see, anything
does so long as we do not suggest to ourselves the thoughts
we *ought* to think on the subject in question. The will does
not want the support of arguments but the recreation of
rest, change, diversion. In a surprisingly short time it is able
to return to the charge and to choose this day the path of
duty, however dull or tiresome, difficult or dangerous. This
'way of the will' is a secret of power, the secret of self-government, with which people should be furnished, not
only for ease in practical right doing, or for advance in the
religious life, but also for their intellectual well-being. Our
claim to free will is a righteous claim; will can only be free,
whether its object be right or wrong; it is a matter of choice   137
and there is no choice but free choice. But we are apt to
translate free will into free thought. We allow ourselves to

sanction intellectual anarchism and forget that it rests with the will to order the thoughts of the mind fully as much as the feelings of the heart or the lusts of the flesh. Our thoughts are not our own and we are not free to think as we choose. The injunction,—"Choose ye this day," applies to the thoughts which we allow ourselves to receive. Will is the one free agent of Mansoul, will alone may accept or reject; and will is therefore responsible for every intellectual problem which has proved too much for a man's sanity or for his moral probity. We may not think what we please on shallow matters or profound. The instructed conscience and trained reason support the will in those things, little and great, by which men live.

The ordering of the will is not an affair of sudden resolve; it is the outcome of a slow and ordered education in which precept and example flow in from the lives and thoughts of other men, men of antiquity and men of the hour, as unconsciously and spontaneously as the air we breathe. But the moment of choice is immediate and the act of the will voluntary; and the object of education is to prepare us for this immediate choice and voluntary action which every day presents.

While affording some secrets of 'the way of the will' to young people, we should perhaps beware of presenting the ideas of 'self-knowledge, self-reverence, and self-control.' All adequate education must be outward bound, and the mind which is concentrated upon self-emolument, even though it be the emolument of all the virtues, misses the higher and the simpler secrets of life. Duty and service are the sufficient motives for the arduous training of the will that a child goes through with little consciousness. The gradual fortifying of the will which many a schoolboy undergoes is hardly perceptible to himself however tremendous the results may be for his city or his nation. Will, free will, must have an object outside of self; and the poet has said the last word so far as we yet know,–

138

> "Our wills are ours we know not how;
> Our wills are ours to make them Thine."

Chapter 9

2.—*The Way of the Reason*

We should teach children, also, not to lean (too confidently) unto 139 *their own understanding because the function of reason is to give logical demonstration of (a) mathematical truth and (b) of initial ideas accepted by the will. In the former case reason is, perhaps, an infallible guide but in the latter is not always a safe one, for whether the initial idea be right or wrong reason will confirm it by irrefragible proofs.*

Therefore children should be taught as they become mature enough to understand such teaching that the chief responsibility which rests upon them as persons is the acceptance or rejection of ideas presented to them. To help them in this choice we should afford them principles of conduct and a wide range of fitting knowledge.

Every child, every man, who comes to a sudden halt watching the action of his own reason, is another Columbus, the discoverer of a new world. Commonly we let reason do its work without attention on our part, but there come moments when we stand in startled admiration and watch the unfolding before us point by point of a score of arguments in favour of this carpet as against that, this route in preference to the other, our chosen chum as against Bob Brown; because every *pro* suggested by our reason is opposed to some *con* in the background. How else should it happen that there is no single point upon which two persons may reason,—food, dress, games, education, politics, religion,—but the two may take opposite sides, and each will bring forward infallible proofs which must convince the other were it not that he too is already convinced by stronger proofs to strengthen his own argument. Every character in history or fiction supports this thesis; and probably we cannot give a better training in right reasoning than by letting children work out the arguments in favour of this or that conclusion.

140

Thus, Macbeth, a great general, returns after a brilliant victory, head and heart are inflated, what can he not achieve? Could he not govern a country as well as rule an army? Reason unfolds the steps by which he might do great things; great things, ay, but are they lawful, these possible exploits? And then in the nick of time he comes across the 'weird Sisters,' as we are all apt to take refuge in fatalism when conscience no longer supports us. He shall be Thane of Cawdor, and, behold, confirmation arrives on the spot. He shall also be king. Well, if this is decreed, what can he do? He is no longer a free agent. And a score of valid arguments unfold themselves showing how Scotland, the world, his wife, himself, would be enhanced, would flourish and be blessed if he had the opportunity to do what was in him. Opportunity? The thing was decreed! It rested with him to find the means, the tools. He was not without imagination, had a poetic mind and shrank before the horrors he vaguely foresaw. But reason came to his aid and step by step the whole bloody tragedy was wrought out before his prescient mind. When we first meet with Macbeth he is rich in honours, troops of friends, the generous confidence of his king. The change is sudden and complete, and, we may believe, reason justified him at every point. But reason did not begin it. The will played upon by ambition had already admitted the notion of towering greatness or ever the 'weird Sisters' gave shape to his desire. Had it not been for this countenance afforded by the will, the forecasts of fate would have influenced his conduct no more then they did that of Banquo.

But it must not be supposed that reason is malign, the 141 furtherer of ill counsels only. Nurse Cavell, Jack Cornwell, Lord Roberts, General Gordon, Madame Curie, leave hints enough to enable us to follow the trains of thought which issued in glorious deeds. We know how Florence Nightingale received, welcomed, reasoned out the notion of pity which obsessed her, and how through many difficulties her great project for the saving of the sick and suffering of her country's army worked itself out; how she was able to convey to those in power the same convincing arguments which moved herself. That was a happy thought of the mediaeval Church which represented the leading idea of each of the

seven Liberal Arts by a chosen exponent able to convince
others by the arguments which his own reason brought
forward. So Priscian taught the world Grammar; Pythagoras, Arithmetic; and the name of Euclid still stands for
the science which appealed to his reason. But it is not only
great intellectual advances and discoveries or world-shaping
events for good or evil, that exhibit the persuasive power
of reason. There is no object in use, great or small, upon
which some man's reason has not worked exhaustively. A
sofa, a chest of drawers, a ship, a box of toy soldiers, have
all been thought out step by step, and the inventor has not
only considered the *pros* but has so far overcome the *cons*
that his invention is there, ready for use; and only here and
there does anyone take the trouble to consider how the
useful, or, perhaps, beautiful article came into existence.
It is worth while to ask a child, How did you think of it?
when he comes to tell you of a new game he has invented,
a new country of the imagination he has named, peopled
and governed. He will probably tell you what first 'put it
into his head' and then how the reasons one after another
came to him. After,—How did *you* think of it?—the next
question that will occur to a child is,—How did *he* think of
it?—and he will distinguish between the first notion that
has 'put it into his head' and the reasoned steps which have
gone to the completion of an object, the discovery of a planet, the making of a law. Sometimes a child should be taken
into the psychology of crime, and he will see that reason
brings infallible proofs of the rightness of the criminal act.

From Cain to the latest great offender every criminal act has been justified by reasoned arguments which come of their own accord to the criminal. We know the arguments before which Eve fell when the Serpent played the part of the 'weird Sisters.' It is pleasant to the eye; it is good for food; it shall make you wise in the knowledge of good and evil—good and convincing arguments, specious enough to overbear the counter-pleadings of Obedience. Children should know that such things are before them also; that whenever they want to do wrong capital reasons for doing the wrong thing will occur to them. But, happily, when they want to do right no less cogent reasons for right doing will appear.

After abundant practice in reasoning and tracing out the reasons of others, whether in fact or fiction, children may readily be brought to the conclusions that reasonable and right are not synonymous terms; that reason is their servant, not their ruler,—one of those servants which help Mansoul in the governance of his kingdom. But no more than appetite, ambition, or the love of ease, is reason to be trusted with the government of a man, much less that of a state; because well-reasoned arguments are brought into play for a wrong course as for a right. He will see that reason works involuntarily; that all the beautiful steps follow one another in his mind without any activity or intention on his own part; but he need never suppose that he was hurried along into evil by thoughts which he could not help, because reason never begins it. It is only when he chooses

143   to think about some course or plan, as Eve standing before the apples, that reason comes into play; so, if he chooses to think about a purpose that is good, many excellent reasons will hurry up to support him; but, alas, if he choose to entertain a wrong notion, he, as it were, rings the bell for reason, which enforces his wrong intention with a score of arguments proving that wrong is right.

A due recognition of the function of reason should be an enormous help to us all in days when the air is full of fallacies, and when our personal modesty, that becoming respect for other people which is proper to well-ordered natures whether young or old, makes us willing to accept conclusions duly supported by public opinion or by those whose opinions we value. Nevertheless, it is something to recognise that probably no wrong thing has ever been done or said, no crime committed, but has been justified to the perpetrator by arguments coming to him involuntarily and produced with cumulative force by his own reason. Is Shakespeare ever wrong? And, if so, may we think that a Richard III who gloats over his own villainy as villainy, who is in fact no hypocrite, in the sense of acting, to himself—is hardly true to human nature? Great is Shakespeare! So perhaps Richard was the exception to the rule which makes a man go out and hang himself when at last he sees his incomparable villainy, and does not Richard say in the end,—"I myself find in myself no pity for myself"? For ourselves and our children it is enough to know that reason will put a good face on any matter we propose; and, that we can prove ourselves to be in the right is no justification for there is absolutely no theory we may receive, no action we may contemplate, which our reason will not affirm. Of course we know by many infallible proofs that Bacon wrote Shakespeare, and an ingenious person has worked out a chain of arguments proving that Dr. Johnson wrote the Bible! Why not? For a nation of logical thinkers, the French made an extraordinary *faux-pas* when they elected the Goddess of Reason to divine honours. But, indeed, perhaps they did it because they are a logical nation; for logic gives us the very formula of reason, and that which is logically proved is not necessarily right. We need no longer wonder that two men equally upright, equally virtuous, selected out of any company, will hold opposite views on almost any question; and each will support his views by logical argument. So we are at the mercy of the *doctrinaire* in religion, the demagogue in politics, and, dare we say, of the dreamer in science; and we think to save our souls by being in the front rank of opinion in one or the other. But not if we have grown up cognisant of the beauty and wonder of the act of reasoning, and also, of the limitations which attend it.

We must be able to answer the arguments in the air, not so much by counter reasons as by exposing the fallacies in such arguments and proving on our own part the opposite position. For example, "that very lovable, very exasperating but essentially real, though often wrong-headed enthusiast," Karl Marx, dominates the socialistic thought of to-day.

Point by point, for good or for evil, the Marxian Manifesto of 1848 is coming into force. "For the most advanced countries," we are told, "the following measures might come into very general application."

(1) "Expropriation of landed property and application of rent to State Expenditure." We have not space to examine the Marxian proposition in detail but let us consider a single fallacy. It is assumed that the rent of landed property is for the sole use, enrichment and enjoyment of the owner. Now the schedule of the Duke of Bedford, for example, published recently, shows that the income derived from park property is inadequate to its upkeep and to the taxes imposed upon the owner. Again, landowners are not only large employers of labour, generally under favourable conditions, but they keep up a very important benefaction; most of the extensive landowners make of their places *public* parks kept in beautiful order at their *private* expense.

(2) "Heavy progressive taxation." The fallacy lies in the fact that the proletariat in whose interest the Manifesto was issued must necessarily on account of their numbers be large taxpayers. Therefore it is upon them that heavy progressive taxation will press—as we have all seen in Russia—to the point of their extinction.

(3) "Abolition of inheritance." A measure designed to reduce all persons to the same level. As we know, the abolition of class is the main object of socialism. But the underlying fallacy is the assumption that class is stable and is not in a state of continual flux, the continual upward and

downward movement as of watery particles in the Ocean. The man at the bottom to-day may be at the top to-morrow, as we see, not only in Soviet Russia, but in most civilised countries. Attempts to control this natural movement are as vain as King Canute's command to the ocean.

(4) "Confiscation of the property of all emigrants and rebels." Assumed authority must be supported by tyranny, that worst tyranny which requires all men to think to order, as they must in a Soviet State, or be penalised to make them powerless. The fallacy lies in a misconception of human nature. There is nothing that men will not sacrifice for an idea, for such an idea as that of freedom of thought and of movement.

(5), (6), (7), deal with centralisation, credit, of transport, of factories, of instruments of production in the hands of the State,—the State, that is, Everyman,—the Proletariat, in fact,—in whose hands all wealth and means of obtaining wealth shall be lodged.

Here we have a logically thought-out preparation for the government of the people, by the people, for the people; 146 but the underlying fallacy is that it makes for revolution which effects no change but a mere change of rulers, better or worse as may be. In the Soviet Republic, according to the law of perpetual social flux, new rulers would come to the top, arbitrary and tyrannical, because not hemmed in by precedent and custom; and children will be at no loss to show how the last state of a nation so governed is worse than the first.

(8) "Compulsory obligation of labour upon all." The initial idea of a Soviet State is that it shall afford due liberty and equal conditions for all. But even in the contemplation of such a State it was necessary to postulate for everybody conscription and the discipline of an army.

(9) "Joint prosecution for Agriculture and Manufacture." The aim being the gradual removal of the distinction of town and country. Here is a point in the Manifesto which we should all like to see in practice but—is it possible?

(10) "Public and gratuitous education for all children." This happily we have seen carried out with the proviso, 'for whom it may be necessary or desirable.' The difficulty lies in the conception of education formed by a Soviet community; and the plea for free education is a specious blind, the intention being such an education as shall train the coming generation in rabid revolutionary principles.

To continue our examination of the Tenth Maxim; the next clause (*b*) requires "abolition of children's labour in factories in its present form." So far so good. Happily we have lived to see this abolition; there may be a sinister reading of the clause but on the surface it carries the assent of all good citizens.

(*c*) "Union of education with material production." Here from motives of economy we are going the way of the Communists in our Continuation Schools; but a fallacy underlies the maxim which may well frustrate our efforts towards the better education of the people. The assumption is that the boy who learns, say, certain manufacturing processes, *pari passu* with his intellectual education does better in the future than he who gives the full period to education. There is no consensus of the opinion of employers to prove that this is the case. On the contrary, given a likely boy, and a manufacturer will be satisfied that he will soon learn his business in the 'works.' But the function of education is not to give technical skill but to develop a person; the more of a person, the better the work of whatever kind; and as I have said before, the idea of the Continuation School is, or should be, a University course in the 'humanities'; not in what have been called the 'best humanities,' *i.e.*, the Classics, though whether these are in any sense 'best' is a moot question, but in the singularly rich 'humanities' which the English tongue affords.

These Ten Marxian Maxims give us ample ground for discussion not for lectures or for oral lessons, but for following for a few minutes any opening suggested by 'current events,' a feature in the children's programme of work. But they must follow arguments and detect fallacies for themselves. Reason like the other powers of the mind, requires material to work upon whether embalmed in history and literature, or afloat with the news of a strike or uprising. It is madness to let children face a debatable world with only, say, a mathematical preparation. If our business were to train their power of reasoning, such a training would no doubt be of service; but the power is there already, and only wants material to work upon.

This caution must be borne in mind. Reason, like all

other properties of a person, is subject to habit and works upon the material it is accustomed to handle. Plato formed a just judgment on this matter, too,* and perceived that mathematics afford no clue to the labyrinth of affairs whether public or private.

We have seen that their reading and the affairs of the day should afford scope and opportunity for the delight in ratiocination proper to children. The fallacies they themselves perpetrate when exposed make them the readier to detect fallacies elsewhere.

What are we to do? Are we to waste time in discussing with children every idle and blasphemous proposition that comes their way? Surely not. But we may help them to principles which should enable them to discern these two characters for themselves. A proposition is idle when it rests on nothing and leads to nothing. Again, blasphemy is a sin, the sin of being impudent towards Almighty God, Whom we all know, without any telling, and know Him to be fearful, wonderful, loving, just and good, as certainly as we know that the sun shines or the wind blows. Children should be brought up, too, to perceive that a miracle is not less a miracle because it occurs so constantly and regularly that we call it a law; that sap rises in a tree, that a boy is born with his uncle's eyes, that an answer that we can perceive comes to our serious prayers; these things are not the less miracles because they happen frequently or invariably, and because we have ceased to wonder about them. No doubt

* *Education of the Young.*

so did the people of Jerusalem when our Lord performed many miracles in their streets.

When children perceive that,—"My Father worketh hitherto and I work"—is the law which orders nations and individuals: that "My spirit shall not always strive with man," is an awful warning to every people and every person; that to hinder the mis-doing, encourage the well-doing of men and nations is incessant labour, the work of the Father and the Son:—to a child who perceives these things miracles will not be matters of supreme moment because all life will be for him matter for wonder and adoration.

Again, if we wish children to keep clear of all the religious clamours in the air, we must help them to understand what religion is—*

> "Will religion guarantee me my private and personal happiness? To this on the whole I think we must answer, No; and if we approach it with a view to such happiness, then most certainly and absolutely No."

Here is a final and emphatic answer to the quasi religious offers which are being clamourously pressed upon hesitating souls. Ease of body is offered to these, relief of mind, reparation of loss, even of the final loss when those they love pass away. We may call upon mediums, converse through table-rappings, be healed by faith,—faith, that is, in the power of a Healer who manipulates us. Sin is not

---

* *What Religion Is*, by Bernard Bosanquet, D.C.L.

for us, nor sorrow for sin. We may live in continual odious self-complacency, remote from the anxious struggling souls about us, because, forsooth, there is no sin, sorrow, anxiety or pain, if we *will* that these things shall not be. That is to say, religion will "guarantee me my private and personal happiness," will make me immune from every distress and misery of life; and this happy immunity is all a matter within the power of my own will; the person that matters in my religion is myself only. The office of religion for me in such a case is to remove all uneasiness, bodily and spiritual, and to float me into a Nirvana of undisturbed self-complacency. But we must answer with Professor Bosanquet, "absolutely NO." True religion will not do this for me because the final form of the religion that will do these things is idolatry, self-worship, with no intention beyond self.

To go on with our quotation,—

150   "Well, but if not that then what? We esteem the thing as good and great, but if it simply does nothing for us, how is it to be anything to us? But the answer was the answer to the question and it might be that to a question sounding but slightly different, a very different answer would be returned. We might ask, for instance, 'does it make my life more worth living?' And the answer to this might be,—'It is the only thing that makes life worth living at all.'"

In a word, "I want, am made for and must have a God."

No doubt through the sweetness of their faith and love children have immediate access to God, and what more would we have? 'Gentle Jesus' is about their path and about their bed; angels minister to them; they enjoy all the immunities of the Kingdom. But we may not forget that reason is as active in them as the affections. Towards the end of the last century people had a straight and easy way of giving a reasonable foundation to a child's belief. All the articles of the Christian Faith were supported by a sort of little catechism of 'Scripture Proofs'; and this method was not without its uses. But, to-day, we have to prove the Scriptures if we rely upon Scripture proofs and we must change our point of attack. Children must know that we cannot prove any of the great things of life, not even that we ourselves live; but we must rely upon that which we know without demonstration. We know, too, and this other certainty must be pressed home to them, that reason, so far from being infallible, is most exceedingly fallible, persuadable, open to influence on this side and that; but is all the same a faithful servant, able to prove whatsoever notion is received by the will. Once we are convinced of the fallibility of our own reason we are able to detect the fallacies in the reasoning of our opponents and are not liable to be carried away by every wind of doctrine. Every mother knows how intensely reasonable a child is and how difficult it is to answer his quite logical and foolishly wrong conclusions. So we need not be deterred from dealing with serious matters with these young neophytes, but only as the occasion occurs; we may not run the risk of boring them with the great questions of life while it is our business to send them forth assured.

We find that, while children are tiresome in arguing about trifling things, often for the mere pleasure of employing their reasoning power, a great many of them are averse to those studies which should, we suppose, give free play to a power that is in them, even if they do not strengthen and develop this power. Yet few children take pleasure in Grammar, especially in English Grammar, which depends so little on inflexion. Arithmetic, again, Mathematics, appeal only to a small percentage of a class or school, and, for the rest, however intelligent, its problems are baffling to the end, though they may take delight in reasoning out problems of life in literature or history. Perhaps we should accept this tacit vote of the majority and cease to put undue pressure upon studies which would be invaluable did the reasoning power of a child wait upon our training, but are on a different footing when we perceive that children come endowed to the full as much with reason as with love; that our business is to provide abundant material upon which this supreme power should work; and that whatever development occurs comes with practice in *congenial fields of thought*. At the same time we may not let children neglect either of these delightful studies. The time will come when they will delight in words, the beauty and propriety of words; when they will see that words are consecrated as the vehicle of truth and are not to be carelessly tampered with in statement or mutilated in form; and we must prepare them for these later studies. Perhaps we should postpone parsing, for instance, until a child is accustomed to weigh sentences for their sense, should let them dally with figures of speech before we attempt minute analysis of sentences, 152 and should reduce our grammatical nomenclature to a minimum. The fact is that children do not generalise, they gather particulars with amazing industry, but hold their impressions fluid, as it were; and we may not hurry them to formulate. If the use of words be a law unto itself, how much more so the language of figures and lines! We remember how instructive and impressive Ruskin is on the thesis that 'two and two make four' and cannot by any possibility that the universe affords be made to make five or three. From this point of view, of immutable law, children should approach Mathematics; they should see how impressive is Euclid's 'Which is absurd,' just as absurd as would be the statements of a man who said that his apples always fell upwards, and for the same reason. The behaviour of figures and lines is like the fall of an apple, fixed by immutable laws, and it is a great thing to begin to see these laws even in their lowliest application. The child whose approaches to Arithmetic are so many discoveries of the laws which regulate number will not divide fifteen pence among five people and give them each sixpence or ninepence; 'which is absurd' will convict him, and in time he will perceive that 'answers' are not purely arbitrary but are to be come at by a little boy's reason. Mathematics are delightful to the mind of man which revels in the perception of law, which may even go forth guessing at a new law until it discover that law; but not every boy can be a champion prize-fighter, nor can every boy 'stand up' to Mathematics. Therefore perhaps the business of teachers is to open as many doors as possible in the belief that Mathematics is one out of many studies which make for education, a study by no means accessible to everyone. Therefore it should not monopolise undue time, nor should persons be hindered from useful careers by the fact that they show no great proficiency in studies which are in favour with examiners, no doubt, because solutions are final, and work can be adjudged without the tiresome hesitancy and fear of being unjust which beset the examiners' path in other studies.

We would send forth children informed by "the reason firm, the temperate will, endurance, foresight, strength and skill," but we must add resolution to our good intentions and may not expect to produce a reasonable soul of fine polish from the steady friction, say, of mathematical studies only.

Chapter 10

The Curriculum *

We, believing that the normal child has powers of mind which fit 154 *him to deal with all knowledge proper to him, give him a full and generous curriculum, taking care only that all knowledge offered to him is vital, that is, that facts are not presented without their informing ideas. Out of this conception comes our principle that:—*

"Education is the Science of Relations"; that is, a child has natural relations with a vast number of things and thoughts: so we train him upon physical exercises, nature lore, handicrafts, science and art, and upon many living books, for we know that our business is not to teach him all about anything, but to help him to make valid as many as may be of—

> *Those first-born affinities*
> *That fit our new existence to existing things."*

In devising a syllabus for a normal child, of whatever social class, three points must be considered:—

---

* All particulars may be had from The Director, Parents' Union School, Ambleside. The illustrations in the way of children's answers for the various sections of this chapter have been omitted for want of space, except in the case of a few answers under Composition.

213

(a) *He requires* much *knowledge, for the mind needs sufficient food as much as does the body.*

(b) *The knowledge should be various, for sameness in mental diet does not create appetite (i.e., curiosity).*

(c) *Knowledge should be communicated in well-chosen language because his attention responds naturally to what is conveyed in literary form.*

155   *As knowledge is not assimilated until it is reproduced, children should "tell back" after a single reading or hearing: or should write on some part of what they have read.*

A single reading *is insisted on, because children have naturally great power of attention; but this force is dissipated by the re-reading of passages, and also, by questioning, summarising, and the like.*

Acting upon these and some other points in the behaviour of mind, we find that the educability of children is enormously greater than has hitherto been supposed, and is but little dependent on such circumstances as heredity and environment.

Nor is the accuracy of this statement limited to clever children or to children of the educated classes: thousands of children in elementary schools respond freely to this method, which is based on the behaviour of mind.

Few things are more remiss in our schools than the curriculum which is supposed to be entirely at the option of the Head: but is it? Most Secondary schools work towards examinations which more or less afford the privilege of entry to the Universities. The standard to be reached is set by these and the Heads of schools hold themselves powerless.

Though Elementary schools no longer work with a view to examination results yet as their best pupils try for scholarships admitting them to secondary schools, they do come indirectly under the same limitations. There is, however, much less liberty in Secondary than in Primary schools with regard to the subjects taught and the time devoted to each. The result is startling. A boy of eight in an Elementary school may shew more intelligence and wider knowledge than a boy of fourteen in a Preparatory school, that is, if he have been taught on the principles I have in view, while the other boy has been instructed with a view to a given standard of scholarship. The Preparatory school boy does, however, reach that standard in Latin, if not in Greek also, and in Mathematics.

If we succeed in establishing a similar standard which every boy and girl of a given age should reach in a liberal range of subjects, a fair chance will be afforded to the average boy and girl while brilliant or especially industrious young people will go ahead. 156

We labour under the mistake of supposing that there is no natural law or inherent principle according to which a child's course of studies should be regulated; so we teach him those things which, according to Locke, it is becoming for a 'gentleman' to know on the one hand, and, on the other, the arts of reading, writing and summing, that he may not grow up an illiterate citizen. In both cases the education we offer is too utilitarian,—an indirect training for the professions or for a craftsman's calling with efforts in the latter case to make a boy's education bear directly on his future work.

But what if in the very nature of things we find a complete curriculum suggested? "The human race has lost its title deeds," said Voltaire, and mankind has been going about ever since seeking to recover them; education is still at sea and Voltaire's epigram holds good. We have not found our title deeds and so we yield to the children no inherent claims. Our highest aim is to educate young people for their uses to society, while every faddist is free to teach what he pleases because we have no title deeds to confront him with. Education, no doubt, falls under the economic law of supply and demand; but the demand should come from the children rather than from teachers and parents; how are their demands to become articulate? We must give consideration to this question because the answer depends on a survey of the composite whole we sum up as 'human nature,' a whole whose possibilities are infinite and various, not only in a budding genius, the child of a distinguished family, but in every child of the streets.

A small English boy of nine living in Japan, remarked,—"Isn't it fun, Mother, learning all these things? Everything seems to fit into something else." The boy had not found out the whole secret; everything fitted into something within himself.

The days have gone by when the education befitting either a gentleman or an artisan was our aim. Now we must deal with a child of man, who has a natural desire to know the history of his race and of his nation, what men thought in the past and are thinking now; the best thoughts of the best minds taking form as literature, and at its highest as poetry, or, as poetry rendered in the plastic forms of art: as a child of God, whose supreme desire and glory it is to know about and to know his almighty Father: as a person of many parts and passions who must know how to use, care for, and discipline himself, body, mind and soul: as a person of many relationships,—to family, city, church, state, neighbouring states, the world at large: as the inhabitant of a world full of beauty and interest, the features of which he must recognise and know how to name, and a world too, and a universe, whose every function of every part is ordered by laws which he must begin to know.

It is a wide programme founded on the educational rights of man; wide, but we may not say it is impossible nor may we pick and choose and educate him in this direction but not in that. We may not even make choice between science and the 'humanities.' Our part it seems to me is to give a child a vital hold upon as many as possible of those wide relationships proper to him. Shelley offers us the key to education when he speaks of "understanding that grows bright gazing on many truths."

Because the relationships a child is born to are very various, the knowledge we offer him must be various too. A lady teaching in Cape Colony writes,—"The papers incorporated in the pamphlet *A Liberal Education: Practice* (by A. C. Drury) testify to—to me—an almost incredible   158 standard of proficiency. The mistakes are just the kind of mistakes that children should make and no more of them than just enough to keep them from being priggish. There are none of those howlers of fact or expression that make one view one's efforts with a feeling of utter despondency."

The knowledge of children so taught is consecutive, intelligent and complete as far as it goes, in however many directions. For it is a mistake to suppose that the greater the number of 'subjects' the greater the scholar's labour; the contrary is the case as the variety in itself affords refreshment, and the child who has written thirty or forty sheets during an examination week comes out unfagged. Not the number of subjects but the hours of work bring fatigue to the scholar; and bearing this in mind we have short hours and no evening preparation.

Section I

THE KNOWLEDGE OF GOD

Of the three sorts of knowledge proper to a child,—the knowledge of God, of man, and of the universe,—the knowledge of God ranks first in importance, is indispensable, and most happy-making. Mothers are on the whole more successful in communicating this knowledge than are teachers who know the children less well and have a narrower, poorer standard of measurement for their minds. Parents do not talk down to children, but we might gather from educational publications that the art of education as regards young children is to bring conceptions down to their 'little' minds. If we give up this foolish prejudice in favour of the grown-up we shall be astonished at the range and depth of children's minds; and shall perceive that their relation to God is one of those 'first-born affinities' which it is our part to help them to make good. A mother knows 159 how to speak of God as she would of an absent father with all the evidences of his care and love about her and his children. She knows how to make a child's heart beat high in joy and thankfulness as she thrills him with the thought, 'my Father made them all,' while his eye delights in flowery meadow, great tree, flowing river. "His are the mountains and the valleys his and the resplendent rivers, whose eyes they fill with tears of holy joy," and this is not beyond children. We recollect how 'Arthur Pendennis' walked in the evening light with his mother and recited great passages from Milton and the eyes of the two were filled 'with tears of holy joy,' when the boy was eight. The teacher of a class has not the same tender opportunities but if he take pains to get a just measure of children's minds it is surprising how much may be done.

The supercilious point of view adopted by some teachers is the cause of the small achievements of their scholars. The 'kiddies' in a big girls' school are not expected to understand and know and they live down to the expectations formed of them. We (of the P.N.E.U.) begin the definite 'school' education of children when they are six; they are no doubt capable of beginning a year or two earlier but the fact is that nature and circumstances have provided such a wide field of education for young children that it seems better to abstain from requiring *direct* intellectual efforts until they have arrived at that age.

As for all the teaching in the nature of 'told to the children,' most children get their share of that whether in the infant school or at home, but this is practically outside the sphere of that part of education which demands a *conscious mental effort*, from the scholar, the mental effort of telling again that which has been read or heard. That is how we all learn, we tell again, to ourselves if need be, the matter we wish to retain, the sermon, the lecture, the conversation. The method is as old as the mind of man, the distressful fact is that it has been made so little use of in general education. Let us hear Dr. Johnson on the subject:—

160

> "'Little people should be encouraged always to tell whatever they hear particularly striking to some brother, sister, or servant, immediately before the impression is erased by the intervention of newer occurrences.' He perfectly remembered the first time he heard of heaven and hell because when his mother had made out such a description of both places as she thought likely to seize the attention of her infant auditor who was then in bed with her, she got up and dressing him before the usual time, sent him directly to call the favourite workman in the house to whom she knew he would communicate the conversation while it was yet impressed upon his

mind. The event was what she wished and it was to that method chiefly that he owed the uncommon felicity of remembering distant occurrences and long past conversations." (Mrs. Piozzi).

Now our objective in this most important part of education is to give the children the knowledge of God. We need not go into the question of intuitive knowledge, but the expressed knowledge attainable by us has its source in the Bible, and perhaps we cannot do a greater indignity to children than to substitute our own or some other benevolent person's rendering for the fine English, poetic diction and lucid statement of the Bible.

Literature at its best is always direct and simple and a normal child of six listens with delight to the tales both of Old and New Testament read to him passage by passage, and by him narrated in turn, with delightful touches of native eloquence. Religion has two aspects, the attitude of the will towards God which we understand by Christianity, and that perception of God which comes from a gradual slow-growing comprehension of the divine dealings with men. In the first of these senses, Goethe was never religious, but the second forms the green reposeful background to a restless and uneasy life and it is worth while to consider how he arrived at so infinitely desirable a possession. He gives us the whole history fully in *Aus Meinem Leben*, a treatise on education very well worth our study. There he says,—

161

"Man may turn where he will, he may undertake what he
will but he will yet return to that road which Dante has
laid down for him. So it happened to me in the present
case: my efforts with the language" (Hebrew, when he
was ten) "with the contents of the Holy Scriptures, resulted in a most lively presentation to my imagination
of that beautiful much-sung land and of the countries
which bordered it as well as of the people and events
which have glorified that spot of earth for thousands of
years. . . . Perhaps someone may ask why I set forth here
in such detail this universally known history so often
repeated, and expounded. This answer may serve, that
in no other way could I show how with the distractions
of my life and my irregular education I concentrated
my mind and my emotion on one point because I can
in no other way account for the peace which enveloped
me however disturbed and unusual the circumstances of
my life. If an ever active imagination of which the story
of my life may bear witness led me here and there, if the
medley of fable, history, mythology, threatened to drive
me to distraction, I betook myself again to those morning lands, I buried myself in the five books of Moses and
there amongst the wide-spreading, shepherd people I
found the greatest solitude and the greatest comfort."

It is well to know how Goethe obtained this repose of
soul, this fresh background for his thoughts, and in all the
errors of a wilful life this innermost repose appears never

to have left him. His eyes, we are told, were tranquil as
those of a god, and here is revealed the secret of that large
tranquility. Here, too, Goethe unfolds for us a principle of
education which those who desire their children to possess
the passive as well as the active principle of religion would
do well to consider; for it is probably true that the teaching
of the New Testament, not duly grounded upon or accompanied by that of the Old, fails to result in such thought
of God, wide, all-embracing, all-permeating, as David, 162
for example, gives constant expression to in the Psalms.
Let us have faith and courage to give children such a full
and gradual picture of Old Testament history that they
unconsciously perceive for themselves a panoramic view
of the history of mankind typified by that of the Jewish
nation as it is unfolded in the Bible. Are our children little
sceptics, as was the young Goethe, who take a laughing joy
in pulling their teachers with a hundred difficulties? Like
that wise old Dr. Albrecht, let us be in no haste to explain.
Let us not try to put down or evade their questions, or
to give them final answers, but introduce them as did he
to some thoughtful commentator who weighs difficult
questions with modesty and scrupulous care. If we act
in this way, difficulties will assume their due measure of
importance, that is to say, they will be lost sight of in the
gradual unfolding of the great scheme whereby the world
was educated. I know of no commentator for children, say,
from six to twelve, better than Canon Paterson Smyth (*The
Bible for the Young*). He is one of the few writers able to

take the measure of children's minds, to help them over real difficulties, give impulse to their thoughts and direction to their conduct.

Between the ages of six and twelve children cover the whole of the Old Testament story, the Prophets, major and minor, being introduced as they come into connection with the Kings. The teacher opens the lesson by reading the passage from *The Bible for the Young*, in which the subject is pictorially treated; for example,—

> "It is the battle field of the valley of Elah. The camp of Israel is on one slope, the big tents of the Philistines on the other. The Israelites are rather small men, lithe and clever, the Philistines are big men, big, stupid, thick-headed giants, the same as when Samson used to fool them and laugh at them long ago. There is great excitement on both sides," etc.

163   There will be probably some talk and discussion after this reading. Then the teacher will read the Bible passage in question which the children will narrate, the commentary serving merely as a background for their thoughts. The narration is usually exceedingly interesting; the children do not miss a point and often add picturesque touches of their own. Before the close of the lesson, the teacher brings out such new thoughts of God or new points of behaviour as the reading has afforded, emphasising the moral or religious lesson to be learnt rather by a reverent and sympathetic manner than by any attempt at personal application.

Forms III and IV (twelve to fifteen) read for themselves the whole of the Old Testament as produced by the Rev. H. Costley-White in his *Old Testament History*. Wise and necessary omissions in this work make it more possible to deal with Old Testament History, in the words of the Authorised Version, than if the Bible were used as a single volume. Then, "each period is illustrated by reference to contemporary literature (e.g., Prophets and Psalms and monuments)." Again, brief historical explanations and general commentary are inserted in their proper places." For example, after Genesis iii, we read, as an introduction to the story of Cain and Abel,—

"The original object of this story was to explain the development of sin amongst mankind and the origin of homicide which in this first instance was actual murder. There are difficulties in the story which do not admit of satisfactory explanation. It may be asked,—'Why did God not accept Cain's offering?' 'How was his displeasure shewn?' 'What was the sign appointed for Cain?' 'Whom did he marry?' The best way to answer such questions is to admit that we do not know, but we may add that these early stories are only a selection which do not necessarily form a consistent and complete whole, and that in this very case there are signs that the original story has been cut down and edited.

"Among the lessons taught are the following—(1) God judges man's motives rather than his acts. The service of the heart is worth more than any ceremonial.

164 (2) It is not the sin of murder that is condemned so much as the sin of jealousy and malice: cf. the Sermon on the Mount, Matt. xxi, 6. (3) The great doctrine of the Brotherhood of Man, that each man is his brother's keeper and has his share of responsibility for the conditions of the lives of others. (4) Sin always brings its own punishment. (5) God remonstrates with man before the climax of sin is reached."

The footnotes which form the only commentary upon the text are commendably short and to the point.

Having received a considerable knowledge of the Old Testament in detail from the words of the Bible itself and having been trained to accept difficulties freely without giving place to the notion that such difficulties invalidate the Bible as the oracle of God and our sole original source of knowledge concerning the nature of Almighty God and the manner of His government of the world, children are prepared for a further study of divinity, still following the Bible text.

When pupils are of an age to be in Forms V and VI (from 15 to 18) we find that Dummelow's *One Volume Bible Commentary* is of great service. It is designed to provide in convenient form,—

"A brief explanation of the meaning of the Scriptures. Introductions have been supplied to the various books and Notes which will help to explain the principal difficulties, textual, moral or doctrinal, which may arise in conjunction with them. A series of articles has also been prefixed dealing with the larger questions suggested by the Bible as a whole. It is hoped that the Commentary may lead to a perusal of many of the books of Holy Scripture which are often left unread in spite of their rare literary charm and abundant usefulness for the furtherance of the spiritual life.... In recent years much light has been thrown upon questions of authorship and interpretation and the contributors to this volume have endeavoured to incorporate in it the most assured results of modern scholarship whilst avoiding opinions of an extreme or precarious kind. Sometimes these results differ from traditional views but in such cases it is not only hoped but believed that the student will find the spiritual value and authority of the Bible have been enhanced rather than diminished by the change."

The Editor has in these words set forth so justly the aims of the Commentary that I need only say we find it of very great practical value. The pupils read the general articles and the introductions to the separate Books; they read too the Prophets and the poetical books with the notes supplied. Thus they leave school with a fairly enlightened knowledge of the books of the Old Testament and of the aids modern scholarship has brought towards their interpretation; we hope also with increased reverence for and delight in the ways of God with men.

The New Testament comes under another category. The same commentaries are used and the same methods followed, that is, the reverent reading of the text, with the following narration which is often curiously word perfect after a single reading; this is the more surprising because we all know how difficult it is to repeat a passage which we have heard a thousand times; the single attentive reading does away with this difficulty and we are able to assure ourselves that children's minds are stored with perfect word pictures of every tender and beautiful scene described in the Gospels; and are able reproduce the austere if equally tender teaching which enforces the object lessons of the miracles. By degrees the Person of Our Lord as revealed in His words and His works becomes real and dear to them, not through emotional appeals but through the impression left by accurate and detailed knowledge concerning the Saviour of the World, Who went about doing good. Dogmatic teaching finds its way to them by inference through a quiet realisation of the Bible records; and loyalty to a Divine Master likely to become the guiding principle of their lives.

I should like to urge the importance of what may be called a poetic presentation of the life and teaching of Our Lord. The young reader should experience in this study a curious and delightful sense of harmonious development, the rounding out of each incident, of the progressive unfolding which characterises Our Lord's teaching; and, let me say here, the custom of narration lends itself surprisingly to this sort of poetic insight. Every related incident stands out in a sort of bas-relief; every teaching so rendered unfolds its meaning; every argument convinces; and the personages reveal themselves to us more intimately than almost any persons we know in real life. Probably very little hortatory teaching is desirable. The danger of boring young listeners by such teaching is great, and there is also the further danger of provoking counter-opinions, even counter-convictions, in the innocent-looking audience. On the whole we shall perhaps do well to allow the Scripture reading itself to point the moral.

"We are at present in a phase of religious thought, Christian and pseudo-Christian, when a synthetic study of the life and teaching of Christ may well be of use. We have analysed until the mind turns in weariness from the broken fragments; we have criticised until there remains no new standpoint for the critic; but if we could only get a whole conception of Christ's life among men and of the philosophic method of His teaching, His own words should be fulfilled and the Son of Man lifted up, would draw all men unto Himself. It seems to me that *verse* offers a comparatively new medium in which to present the great theme. It is more impersonal, more condensed, is capable of more reverent handling than is prose; and what Wordsworth calls the 'authentic comment' may be essayed in verse with more becoming diffidence. Again, the supreme moment of a very great number of lives, that in which a person is brought face to face with Christ, comes before us with great vividness in the Gospel narratives, and it is possible to treat what we may call dramatic situations with more force, and at the same time with more reticence, in verse than in prose.

"We have a single fragment of the great epic which the future may bring forth,—

167
       'Those holy fields
  Over whose acres walked those blessed feet
  Which fourteen hundred years ago were nailed
  For our advantage to the bitter cross.'

"If Shakespeare had given us the whole how rich should we be! Every line of verse dealing directly with our Lord from the standpoint of His personality is greatly treasured. We love the lines in which Trench tells us,—

  "Of Jesus sitting by Samarian well
  Or teaching some poor fishers on the shore.'

and Keble's,—

  'Meanwhile He paces through the adoring crowd
  Calm as the march of some majestic cloud.'

or his,—

  'In His meek power He climbs the mountain's brow.'

Every line of such verse is precious but the lines are few, no doubt because the subject is supremely august. Meantime we are waiting for the great epic: because the need seems to be urgent the writer has ventured to offer a temporary stop-gap in the six volumes of *The Saviour of the World.*" (*From the Preface to the first volume*).

A girl of thirteen and a half (Form IV) in her Easter examination tackled the question: *"The people sat in darkness."* ... *"I am the Light of the World." Shew as far as you can the meaning of these statements.* She was not asked to write in verse, and was she not taught by a beautiful instinct to recognise that the phrases she had to deal with were essential poetry and that she could best express herself in verse?

> The people sat in darkness—all was dim,
> No light had yet come unto them from Him,
> No hope as yet of Heaven after life,
> A peaceful haven far from war and strife.
> Some warriors to Valhalla's halls might go
> And fight all day, and die. At evening, lo!
> They'd wake again, and drink in the great hall.
> Some men would sleep for ever at their fall;
> Or with their fickle Gods for ever be:
> So all was dark and dim. Poor heathens, see!
> *The Light ahead*, the clouds that roll away,
> The golden, glorious, dawning of the Day;
> And in the birds, the flowers, the sunshine, see
> The might of Him who calls, "Come unto Me.'"

168

A girl of seventeen (Form V) answered the question: *Write an essay or a poem on the Bread of Life*, by the following lines,

"'How Came He here,' ev'n so the people cried,
Who found Him in the Temple: He had wrought
A miracle, and fed the multitude,
On five small loaves and fish: so now they'd have
Him king; should not they then have ev'ry good,
Food that they toiled not for and clothes and care,
And all the comfort that they could require?—
So thinking sought the king. . . .

                        Our Saviour cried:
'Labour ye not for meat that perisheth,
But rather for the everlasting bread,
Which I will give'—Where is this bread, they cry,
They know not 'tis a heavenly bread He gives
But seek for earthly food—'I am the Bread of Life
And all who come to Me I feed with Bread.
Receive ye then the Bread. Your fathers eat
Of manna in the wilderness—and died—
But whoso eats this Bread shall have his part
In everlasting life: I am the Bread,
That cometh down from Heaven; unless ye eat
Of me ye die, but otherwise ye live.'
So Jesus taught, in Galilee, long since.

"The people murmured when they heard His Word,
How can it be? How can He be our Bread?

They hardened then their hearts against His Word,
They would not hear, and could not understand,
And so they turnéd back to easier ways,
And many of them walked with Him no more.
May He grant now that we may hear the Word
And harden not our hearts against the Truth
That Jesus came to teach: so that in vain   169
He may not cry to hearts that will not hear,
'I am the Bread of Life, for all that come,
I have this gift, an everlasting life,
And room within my Heavenly Father's House."

The higher forms in the P.U.S. read *The Saviour of the World* volume by volume together with the text arranged in chronological order. The lower forms read in turns each of the Synoptic Gospels; Form IV adds the Gospel of St. John and The Acts, assisted by the capital Commentaries on the several Gospels by Bishop Walsham How, published by the S.P.C.K. The study of the Epistles and the Book of Revelation is confined for the most part to Forms V and VI. The Catechism, Prayer-book, and Church History are treated with suitable text-books much in the same manner and give opportunities for such summing-up of Christian teaching as is included in the so-called dogmas of the Church. We find that Sundays together with the time given to preparation for Confirmation afford sufficient opportunities for this teaching.*

---

* Examples of the work of scholars of various ages illustrating what has been said may be seen at the P.N.E.U. Office.

Section II
THE KNOWLEDGE OF MAN
(*a*) HISTORY

I have already spoken of history as a vital part of education and have cited the counsel of Montaigne that the teacher 'shall by the help of histories inform himself of the worthiest minds that were in the best ages.' To us in particular who are living in one of the great epochs of history it is necessary to know something of what has gone before in order to think justly of what is occurring to-day. The League of Nations, for example, has reminded us not only of the Congress of Vienna but of the several Treaties of Perpetual Peace which have marked the history of Europe. It is still true that,—

> "Things done without example, in their issue
> Are to be feared. Have you a precedent
> Of this commission?" (*Henry VIII.*)

We applaud the bluff King's wisdom and look uneasily for precedents for the war and the peace and the depressing anxieties that have come in their train. We are conscious of a lack of sound judgment in ourselves to decide upon the questions that have come before us and are aware that nothing would give us more confidence than a pretty wide acquaintance with history. The more educated among our 'Dominion' cousins complain that their young people have no background of history and as a consequence 'we are the people' is their master thought; they would face even the loss of Westminster Abbey without a qualm. What is it to them where great events have happened, great persons lived and moved? And, alas, this indifference to history is not confined to the Dominions; young people at home are equally indifferent, nor have their elders such stores of interest and information as should quicken children with the knowledge that always and everywhere there have been great parts to play and almost always great men to play those parts: that any day it may come to anyone to do some service of historical moment to the country. It is not too much to say that a rational well-considered patriotism depends on a pretty copious reading of history, and with this rational patriotism we desire our young people shall be informed rather than with the jingoism of the emotional patriot.

If there is but little knowledge of history amongst us, no doubt our schools are in fault. Teachers will plead that there is no time save for a sketchy knowledge of English history given in a course of lectures of which the pupils take notes and work up reports. Most of us know how unsatisfying is such a course however entertaining. Not even Thackeray could introduce the stuff of knowledge into his lectures on *The Four Georges*. Our knowledge of history should give us something more than impressions and opinions, but, alas, the lack of time is a real difficulty.

Now the method I am advocating has this advantage; it multiplies time. Each school period is quadrupled in time value and we find that we get through a surprising amount of history in a thorough way, in about the same time that in most schools affords no more than a skeleton of English History only. We know that young people are enormously interested in the subject and give concentrated attention if we give them the right books. We are aware that our own discursive talk is usually a waste of time and a strain on the scholars' attention, so we (of the P.N.E.U.) confine ourselves to affording two things,—knowledge, and a keen sympathy in the interest roused by that knowledge. It is our part to see that every child *knows* and *can tell*, whether by way of oral narrative or written essay. In this way an unusual amount of ground is covered with such certainty that no revision is required for the examination at the end of the term. A *single reading* is a condition insisted upon because a naturally desultory habit of mind leads us all to put off the effort of attention as long as a second or third chance of coping with our subject is to be hoped for. It is, however, a mistake to speak of the 'effort of attention.' Complete and entire attention is a natural function which requires no effort and causes no fatigue; the anxious labour of mind of which we are at times aware comes when attention wanders and has again to be brought to the point; but the concentration at which most teachers aim is an innate provision for education and is not the result of training or effort. Our concern is to afford matter of a sufficiently literary character, together with the certainty that no second or third opportunity for knowing a given lesson will be allowed.

The personality of the teacher is no doubt of much value

but perhaps this value is intellectual rather than emotional. The perception of the teacher is keenly interested, that his mind and their minds are working in harmony is a wonderful incentive to young scholars; but the sympathetic teacher who believes that to attend is a strain, who makes allowance for the hundred wandering fancies that beset a child—whom he has at last to pull up with effort, tiring to teacher and pupil—hinders in his good-natured efforts to help.

The child of six in IB has, not stories from English History, but a definite quantity of consecutive reading, say, forty pages in a term, from a well-written, well-considered, large volume which is also well-illustrated. Children cannot of course themselves read a book which is by no means written down to the 'child's level' so the teacher reads and the children 'tell' paragraph by paragraph, passage by passage. The teacher does not talk much and is careful never to interrupt a child who is called upon to 'tell.' The first efforts may be stumbling but presently the children get into their 'stride' and 'tell' a passage at length with surprising fluency. The teacher probably allows other children to correct any faults in the telling when it is over. The teacher's own really difficult part is to keep up sympathetic interest by look and occasional word, by remarks upon a passage that has been narrated, by occasionally shewing pictures, and so on. But she will bear in mind that the child of six has begun the serious business of his education, that it does not matter much whether he understands this word or that, but that it matters a great deal that he should learn to deal directly with books. Whatever a child or grown-up person can tell, that we may be sure he knows, and what he cannot tell, he does not know. Possibly this practice of 'telling' was more used in the sixteenth and seventeenth centuries than it is now. We remember how three gentlemen meet in *Henry VIII* and one who has just come out of the Abbey from witnessing the coronation of Anne Boleyn is asked to tell the others about it, which he does with the vividness and accuracy we obtain from children. In this case no doubt the 'telling' was a stage device, but would it have been adopted if such narration were not commonly practised? Even in our own day a good *raconteur* is a welcome guest; and a generation or two ago the art was studied as a part of gentlemanly equipment. The objection occurs that such a social accomplishment is unnecessary for children and is a mere exercise of memory. Now a passage to be memorised requires much conning, much repetition, and meanwhile the learners are 'thinking' about other matters, that is, the *mind* is not at work in the act of memorising. To read a passage with full attention and to tell it afterwards has a curiously different effect. M. Bergson makes the happy distinction between *word* memory and *mind* memory, which, once the force of it is realised, should bring about sweeping changes in our methods of education.

Trusting to mind memory we visualise the scene, are convinced by the arguments, take pleasure in the turn the sentences and frame our own upon them; in that particular passage or chapter has been received us and become a part of us just as literally as was yesterday's dinner; nay, more so, for yesterday's dinner is of little account tomorrow; but several months, perhaps hence, we shall be able to narrate the passage we had, so to say, consumed and grown upon with all the vividness, detail and accuracy of the first telling. All powers of the mind which we call faculties have brought into play in dealing with the intellectual matter thus afford- ed; so we may not ask questions to help the child to reason, paint fancy pictures to help him to imagine, draw out moral lessons to quicken his conscience. These things take place as involuntarily as processes of digestion.

Children of seven are promoted to Form IA in which they remain for a couple of years. They read from the same capital book, Mrs. Marshall's *Our Island Story*, and about the same number of pages in a term; but while the readings in IB are confined to the first third of the book embodying the simpler and more direct histories, those in IA go on to the end of the volume and children learn at any rate to love English history. "I'd a lot sooner have history than my dinner," said a sturdy boy of seven by no means inclined to neglect his dinner.

In IA the history is amplified and illustrated by short biographies of persons connected with the period studied, Lord Clive, Nelson, etc.; and Mrs. Frewen Lord's delight- ful *Tales from Westminster Abbey* and *from St. Paul's* help the children immensely in individualising their heroes. It is good to hear them 'tell' of Franklin, Nelson, Howard,

174

Shaftesbury, and their delight in visiting the monuments is very great. One would not think that Donne would greatly interest children but the excitement of a small party in noticing the marks of the Great Fire still to be seen on his monument was illuminating to lookers-on.

Possibly there is no sounder method of inculcating a sane and serviceable patriotism than this of making children familiar with the monuments of the great event if they have not the opportunity to see them. Form II (ages 9 to 12) have a more considerable historical programme which they cover with ease and enjoyment. They use a more difficult book than in IA, an interesting and well-written history of England of which they read some fifty pages or so in a term. IIA read in addition and by way of illustration the chapters dealing with the social life of the period in a volume, treating of social life in England. We introduce children as early as possible to the contemporary history of other countries as the study of English history alone is apt to lead to a certain insular and arrogant habit of mind.

Naturally we begin with French history and both divisions read from the *First History of France*, very well written, the chapters contemporary with the English history they are reading. The readiness with which children write or tell of Richelieu, Colbert, Bayard, justifies us in this early introduction of foreign history; and the lucidity and clearness with which the story is told in the book they use results on the part of the children in such a knowledge of the history of France as throws light on that of their own country and certainly gives them the sense that history was progressing everywhere much as it was at home during the period they are reading about.

The study of ancient history which cannot be contemporaneous we approach through a chronologically-arranged book about the British Museum (written for the scholars of the P.U.S. by the late Mrs. W. Epps who had the delightful gift of realising the progress of the ages as represented in our great national storehouse). I have already instanced a child's visit to the Parthenon Room and her eager identification of what she saw with what she had read, and that will serve to indicate the sort of key to ancient history afforded by this valuable book. Miss G. M. Bernau has added to the value of these studies by producing a 'Book of Centuries' in which children draw such illustrations as they come across of objects of domestic use, of art, etc., connected with the century they are reading about. This slight study of the British Museum we find very valuable; whether the children have or have not the opportunity of visiting the Museum itself, they have the hope of doing so, and, besides, their minds are awakened to the treasures of local museums.

176

In Form III children continue the same history of England as in II, the same French history and the same British Museum Book, going on with their 'Book of Centuries.' To this they add about twenty to thirty pages a term from a little book on Indian History, a subject which interests them greatly.

Slight studies of the history of other parts of the British Empire are included under 'Geography.'

In Form IV the children are promoted to Gardiner's

Student's History of England, clear and able, but somewhat stiffer than that they have hitherto been engaged upon, together with Mr. and Mrs. Quennell's *History of Everyday Things in England* (which is used in Form III also). Form IV is introduced to outlines of European history. *The British Museum for Children* and 'Book of Centuries' are continued.

It is as teachers know a matter of extreme difficulty to find the exactly right book for children's reading in each subject and for some years we have been regretting the fact that Lord's very delightful *Modern Europe** has been out of print.

The history studies of Forms V and VI (ages 15 to 18) are more advanced and more copious and depend for illustration upon readings in the literature of the period. Green's *Shorter History of the English People* is the textbook in English history, amplified, for example, by Macaulay's *Essays on Frederick the Great* and the *Austrian Succession*, on *Pitt* and *Clive*. For the same period we use an American history of Western Europe and a very admirable history of France, well-translated from the original of M. Duruy. Possibly Madame de Staël's *L'Allemagne* or some other historical work of equal calibre may occur in their reading of French. It is not possible to continue the study of Greek and Roman history in detail but an admirably written survey informed with enthusiasm is afforded by Professor de Burgh's *The Legacy of the Ancient World*. The pupils make history charts for every hundred years on the plan either

---

* This book is now in print again.

adapted or invented by the late Miss Beale of Cheltenham, a square ruled into a hundred spaces ten in each direction with the symbol in each square showing an event which lends itself to illustration during that particular ten years. Thus crossed battle axes represent a war.

The geographical aspects of history fall under 'Geography' as a subject. This course of historical reading is valued exceedingly by young people as affording a knowledge of the past that bears upon and illuminates the present. The writer recollects meeting a brilliant group of Oxford undergraduates, keen and full of interest, but lamentably ignorant, who said, "We want to know something about history. What do you advise us to read? We know nothing." Perhaps no youth should go to College without some such rudimentary course of English, European, and, especially, French history, as is afforded by the programmes.* Such a general survey should precede any special course and should be required before the more academic studies designed to prepare students for 'research work.'

It will be observed that the work throughout the Forms is always chronologically progressive. The young student rarely goes over old ground; but should it happen that the whole school has arrived at the end of 1920, say, and there is nothing for it but to begin again, the books studied throw new light and bring the young students into line with modern research.

But any sketch of the history teaching in Forms V and

---

* Of the Parents' Union School.

178 VI in a given period depends upon a notice of the 'literature' set; for plays, novels, essays, 'lives,' poems, are all pressed into service and where it is possible, the architecture, painting, etc., which the period produced. Thus questions such as the following on a term's work both test and record the reading of the term,—"Describe the condition of (*a*) the clergy, (*b*) the army, (*c*) the navy, (*d*) the general public in and about 1685." "Trace the rise of Prussia before Frederick the Great." "What theories of government were held by Louis XIV? Give some account of his great ministers." "Describe the rise of Russia and its condition at the opening of the eighteenth century." "Suppose Evelyn (Form VI) or Pepys (Form V) in counsel at the League of Nations, write his diary for three days." "Sketch the character and manners of Addison. How does he appear in *Esmond*?"

It is a great thing to possess a pageant of history in the background of one's thoughts. We may not be able to recall this or that circumstance, but, 'the imagination is warmed'; we know that there is a great deal to be said on both sides of every question and are saved from crudities in opinion and rashness in action. The present becomes enriched for us with the wealth of all that has gone before.

Perhaps the gravest defect in school curricula is that they fail to give a comprehensive, intelligent and interesting introduction to history. To leave off or even to begin with the history of our own country is fatal. We cannot live sanely unless we know that other peoples are as we are with a difference, that their history is as ours, with a difference, that they too have been represented by their poets and their artists, that they too have their literature and their national life. We have been asleep and our awaking is rather terrible. The people whom we have not taught, rise upon us in their ignorance and 'the rabble,'—

> "As the world were now but to begin 179
>   Antiquity forgot, custom not known.
> They cry,—'Choose we!'" (*Hamlet.*)

Heaven help their choice for choosing is indeed with them, and little do they know of those two ratifiers and props of every present word and action, Antiquity and Custom! It is never too late to mend but we may not delay to offer such a liberal and generous diet of History to every child in the country as shall give weight to his decisions, consideration to his actions and stability to his conduct.; that stability, the lack of which has plunged us into many a stormy sea of unrest.

It is to be noted that 'stability' is the mark of the educated classes. When we reflect upon the disturbance of the national life by labour unrest and again, upon the fact that political and social power is passing into the hands of the majority, that is of the labouring classes, we cannot but feel that there is a divine fitness, a providential adaptation in the circumstance that the infinite educability of persons of all classes should be disclosed to us as a nation at a time when an emotional and ignorant labouring class is a peculiar danger. I am not sure that the education implied in the old symbol of the ladder does make for national tranquility. It is right that equal opportunity of being first should be afforded to all but that is no new thing. Our history is punctuated by men who have risen, and the Roman Church has largely founded herself as has the Chinese Empire upon this doctrine of equal opportunity. But let us remember that the men who climb are apt to be uneasy members of society; the desire for knowledge for its own sake, on the other hand, finds satisfaction in knowledge itself.

The young men see visions; the hardships of daily life are ameliorated, and while an alert and informed mind leads to decency and propriety of living it does not lead to the restless desire to subvert society for the sake of the chances offered by a general upheaval. Wordsworth is right:—

"If rightly trained and bred Humanity is humble."

We live in times critical for everybody but eminently critical for teachers because it rests with them to decide whether personal or general good should be aimed at, whether education shall be merely a means of getting on or a means of general progress towards high thinking and plain living and therefore an instrument of the greatest national good.*

---

* Examination papers giving some idea of the scope of the history studies in the P.U.S. may be seen at the P.N.E.U. Office.

II

THE KNOWLEDGE OF MAN
(*b*) LITERATURE

Except in Form I the study of Literature goes *pari passu* with that of History. Fairy tales, (Andersen or Grimm, for example), delight Form IB, and the little people re-tell these tales copiously, vividly, and with the astonishing exactness we may expect when we remember how seriously annoyed they are with the story-teller who alters a phrase or a circumstance. *Aesop's Fables*, too, are used with great success, and are rendered, after being once heard, with brevity and point, and children readily appropriate the moral. Mrs. Gatty's *Parables From Nature*, again, serve another purpose. They feed a child's sense of wonder and are very good to tell. There is no attempt to reduce the work of this form, or any other, to a supposed 'child level.' Form IA (7 to 9) hears and tells chapter by chapter *The Pilgrim's Progress* and the children's narrations are delightful. No beautiful thought or bold figure escapes them. Andrew Lang's *Tales of Troy and Greece*, a big volume, is a *pièce de resistance* going on from term to term.

    181

The great tales of the heroic age find their way to children's hearts. They conceive vividly and tell eagerly, and the difficult classical names instead of being a stumbling-block are a delight, because, as a Master of a Council school says,—

> "Children have an instinctive power by which they are able to sense the meaning of a whole passage and even some difficult words."

That the sonorous beauty of these classical names appeals to them is illustrated by a further quotation from the same Master,—

> "A boy of about seven in my school the other day asked his mother why she had not given him one of those pretty names they heard in the stories at school. He thought Ulysses a prettier name than his own, Kenneth, and that the mother of his playmate might have called him Achilles instead of Alan."

There is profound need to cultivate delight in beautiful names in days when we are threatened with the fear that London itself should lose that rich halo of historic associations which glorifies its every street and alley, that it may be made like New York, and should name a street X500,—like a workhouse child without designation; an age when we express the glory and beauty of the next highest peak of the Himalayas by naming it D2! In such an age, this, of their inherent aptitude for beautiful names, is a lode of much promise in children's minds. The Kaffir who announced that his name was 'Telephone' had an ear for sound. Kingsley's *Water Babies, Alice in Wonderland*, Kipling's *Just So Stories*, scores of exquisite classics written for children, but not written down to them, are suitable at this stage.

Form IIB has a considerable programme of reading, that is, not the mere mechanical exercise of reading but the reading of certain books. Therefore it is necessary that

182

two years should be spent in Form IA and that in the second of these two years the children should read a good deal of the set work for themselves. In IIB they read their own geography, history, poetry, but perhaps Shakespeare's *Twelfth Night*, say, *Scott's Rob Roy*, *Gulliver's Travels*, should be read to them and narrated by them until they are well in their tenth year. Their power to understand, visualise, and 'tell' a play of Shakespeare from nine years old and onwards is very surprising. They put in nothing which is not there, but they miss nothing and display a passage or a scene in a sort of curious relief. One or two books of the calibre of *The Heroes of Asgard* are also included in the programme for the term.

The transition to Form IIA is marked by more individual reading as well as by a few additional books. The children read their 'Shakespeare play' in character. Certain Council School boys, we are told, insist on dramatising Scott as they read it. Bulfinch's *Age of Fable* admits them to the rich imaginings of peoples who did not yet know. Goldsmith's poems and Stevenson's *Kidnapped*, etc., may form part of a term's work, and in each and all children shew the same surprising power of knowing, evinced by the one sure test,— they are able to 'tell' each work they have read not only with accuracy but with spirit and originality. How is it possible, it may be asked, to show originality in 'mere narration'? Let us ask Scott, Shakespeare, Homer, who told what they knew, that is narrated, but with continual scintillations from their own genius playing upon the written word. Just so in their small degree do the children narrate; they see it all so vividly that when you read or hear their versions the theme is illuminated for you too.

Children remain in Form II until they are twelve, and here I would remark on the evenness with which the power of children in dealing with books is developed. We spread an abundant and delicate feast in the programmes and each small guest assimilates what he can. The child of genius and imagination gets greatly more than his duller comrade but all sit down to the same feast and each one gets according to his needs and powers.

The surprises afforded by the dull and even the 'backward' children are encouraging and illuminating. We think we know that man is an educable being, but when we afford to children all that they want we discover how straitened were our views, how poor and narrow the education we offered. Even in so-called deficient children we perceive,—

> "What a piece of work is man. . . . In apprehension, how like a god!"

In Forms III and IV we introduce a *History of English Literature* carefully chosen to afford sympathetic interest and delight while avoiding stereotyped opinions and stale information. The portion read each term (say fifty pages) corresponds with the period covered in history studies and the book is a great favourite with children. They have of course a great *flair* for Shakespeare, whether *King Lear,*

Twelfth Night, *Henry V*, or some other play, and *The Wa-verleys* usually afford a contemporary tale. There has been discussion in Elementary Schools as to whether an abridged edition would not give a better chance of getting through the novel set for a term, but strong arguments were brought forward at a conference of teachers in Gloucester in favour of a complete edition. Children take pleasure in the 'dry' parts, descriptions and the like, rendering these quite beautifully in their narrations. Form IV may have quite a wide course of reading. For instance if the historical period for a term include the Commonwealth, they may read *L'Allegro*, and *Il Penseroso*, *Lycidas*, and contemporary poets as represented in a good anthology, or, for a later period, Pope's *Rape of the Lock*, or Gray's poems, while Form III read poems of Goldsmith and Burns. The object of children's literary studies is not to give them precise information as to who wrote what in the reign of whom?—but to give them a sense of the spaciousness of the days, not only of great Elizabeth, but of all those times of which poets, historians and the makers of tales, have left us living pictures. In such ways the children secure, not the sort of information which is of little cultural value, but wide spaces wherein imagination may take those holiday excursions deprived of which life is dreary; judgment, too, will turn over these folios of the mind and arrive at fairly just decisions about a given strike, the question of Poland, Indian Unrest. Every man is called upon to be a statesman seeing that every man and woman, too, has a share in the government of the country; but statesmanship requires imaginative conceptions, formed upon pretty wide reading and some familiarity with historical precedents.

The reading for Forms V and VI (ages 15 to 18) is more comprehensive and more difficult. Like that in the earlier Forms, it follows the lines of the history they are reading, touching current literature in the occasional use of modern books; but young people who have been brought up on this sort of work may, we find, be trusted to keep themselves *au fait* with the best that is being produced in their own days. Given the proper period, Form V would cover in a term Pope's *Essay on Man*, Carlyle's *Essay on Burns*, Frankfort Moore's *Jessamy Bride*, Goldsmith's *Citizen of the World* (edited), Thackeray's *The Virginians*, the contemporary poets from an anthology. Form VI would read Boswell, *The Battle of the Books*, Macaulay's *Essays* on Goldsmith, Johnson, Pitt; the contemporary poets from *The Oxford Book of Verse*, and both Forms read *She Stoops to Conquer*. This course of reading, it will be seen, is suggestive and will lead to much reading round and about it in later days. As for the amount covered in each Form, it is probably about the amount most of us cover in the period of time included in a school term, but while we grown-up persons read and forget because we do not take the pains to *know* as we read, these young students have the powers of perfect recollection and just application because they have read with attention and concentration and have in every case reproduced what they have read in narration, or, the gist of some portion of it, in writing.

185

The children's answers* in their examination papers, show that literature has become a living power in the minds of these young people.

II

THE KNOWLEDGE OF MAN
(c) MORALS AND ECONOMICS: CITIZENSHIP

Like Literature this subject, too, is ancillary to History. In Form I, children begin to gather conclusions as to the general life of the community from tales, fables and the story of one or another great citizen. In Form II, Citizenship becomes a definite subject rather from the point of view of what may be called the inspiration of citizenship than from that of the knowledge proper to a citizen, though the latter is by no means neglected. We find Plutarch's *Lives* exceedingly inspiring. These are read by the teacher (with suitable omissions) and narrated with great spirit by the children. They learn to answer such questions as,—"In what ways did Pericles make Athens beautiful? How did he persuade the people to help him?" And we may hope that the idea is engendered of preserving and increasing the beauty of their own neighbourhood without the stale- 186 ness which comes of much exhortation. Again, they will answer,—"How did Pericles manage the people in time of war lest they should force him to act against his own judgment?" And from such knowledge as this we may suppose

---

* Examination Papers can be seen at the P.N.E.U. Office

that the children begin to get a sympathetic view of the problems of statesmanship. Then, to come to our own time, they are enabled to answer,—"What do you know of (*a*) County Councils, (*b*) District Councils, (*c*) Parish Councils?"—knowledge which should make children perceive that they too are being prepared to become worthy citizens, each with his several duties. Our old friend Mrs. Beesley's *Stories from the History of Rome* helps us here in Form IIB instead of Plutarch, illumined by Macaulay's *Lays of Ancient Rome*. In giving children the knowledge of men and affairs which we class under 'Citizenship' we have to face the problem of good and evil. Many earnest-minded teachers will sympathise with one of their number who said,—

> "Why give children the tale of Circe, in which there is such an offensive display of greediness, why not bring them up exclusively on heroic tales which offer them something to live up to? Time is short. Why not use it all in giving examples of good life and instruction in good manners?"

Again,—

> "Why should they read any part of *Childe Harold*, and so become familiar with a poet whose works do not make for edification?"

Now Plutarch is like the Bible in this, that he does not label the actions of his people as good or bad but leaves the

conscience and judgment of his readers to make that classification. What to avoid and how to avoid it, is knowledge
as important to the citizen whether of the City of God or
of his own immediate city, as to know what is good and
how to perform the same. Children recognise with incipi-
ent weariness the doctored tale as soon as it is begun to be   187
told, but the human story with its evil and its good never
flags in interest. Jacob does not pall upon us though he
was the elect of God. We recognise the justice of his own
verdict on himself, "few and evil have been the days of my
life." We recognise the finer integrity of the foreign kings
and rulers that he is brought in contact with, just as in the
New Testament the Roman Centurion is in every case a
finer person than the religious Jew. Perhaps we are so made
that the heroic which is all heroic, the good which is all
virtuous, palls upon us, whereas we preach little sermons
to ourselves on the text of the failings and weaknesses of
those great ones with whom we become acquainted in our
reading. Children like ourselves must see life whole if they
are to profit. At the same time they must be protected from
grossness and rudeness by means of the literary medium
through which they are taught. A daily newspaper is not
on a level with Plutarch's *Lives*, nor with Andrew Lang's
Tales of Troy and Greece, though possibly the same class
of incidents may appear in both. The boy, or girl, aged
from ten to twelve, who is intimate with a dozen or so of
Plutarch's *Lives*, so intimate that they influence his thought
and conduct, has learned to put his country first and to see
individuals only as they serve or dis-serve the State. Thus he

gets his first lesson in the science of proportion. Children familiar with the great idea of a State in the sense, not of a government but of the people, learn readily enough about the laws, customs and government of their country; learn, too, with great interest something about themselves, mind and body, heart and soul, because they feel it is well to know what they have it in them to give to their country.

We labour under a difficulty in choosing books which has exercised all great thinkers from Plato to Erasmus, from Erasmus to the anxious Heads of schools to-day, I mean the coarseness and grossness which crop up in scores of books desirable otherwise for their sound learning and judgment. Milton assures us with strong asseveration that to the pure all things are pure; but we are uneasy. When pupils in the higher forms read the *Areopagitica* they are safeguarded in some measure because they perceive that to see impurity is to be impure. The younger children are helped by the knowledge we offer them in *Ourselves*, and chastely taught children learn to watch over their thoughts 'because of the angels.' So far as we can get them we use expurgated editions; in other cases the book is read aloud by the teacher with necessary omissions. We are careful not to associate the processes of nature whether in the plant or animal world with possible thoughts of impurity in the mind of a child. One point I should like to touch upon in this connection. The excessive countenance sometimes afforded to games by the Heads of schools is not altogether for the sake of distinction in the games. "I keep under my body," says St.

Paul, and games which exhaust the physical powers have as their unspoken *raison d'être* the desire to keep boys and girls decent. No doubt they do so to some extent though painful occurrences come to light in even the best schools. Now a fact not generally recognised is that offences of the kind which most distress parents and teachers are *bred in the mind* and in an empty mind at that. That is why parents, who endeavour to save their sons from the corruption of the Public School by having them taught at home, are apt to miss their mark. The abundant leisure afforded by home teaching offers that empty chamber swept and garnished which invites sins that can be committed in thought and in solitude. Our schools err, too, in not giving anything like enough work of the kind that from its absorbing interest compels reflection and tends to secure a mind continually and wholesomely occupied. Supply a boy with abundant 189 mental pabulum, not in the way of desultory reading, (that is a sort of idleness which leads to mischief), but in the way of matter to be definitely known, give him much and sound food for his imagination, speculation, aspiration, and you have a wholesome-minded youth to whom work is a joy and games not a strain but a healthy relaxation and pleasure. I make no apology for what may appear like a divergence from the subject of citizenship, because all boys and girls should know that they owe a sound mind and a sound body as their personal contribution alike to their city and their State.

Ourselves, our Souls and Bodies (by the Writer) is much

used in the P.U.S., as I know of no other attempt to present such a ground plan of human nature as should enable the young student to know where he is in his efforts to 'be good' as the children say. The point of view taken in this volume is, that all beautiful and noble possibilities are present in every one; but that each person is subject to assaults and hindrances in various ways of which he should be aware in order that he may watch and pray. Hortatory teaching is apt to bore both young people and their elders; but an ordered presentation of the possibilities and powers that lie in human nature and of the risks that attend these, can hardly fail to have an enlightening and stimulating effect.

But the objects we have in view in teaching 'Everyday Morals' and 'Citizenship' cannot be better illustrated than by a few papers* written by children of various ages, dealing with self management, and exemplifying the virtues that help and serve city and country. "Oh dear," said a little girl coming out of a bath, "I'm just like Julius Caesar, I don't care to do a thing at all if I'm not best at it." So, in unlikely ways and from unlikely sources, do children gather that little code of principles which shall guide their lives.

II

THE KNOWLEDGE OF MAN

(*d*) COMPOSITION

190   Composition in Form I (A and B) is almost entirely oral and is so much associated with Bible history, English

---

* Examination Papers can be seen at the P.N.E.U. Office.

history, geography, natural history, that it hardly calls for a special place on the programme, where however it does appear as 'Tales.' In few things do certain teachers labour in vain more than in the careful and methodical way in which they teach composition to young children. The drill that these undergo in forming sentences is unnecessary and stultifying, as much so perhaps as such drill would be in the acts of mastication and deglutination. Teachers err out of their exceeding goodwill and generous zeal. They feel that they cannot do too much for children and attempt to do for them those things which they are richly endowed to do for themselves. Among these is the art of composition, that art of 'telling' which culminates in a Scott or a Homer and begins with the toddling persons of two and three who talk a great deal to each other and are surely engaged in 'telling' though no grown-up, not even a mother, can understand. But children of six can tell to amazing purpose. The grown-up who writes the tale to their 'telling' will cover many pages before getting to the end of "Hans and Gretel" or "The Little Match Girl" or a Bible story. The facts are sure to be accurate and the expression surprisingly vigorous, striking and unhesitating. Probably few grown-ups could 'tell' one of Aesop's *Fables* with the terse directness which children reproduce. Neither are the children's narrations incoherent; they go on with their book, week by week, whatever comes at a given time,—whether it be Mrs. Gatty's *Parables From Nature*, Andersen or Grimm or *The Pilgrim's Progress*, from the point where they left 191 off,—and there never is a time when their knowledge is scrappy. They answer such questions as—"Tell about the meeting of Ulysses and Telemachus," or, "about Jason and Hera." "Tell how Christian and Hopeful met with Giant Despair," or, "about the Shining Ones."

Children are in Form IA from 7 to 9 and their reading is wider and their composition more copious. They will 'tell' in their examinations about the Feeding of the Four Thousand, about the Building of the Tabernacle, How Doubting Castle was demolished, about the burning of Old St. Paul's, How we know that the world is round and a great deal besides; for all their work lends itself to oral composition and the power of such composition is innate in children and is not the result of instruction. Two or three points are important. Children in IB require a quantity of matter to be read to them, graduated, not according to their powers which are always present, but they require a little time to employ their power of fixed attention and that other power which they possess of fluent narration. So probably young children should be allowed to narrate paragraph by paragraph, while children of seven or eight will 'tell' chapter by chapter. Corrections must not be made during the act of narration, nor must any interruption be allowed.

Children must not be teased or instructed about the use of stops or capital letters. These things too come by nature to the child who reads, and the teacher's instructions are apt to issue in the use of a pepper box for commas. We do not say that children should never read well-intentioned second-rate books, but certainly they should not read these in school hours by way of lessons. From their earliest days they should get the habit of reading literature which they should take hold of for themselves, much or little, in their own way. As the object of every writer is to explain himself in his own book, the child and the author must be trusted together, without the intervention of the middle-man. What his author does not tell him he must go without knowing for the present. No explanation will really help him, and explanations of words and phrases spoil the text and should not be attempted unless children ask, What does so and so mean? when other children in the class will probably tell.

192

Form II (A and B), (ages 9 to 12). Children in this Form have a wider range of reading, a more fertile field of thought, and more delightful subjects for composition. They write their little essays themselves, and as for the accuracy of their knowledge and justice of their expression, why, 'still the wonder grows.' They will describe their favourite scene from *The Tempest* or *Woodstock*. They write or 'tell' stories from work set in Plutarch or Shakespeare or tell of the events of the day. They narrate from English, French and General History, from the Old and the New Testament, from *Stories from the History of Rome*, from Bulfinch's *Age of Fable*, from, for example, Goldsmith's or Wordsworth's poems, from *The Heroes of Asgard*: in fact, Composition is not an adjunct but an integral part of their education in every subject. The exercise affords very great pleasure to children, perhaps we all like to tell what we know, and in proportion as their composition is entirely artless, it is in the same degree artistic and any child is apt to produce a style to be envied for its vigour and grace. But let me again say there must be no attempt to teach composition. Our failure as teachers is that we place too little dependence on the intellectual power of our scholars, and as they are modest little souls what the teacher kindly volunteers to do for them, they feel that they cannot do for themselves. But give them a fair field and no favour and they will describe their favourite scene from the play they have read, and much besides.

193   Forms III and IV. In these Forms as in I and II what called 'composition' is an inevitable consequence of a free yet exact use of books and requires no special attention until the pupil is old enough to take of his own accord a critical interest in the use of words. The measured cadences of verse are as pleasing to children as to their elders. Many children write verse as readily as prose, and the conciseness and power of bringing their subject matter to a point which this form of composition requires affords valuable mental training. One thing must be borne in mind. Exercises in scansion are as necessary in English as in Latin verse. Rhythm and accent on the other hand take care of themselves in proportion as a child is accustomed to read poetry. In III and IV as in the earlier Forms, the matter of their reading during the term, topics of the day, and the passing of the Seasons, afford innumerable subjects for short essays or short sets of verses of a more abstract nature in IV than in III: the

point to be considered is that the subject be one on which, to quote again Jane Austen's expression, the imagination of the children has been 'warmed.' They should be asked to write upon subjects which have interested them keenly. Then when the terminal examination comes they will respond to such a question as,—"Write twelve lines (which must scan) on 'Sir Henry Lee,' or 'Cordelia,' or Pericles, or Livingstone," or, to take a question from the early days of the War, "Discuss Lord Derby's Scheme. How is it working?"; or, (IV) an essay on "The new army in the making, shewing what some of the difficulties have been and what has been achieved."

Forms V and VI. In these Forms some definite teaching in the art of composition is advisable, but not too much, lest the young scholars be saddled with a stilted style which may encumber them for life. Perhaps the method of a University tutor is the best that can be adopted; that is, a point or two   194 might be taken up in a given composition and suggestions or corrections made with little talk. Having been brought up so far upon stylists the pupils are almost certain to have formed a good style; because they have been thrown into the society of *many* great minds, they will not make a servile copy of any one but will shape an individual style out of the wealth of material they possess; and because they have matter in abundance and of the best they will not write mere verbiage. Here is an example of a programme set for a term's work in these two Forms,—"A good précis; Letters to *The Times* on topics of the day; subjects taken from the term's work in history and literature; or notes on a picture study; dialogues between characters occurring in your literature and history studies; ballads on current events; (VI) essays on events and questions of the day; a patriotic play in verse or prose." Here are questions set for another term,—"Write a paean, rhymed or in blank verse, on the Prince of Wales's tour in the Dominions." "An essay, dated 1930, on the imagined work of the League of Nations." Form V, "Write a woeful ballad touching the condition of Ireland, or, a poem on the King's garden party to the V.C.'s." "An essay on the present condition of England, or, on President Wilson."

The response of the young students to such a scheme of study is very delightful. What they write has literary and sometimes poetic value, and the fact that they can write well is the least of the gains acquired. They can read, appreciating every turn of their author's thought; and they can bring cultivated minds to bear on the problems of the hour and the guiding of the State; that is to say, their education bears at every point on the issues and interests of every day life, and they shew good progress in the art of becoming the magnanimous citizens of the future. Here are a few examples* of the compositions of the several Forms.

---

* These answers are uncorrected and are taken from Examination papers not sent back. Most parents and teachers have their papers returned.

(F. B. IIA. Council School.)

ARMISTICE DAY

Soldiers dying, soldiers dead,
Bullets whizzing overhead.
Tommies standing cheerily by.
Waiting for their time to die;
Soon the lull of firing comes,
And naught is heard but the roll of drums.
And now the last shell crashes down,
A soldier reels in pain
Too late the glad news comes to him.
He never moves again,
He is the Unknown Warrior,
A man without a name.
Two years have passed and home he comes,
To the hearts that loved him well,
Who is the Unknown Warrior,?
No lips the tale can tell,
His tomb is in the Abbey,
Where the souls of Heroes dwell.
A nations sorrow and a nations tears,
Have gone with the nameless man,
Who knows, who can tell, the Warriors name,
We think that no man can,
So let our sorrow turn to joy
On the grave of the Unknown man.

196   **(A. B. 13 ¾. III)**

Write some lines, in blank verse, that must scan on one of the following: (a), Scylla and Charybdis; (b), The White Lady of Avenel; (c), The Prince of Wales in India.

THE WHITE LADY OF AVENEL

The sun had set and night was drawing on,
The hills stood black against the twilight sky.
A faint young crescent moon shone dimly forth
Casting a pale and ghostly radiance
Upon the group of pine trees on the hill,
And silvering the rivers eddying swirl.
Now all was silent, not a sound disturbed
The summer night, and not a breath of wind
Stirred in the pines. All nature slept in peace.
But what was that, standing up in the shade?
A woman, straight, and slim, all clad in white,
Upon her long soft hair a misty crown,
And ever and anon she deeply sighed,
Leaning against the rugged mountain rock,
Like to a moon beam, or a wisp of smoke.
And on her shimmering, moonlit, robe she wore
A golden girdle, in whose links was woven
The fortunes of the house of Avenel.
 A cloud past o'er the moon, and the slim ghost
Faded and disappeared into the air.
A breeze sprang up among the pine trees tall;
And then the river murmuring on its way
Whispered a sad lament unto the night.

(K.L. 13½. III.)

Write in Ballad Metre some lines on "Armistice Day" or "Echo."

ARMISTICE DAY, OR THE UNKNOWN WARRIOR

Within the ancient Abbey's sacred pyle,
Which proudly guards the noblest of our dead.
Where kings and statesmen lie in every aisle,
And honoured poets, soldiers, priests are laid;

Behold a stranger comes. From whence is he?
Is he of noble birth; of rank or fame?
Was he as great as any whom we see
Around, who worked to make themselves a name?

Surely he is a prince. nay, e'en a king?
For see the waiting thousands gathered here;
And hear the streets of ancient London ring
To the slow tramp of men who guard his bier!

And, surely, 'tis the King himself who comes
As chiefest mourner on this solemn day,
And these who walk behind him are his sons—
All here to mourn this man. Who is he? Say!

How long the ranks of men who follow him
To his last resting-place—the House of God.
Our bishops, soldiers, statemen all are here,
Gathered to lay him in his native sod.

197

You ask "Is he a prince?" I answer "No!
Though none could be interred with greater state!
This man went forth to guard us from a foe,
Which threatened this our land—He did his
    work!

He raised the flag of Liberty on high
And challenging the powers of Wrong and Might
He gave up all he had without a sigh
And died for the good cause of God and Right.

Nor is a sense of humour wanting,—

(M.O. 13. III.)
Write in Ballad Metre some lines on "Echo."

ECHO

Jupiter once went away from his wife
    To flirt with some nymphs in a wood
But Juno, suspecting that he was with them
    Came after as fast as she could.

198   Now Echo, a nymph, knew that Juno was there
    That the nymphs they would soon be found out,
And so she kept Juno away from the wood
    For if they had gone she did doubt.

But Juno knew all; and her anger was great
　　And Echo this dreadful thing heard
"Since you are so fond of talking, from now
　　You only shall have the last word!"

Now Echo went far from the dwellings of men
　　And spent her sad life all alone
And often she'd weep and think of the past
　　And over her fate make her moan.

Echo loved a Greek youth, but he could not love her.
　　And she watched him all day from her bower
Till she pined away, all but her voice, which lives still,
　　And the youth was turned into a flower.

(R. C. 15. III. Elementary, Convent School.)
*Write some verses on (a) 'Dandie Dinmont,' or, (b) 'Atalanta,' or,
(c) Allenby.*

　　　　Atlanta was a huntress,
　　　　Who dearly loved the chase.
　　　　She out-ran the deer in fleetness,
　　　　And possessed a lovely face,

　　　　Many eager suitors sought her,
　　　　But they sought her all in vain,
　　　　For she vowed she'd never marry
　　　　And her suitors all were slain.

She had heeded well the warning,
From a witch well skilled in lore,
Who had told her if she married,
Happiness was hers no more.

Then a youth whom Venus favoured,
Came one day to run the race,
And by throwing golden apples,
He out-ran her in the chase.

199   In their hour of joy and triumph
Venus they forget to thank,
And the goddess sore offended,
Lowered them to the wild beast's rank.

(J. T. III.)

Phaëton was a wilful youth who always got his way.
He asked to drive his father's charge upon a certain day.
But Phoebus knowing well what danger lurketh in the sky;
Implored of him to wish again and not that task to try,
But Phaëton determined was to best this dangerous way,
And leaped into the chariot to spite his father's sway.
The horses started forward at a dashing headlong pace,
Phaëton tried to hold them back and modify the race.
With dreadful swiftness on he flew, losing his proper road,
The earth and sky began to smoke in an alarming mode.
At length when all had burst in flames, Jupiter cried aloud,
Phaëton who had lost his head was killed beneath a cloud.

(H.E.M. 15 ⁸⁄₁₂. IV.)

Write thirty lines of blank verse on (a), "A Spring Morning" (following "A Winter Morning Walk"), or, (b), Pegasus, or, (c), Allenby.

A SPRING MORNING.

'Tis Spring; and now the birds with merry song
Sing with full-throated voice to the blue sky
On which small clouds float, soft as a dove's wing.
Against the blue the pale-green leaflet gleams.
The darker green of elder, further down,
Sets off the brilliance of the hawthorn-hedge.
Close to the ground, the purple violet peeps
From out its nest of overhanging leaves.
On yonder bank the daffodils toss their heads
Under the shady lichen trees so tall.
Close by a chestnut, bursting into leaf,
Drops down it's sticky calyx on the ground;
An early bumble-bee dives headlong in
To a half-opened flower of early pear.
O'erhead, in the tall beech trees, busy rooks,
With great caw-caws and many angry squawks   200
Build their great clumsy nests with bits of twig
And little sticks just laid upon a bough.
And by the long, straight, path tall fir trees wave
Their graceful heads in the soft whisp'ring breeze
And pressed against one ruddy trunk, an owl
In vain tries to avoid the light of day,
But blinks his wise old eyes, and shakes himself,

And nestles close amid the sheltering leaves.
Now on the rhubarb-bed we see, glad sight,
Large red buttons, which promise fruit quite soon
And further down the lettuce shoots up pale
Next to a row of parsley, getting old.
But see the peas, their curly tendrils green
Clinging to their stout pea-sticks for support.

(B. B. 15. IV.)

A SPRING MORNING

Soft on the brown woods
A pale light gleams,
And slowly spreading seems
To change the brown wood to a land of dreams,
Where beneath the trees
The great god Pan,
Doth pipe, half goat, half man,
To satyrs dancing in the dawning wan.
And then comes Phoebus,
The visions fade
And down the dewy glade
The rabbits scuttle o'er the rings they made.
In the fields near-by
The cattle rise
And where the river lies
A white mist rises to the welcoming skies.
Where the downs arise

And blue sky crowns
Their heads, fast o'er the mounds
The mist is driv'n to where the ocean sounds.
White wings against blue sky,
Gulls from the cliffs rise,
Watching, with eyes
That see from shore to where the sky line lies,
Where blue sea fades in bluer skies
Soft, doth the tide creep
O'er the golden sands
With sea-weed strands
Which, mayhap, knew the dawn of other lands.

201

(R. B. IV.)

Write thirty lines of blank verse on "Pegasus."

The sky was blue and flecked with tiny clouds
Like sheep they ran before the driving wind
The sun was setting like a big red rose
The clouds that flew by him like rose-buds were
And as I gaz'd I saw a little cloud
White as the flower that rises in the spring
Come nearer, nearer, nearer as I looked
And as it came it took a diff'rent shape
It seemed to turn into a fairy steed.
White as the foam that rides the roaring waves
Still it flew on until it reached the earth
And galloping full lightly came to me
And then I saw it was a wondrous thing

It leapt about the grass and gently neighed
I heard its voice sound like a crystal flute
"Oh come" he said "with me ascend the sky
Above the trees, above the hills we'll soar
Until we reach the home of all the gods
There will we stay and feast awhile with them
And dance with Juno and her maidens fair
And hear dear Orpheus and the pipes of Pan
And wander, wander, wander up above"
"Oh fairy steed, oh angel steed" I said
Horse fit for Jupiter himself to ride
What is thy name I pray thee tell me this"
Then came the magic voice of him again
"If thou wilt know my name then come with me."
Yet tell me first I hesitating said
He told me and when I had heard the name
I leapt upon his back and flew with him.

202   **(A. B. 16. V.)**

Some verses, in the metre of Pope's "Essay on Man," on the meeting of the League of Nations.

From each proud kingdom and each petty state
The statesmen meet together to debate
Upon the happy time when wars shall cease
And joy shall reign, and universal peace.
No more shall day with radiance cruelly bright
Glare down upon the carnage of the fight.
No more shall night's dark cloak be rent aside

By flashing shells and searchlight's stealthy glide
No more shall weary watchers wait at home
With straining eyes for those that cannot come
The nations shall forget their strife and greed
The strong shall help the weak in time of need
May they succeed in every peaceful plan
If war can cease as long as man is man.

(E. H. 16 $^{11}/_{12}$. V.)
*Gather up in blank verse the impressions you have received from
your reading of Tennyson's poems.*

Take up a volume of the poet's works,
Read on, lay it aside, and take thy pen,
Endeavour in a few, poor, worthless lines
To give expression of thy sentiments. . . .
Surely this man loved all the joys of life,
Saw beauty in the smallest and the least,
Put plainer things that hitherto were dim,
And lit a candle in the darkest room.
His thoughts, now sad, now gay, may surely be
The solace sweet for many a weary hour,
His words, drunk deeply, seem to live and burn
Clear, radiant, gleaming from the printed page,
Nature to him was dear and so has made
Her wiles for other men a treasure vast.
Old Books, his master mind could comprehend
Are shown to us as pictures to a child,
Read on—and when the volume's put away,

Muse on the learnings thou hast found therein;
The time thus spent thou never will repent,
For love of good things all should seek and find.

203   **(E. P. H. 16 $^{11}/_{12}$. V.)**

A LULLABY SONG

The little waves are sighing on the shore,
And the little breezes sobbing in the trees;
But the little stars are shining,
In the sky's blue velvet lining,
And Lady Sleep is tapping at the door.

The little gulls are flying home to shore,
And the little lights are flashing from the ships,
But close your eyes, my sweet,
And be ready then to greet
Dear Lady Sleep who's tapping at the door.

The wind is rising all around the shore,
And the fishing boats speed home before the gale;
But hark not to the rain
That is lashing on the pane,
For Lady Sleep has entered by the door.

The storm has sunk the ships and swept the shore,
But there's weeping in the town and on the quay,

But, sweet, you're dreaming fast
Even though the dawn be past,
And Lady Sleep has gone, and closed the door.

(M. H. 17 ⅓. VI.)
Write a letter in the manner of Gray on any Modern Topic.

Mr. Gray to Mr. —— At Torquay.

My dear ——

"Savez vous que je vous hais, que je vous deteste—voici des termes un peu forts," still, I think that they are justified, imagine leaving a friend for two months in this place without once taking up the pen upon his behalf. If this neglect be due only to your low spirits, I will for once pardon you but only upon condition that you should come down here to visit me and at the same time strengthen your constitution. I can promise you but little diversion, but I think that the scenery will repay the journey—not to speak of myself. You will also be able to study many "venerable vegetables" which are not usually to be found in England. But, I waste your time and my paper with these "bêtises" and I know well upon what subject your mind is at present dwelling—which of us indeed is not thinking of Ireland. I would give much to hear your views upon the subject. For my part it seems to me that there can be but one true view, and it surprises me mightily to hear so much discussion upon

204

the subject. Are we not truly a peculiar nation who pass bills of Home Rule etc with much discussion and debate, when neither of the two parties concerned will accept the conditions that we offer them? The one considering they give too little freedom, and the other too much. Accursed be the man who invented a bill which was and will be the cause of so much trouble "in saecula saeculorum." Surely we need not have any doubt as to what line of action we should adopt, surely it has not been the habit of England to let her subjects revolt without an attempt to quell them, surely the government will not stand by and see its servants murdered, and the one loyal province oppressed. But alas many things are possible with such a government. Here it is said by people who have been driven from that country by incendiaries that the Government will let things take their course till everything is in such a condition that the Premier will rise in the house and say "You see how things stand—it is no use trying to control Ireland, let us leave it to the Seinn Feiners, and live happily ever afterwards, free from such unprofitable cares,"

Such is the talk, but I believe it not. We have as a nation always muddled things but we have muddled through triumphant in the end. It is so obvious that our interests and those of Ireland co-incide, that even to contemplate separation is to me incredible.

Thus I remain your harassed friend, etc.

(N. S. 15 ¹⁰⁄₁₂. VI.)
Gather up in blank verse the impressions you have received from
your reading of Tennyson's poem.

ON READING TENNYSON'S POEMS.

Oh! Prophet of an era yet to come,
When men shall sing where men were wont to speak
In words which even Englishmen knew not
And when I read thy songs, at once I felt
The breath of Nature that was lurking there,
And then I knew that all thy life thou dwelt   205
Amid the changing scenes of Nature's play,
And knew the very language of the birds,
And drank the essence of the honeysuckle.
And when thou wast but young, I knew thy thoughts,
Thy Doubts and struggles, for thou gave them me;
And yet, had I been thee, my thoughts would still
Have rested deep within my heart; but still
T'would be relief to pour out all my woes
In the sweet flow of sympathetic verse.
Thy epithets produce a vivid scene
Of knights in armour or of maiden fair,
And yet, methinks, the fairness of her face
Doth sometimes cover many a fault below.
But to thy genius and thy work for ever
Be owed a debt of thankfulness that we
No longer tread the paths of level Pope
Or read those words that are not English-born.

(K. B. 16. V.)

The Clouds

Among the spirits of the nearer air
There are three children of the sun and sea—
The Genii of the clouds; it is their care
To give the ocean's bounty to the earth:
Oft they retain it in a time of dearth,
But they give all, however much it be.

The youngest of the three is very fair;
She is a maiden beautiful and sweet,
Of ever varying mood, changeful as air.
Now, plunged in merriment, she takes delight
In all she sees, now tears obscure her sight;
A breeze-swept lake shows not a change more fleet.

The fleecy clouds of April own her sway—
They, golden, lie against the golden sun,
Or sport across the blue when she is gay;
But when, anon, her girlish passions rise,
She marshalls them across the sunny skies
To flood the earth, then stops ere half begun.

206

Her elder brother is of different mien,
The clouds he governs are of different mould;
When the earth pants for moisture he is seen

To spread his clouds across the filmy blue.
When his rain falls, it steady is and true;
Persistent, gentle, ceaseless, yet not cold.

From the grey bowl with which he caps the earth,
It sweetly falls with earth-renewing force.
Not April's rapid change from grief to mirth
Excites its fall, but calm, determined thought
Of middle age, of deeds from judgment wrought;
He recks not blame, but still pursues his course.

Aged, yet of awesome beauty is the third,
Of flashing eye and sullen, scornful brow—
With an imperious hand she guides her herd
Of wild, tempestuous mood; quick roused to ire
Is she, slow to forgive, of vengeance dire;
Before her awful glance the tree-tops bow.

And when enraged, she stretches forth a hand—
A long, thin hand—to North, South, East and
     West,
And draws from thence clouds num'rous as the
     sand;
They crowd on the horizon, and blot out
The sun's fair light; then, like a giant's shout,
The thunder booms at her dread spear's behest.

(A.P. V.)

Sketch a scene between a "Mr. Woodhouse" of to-day and a neighbour of his.

SCENE:—MR. WOODHOUSE'S PRIVATE STUDY.

Persons present:—Owner of study, and Miss Syms, a very modern young lady.

Mr. Woodhouse.—"Oh, good afternoon Miss Syms, I am charmed to see you. Dear, dear, how dark it is. One might almost think it were evening, if the clock opposite did not directly oppose the fact."

Miss S.—"Oh, I don't know, it's not so bad out. I'm awfully sorry to blow in like this, but I came to enquire after Miss Woodhouse's cold. Is she better?

Mr. W.—"How very thoughtful of you! No, I am afraid dear Emma is very indisposed. It is so trying having an invalid in the house, it makes me quite miserable when I think of my poor daughter having to stay all alone, in bed. But really, that is almost the best place in this dreadful weather. Do you really mean to say that you have been taking a walk."

Miss S.—"Yes, why on earth shouldn't I? It's about the only way to get really warm."

Mr. W.—" If the liberty might be allowed me, (dryly) I should say, that it was the one way in which to get a feverish cold, besides making oneself thoroughly miserable; and the ground is so damp under foot!"

Miss S.—"Oh. it hasn't been raining much lately. I

only got caught in a little shower, (visible start from Mr. W.). (coyly,) Excuse me, but is that a box of cigarettes up there on the mantlepiece?"

Mr. W.—"Cigarettes? Oh, no! I couldn't think of keeping them near the house. I *never* smoke. It irritates my throat, which is naturally weak."

Miss S.—"But don't your visitors ever take the liberty of enjoying something of the sort? Besides, what about Miss Woodhouse?"

Mr. W.—(horrified,) "Dear Emma smoke a cigarette!! Why, I never heard of such a thing. What would she say if I told her. Dear Emma smoke, no, no, certainly not.

Miss S.—(laughing,) "Oh, I am sure I'm very sorry. I didn't mean to offend.

How do you think the old Johnnies in Ireland are behaving themselves?"

Mr. W.—(coldly.) "I *beg* your pardon."

Miss S.—(sweetly,) "I said, how do you think matters are looking, in Ireland."

Mr. W.—"I am sorry, I think I could not have heard aright before.—Matters in Ireland, yes, oh I think the Irish rebels are positively awful. To think of breaking into houses, and turning the poor inhabitants out into the cold streets, (where they probably nearly die of cold), it is too dreadful!"

Miss S.—"Oh, I s'pose they are rather brutes sometimes. But in a way I almost sympathise with them. I wouldn't like to have to knuckle under to the English (catching sight of Mr. W.'s expression of horror and pained surprise,) I really think I'd better get a move on. Please don't look at me like that! I really don't mean half I say. Cheerio!!

208 *Mr. W.*—"Good afternoon Miss Syms, it was so kind of you to come. (aside) Oh, how unfeeling of dear Emma to have a cold, if it means visitors like this every hour. (aloud,) Good afternoon, can you find your way out. I really shall catch cold if I move out of this room!!

(E.G. 17. V.)
Write some lines on "'Spring" in the metre of "Allegro."

SPRING

Begone! for a short space
Ye whistling winds, and fogs, and snowy clouds,
 And frosts that with fair lace
Each window-pane in dainty pattern shrouds,
 Offsprings of Winter, ye!
Begone! find out some icy arctic land.
 Upon that cheerless strand
'Mongst piercing ice, and chilling glaciers dwell
 Such regions suit ye well,
 Go, cold Winter, well are we rid of thee!
 Come Spring, thou fairest season come!
 With the bee's enchanting hum,
 And the dainty blossoms swinging

On the tree, while birds are singing.
See how they clothe the branches gray
In dress of freshest pink, all day,
Then when the dewy evening falls
They close their flowers till Morning calls.
Sweet Morn! Spring leads thee by the hand
And bids thee shine o'er all the land;
Thou send'st forth beams of purest gold,
To bid the daffodils unfold,
While Spring bends down with her fresh lips
To kiss the daisie's petal tips.
And as she walks o'er the green sward
A cheerful mavis, perfect bard
Breaks into song; his thrilling notes
Are echoed from a hundred throats
Of eager birds, who love to sing
To their sweet mistress, fairest Spring.
Then as she sits on mossy throne   209
A scarlet lady-bird, alone,
Bids her good welcome; and above
Is heard the cooing of the dove.
Two butterflies in russet clad
Fly round her head with flutt'rings glad;
While at her side a giddy fly
Buzzes his joy that she is nigh,
Oh! Spring my heart's desire shall be
That thou wilt ever dwell with me!

II

THE KNOWLEDGE OF MAN

(*e*) LANGUAGES

English is rather a logical study dealing with sentences and the positions that words occupy in them than with words and what they are in their own right. Therefore it is better that a child should begin with a sentence and not with the parts of speech, that is, he should learn a little of what is called analysis before he learns to parse. It requires some effort of abstraction for a child to perceive that when we speak, we speak about something and say something about it; and he has learned nearly all the grammar that is necessary when he knows that when we speak we use sentences and that a sentence makes sense; that we can put words together so as to make utter nonsense, as,—"Tom immediately candlestick uproarious nevertheless"—a string of words making perfect nonsense and therefore not a sentence. If we use words in such a way as to make sense we get a sentence; "John goes to school" is a sentence. Every sentence has two parts, (1), the thing we speak of, and (2), what we say about it. We speak of John, we say about him that he goes to school. At this stage the children require many exercises in finding out the first and second parts of simple sentences. When they are quite familiar with the fact that the first part of a sentence is what we speak about, they may get a name for it, subject, which will be made simpler to them if they know the word subject means that which we talk about. For instance, we may say, the subject of conversation was parsley, which is another way of saying

210

the thing we were speaking about was parsley. To sum up such a lesson, the class should learn,—Words put together so as to make sense form a sentence. A sentence has two parts, that which we speak of and what we say about it. That which we speak of is the subject.

Children will probably be slow to receive this first lesson in abstract knowledge, and we must remember that knowledge in this sort is difficult and uncongenial. Their minds deal with the concrete and they have the singular faculty of being able to make concrete images out of the merest gossamer of a fairy tale. A seven year old child sings,—

"I cannot see fairies,
I dream them.
There is no fairy that can hide from me;
I keep on dreaming till I find him.
There you are, Primrose! I see you, Blackwing!"

But a child cannot dream parts of speech, and any grown-up twaddle attempting to personify such abstractions offends a small person who with all his love of play and nonsense has a serious mind. Most children can be got to take in the notion of a sentence as, words making sense, especially if they are allowed a few excursions into non-sense, the gibberish of strings of words which do not make sense. Again, by dint of many interesting exercises in which they never lose sight of the *subject*, they get hold of that idea also.

One more initial idea is necessary if children are not to

21   wander blindfold through the mazes of grammar 'as she is' not 'spoke,' but writ in books. They must be familiar with verbs and perhaps the simplest way to approach this idea is to cause them to make sentences with two words, the thing they speak of and what they say about it,—Mary sings, Auntie knits, Henry runs. In each of these examples, the child will see the thing we speak of and what we say about it.

But these are matters familiar to all teachers and we have nothing new in the teaching of grammar to suggest; but we probably gain in the fact that our scholars pay full attention to grammar, as to all other lessons. We look forward hopefully to the result of efforts so to unify grammar that it will no longer perplex the student, as English, Latin, French grammar, each with its own nomenclature.

Children in Form IIB have easy French Lessons with pictures which they describe, but in IIA while still engaged on the *Primary French Course* children begin to use the method which is as full of promise in the teaching of languages as in English, that is, they are expected to narrate the sentence or paragraph which has been read to them. Young children find little difficulty in using French vocables, but at this stage the teacher should with the children's help translate the little passage which is to be narrated, then re-read it in French and require the children to narrate it. This they do after a time surprisingly well, and the act of narrating gives them some command of French phrases as far as they go, much more so than if they learnt the little passage off by heart. They learn French songs in both divisions and act *French Fables* (by Violet Partington) in Form IIA. This method of closely attentive reading of the text followed by narration is continued in each of the Forms. Thus Form II is required to "Describe in French, picture 20." "Narrate the story *Esope et le Voyageur.*" Part of the term's work in Form III is to "Read and narrate *Nouveaux Contes Français*, by Marc Ceppi." Form IV is required amongst other things to "Read and narrate Molière's *Les Femmes Savantes.*" Forms V and VI are required to "Write a résumé of *Le Misanthrope* or L'Avare," "Translate into French, *Modern Verse*, page 50, 'Leisure.'"

212

We have not space to follow in detail the work of the P.U.S. in French, which of course includes the usual attention to French Grammar but it may interest the reader to see the sort of thing that students of the House of Education are able to accomplish in the way of narration. The French mistress gives, let us suppose, a lecture in history or literature lasting, say, for half an hour. At the end the students will narrate the substance of the lecture with few omissions and few errors. Here is an example of the sort of thing Mr. Household heard, on the occasion of a short visit to the House of Education, Ambleside,—

"A French lesson was given to the second-year students by the French mistress, a native of Tournai, who came to Ambleside in 1915. She had been teaching in England for some years but had not previously come into contact with Miss Mason's methods. Those methods were exactly followed during the lesson. There was the book of recognised literary merit, the single reading, and the immediate narration—of course in French. The book was Alphonse Daudet's *Lettres de Mon Moulin*, and the story read was 'La Chèvre de M. Seguin.' Before the reading began, a few—a very few—words of explanation were given—of course, in French. Then nine pages of the story were read straight through by the mistress, without pause or interruption of any kind, at the same pace that one would read an English story. The students followed by ear only: they had no books. As soon as the reading ended, on the instant, without hesitation of any kind, narration began in French, different members of the class taking up the story in turn till it was finished. All were good; some astonishingly good. To all French was a tongue in which they could think and speak with considerable facility. Yet the time given to French is two hours and three-quarters a week only. Such results com-

213 pel attention. It may be added that last year the writer heard a history lecture on the reign of Louis XI given in French by the same mistress to the then senior students, and the content of the lecture was narrated in a similar manner, with the same astonishing success."

This hitherto unused power of concentrated attention in the study of languages whether ancient or modern appears to hold promise of making us at last a nation of linguists. We have attained very good results in Italian and German by this same method, both in the House of Education and the Practising School belonging to it, and we are in a fair way to produce noticeable results in Latin. The classical mistress writes,—

> "Latin is taught at the House of Education by means of narration after each section has been thoroughly studied in grammar, syntax and style. The literature studied increases in difficulty as the pupil advances in grammar, etc. Nothing but good Latin is ever narrated, so the pupil acquires style as well as structure. The substance of the passage is usually reproduced with the phraseology and style of the original and both students and children learn what is really Latin and realise that it is a language and not a mere grammar."

Here we get Grammar, that is, construction, learned as we learn it in English, at the lips of those who, know, and the extraordinary readiness in acquiring new words shewn by the scholars promises English folk the copious vocabulary in one or another foreign language, the lack of which is a national distress.

II
THE KNOWLEDGE OF MAN
(f) ART

There are few subjects regarded with more respect and less confidence in our schools than this of 'Art.' Of course, we say, children should have their artistic powers cultivated,

214 especially those who have such powers, but *how* is the question. The neat solution offered by South Kensington in the sixties,—freehand drawing, perspective, drawing from the round, has long been rejected; but nothing definite has taken its place and we still see models of cones, cubes and so on, disposed so that the eye may take them in freely and that the hand may perhaps produce what the eye has seen. But we begin now to understand that art is not to be approached by such a macadamised road. It is of the spirit, and in ways of the spirit must we make our attempt. We recognise that the power of appreciating art and of producing to some extent an interpretation of what one sees is as universal as intelligence, imagination, nay, speech, the power of producing words. But there must be knowledge and, in the first place, not the technical knowledge of how to produce, but some reverent knowledge of what has been produced; that is, children should learn pictures, line by line, group by group, by reading, not books, but pictures themselves. A friendly picture-dealer supplies us with half a dozen beautiful little reproductions of the work of some single artist, term by term. After a short story of the artist's life and a few sympathetic words about his trees or his skies, his river-paths or his figures, the little pictures are studied one at a time; that is, children learn, not merely to see a picture but *to look at it*, taking in every detail. Then the picture is turned over and the children tell what they have seen,—a dog driving a flock of sheep along a road but nobody with the dog. Ah, there is a boy lying down

by the stream drinking. It is morning as you can see by the light so the sheep are being driven to pasture, and so on; nothing is left out, the discarded plough, the crooked birch, the clouds beautiful in form and threatening rain, there is enough for half an hour's talk and memory in this little reproduction of a great picture and the children will know it wherever they see it, whether a signed proof, a copy in oils, or the original itself in one of our galleries. We hear of a small boy with his parents in the National Gallery; the boy, who had wandered off on his own account, came running back with the news,—"Oh, Mummy, there's one of our Constables on that wall." In this way children become acquainted with a hundred, or hundreds, of great artists during their school-life and it is an intimacy which never forsakes them. A group of children are going up to London for a treat. "Where would you like to go?" "Oh, Mummy, to the National Gallery to see the Rembrandts." Young people go to tea in a room strange to them and are delighted to recognise two or three reproductions of De Hooch's pictures. In the course of school-life children get an Open Sesame to many art galleries, and to many a cultivated home; and life itself is illustrated for them at many points. For it is true as Browning told us,—

> "For, don't you mark, we're made so that we love
> First when we see them painted, things we have passed
> Perhaps a hundred times nor cared to see."

Here is an example of how beautiful and familiar things give quite new delight when they are pictured. A lady writes,—

> "I was invited to a small village to talk about the P.U. School. Twelve really interested women came in spite of heavy rain.... I suggested introducing them to some of the friends their children had made and we had a delightful picture talk with Jean B. Corot, delightful to me because of the way one woman especially narrated. She did it as if she had been set free for the first time for months. It was the 'Evening' picture with a canal on the right and that splendid mass of quiet trees in the centre. The others gave bits of the picture but she gave the whole thing. It was a green pasture to her."

The noteworthy thing is that these women were familiar with all such details as Corot offers in their own beautiful neighbourhood, but Browning is right; we learn to see things when we see them painted.

It will be noticed that the work* done on these pictures is done by the children themselves. There is no talk about schools of painting, little about style; consideration of these matters comes in later life, but the first and most important thing is to know the pictures themselves. As in a worthy book we leave the author to tell his own tale, so do we trust a picture to tell its tale through the medium

* Examination answers can be seen at the P.N.E.U. Office.

the artist gave it. In the region of art as else-where we shut out the middleman.

Forms V and VI are asked to,—"Describe, with study in sepia, Corot's 'Evening.'" Beyond this of a rough study from memory of a given picture or of any section of it, these picture studies do not afford much material for actual drawing; they are never copied lest an attempt to copy should lessen a child's reverence for great work. We are shy in speaking of what we do in actual drawing since Herr Cizek came among us and shewed what great things children could do with scarcely any obvious teaching and but little suggestion. But probably such work is only to be done under the inspiration of an artist of unusual powers and I am writing for teachers who depend upon their children rather than upon themselves. They illustrate favourite scenes and passages in the books read during the term and the spirit with which the illustrations are drawn and the fitting details introduced make the teacher aware of how much more the children have seen in the passage than he has himself. Their courage in grappling with points of technique is very instructive. They tackle a crowd with wonderful ingenuity, a crowd listening to Mark Antony's oration, cheering the Prince of Wales in India, in fact wherever a crowd is wanted it is suggested pretty much as an artist would give it by a show of heads. Like those Viennese children they use all their paper, whether for a landscape or the details in a room. They give you horses leaping brooks, dogs running after cats, sheep on the road, always with a sense of motion.

217   It is evident that children study the figures they see with due attention and will give you a gardener sharpening his scythe, their mother sewing, a man rowing, or driving, or mowing. Their chairs stand on four legs and their figures on two feet in a surprising way, and they are always on the watch to correct their errors by what they see. They have a delightful and courageous sense of colour, and any child will convince you that he has it in him to be an artist. Their field studies give them great scope. The first buttercup in a child's nature note book is shockingly crude, the sort of thing to scandalise a teacher of brush-drawing, but by and by another buttercup will appear with the delicate poise, uplift and radiance of the growing flower.

Drawing is generally so well taught now that we need do no more than emphasize one or two special points in our work, such as the definite study of pictures and the illustrations of Nature Note Books.

We do what is possible to introduce children to Architecture; and we practise clay-modelling and the various artistic handicrafts, but there is nothing unusual in our work in these directions.*

With Musical Appreciation the case is different; and we cannot do better than quote from an address made by Mrs. Howard Glover at the Ambleside Conference of the Parents' Union, 1922:—

"Musical Appreciation—which is so much before the eye at the present moment—originated in the P.N.E.U.

---

* For details see the Parents' Union School programmes.

about twenty-five years ago. At that time I was playing to my little child much of the best music in which I was interested, and Miss Mason happened to hear of what I was doing. She realised that music might give great joy and interest to the life of all, and she felt that just as children in the P.U.S. were given the greatest literature and art, so they should have the greatest music as well. She asked me to write an article in the *Review* on the result of my observations, and to make a programme of music each term which might be played *to* the children. From that day to this, at the beginning of every term a programme has appeared; thus began a movement which was to spread far and wide.

218

"Musical Appreciation, of course, has nothing to do with playing the piano. It used to be thought that 'learning music' must mean this, and it was supposed that children who had no talent for playing were unmusical and would not like concerts. But Musical Appreciation had no more to do with playing an instrument than acting had to do with an appreciation of Shakespeare, or painting with enjoyment of pictures. I think that all children should take Musical Appreciation and not only the musical ones, for it has been proved that only three per cent of children are what is called 'tone-deaf'; and if they are taken at an early age it is astonishing how children who appear to be without ear, develop it and are able to enjoy listening to music with understanding."

Section III

THE KNOWLEDGE OF THE UNIVERSE
(*a*) SCIENCE*

Huxley's axiom that science teaching in the schools should be of the nature of 'common information' is of use in defining our limitations in regard to the teaching of science. We find another limitation in the fact that children's minds are not in need of the mental gymnastics that such teaching is supposed to afford. They are entirely alert and eager to know. Books dealing with science as with history, say, should be of a literary character, and we should probably be more scientific as a people if we scrapped all the textbooks which swell publishers' lists and nearly all the chalk expended so freely on our blackboards. The French mind has appreciated the fact that the approach to science as to other subjects should be more or less literary, that the principles which underlie science are at the same time so simple, so profound and so far-reaching that the due setting forth of these provokes what is almost an emotional response; these principles are therefore meet subjects for literary treatment, while the details of their application are so technical and so minute as,—except by way of illustration,—to be unnecessary for school work or for general knowledge. We have not a copious scientific literature in English but we have quite enough to go on with in our schools. We find

219

---

* Specimens of the children's Examination work can be seen at the P.N.E.U. Office.

an American publication called *The Sciences* (whose author would seem to be an able man of literary power) of very great value in linking universal principles with common incidents of every day life in such a way that interest never palls and any child may learn on what principles an electric bell works, what sound means, how a steam engine works, and many other matters, explained here with great lucidity. Capital diagrams and descriptions make experiments easy and children arrive at their first notions of science without the verbiage that darkens counsel. Form IIA read *Life and Her Children* by Arabella Buckley and get a surprising knowledge of the earlier and lower forms of life. IIB take pleasure in Kingsley's *Madam How and Lady Why*. They are expected to do a great deal of out-of-door work in which they are assisted by *The Changing Year*, admirable month by month studies of what is to be seen out-of-doors. They keep records and drawings in a Nature Note Book and make special studies of their own for the particular season with drawings and notes.

The studies of Form III for one term enable children to—"Make a rough sketch of a section of ditch or hedge or sea-shore and put in the names of the plants you would expect to find." "Write notes with drawings of the special study you have made this term," "What do you understand by calyx, corolla, stamen, pistil? In what ways are flowers fertilised?" "How would you find the Pole Star? Mention six other stars and say in what constellations they occur." "How would you distinguish between Early, Decorated and Perpendicular Gothic? Give drawings." Questions like these, it will be seen, cover a good deal of field work, and the study of some half dozen carefully selected books on natural history, botany, architecture and astronomy, the principle being that children shall observe and chronicle, but shall not depend upon their own unassisted observation.

The study of natural history and botany with bird lists and plant lists continues throughout school life, while other branches of science are taken term by term.

The questions for Form IV for one term illustrate the various studies of the scholars in natural history, general science, hygiene and physiology; in fact, their studies are so various that it is difficult to give each a separate title in the programme:—

GEOGRAPHY.
1. Write a short sketch of Central Asia, with map.
2. Compare Palestine with the Yorkshire moors. Describe the valley of the Jordan.
3. "There is but one Nelson." Illustrate by half-a-dozen instances.
4. What is said in *Eöthen* of the Church of the Holy Sepulchre?

NATURAL HISTORY.
1. What do you know of (*a*), the manatee, (*b*), the whale-bone whale (sketch of skeleton), (*c*), porpoises and dolphins?

or, 1. Describe (*a*), quartz crystals, (*b*), felspar, (*c*), mica, (*d*), hornblende. In what rock do these occur?

2. What do you know of insectivorous plants? Name those you know.

3. What circumstances strike you in a walk in summer?

GENERAL SCIENCE

1. What do you understand by,—(*a*), electrical attraction, (*b*), repulsion, (*c*), conductors, (*d*), insulators, (*e*), methods of obtaining electricity?

2. Prove that "you never see matter itself," and show how sight gives us knowledge.

PHYSIOLOGY.

1. Describe the structure of the human ear.

Perhaps *Some Wonders of Matter* by Bishop Mercer is the most inspiring of the half-dozen volumes in current use in Form IV for this section of their work. The questions indicate the varied nature of the work and the answers shew that in every case the knowledge is fairly wide and thorough. All the children in the school are usually ready to answer each question on the work of the term.

Forms V and VI again cover a wide field as the following questions on a term's work sufficiently indicate,—

GEOGRAPHY.

VI. 1. Show how the discovery of the New World affected England in commerce and war.

2. According to what general law is life distributed on the earth?

3. Describe the Siege of Mexico by Cortes, and its surrender.

VI. & V. 4. How has the war affected (*a*), Luxembourg, (*b*), the Eastern frontier of Belgium, (*c*), Antwerp and the Scheldt?

V. 1. Show how the Restoration affected our American possessions.

2. Show accurately how longitude is determined.

3. Sketch the history and character of Montezuma.

GEOLOGY AND SCIENCE.

VI. 1. Discuss fully (*a*), the cause of radio-activity, (*b*), gravitation.

2. What have you to say of the scenic aspects of the English Trias? Name a dozen of the fossils. Sketch half-a-dozen.

V. 1. Give as full an explanation as you can of colour.

2. Describe the composition of the igneous rocks. Where do they appear?

BIOLOGY, BOTANY, ETC.

VI. 1. What are the characters of the backboneless animals? Describe half-a-dozen examples.

2. Describe and account for the vegetation of (a), 222
woodlands, (*b*), heath, (c), moorland, (d),
meadow.

V. 1. How would you classify the industries of animals?
Give examples.

2. Describe the flora of the seashore.

VI. & V. 3. Describe, with drawings, the special study you
have made this term.

ASTRONOMY.

VI. 1. What do you understand by precession? Describe
the precession and mutation of the earth's axis.

V. 1. Write an essay on the planet Mercury.

If we wanted an excuse for affording children a wide
syllabus introducing them at any rate to those branches of
science of which every normal person should have some
knowledge, we find it in the deprecatory words of Sir Richard Gregory in his Presidential Address in the Education
Science Section of the British Association. He said that,—

"Education might be defined as a deliberate adjustment
of a growing human being to its environment, and the
scope and character of the subjects of instruction should
be determined by this biological principle. What was
best for one race or epoch need not be best for another.
The essential mission of school science was to prepare
pupils for civilised citizenship by revealing to them

something of the beauty and the power of the world in which they lived, as well as introducing them to the methods by which the boundaries of natural knowledge had been extended. School science, therefore, was not intended to prepare for vocations, but to equip pupils for life. It should be part of a general education, unspecialised, but in no direct connexion with possible university courses to follow. Less than three per cent of the pupils from State-aided secondary schools proceeded to universities, and yet most of the science courses in these schools were based on syllabuses of the type of university entrance examinations. The needs of the many were sacrificed to the few.

"Too much importance was attached to what could be covered by personal experiment and observation. Every science examination qualifying for the first school certificate, which now represented subjects normally studied up to about sixteen years of age, was mainly a test of practical acquaintance with facts and principles encountered in particular limited fields, but not a single one afforded recognition of a broad and ample course of instruction in science such as was a necessary complement to laboratory work.

"The numbers [of examination candidates] suggested that general scientific teaching was almost non-existent. The range of instruction in the portions of subjects taken, moreover, was almost confined to what could be taught in a laboratory. Reading or teaching for interest or to learn how physical science was daily extending the power of man received little attention because no credit for knowledge thus gained was given in examinations. There was very special need for the reminder that science was not all measurement, nor all measurement science."

It is reassuring to see methods that we have pursued for over thirty years with admirable results recommended thus authoritatively. The only sound method of teaching science is to afford a due combination of field or laboratory work, with such literary comments and amplifications as the subject affords. For example, from *Ethics of the Dust* children derive a certain enthusiasm for crystals as such that their own unaided observation would be slow to afford. As a matter of fact the teaching of science in our schools has lost much of its educative value through a fatal and quite unnecessary divorce between science and the 'humanities.'

The nature note books which originated in the P.U.S. have recommended themselves pretty widely as travelling companions and life records wherein the 'finds' of every season, bird or flower, fungus or moss, is sketched, and described *somewhat* in the manner of Gilbert White. The nature note book is very catholic and finds room for the stars in their courses and for, say, the fossil anemone found on the beach at Whitby. Certainly these note books do a good deal to bring science within the range of common thought and experience; we are anxious not to make science a utilitarian subject.

224　*Geography*

The teaching of Geography suffers especially from the utilitarian spirit. The whole tendency of modern Geography, as taught in our schools, is to strip the unfortunate planet which has been assigned to us as our abode and environment of every trace of mystery and beauty. There is no longer anything to admire or to wonder at in this sweet world of ours. We can no longer say with Jasper Petulengro,—"Sun, moon and stars are sweet things, brother; there is likewise the wind on the heath." No, the questions which Geography has to solve henceforth are confined to how and under what conditions is the earth's surface profitable to man and desirable for his habitation. No more may children conceive themselves climbing Mont Blanc or Mount Everest, skating on the Fiords of Norway or swimming in a gondola at Venice. These are not the things that matter, but only how and where and why is money to be made under local conditions on the earth's surface. It is doubtful whether this kind of teaching is even lucrative because the mind works on great ideas, and, upon these, works to great ends. Where science does not teach a child to wonder and admire it has perhaps no educative value.

Perhaps no knowledge is more delightful than such an intimacy with the earth's surface, region by region, as should enable the map of any region to unfold a panorama of delight, disclosing not only mountains, rivers, frontiers, the great features we know as 'Geography,' but associations, occupations, some parts of the past and much of the present,

of every part of this beautiful earth. Great attention is paid
to map work; that is, before reading a lesson children have
found the places mentioned in that lesson on a map and
know where they are, relatively to other places, to given
parallels, meridians. Then, bearing in mind that children
do not generalise but must learn by particulars, they read   225
and picture to themselves the Yorkshire Dales, the Sussex
Downs, the mysteries of a coal-mine; they see 'pigs' of iron
flowing forth from the furnace, the slow accretions which
have made up the chalk, the stirring life of the great towns
and the occupations of the villages. Form II (A and B) are
engaged with the counties of England, county by county,
for so diverse are the counties in aspect, history and occupations, that only so can children acquire such a knowledge of
England as will prove a key to the geography of every part
of the world, whether in the way of comparison or contrast.
For instance, while I write, the children in IIA are studying
the counties which contain the Thames basin and "Write
verses on 'The Thames'" is part of their term's work. *Our
Sea Power*, by H. W. Household, is of extraordinary value
in linking England with the world by means of a spirited
account of the glorious history of our navy, while the late
Sir George Parkin, than whom there is no better qualified
authority, carries children round the Empire. They are
thrown on their own resources or those of their teachers
for what may be called current Geography. For instance,
"Learn what you can about *The Political Map of Europe after
the Great War*. (Evans, 4*d*.)."

In Form III the Geography is still regional, that is, children are led to form an intimate acquaintance with the countries of Europe so that the map of any country calls up in a child's imagination a wonderful panorama of the diversities of the country, of the people, their history and occupations. It is evident that this kind of geographical image cannot be secured in any other way than by considering Europe country by country. They begin with a general survey of the seas and shores of the continent, of the countries and peoples, of the diversities of tongues and their historical origin, of the plains and mountains, of the rivers and their basins; a survey after which they should be able to answer such questions as,—"Name three rivers which flow into the Baltic." "What lands form the southern and eastern shores of the Mediterranean?" "What countries are washed by the Baltic?" "Between what parallels does Europe extend? What other continents lie partly within the same parallels?" The young scholars are at home with the map of Europe before they consider the countries separately.

The picture we present of the several countries is meant to be before all things interesting and at the same time to provide an intelligent and fairly exhaustive account of the given country. Whatever further knowledge a child acquires will fit in to this original scheme. For example, "The Rhône Valley and the Border lands."*

"The warm and fertile Rhône valley belongs in climate to
   the southern region, where, although the vine is grown,

---

* *The Ambleside Geography*; Book IV, by the Writer.

large plantations of olive and mulberry occupy much
of the land. We are apt to think of the South of France
as the sunny south, the sweet south, 'but,' says a writer
whom we have already quoted, 'it is austere, grim, som-
bre' . . . but the mulberry feeds the silkworm and so
furnishes material for the great manufacture of France.
Lyons, the second city of France, is the seat of the silk
manufacture including those of velvets and satins. It is
seated upon a tongue of land at the confluence of the
rapid Rhône and the sluggish Saône, and along the banks
of both rivers are fine quays.

This extract indicates how geographical facts are introduced
incidentally, pretty much as a traveller comes across them.
The work for one term includes Belgium, Holland, Spain
and Portugal, and the interests connected with each of
these countries are manifold. For example,—

"On the seashore near Leyden is Katwyck where the
expiring Rhine is helped to discharge itself into the sea
by means of a wide artificial channel provided with no
less than thirteen pairs of enormous floodgates. These
are shut to keep out the sea when the tide is coming in,
and open to let the streams pass out during ebb tide.
Notwithstanding these great works the once glorious
Rhine makes but an ignoble exit. The delta of this river
may be said to include the whole breadth of Holland."*

227

* *Ambleside Geography*: Book IV.

It will be noticed that an attempt is made to shew the romance of the natural features, the history, the industries, so that a country is no more a mere matter of names on a map, or of sections shewn by contour lines. Such generalisations are not Geography but are slow conclusions which the mind should come to of itself when it acquires intimacy with a region. Something of a literary character is preserved in the Geography lessons. The new feature in these is the study of maps which should be very thorough. For the rest the single reading and narration as described in connection with other work is sufficient in this subject also. Children cannot tell what they have not seen with the mind's eye, which we know as imagination, and they cannot see what is not told in their books with some vividness and some grasp of the subject. The thoroughness of the map study is shewn by such a question to be answered from memory as,—"What part of Belgium does the Scheldt drain? Name any of its feeders. Name ten famous places in its basin. What port stands at the head of its estuary?" We find great light thrown upon the geography of the Empire in a little book of literary quality, *Fighting for Sea Power in The Days of Sail.*

There are two rational ways of teaching Geography. The first is the inferential method, a good deal in vogue at the present time; by it the pupil learns certain geographical principles which he is expected to apply universally. This method seems to me defective for two reasons. It is apt to be misleading as in every particular case the general principle is open to modifications; also, local colour and personal and historical interests are wanting and the scholar does not form an intellectual and imaginative conception of the region he is learning about. The second which might be called the panoramic method unrolls the landscape of the world, region by region, before the eyes of the scholar with in every region its own conditions of climate, its productions, its people, their industries and their history. This way of teaching the most delightful of all subjects has the effect of giving to a map of a country or region the brilliancy of colour and the wealth of detail which a panorama might afford, together with a sense of proportion and a knowledge of general principles. I believe that pictures are not of very great use in this study. We all know that the pictures which abide with us are those which the imagination constructs from written descriptions.

The Geography for Form IV* includes Asia, Africa, America and Australasia. But the same principle is followed: vivid descriptions, geographical principles, historical associations and industrial details, are afforded which should make, as we say, an impression, should secure that the region traversed becomes an imaginative possession as well as affording data for reasonable judgments. The pupil begins with a survey of Asia followed by a separate treatment of the great countries and divisions and of the great physical features. Thus of Siberia we read,—

---

* *The Ambleside Geography*: Book V, by the Writer.

"All travellers unite in praise of the free Siberian peasant. As soon as one crosses the Urals one is surprised by the extreme friendliness and good nature of the inhabitants as much as by the rich vegetation of the well-cultivated fields and the excellent state of the roads in the southern part of the government of Tobolsk."

or,—

229

"The glossy jet black soft thick fur of the sea-otter is the most valuable of all the Russian skins. Next ranks the skin of the black fox. But though a thousand of its skins are worth no more than one skin of the sea-otter, the little grey squirrel whose skins are imported by the million really plays the most important part in the Siberian fur trade."

Of Further India,—

"Pigou, the middle division, is really the vast delta of the Irrawaddy, a low-lying country which yields enormous quantities of rice while on the higher grounds which wall in the great river are the finest teak forests in the world."

Africa follows Asia with the discoveries of Livingstone, Speke, Burton, Grant, etc. We get an account of African village life and among the chapter headings are Abyssinia, Egypt, Up the Nile, The Soudan, The Sahara, The Barbary States, South Africa, Cape Colony, The Islands. America follows with an account of the progress of discovery, a geographical sketch of South America, the Andes and the Mountain States, Chili, Peru, Bolivia, etc., the Great Plains of South America, Central America, North America, Canada, a historical sketch of the United States, the Eastern States, States of the Mississippi valley, the prairies, the Western States and territories, California. In the section on the Eastern States we read,—

"Stretching from this chain (the Alleghanies) is the great Appalachian coalfield which extends through Pennsylvania, Virginia and Ohio, with a length of 720 miles containing, it is said, coal enough to supply the world for four thousand years! Iron occurs with the coal in great abundance. Most of this coal is of the kind called Anthracite. It is extremely slow in burning, emits no smoke, but has a painfully drying effect upon the air of a room. Sir Charles Lyall speaking of Pottsville on this coal-field says,—'Here I was agreeably surprised to see a flourishing manufacturing town with the tall chimneys of a hundred furnaces burning night and day, yet quite free from smoke. Leaving this clear atmosphere and going down into one of the mines it was a no less pleasing novelty to find that we could handle the coal without soiling our fingers.'"

But enough has been said to indicate the sort of intimacy that scholars in Form IV get with all quarters of the 230 world, their geography, landscape, histories and industries, together with the study of the causes which affect climate and industries. Geikie's *Physical Geography* affords an admirable introduction to the principles of physical geography.

Forms V and VI are expected to keep up with the newspapers and know something about places and regions coming most into note in the current term. Also, in connection with the history studied, Seeley's *Expansion of England*, *The Peoples and Problems of India*, Geikie's *Elementary Lessons in Physical Geography*, Mort's *Practical Geography*, and Kipling's *Letters of Travel* are included in the reading of one term. In these Forms the young students are expected to apply their knowledge to Geography, both practical and theoretical, and to make much use of a good Atlas without the map questions which have guided the map work of the lower Forms.

III

THE KNOWLEDGE OF THE UNIVERSE

(*b*) MATHEMATICS

The question of Arithmetic and of Mathematics generally is one of great import to us as educators. So long as the idea of 'faculties' obtained no doubt we were right to put all possible weight on a subject so well adapted to train the reasoning powers, but now we are assured that these powers do not wait upon our training. They are there in any case; and if we keep a chief place in our curriculum for Arithmetic we must justify ourselves upon other grounds.

We take strong ground when we appeal to the beauty and truth of Mathematics; that, as Ruskin points out, two and two make four and cannot conceivably make five, is an inevitable law. It is a great thing to be brought into the presence of a law, of a whole system of laws, that exist without our concurrence,—that two straight lines cannot enclose a space is a fact which we can perceive, state, and act upon but cannot in any wise alter, should give to children the sense of limitation which is wholesome for all of us, and inspire that *sursum corda* which we should hear in all natural law. 231

Again, integrity in our dealings depends largely upon 'Mr. Micawber's' golden rule, while 'Harold Skimpole's' disregard of these things is a moral offence against society. Once again, though we do not live on gymnastics, the mind like the body, is invigorated by regular spells of hard exercise.

But education should be a science of proportion, and any one subject that assumes undue importance does so at the expense of other subjects which a child's mind should deal with. Arithmetic, Mathematics, are exceedingly easy to examine upon and so long as education is regulated by examinations so long shall we have teaching, directed not to awaken a sense of awe in contemplating a self-existing science, but rather to secure exactness and ingenuity in the treatment of problems.

What is better, it will be said, than a training in exactness and ingenuity? But in saying so we assume that this exactness and ingenuity brought out in Arithmetic serve us in every department of life. Were this the case we should indeed have a royal road to learning; but it would seem that no such road is open to us. The habits and powers brought to bear upon any one educational subject are exercised upon that subject simply. The familiar story of how Sir Isaac Newton teased by his cat's cries to be let in caused a large hole in the door to be made for the cat and a small one for the kitten, illustrates not a mere amusing lapse in a great mind but the fact that work upon special lines qualifies for work upon those lines only. One hears of more or less deficient boys to whom the study of *Bradshaw* is a delight, of an admirable accountant who was otherwise a little 'deficient.'

232

The boy who gets 'full marks' in Arithmetic makes a poor show in history because the accuracy and ingenuity brought out by his sums apply to his sums only: and as for the value of Arithmetic in practical life, most of us have private reasons for agreeing with the eminent staff officer who tells us that,—

> "I have never found any Mathematics except simple addition of the slightest use in a work-a-day life except in the Staff college examinations and as for mental gymnastics and accuracy of statement, I dispute the contention that Mathematics supply either any better than any other study."

We have most of us believed that a knowledge of the theory and practice of war depended a good deal upon Mathematics, so this statement by a distinguished soldier is worth considering. In a word our point is that Mathematics are to be studied for their own sake and not as they make for general intelligence and grasp of mind. But then how profoundly worthy are these subjects of study for their own sake, to say nothing of other great branches of knowledge to which they are ancillary! Lack of proportion should be our *bête noire* in drawing up a curriculum, remembering that the mathematician who knows little of the history of his own country or that of any other, is sparsely educated at the best.

At the same time Genius has her own rights. The born mathematician must be allowed full scope even to the omission of much else that he should know. He soon asserts himself, sees into the intricacies of a problem with half an eye, and should have scope. He would prefer not to have much teaching. But why should the tortoise keep pace with the hare and why should a boy's success in life depend upon drudgery in Mathematics? That is the tendency at the pres- 233 ent moment to close the Universities and consequently the Professions to boys and girls who, because they have little natural aptitude for mathematics, must acquire a mechanical knowledge by such heavy all-engrossing labour as must needs shut out such knowledge of the 'humanities' say, as is implied in the phrase 'a liberal education.'

The claims of the London Matriculation examination, for example, are acknowledged by many teachers to be incompatible with the wide knowledge proper to an educated person.

Mathematics depend upon the teacher rather than upon

the text-book and few subjects are worse taught; chiefly because teachers have seldom time to give the inspiring ideas, what Coleridge calls, the 'Captain' ideas, which should quicken imagination.

How living would Geometry become in the light of the discoveries of Euclid as he made them!

To sum up, Mathematics are a necessary part of every man's education; they must be taught by those who know; but they may not engross the time and attention of the scholar in such wise as to shut out any of the score of 'subjects,' a knowledge of which is his natural right.

It is unnecessary to exhibit mathematical work done in the P.U.S. as it is on the same lines and reaches the same standard as in other schools. No doubt his habit of entire attention favours the P.U.S. Scholar.

III

THE KNOWLEDGE OF THE UNIVERSE
(*c*) PHYSICAL DEVELOPMENT, HANDICRAFTS

234 It is unnecessary, too, to say anything about games, dancing, physical exercises, needlework and other handicrafts as the methods employed in these are not exceptional.*

---

* For details see the Parents' Union School programmes.

Book 2

THEORY APPLIED

Chapter 1

A Liberal Education in Elementary Schools

I need not waste time in attempting to convince the reader of what we all know, that a liberal education is, like justice, religion, liberty, fresh air, the natural birthright of every child. Neither need we discuss the scope of such an education. We are aware that good life implies cultivated intelligence, that, according to the Platonic axiom, 'Knowledge is virtue,' even though there be many exceptions to the rule. Educated teachers are not slow to perceive the part the Humanities play in a worthy scheme of education, but they are faced by enormous difficulties which are admirably summed up in a recent work,—*

"The tragedy of modern education has been the prolonged failure of Humanism to secure conditions under

---

* *Citizens to Be*, by Miss M. L. V. Hughes.

which its purpose might be realised for the people at large."

It is because we (of the Parents' Union School) have succeeded in offering Humanism under such conditions that we believe the great problem of education is at last solved. We are able to offer the Humanities (in the mother tongue) to large classes of children from illiterate homes in such a way that the teaching is received with delight and freely assimilated. One swallow does not make a summer, we all know, but the experience of one school shows that it is possible to carry out a pretty full literary programme joyously and without effort while including all the usual school activities. Wireless telegraphy was, so to speak, in the air before the first Marconi message was sent, but that first wireless message made it possible for any passenger on board a Channel steamer to send such a message. Just so, the experiment in the Drighlington School (Yorkshire) placed the conditions for a humanistic education at the service of any teacher. I am much impressed by the amount of work of this kind which is already being done in our schools. I heard the other day of a man whose whole life had been elevated by a single inspiring (poetic) sentence which he heard as a schoolboy; we have been told that the 'man in the street' cannot resist a row of books; we are told, too, that the War has made us a nation of readers, both at home and in the trenches, readers largely of the best books in poetry and history; is there no credit due to the schools for these things? But teachers are not satisfied; their reach is greater than their grasp and they are more aware of the sordid lives about them, of the "dull, unfeeling, barren ignorance" which prevails, than of any success they have yet attained. Therefore they fret under the time limitations which seem to make it impossible to do anything worth while in such vast subjects as History and Literature, for example.

I wonder does this uneasiness point to a fact which we are slow to realise,—that the requirements of the mind are very much like those of the body? Both require as conditions of health,—activity, variety, rest and, above all, food. There has been some tendency among us to offer gymnastics, whether intellectual or physical, by way of a square meal of knowledge, which is as if one were to invite a boy to Swedish Drill by way of his dinner; and that wretched misnomer 'education' is partly to blame. Now, potency, not property, 237 is the characteristic of mind. A child is able to deal with much knowledge, but he possesses none worth speaking of; yet we set to work to give him that potency which he already possesses rather than the knowledge which he lacks; we train his reason, cultivate his judgment, exercise this and the other faculty, which we have no more to do with than with the digestive processes of a healthy child; we know that the more we meddle with these the worse for the child; but what if the devitalisation we notice in so many of our young people, keen about games but dead to things of the mind, is due to the processes carried on in our schools, to our plausible and pleasant ways of picturing, eliciting, demonstrating, illustrating, summarising, doing all those things for children which they are born with the potency to do for themselves? No doubt we do give intellectual food, but too little of it; let us have courage and we shall be surprised, as we are now and then, at the amount of intellectual strong meat almost any child will take at a meal and digest at his leisure.

Perhaps the first thing for us to do is to get a just perception of what I may call the relativity of knowledge and the mind. The mind receives knowledge, not in order that it may know, but in order that it may grow, in breadth and depth, in sound judgment and magnanimity; but in order to grow, it *must know*.

The fact is that we are handicapped, not so much by the three or four difficulties I have already indicated, as by certain errors of judgment, forms of depreciation, which none of us escape because they are universal. We as teachers depreciate ourselves and our office; we do not realise that in the nature of things the teacher has a prophetic power of appeal and inspiration, that his part is not the wearies task of spoon-feeding with pap-meat, but the delightful commerce of equal minds where his is the part of guide, philosopher and friend. The friction of wills which makes school work harassing ceases to a surprising degree when we deal with the children, mind to mind, through the medium of knowledge.

238

Next, we depreciate children, even though most teachers

lay down their lives for their charges with amazing devotion. We have been so long taught to regard children as products of education and environment, that we fail to realise that from the first they are persons; and, as Carlyle has well said,—

> "The mystery of a person, indeed, is ever divine, to him that has a sense for the godlike."

We must either reverence or despise children; and while we regard them as incomplete and undeveloped beings who will one day arrive at the completeness of man, rather than as weak and ignorant persons, whose ignorance we must inform and whose weakness we must support, but whose potentialities are as great as our own, we cannot do otherwise than despise children, however kindly and even tenderly we commit the offence.

As soon as he gets words with which to communicate with us, a child lets us know that he thinks with surprising clearness and directness, that he sees with a closeness of observation that we have long lost, that he enjoys and that he sorrows with an intensity we have ceased to experience, that he loves with an abandon and a confidence which, alas, we do not share, that he imagines with a fecundity no artist among us can approach that he acquires intellectual knowledge and mechanical skill at a rate so amazing, that, could the infant's rate of progress be kept up to manhood, he would surely appropriate the whole field of knowledge in a single lifetime! (It is worth while in this connection to re-read the early chapters of *David Copperfield*.)

     I am considering a child as he is, and am not tracing him, either with Wordsworth, to the heights above, or, with the evolutionist, to the depths below; because a person is a mystery, that is, we cannot explain him or account for him, but must accept him as he is. This wonder of personality does not cease, does not disappear, when a child goes to school; he is still 'all there' in quite another sense from that of the vulgar catchword. But we begin to lose the way to his mind from the day that he enters the schoolroom; the reason for this is, we have embraced the belief that 'knowledge is sensation,' that a child knows what he sees and handles rather than what he conceives in his mind and figures in his thoughts. I labour this point because our faith in a child's spiritual, *i.e.*, intellectual educability is one of our chief assets. Having brought ourselves face to face with the wonder of mind in children, we begin to see that knowledge is the aliment of the mind as food is that of the body. In the days before the War, a lifetime ago it seems, our insular contempt for knowledge was a by-word; except for a schoolmaster or other thinker here and there, nobody took knowledge seriously; we announced boldly that it did not matter what a child learned but only how he learned it. As for mere 'book-learning,' for that we had a fine contempt! But we have changed all that. We are beginning to suspect that ignorance is our national stumbling-block, a chief cause of those difficulties at home which hinder our efforts abroad. For ignorance there is only one cure, and that is, knowledge; his school is the seat of knowledge for a child, and whatever else his teachers do for him, first of all they must sustain him with knowledge, not in homoeopathic doses, but in regular, generous servings. If we ask, what is knowledge?—there is no neat and ready answer at hand. Matthew Arnold, we know, classifies all knowledge under three heads,—the knowledge of God, divinity, the knowledge of man, known as the 'humanities' and the knowledge of the physical world, science, and that is enough to go on with. But I should like to question this division and to class 240 all three parts of knowledge under the head of Humanism, which should include all knowledge that makes a direct appeal to the mind through the channel of literary form; now, the substance of Divinity is contained in one of the three great literatures of the world, and Science, in France if not usually in England, is embodied in a beautiful and poetic literature of great clarity, precision and grace. Is it not then allowable to include all knowledge of which literature is a proper medium under the head of 'Humanism'? One thing at any rate we know with certainty, that no teaching, no information becomes knowledge to any of us until the individual mind has acted upon it, translated it, transformed, absorbed it, to reappear, like our bodily food, in forms of vitality. Therefore, teaching, talk and tale, however lucid or fascinating, effect nothing until self-activity be set up; that is, self-education is the only possible education; the rest is mere veneer laid on the surface of a child's nature.

I have endeavoured to call your attention to a certain undervaluing of children and undervaluing of knowledge which seem to me to mar our twentieth century ideal of education, fine as that is. If we realise that the mind and knowledge are like two members of a ball and socket joint, two limbs of a pair of scissors, fitted to each other, necessary to each other and acting only in concert, we shall understand that our function as teachers is to supply children with the rations of knowledge which they require; and that the rest, character and conduct, efficiency and ability, and, that finest quality of the citizen, magnanimity, take care of themselves. "But how?" cries the teacher, whose life is spent in the labour of Sisyphus. I think we have chanced on a way that, at any rate, works to admiration, the principles and practice of which I am anxious to bring before you.

241   Let me first repeat* a few of the results that have been made good by thousands of children, and within the last few years by many Council Schools throughout the country:—

The children, not the teachers, are the responsible persons; they do the work by self-effort. The teachers give the uplift of their sympathy in the work and where necessary elucidate, sum up or enlarge, but the actual work is done by the scholars.

These read in a term from one thousand to between two and three thousand pages, according to age and class, in a large number of set books; the quantity set for each lesson allows of only a single reading.

---

* cf. "Introduction."

The reading is tested by narration, or by writing on a test passage. No revision is attempted when the terminal examination is at hand; because too much ground has been covered to allow of any 'looking up.'

What the children have read they know, and write on any part of it with ease and fluency, in vigorous English. They usually spell well.

During the examinations, which last a week, the children cover say from twenty to sixty sheets of Cambridge paper, according to age and class; but if ten times as many questions were set on the work studied most likely they would cover ten times as much paper.

It rarely happens that all the children in a class are not able to answer all the questions set in such subjects as history, literature, citizenship, geography, science. But here differences manifest themselves; some children do better in history, some in science, some in arithmetic, others in literature; some, again, write copious answers and a few write sparsely; but practically all know the answers to the set questions.

In the course of an examination they deal freely with a great number of substantives, including many proper names; I once had the names used by a child of ten in an examination paper counted; there were well over a hundred, of which these are the 'A's'— 242

Africa, Alsace-Lorraine, Abdomen, Antigonons, Antennae, Aphis, Antwerp, Alder, America, Amsterdam, Austria-Hungary, Ann Boleyn, Antarctic, Atlantic;

and these are the 'M's,'—

> Megalopolis, Maximilian, Milan, Martin Luther, Mary
> of the Netherlands, Messina, Macedonia, Magna Charta,
> Magnet, Malta, Metz, Mediterranean, Mary Queen of
> Scots, Treaty of Madrid;

and upon all these subjects the children wrote as freely and fully as if they were writing to an absent sister about a new family of kittens!

The children write with perfect understanding as far as they go and there is rarely a 'howler' in hundreds of sets of papers. They have an enviable power of getting at the gist of a book or subject. Sometimes they are asked to write verses about a personage or an event; the result is not remarkable by way of poetry, but sums up a good deal of thoughtful reading in a delightful way; for example,—the reading of *King Lear* is gathered in twelve lines on 'Cordelia,'—

CORDELIA

> Nobliest lady, doomed to slaughter,
> An unlov'd, unpitied daughter,
> Though Cordelia thou may'st be,
> "Love's" the fittest name for thee;
> If love doth not, maid, bestow
> Scorn for scorn, and "no" for "no,"
> If love loves through scorn and spite,
> If love clings to truth and right,

If love's pure, maid, as thou art,
If love has a faithful heart,
Thou art then the same as love;
Come from God's own realms above!

M. K. C. 10 Form II.

A life of Livingstone (read in connection with the 243 Geography of Africa) is thus epitomised,—

LIVINGSTONE

"The whole of Africa is desert bare,
Except around the coast." So people said,
And thought of that great continent no more.
"The smoke of thousand villages I've seen!"
So cried a man. He knew no more. His words
Sank down into one heart there to remain.
The man who heard rose up and gave his all:
Into the dark unknown he went alone.
What terrors did he face? The native's hate,
The fever, tetse-fly and loneliness.
But to the people there he brought great Light.
Who was this man, the son of some great lord?
Not so. He was a simple Scottish lad
Who learnt to follow duty's path. His name
Was Livingstone, he will not be forgot.

E. P. (15.) Form IV.

And here is a rendering of Plutarch's *Life of Pericles* by a girl of fourteen in Form IV,—

Oh! land, whose beauty and unrivalled fame;
Lies dead, obscure in Time's great dusty vault.
Not so in memory, for truly here,
Each and alike look up and do revear
Those heroes of the hidden past. Plato,
Who's understanding reached the wide world's end;
Aristides, that just and noble man.
And last, not least, the great wise Pericles
Who's socialistic views and clever ways
For governing the rich and poor alike
Were to be envied. In his eyes must Greece
Live for ever as the home of beauty.
So to the Gods great marble shrines he made,
Temples and theatres did he erect;
So that the beauty of his beloved Greece
Might live for ever. And now when seeing
What is left of all those wondrous sights
We think not of the works *themselves*
But rather of the man who had them built.

244   One wonders is 'socialistic' used for democratic; any way, the notion is original. There is little to be said for the technique of the verses but I think the reader will agree that each set shows thoughtful appreciation of some part of the term's reading. The verses are uncorrected.

Much use is made according to this method of the years from 6 to 8, during which children must learn to read and write; they get at the same time, however, a good deal of consecutive knowledge of history and geography, tale and fable, some of which at the end of the term they dictate in answer to questions and their answers form well-expressed little essays on the subjects they deal with.

The time appropriated in the time-table at this stage to the teaching of some half-dozen more or less literary subjects such as Scripture, and the subjects I have indicated, is largely spent by the teachers in reading, say, two or three paragraphs at a time from some one of the set books, which children, here and there in the class, narrate. The teacher reads with the intention that the children shall know, and therefore, with distinctness, force, and careful enunciation; it is a mere matter of sympathy, though of course it is the author and not himself, whom the teacher is careful to produce. This practice, of the teacher reading aloud and the class narrating, is necessarily continued through all the classes of an elementary school, because some of the books used are rather costly and only one copy is furnished. I wonder does this habit of listening with close attention to what is read aloud tend to equalise the children of the 'uneducated' with those of the educated classes? Certainly, the work of the two is surprisingly equal. By the way, there is no selection of subjects, passages or episodes on the ground of interest. The best available book is chosen and read through in the course, it may be, of two or three years.

245   Let me add that the appeal of these principles and this method is not to the clever child only but to the average and even to the 'backward' child; indeed we have had several marked successes with backward children. Just as we all partake of that banquet which is 'Shakespeare' according to our needs and desires, so do the children behave at the ample board set before them; there is enough to satisfy the keenest intelligence while the dullest child is sustained through his own willing effort. This scheme of fairly wide and successful intellectual work is carried out in the same or less time than is occupied in the usual efforts in the same directions; there are no revisions, no evening preparations (because far more work is done by the children in ordinary school-time than under ordinary school methods, when the child is too often a listener only): no note-taking, because none are necessary, the children having the matter in their books and knowing where to find it; and as there is no cramming or working up of subjects there is much time to spare for vocational and other work of the kind.

Such an education as I am urging should act as a social lever also; everyone is much occupied with problems concerning amelioration of life for our 'poorer classes' but do we sufficiently consider that, given a better education, the problems of decent living will for the most part be solved by the people themselves?

Like all great ventures of life this that I propose is a venture of faith, faith in the saving power of knowledge and in the assimilative power of children. Its efficacy depends upon the fact that it is in the nature of things, that is, in the nature of knowledge and in the nature of children. Bring the two together in ways that are sanctioned by the laws of mind and, to use a figure, a chemical combination takes place and a new product appears, a person of character and intelligence, an admirable citizen whose own life is too full and rich for him to be an uneasy member of society.

246

Education is part and parcel of religion and every enthusiastic teacher knows that he is obeying the precept,—'feed my lambs'—feed with all those things which are good and wholesome for the spirit of a man; and, before all and including all, with the knowledge of God.

I have ventured to speak of the laws of mind, or spirit, but indeed we can only make guesses here and there and follow with diffidence such light as we get from the teachings of the wise and from general experience; general experience, because peculiar experience is apt to be misleading; therefore, when I learned that long tried principles and methods were capable of application to the whole of a class of forty children in the school of a mining village, I felt assured that we were following laws whose observance results in education of a satisfying kind.

The mind requires sustenance as does the body, that it may increase and be strong; so much everybody knows. A long time ago it was perceived that the pabulum given in schools was of the wrong sort; Grammar rules, lists of names and dates and places,—the whole stock in trade of the earlier schoolmaster—was found to be matter which the minds of children reject: and, because we were wise enough to see that the mind functions for its own nourishment whether in rejecting or receiving, we changed our tactics, following, so we thought, the lead of the children. We did well, and therefore are prepared, if necessary, to do better. What, then, if our whole educational equipment, our illustrations, elucidations, questionings, our illimitable patience in getting a point into the children, were all based on the false assumption of the immature, which we take to connote the imperfect, incomplete minds of children? "I think I could understand. Mummy, if you did not explain quite so much,"—is this the inarticulate cry of the school child to-day? He really is capable of much more than he gets credit for, but we go the wrong way about getting his capable mind into action.

247

We err when we allow our admirable teaching to intervene between children and the knowledge their minds demand. The desire for knowledge (curiosity) is the chief agent in education: but this desire may be made powerless like an unused limb by encouraging other desires to intervene, such as the desire for place (emulation), for prizes (avarice), for power (ambition), for praise (vanity). But I am told that marks, places and prizes (except for attendance) do not figure largely in Elementary Schools, therefore the love of knowledge for its own sake is likely to have a freer course in these schools than in others.

That children are born persons,—is the first article of the educational *credo* which I am concerned to advance;

this implies that they come to us with power of attention, avidity for knowledge, clearness of thought, nice discrimination in books even before they can read, and the power of dealing with many subjects.

Practical teachers will say, guarantee to us the attention of our scholars and we will guarantee their progress in what Colet calls 'good literature.' I have already explained* how I came to a solution of this puzzling problem,—how to secure attention.

Let me add again that the principles and methods I have indicated are especially suitable for large classes; what is called the 'sympathy of numbers' stimulates the class, and the work goes with added impetus: each child is eager to take part in narration or to do written work well. By the way, only short test answers are required in writing, so that the labour of correction is minimised. To two further points I must invite attention; the choice of books and the character of the terminal examinations. I do not know better how to describe the sort of books that children's minds will consent to deal with than by saying that they must be literary in character. A child of seven or eight will narrate a difficult passage from *The Pilgrim's Progress*, say, with extraordinary zest and insight; but I doubt if he or his elders would retain anything from that excellent work, Dr. Smiles's *Self-Help!* The completeness with which hundreds of children reject the wrong book is a curious and instructive experience, not less so than the avidity and joy with which they drain

---

* pp. 13 to 15.

the right book to the dregs; children's requirements in the matter seem to be quantity, quality and variety: but the question of books is one of much delicacy and difficulty. After the experience of over a quarter of a century* in selecting the lesson books proper to children of all ages, we still make mistakes, and the next examination paper discovers the error! Children cannot answer questions set on the wrong book; and the difficulty of selection is increased by the fact that what they like in books is no more a guide than what they like in food.

The moment has come to try the great cause of *Education v. Civilisation*, with the result, let us hope, that the latter will retire to her proper sphere of service in the amelioration of life and will not intrude on the higher functions of inspiration and direction which belong to Education. Both Civilisation and Education are the handmaids of Religion, but, each in its place, and the one may not thrust herself into the office of the other. It is a gain, any way, that we are within sight of giving to all members of the working classes notwithstanding their limited opportunities that stability of mind and magnanimity of character which are the proper outcome and the unfailing test of a LIBERAL ED-
249   UCATION; also it is to the good that "the grand elementary principle of pleasure" should be discovered in unexpected places, in what is too often the drudgery of the schoolroom.

Milton's ideal of a "complete and generous education" meets our occasions;—"that which fits a man to perform

---

* The P.U.S. was started in 1890.

justly, skilfully and magnanimously all the offices both private and public of peace and war"; and perhaps it remains for our generation to prove that this ideal is open to and necessary for persons of all sorts and conditions. It has been well said that,—

> "Just as there is only one kind of truth common to us all, so there is only one education common to us all. In the case of the education of the people the only question is: How is this common education to be developed under the circumstances of simple conditions of life and large masses of people? That this should be accomplished is the decisive mark of all real education."

The writer (Eucken) offers no solution of this problem: and it remains with the reader to determine each with himself whether that solution which I here propose is or is not worth a trial.

Chapter 2

A Liberal Education in Secondary Schools

Mighty is the power of persistent advertisement. The author of *The Pagan* may or may not be bringing an indictment against Pelmanism, but without any doubt 'Pelmanism' is bringing an indictment against secondary education. Half a million souls, Judges and Generals, Admirals and Barristers, are protesting that they have not been educated. No doubt the spirit that informs advertisements is often a lying spirit but claims so well attested as these may have something in them, and we who are engaged in secondary education are uneasy. Again, we have the Board of Education desiring that returns should be made promptly of all schools not already in communication with the State, which, by the way, is taking paternal action in several directions to secure a liberal education for *all* His Majesty's lieges. "Pay the schoolmaster well and you will get education" is the panacea of the moment, and so we get in one neighbourhood a village schoolmaster with a salary of £350 and a house, and a singularly able curate, an Oxford man, with a wife and family and no house who flourishes on £150 a year! Work, however, is more than wages, and this exclusive stress on high salaries is a tacit undervaluing of teachers. Most of us know of fine educational work being done with little inducement in the way of either pay or praise. The real drawback to a teacher's work and the stumbling-block in the way of a liberal education is the monotonous drudgery of teaching continually what no one wants to learn. Before the War, the President of the British Association complained that education was uninteresting alike to pupils, teachers and parents. That is why we are always learning and never knowing, and why teachers exert themselves to invent a 'Play Way,' why handicrafts, 'Eurhythmies' and the like are offered, not as adjuncts to, but as substitutes for, education, why our Public Schools are exhorted to change their ways and our lesser private schools are threatened with extinction.

And with all this the intelligence and devotion, the enthusiasm and self-sacrificing zeal of teachers generally is amazing. They realise that education is, not merely an interest, but a passion; and this is true not only of the heads and the staffs of great schools but of those hundreds of little private schools scattered over the country.

We have all heard of "the two Miss Prettymans, who kept a girls' school at Silverbridge. Two more benignant ladies than the Miss Prettymans never presided over such an establishment." As for Miss Annabella Prettyman, the elder, "it was considered . . . that she did all the thinking, that she knew more than any other woman in Barsetshire, and that all the Prettyman schemes for education emanated from her mind. It was said, too, by those who knew them best, that her sister's good-nature was as nothing to hers, that she was the most charitable, the most loving, the most conscientious of schoolmistresses." To be sure Miss Ann, the younger sister, knew more about Roman History and Roman Law than about current history and English Law, but what would you have?

Here was a type of school with which Trollope was familiar generations ago, and perhaps it would not be hard to find such another school in every 'Silverbridge' of to-day. 252 To-day, however, we are uneasy, and in our unrest produce "Joan and Peter" types of education; that is, small schools indulge in freaks and great schools with much reason to believe in themselves are aware of a hitch somewhere, for they fail to turn out many boys or girls who have intellectual interests, or have that flexibility of mind which Matthew Arnold tells us their Academy gives to our neighbours across the Channel. There is that bugbear of 'Pelmanism' urging a charge of inadequacy against our methods; there is always some new book by a man who brings railing accusations against his particular school; and here is a tempered protest from Colonel Repington which is telling:—

> "When I look back upon Eton schooling I regard it with
> mixed feelings, for I loved my five years at Eton, gloried
> in its beauties and traditions, and was in upper division

when I left. But all the same I was conscious that Eton was not teaching me the things that I wanted to know, and was trying to teach me things that revolted me, particularly mathematics and classics. I wanted to learn history, geography, modern languages, literature, science, and political economy, and I had a very poor chance at Eton of obtaining anything but a smattering of any one of them. I do not agree that we learnt nothing or were lazy. We worked very hard, but at what, to my mind, were useless things, and, with my feet planted firmly in the ground, I resisted in a mulish way all attempts to teach me dead languages and higher mathematics. I believe that I was right. Classics have left nothing with me but some ideas that I could have learnt better from a crib."

Probably the writer is mistaken as to what he owes to Eton. Without those five years he might not have become the authority on the theory and practice of war he is admitted to be. Who knows how much 'Caesar' may have influenced him as a small boy! No doubt Public Schools have many defects but they also have the knack of turning out men who do the work of the world. We know about the 'playing fields,' but perhaps when all is said it is the tincture of the classics that every public schoolboy gets which makes him 'to differ.' Nevertheless such protests as 'Eton was not teaching me the things I wanted to know' deserve consideration.

253

It is easy to condemn the schools, but the fact is, a human being is born with a desire to know much about an enormous number of subjects. How is the school time table to get them all in or an adequate treatment of any one of them? Then, boys (and girls too) offer a resisting medium of extraordinary density. Every boy 'resists in a mulish way' attempts to teach him, not only dead languages and higher mathematics, but literature and science and every subject the master labours at; with the average boy a gallon of teaching produces scarce a gill of learning, and what is the master to do? It is something to know, however, that behind all this 'mulishness' there is avidity for knowledge, not so much for the right sort (every sort is the right sort), but put in the right way, and we cannot say that every way is the right way.

I put before the reader what we (of the P.N.E.U.) have done towards the solution of this educational problem with sincere diffidence, but also with courage, because I know that no persons are more open to conviction on reasonable grounds than are many distinguished Headmasters and Mistresses; may they, if convinced, have the courage of their convictions!

So little is known about the behaviour of mind that it is open to anyone to make discoveries in this *terra incognita*. I speak, not of psychology, of which we hear a great deal and know very little, but of mind itself, whose ways are subtle and evasive; nevertheless that education only is valid which has mind for its objective. The initial difficulty is the enormous field of knowledge to which a child ought to be introduced in right of his human nature and of those

254 "first born affinities" which he lives to make good. First and chiefest is the knowledge of God, to be got at most directly through the Bible; then comes the knowledge of man, to be got through history, literature, art, civics, ethics, biography, the drama, and languages; and lastly, so much knowledge of the universe as shall explain to some extent the phenomena we are familiar with and give a naming acquaintance at any rate with birds and flowers, stars and stones; nor can this knowledge of the universe be carried far in any direction without the ordering of mathematics. The programme is immense and school life is limited. What we may call the 'Academic' solution of the problem is,— teach a boy to know one thing thoroughly, say, Greek or Chemistry or Mathematics, and you give him the key to all knowledge. Therefore, we are told, it is not what you know that matters, but how you learn it; and a grammar grind, a mathematics grind or a laboratory 'stunt,' with a few odd matters thrown in, is supposed to answer all the purposes of education. The plan answers fairly well with the dozen best boys or girls in any school, because these are so keen and intelligent that they forage for themselves in various directions; but it does not answer with the average pupil, and he is coming in for his share of public attention. Shortly we shall have a new rule,—every school must educate *every* scholar in the three sorts of knowledge proper to him as a human being. What is knowledge? some one will say, and there is no pat, neatly-framed answer to be given; only this we can assert,—Knowledge is that which we know; and the

learner knows only by a definite act of knowing which he performs for himself. But appalling *incuria* blocks the way. Boys and girls do not want to know; therefore they do not know; and their future intellectual requirements will be satisfied by bridge at night and golf by day.

It has come to us of the Parents' Union School to discover great avidity for knowledge in children of all ages and of every class, together with an equally remarkable power of attention, retention, and intellectual reaction upon the pabulum consumed. The power which comes into play in the first place is, of course, attention, and every child of any age, even the so-called 'backward' child seems to have unlimited power of attention which acts without mark, prize, place, praise or blame. This fact clearly recognised opens great possibilities to the teacher; though his first impulse be to deny statements which seem to him sweeping and absurd. But the education of the future will probably offer us intellectual assets in human nature as surprising as the ethical values exhibited by the War.

We have not attained but I think we are on the way to attainment. After over a quarter of a century of experiment on a wide scale and consequent research, we have discovered what children are able to know and desire to know; what their minds will act upon in the ways of judgment and imagination; what they are incapable of knowing; and under what conditions knowledge must be offered to them. We do not want a 'play-way', nor need we substitute arts and crafts or eurhythmies or even 'rugger' and

255

the swimming bath, as things that boys take to, whereas learning goes against the grain. Physical and mechanical training are necessary for the up bringing of the young, but let us regard them for the moment as training rather than education,—which ought to concern itself with things of the mind. Education as we know it is admirably designed to 'develop the faculties'; but if "All that's an exploded idee," if there be no faculties to develop, but only mind,—alert, self-active, discriminating, logical, capable alike of great flights and of minute processes—we must necessarily alter our educational tactics. Mind is benefitted by occasional gymnastics just as is 'Brother Body,' but cannot subsist on

256　these any more than 'Body' can live on Swedish drill.

As I have said, knowledge, that is, roughly, ideas clothed upon with facts, is the proper pabulum for mind. This food a child requires in large quantities and in great variety. The wide syllabus I have in view is intended in every point to meet some particular demand of the mind, and the curious thing is that in a syllabus embracing a score of subjects the young learner is quite unconfused, makes no howlers, and never mixes, say, a fact of English with a fact of French history.

Again, we have made a rather strange discovery,—that the mind refuses to know anything except what reaches it in more or less literary form. It is not surprising that this should be true of children and persons accustomed to a literary atmosphere but that it should be so of ignorant children of the slums points to a curious fact in the behaviour of mind. Persons can 'get up' the driest of pulverised text-books and enough mathematics for some public examination; but these attainments do not appear to touch the region of mind. When we get a young Pascal who enters voluntarily and eagerly into the study of mathematics he finds himself in a region of high thinking and self-existent law of the very nature of poetry; minds of this calibre assert themselves; but this is a gift and does not come of plodding. For the general run of scholars probably the "Association of Head Mistresses" are right and a less exacting standard should be set for public examinations.

Of Natural Science, too, we have to learn that the way into the secrets of nature is not through the barbed wire entanglements of science as she is taught but through field work or other immediate channel, illustrated and illuminated by books of literary value.

The French Academy was founded to advance *Science* and Art, a fact which may account for the charming lucidity and the exquisite prose of many French books on scientific subjects. The mind is a crucible which brings enormous power to act on what is put into it but has no power to distil from sand and sawdust the pure essence of ideas. So much for the manner of food which that organism (if I may be allowed the figure) called the mind requires for its daily subsistence. How various this sustenance must be I have already indicated and we remember how urgently Dr. Arnold insisted on 'very various reading' in the three parts of knowledge, knowledge of God, of man, and of the universe.

But the mind was a deceiver ever. Every teacher knows how a class will occupy itself diligently by the hour and accomplish nothing, even though the boys think they have been reading. We all know how ill we could stand an examination on the daily papers over which we pore. Details fail us, we can say,—"Did you see such and such an article?" but are not able to outline its contents. We try to remedy this vagueness in children by making them take down, and get up, notes of a given lesson: but we accomplish little. The mind appears to have an outer court into which matter can be taken and again expelled without ever having entered the inner place where personality dwells. Here we have the secret of learning by rote, a purely mechanical exercise of which no satisfactory account has been given, but which leaves the patient, or pupil, unaffected. Most teachers know the dreariness of piles of exercises into which no stray note of personality has escaped. Now there is a natural provision against this mere skimming of the ground by the educational plough. Give children the sort of knowledge that they are fitted to assimilate, served in a literary medium, and they will pay great attention. What next? A clever *questionnaire*? Questions, as Dr. Johnson told us, are an intrusion and a bore; but here we have a word of ancient wisdom for our guidance; "The mind can know nothing except what it can express in the form of an answer to a question put by the mind to itself." Observe, not a question put by an outsider, but, put by the mind to itself. We all know the trick of it. If we want to tell the substance of a conversation, a sermon, a lecture, we 'go over it in our minds' first and the mind puts its question to itself, the same question over and over again, no more than,—What next?—and lo, we have it, the whole thing complete! We remember how one of Burke's pamphlets, by no means light affairs, was told almost verbatim at a College supper. We admire such a feat and think it quite out of our reach but it is the sort of thing that any boy or girl of fifteen could do if allowed to read the pamphlet only once; a second reading would be fatal because no one can give full attention to that which he has heard before and expects to hear again. Attention will go halt all its days if we accustom it to the crutch. We as teachers offend deeply in this matter. We think that we shall be heard for our much speaking and we repeat and enforce, explain and illustrate, not altogether because we love the sound of our own voices, but because we depreciate knowledge, we depreciate children, and we do not understand that the mind and knowledge are as the two members of a ball and socket joint, each of them irrelevant without the other. 'Education' will have turned over a new leaf once we realise that knowledge is to the mind as food is to the body, without which the one faints and flags and eventually perishes as surely as does the other.

The way to bring this panacaea into use is exceedingly simple. Let the child (up to any age while he is an infant in the eye of the law) tell what he has read in whole or in part on the instant, and again, in an examination paper months later. 'Mere verbal memory,' some reader will say, and there is no answer to be given but that which one must give to oneself. Let the objector read an essay of Lamb's, say, or of

259   Matthew Arnold's, *Lycidas* or the 'raven' scene in *Barnaby Rudge* and then put himself to sleep or wile away an anxious or a dull hour by telling to himself what he has read. The result will be disappointing; he will have forgotten this and that turn of thought, link in the chain of argument, but he will know the whole thing in a surprising way; the incidents, the figures, the delicate play of thought in the author will be brought out in his mind like the figures in the low relief which the sculptor produces from his block. He finds he has taken in 'mind stuff' which will come into use in a thousand ways perhaps as long as he lives.

Here we get the mind forces which must act continuously in education,—attention, assimilation, narration, retention, reproduction. But what of reason, judgment, imagination, discrimination, all the corps of 'faculties' in whose behoof the teacher has hitherto laboured? These take care of themselves and play as naturally and involuntarily upon the knowledge we receive with attention and fix by narration as do the digestive organs upon duly masticated food-stuff for the body. We must feed the mind as the body fitly and freely; and the less we meddle with the digestive processes in the one as in the other the more healthy the life we shall sustain. It is an infinitely great thing, that mind of man, present in completeness and power in even the dullest of our pupils; even of him it may be said,—

"Darkness may bound his Eyes, not his Imagination. In his Bed he may lie, like Pompey and his Sons, in all quarters of the Earth, may speculate the Universe, and enjoy the whole World in the Hermitage of Himself."

We are paying in our education of to-day for the wave of materialism that spread over the country a hundred years ago. People do not take the trouble to be definitely materialistic now, but our educational thought has received a trend which carries us whither we would not. Any apostle of a new method is welcome to us. We have ceased to believe in mind, and though we would not say in so many words that "the brain secretes thought as the liver secretes bile," yet the physical brain rather than the spiritual mind is our objective in education; therefore, "things are in the saddle and ride mankind," and we have come to believe that children are inaccessible to ideas or any knowledge.

260

The message for our age is, Believe in mind, and let education go straight as a bolt to the mind of the pupil. The use of books is a necessary corollary, because no one is arrogant enough to believe he can teach every subject in a full curriculum with the original thought and exact knowledge shown by the man who has written a book on perhaps his life-study. But the teacher is not moved by arrogance but by a desire to be serviceable. He believes that children cannot understand well-written books and that he must make of himself a bridge between the pupil and the real teacher, the man who has written the book.

Now we have proved that children, even children of the slums, are able to understand any book suitable for their age: that is, children of eight or nine will grasp a chapter in *Pilgrim's Progress* at a single reading; children of fourteen, one of Lamb's Essays or a chapter in *Eöthen*, boys and girls of seventeen will 'tell' *Lycidas*. Given a book of literary quality suitable to their age and children will know how to deal with it without elucidation. Of course they will not be able to answer questions because questions are an impertinence which we all resent, but they will tell you the whole thing with little touches of individual personality in the narrative. Perhaps this is the key to the enormous difficulty of humanistic teaching in English. We are no longer overpowered by the mass of the 'humanities' confronted with the slow process of getting a child to take in anything at all of the author he is reading. The slow process is an invention of our own. Let the boy read and he knows, that is, if he must tell again what he has read.

This, of telling again, sounds very simple but it is really a magical creative process by means of which the narrator sees what he has conceived, so definite and so impressive is the act of narrating that which has been read only once. I dwell on the single reading because, let me repeat, it is impossible to fix attention on that which we have heard before and know we shall hear again.

Treat children in this reasonable way, mind to mind; not so much the mind of the teacher to that of the child,—that would be to exercise undue influence—but the minds of a score of thinkers who meet the children, mind to mind, in their several books, the teacher performing the graceful office of presenting the one enthusiastic mind to the other. In this way children cover an incredible amount of ground in the time at their disposal.

Perhaps there is no better way of measuring a person of liberal education than by the number of substantives he is able to use with familiarity and discrimination. We remember how Scott tried a score of openings with the man on the coach and got no further until he hit upon 'bent leather'; then the talk went merrily for the man was a saddler. We have all had such experiences and know to our shame that we ourselves have victimised interlocutors who have not been able to find our particular 'bent leather.' Now, this is a matter for teachers to consider. There are a thousand subjects on which we should have definite knowledge and be able to speak with intelligence; and, indeed, do we not set 'general knowledge' papers, with the result that boys and girls are 'out' for scrappy information and provide material for comic paragraphs? There is no remedy for this state of things but a great deal of *consecutive* reading from very various books, all of some literary value; and this we find can be accomplished readily in school hours because one reading is sufficient; nor should there be any revision 262 for the distant examination. Here is an uncorrected list of 200 names, used with ease and fitness in an examination on one term's work by a child of eleven in Form II.

Abinadab, Athenian, Anne Boleyn, Act of Uniformity, Act of Supremacy, America, Austria, Alcibiades, Athens, Auckland, Australia, Alexandria, Alhambra.

Bible, Bishop of Rochester, Baron, Bean-shoots, Bluff, Bowen Falls, Bishoprics, Blind Bay, Burano.

Currants, Cupid, Catholic, Court of High Commission, Cranmer, Charles V, Colonies, Convent, Claude, Calais, Cook Strait, Canterbury Plain, Christchurch, Cathedral, Canals, Caliph of Egypt, Court of the Myrtles, Columbus, Cordova.

David, Defender of the Faith, Duke of Guise, Dunedin, Doge's Palace.

England, Emperor, Empire, Egmont (Count), English Settlement.

Flour, Fruits, French, Francis I, Francis of Guise, Ferdinand, Foveau Strait, Fuchsias, Fiords, Ferns.

Greek, Germany, Gondolas, "Gates of the Damsels," Gondoliers, Granada, Gate of Justice, Gypsies.

Henry VIII, History, Hooper, Henry II, Hungary, Haeckel.

Israel, Italian (language), Italy, Infusoria.

Jesse, Jonathan, Joseph, John, Jerusalem, James, Jane Seymour.

King of Denmark, King of Scotland, Kiwi.

"Love-in-idleness," Lord Chancellor, Lord Burleigh, Lord Robert Dudley, Lime, Lyttleton, N.Z., Lake Tango.

Mary (The Virgin), More (Sir Thomas), Music,

Martyr's Memorial, Milan, Metz, Monastery, Mary, Queen of Scots, Mediterranean, Microscope, Messina, Middle Island, Mount Egmont, Mount Cook, Milford Sound, Museum, Moa, Maoris, Mussulman, Moorish King.

Naomi, Netherlands, Nice, New Zealand, North Island, Napier, Nelson.

Oberon, Oxford, Orion.

Pharisees, Plants, Parliament, Puck, Pope, Protestant, Poetry, Philosophy, *"Paix des Dames,"* Philip II, Paris, Planets, "Pink Terraces," Piazetta, Philip of Burgundy.

Queen Catherine, Queen Elizabeth, Queen Mary, Queen Isabella, Queen Juana.

Ruth, Robin Goodfellow, Ridley, Reformation, Radiolaria, Rotomaliana (Lake), Rea.

263

Saul, Samuel, Simeon, Simon Peter, Sunshine, Sugar-cane, Spices, Sultan, Spain, St. Quentin, Socrates, Stars, Sycamore, Seed-ball, Stewart Island, Seaports, Southern Alps, Scotch Settlement, St. Mark, St. Theodore, St. Maria Formosa (Church), Sierra Navada.

Temple, Titania, Testament, Treaty, Turks, Toul, Thread Slime, Tree Ferns, Timber Trees, Trieste, Toledo.

Verdure, Venus (Planet), Volcano, Volcanic Action, Venice.

Wheat, Wiltshire, William Cecil, Walsingham, Winged Seed, Wellington, Waikato.

Zaccharias, Zebedee.

The fitness and simplicity with which these substantives are employed is evidenced in the complete sets of papers that follow.*

Supposing we have succeeded in shifting a conscientious and intelligent teacher from one mental position to another, suppose that he give up the notion of developing 'faculties' because he perceives that mind is complete and sufficient and wants nothing but its proper pabulum; that, again, he yield his place as the medium of all knowledge because his boys are qualified to deal with knowledge at first hand from the right books; suppose he scrap all the text-books and compendiums he has in use, perceiving that only that curious outsider, the verbal memory, and not the mind, will consent to deal with these dry-as-dust compilations; suppose he concede that much knowledge of various sorts and therefore a wide curriculum is necessary for the production of an intelligent and magnanimous citizen; supposing he has proved that any boy can face such a curriculum because all boys have immense power of attention and are able to know their work after a single reading,—surely he has still one or two strongholds that have not been attacked! What he aims at, he will tell you, is, not to open avenues of approach to the subjects about which intelligent citizens should know something, but to give pretty thorough knowledge in two or three directions and to turn out straight Englishmen; that is, he looks upon

264

---

* These are omitted for want of space but other sets can be seen at the Office of the P.N.E.U.

school as a nursery for the formation of character rather than for the acquisition of knowledge. As for the one or two subjects, practically, classics and mathematics, I have nothing to say; those subjects are of real value and also under existing regulations pretty high attainments in them are necessary as a preliminary to professional advancement. It is possible that when a boy has the habit of covering the ground rapidly he may get more into the given 'period' and leave a margin for the wider range of subjects proper to a liberal education. Experiments in this direction are being tried in one of our great Grammar Schools, and how important such experiments are to us as a democracy, I need not be at pains to show. There is every promise that the 'masses' will learn to read in their schools in such wise as to produce in a terminal examination as considerable a list of names as those on the preceding page. If the masses know 'Sancho Panza,' Elsinore, 'Excalibur,' 'Rosinante,' 'Mrs. Jellaby,' redstart, 'Bevis,' bogbean,—the classes must know these things too with easy intimacy. If the one class is familiar with the pictures of the Van Eycks, with 'Comus,' 'Duessa,' 'Baron of Bradwardine,' the other class must know them too, and be able to use the knowledge with such effect as does the 'Honourable Member' when he quotes a familiar tag from Horace. He touches a spring to which all hearts rise, because allusions to what we know are like the light on 'old familiar faces.' What we want is a common basis of thought, such a ground work as we get from having read the same books, grown familiar with the same pictures, the

265   same musical compositions, the same interests; when we have such a fundamental basis, we shall be able to speak to each other whether in public speaking or common talk; we shall "all hear . . . in our own tongue the wonderful works of God" because we have learned a common speech through those who in their books have lived to educate the race. And how persuasively shall we speak to those who know, and therefore do not present the dead front of opposition—the natural resource of ignorance!

A democratic education must have new features. We must all be able to 'take the front' of men and women by speaking of that which they have known and felt and already found joy in. So shall we cease to present motives of self interest and personal advantage as incentives to public action; we shall touch springs of poetry, of heroism, to which all natures have the habit of rising and thus shall we build "Jerusalem in England's green and pleasant land." Towards this, we must have read the same books, only in English rather than in Latin or Greek, because the people will probably never have time to attain proficiency in these; neither, as a matter of fact, has the average boy at our great schools. If we must still have an exclusive education to which only the few best in a school can attain,—and it seems to me that we must, that this is, in fact, the one thing we have achieved, an education that has accomplished great results in character and conduct;—but if we would keep this possession, we must at the same time broaden its base and narrow its bounds. We must give wide reading in the lower forms, reading that everybody has read, and we must so compress our classical and mathematical work in the higher Forms that much history and 'English' may be included. I speak without authority but is it not true that there is overlapping in the passage from Preparatory to Public School, from one Form to a higher, from the Sixth to the University? Probably it will be found possible to give the old training which has produced such notable results, but to make it an inclusive not an exclusive education, to 266 take in the books which everyone should know, the pictures everyone should be familiar with, the history, the travel, in which we should all be at home, some understanding of the phenomena which come before us all. Once we give up the notion that education is a development of the 'faculties' to be accomplished by the teacher, and realize that it is on the contrary an appropriation of wide knowledge which the pupil must get for himself, there is some fear that the old exclusive education must go by the board; but this would be a national calamity. We must keep that to which we have attained and add to it the wide reading of a liberal education. The careers of 'Joan' and 'Peter,' as depicted by Mr. Wells are instructive. Peter is not entered for a recognised Public School for his guardian had many things against such schools, but games are his chief concern. Later we find the two at College, and of Joan it is said, "No religion has convinced her of a purpose in her life, neither Highmorton nor Cambridge has suggested any mundane devotion to her nor pointed her ambitions to a career. The only career these feminine schools and Colleges recognised was a career of academic success and teaching." The implicit charge against the schools is that they try each in its own way to find a substitute for the saving grace of knowledge. Academic success and knowledge are not the same thing and many excellent schools fail to give their pupils delight in the latter for its own sake or to bring them in touch with the sort of knowledge that influences character and conduct. The slow, imperceptible, sinking in of high ideals is the gain that a good school should yield its pupils.

We have, if not a higher, yet another standard which it may be interesting to consider. We offer children knowledge for its own sake and our pupils discover that 'studies serve for delight.' We do not give our best attention to brilliant children, it is not necessary; these work well on their own account and so do the average and even the dull pupils. Historical characters become real to them and a fairly wide historical field comes under their purview; they do not grow up in crass ignorance of the history of foreign countries; they understand, for example, the India of to-day the better because they have some slight intimacy with Akbar as a contemporary of Elizabeth. They take to themselves a lesson from the youthful presumption of 'Phaëton'; 'Midas' and 'Circe,' Xerxes and Pericles enrich the background of their thoughts. The several Forms get through a great deal of reading because we have discovered that a single reading suffices to secure a clear knowledge (as far as it goes) of a subject, given the right book. Therefore, many books are necessary, and each is read consecutively so that the knowledge acquired is not scrappy and insecure. I know that teachers enjoy the work set term by term fully as much as do the children and that a schoolroom life in which there is no monotony, no dulness, little or no idleness or inattention, does away with the necessity to make games the paramount interest of the school—to make them indeed a stern necessity rather than a joyous relaxation.

The introduction of the methods I advocate has a curious effect on a whole family. The old nurse and the gardener are told of the adventures of 'Waverley.' "A.B. has named a moss her father picked on the tip-top of Ben Lawers. It is very rare and only grows on Ben Lawers and one other mountain. She is so pleased," and so, no doubt, is her father! The whole household thinks of and figures to itself great things, for nothing is so catching as knowledge and that fine temper of mind that knowledge brings with it. Children so taught are delightful companions because they have large interests and worthy thoughts; they have much to talk about and such casual talk benefits society. The fine sense, like an atmosphere, of things worth knowing and worth living for, this it is which produces magnanimous citizens, and we feel that Milton was right in claiming magnanimity as the proper outcome of education.

When we compare the large number of books, of historical and literary personages, the range of natural phenomena, with which children brought up on these lines are acquainted, with the sterile syllabus, not very well mastered, which is the schoolboy's normal fare, we find matter for reflection. Yet I suppose that in few things is the general moral and intellectual progress evidenced more than in the culture common among the teachers of secondary schools. Every Head knows how to draw up the best possible syllabus and to secure good work, if upon narrow lines, but we (of the P.N.E.U.) work at an advantage when, as I have said, we recognise one or two natural laws.

I have no doubt that some of my readers are interested in the work we are doing in Elementary schools,—a work the more astonishing because children who have little vocabulary to begin with, no trace of literary background, show themselves able to hear or read a work of literary value and after a single reading to narrate pages with spirit and accuracy, not hedging at the longest names nor muddling complicated statements. This was a revelation to us, and it signifies that a literary education is open to all, not after tedious and laborious preparation, but immediately. The people wait only for the right books to be put into their hands and the right method to be employed.

Let me repeat that we live in times critical for everybody, but eminently critical for teachers, because it rests with them whether personal or general good shall be aimed at, whether education shall be merely a means of getting on, or a means of general progress towards high thinking and plain living, and therefore an instrument of the greatest national good.

Let me beg that Heads of schools, so far in sympathy

with me that they perceive we are at the parting of the ways, will consider a method which brings promise of relief.

We are in a condition, for example, to answer the questions to be considered by the Departmental Committee on English:—

> "Can history and literature be brought into closer relations with the school curriculum than is the case at present? How much grammar is necessary? Could not oral composition and drama and debate, do something to cure our national *aphasia*? How can the preparatory schools improve their English teaching? How can the school essay be redeemed from barrenness? How can examinations be made a test of English without destroying the love of literature?"

These questions might have been framed with a view to bring out the attainments of the Parents' Union School. History, European as well as English, runs in harness with literature. Some Syntax is necessary and a good deal of what may be called historical Grammar, but, *not* in order to teach the art of correct writing and speaking; this is a native art, and the beautiful consecutive and eloquent speech of young scholars in narrating what they have read is a thing to be listened to not without envy. As to *aphasia*, to quote a Director of Education on this subject,—"Conversational readiness becomes a characteristic. A quarter of a century of these methods with all the children of

England and the strong silent Englishman should be a rare bird!" A schoolmaster remarks that his big boys are now eager to speak at some length—a thing new in his experience. Consider what an asset this should be to a country whose safety will depend more and more upon the power in the middle classes of clear and conclusive speech. Oral composition is the habit of the school from the age of six 270　to eighteen. "Children of ten who read Shakespeare" is the heading of an article in a local newspaper which sent a reporter to investigate the P.N.E.U. method at work in a school as the result of an article in the *Nineteenth Century and After* written by the Headmaster. As for preparatory schools, we can do no more than offer them a method the results of which in teaching English are rather surprising. The final question as to how examinations may be made a source of intellectual profit is I think sufficiently answered in the P.U.S. children's examination papers.

We do not invite Heads of schools to take up work lightly, which implies a sound knowledge of certain principles and as faithful a practice. The easy tolerance which holds smilingly that everything is as good as everything else, that one educational doctrine is as good as another, that, in fact, a mixture of all such doctrines gives pretty safe results,—this sort of complacent attitude produces lukewarm effort and disappointing progress. I feel strongly that to attempt to work this method without a firm adherence to the few principles laid down would be not only idle but disastrous. "Oh, we could do anything with books like those," said a master; he tried the books and failed conspicuously because he ignored the principles. We teachers are really modest and diffident and are not prepared to say that we are more capable of handling a subject than is a carefully chosen author who writes especially upon that subject. "Yes, but," says a young and able teacher, "we know better how to reach the minds of children than does the most eloquent author speaking through the dull pages of a book." This is a contention of which we have finally disposed. We have shown that the mass of knowledge, evoking vivid imagination and sound judgment, acquired in a term from the proper books, is many times as great, many times more thoroughly visualised by the scholars, than had they waited upon the words of the most able and effective teacher. This is why we insist upon the use of books. It is not that teachers are not eminently capable but because information does not become knowledge unless a child perform the 'act of knowing' without the intervention of another personality.

Heads of schools are a generous folk and perhaps they have some reason to think parents are niggardly, but the provision of the necessary books by the parents is a *sine quâ non*. It is our part to see to it that books take root in the homes of our scholars and we must make parents understand that it is impossible to give a liberal education to children who have not a due provision of very various books. Moreover, it is impossible to teach children to spell when they do not read for themselves; we hear complaints of the difficulties of spelling, of the necessity to do violence to the language which is dear to us all in order to make 'spelling made easy'; but in thousands of cases that come before us we find that children who use their books for themselves spell well because they visualise the words they read. Those who merely listen to their teacher have no guide (in English at any rate) to the spelling of the words they hear. We are, perhaps, opposed to oral lessons or lectures except by way of occasional review or introduction. For actual education children must do their own work out of their own books under the sympathetic guidance of an intelligent teacher. We find, I may add, that once parents recognise how necessary a considerable supply of books is, they make no difficulty about getting those set in our programmes. Mr. Fisher says,—"there are books and textbooks," and the day is at hand when we shall all see that the latter are of no educational value. We rarely use text-books in the Parents' Union School but confine ourselves as far as possible to works with the imaginative grasp, the touch of originality, which distinguish a book from a text-book. Perhaps we should apologise for ourselves as purveyors not precisely of books but of lists of books. Every headmaster or mistress is able to draw up such lists, but think of the labour of keeping some 170 books in circulation with a number of changes every term! Here is our excuse for offering our services to much-occupied teachers. There has been talk from time to time about interfering with the liberty of teachers to choose their own books, but one might as well contend for everyman's liberty to make his own boots! It is one of those questions of the division of labour which belong to our civilisation; and if the question of liberty be raised at all, why should we not go further and let the children choose their books? But we know very well that the liberty we worship is an elusive goddess and that we do not find it convenient to do all those things we are at liberty to do.

The terminal examinations are of great importance. They are not merely and chiefly tests of knowledge but records which are likely to be permanent. There are things which every child must know, every child, for the days have gone by when 'the education befitting a gentleman' was our aim.

The knowledge of God is the principal knowledge, and no teaching of the Bible which does not further that knowledge is of religious value. Therefore the children read, or if they are too young to read for themselves the teacher reads to them, a passage of varying length covering an incident or some definite teaching. If there are remarks to be made about local geography or local custom, the teacher makes them before the passage has been read, emphasizing briefly but reverently any spiritual or moral truth; the children narrate what has been read after the reading; they do this with curious accuracy and yet with some originality, conveying the spiritual teaching which the teacher has indicated. Now this is no parrot-exercise, but is the result of such an assimilation of the passage that it has become a part of the young scholar. It is only by trying the method oneself on such an incident, for example, as the visit of Nicodemus or the talk with the woman of Samaria, that we realise the wonderful clearness with which each incident is brought out, the fullness of meaning with which every phrase is invested by such personal effort. This method of teaching is especially valuable in dealing with the Gospel history, but none of us who read during the War the daily lessons appointed by the Church could fail to be struck by the fact that the law and the prophets still interpret the ways of God, and we shall not do well if we tacitly treat the Old Testament as out-of-date as a guide to life.

Next in order to religious knowledge, history is the pivot upon which our curriculum turns. History is the rich pasture of the mind—which increases upon the knowledge of men and events and, more than all, upon the sense of nationhood, the proper corrective of the intolerable individualism of modern education. Let Amyot tell us,—

> "How greatly is the reading of histories to be esteemed, which is able to furnish us with more examples in one day, than the whole course of the longest life of any man is able to do. Insomuch that they which exercise themselves in reading as they ought to do, although they be but young, become such in respect of understanding of the affairs of this world, as if they were old and gray-headed and of long experience. Yea, though they never have removed out of their houses, yet are they advertised, informed and satisfied of all things in the world."

Hence, the great value of the Old Testament,—history and poetry, the law and the prophets; and perhaps no one was more sensible of this educative value of the Scriptures than Goethe, though he was little sensible of their more spiritual worth. We endeavour to bring records contemporary with the Bible before children, using the contents of certain Rooms of the British Museum as a basis. Episodes of Greek and Roman history come in, partly for their historical, partly for their distinctly ethical value. Plutarch is, of course, our great authority.

> "(Plutarch) hath written the profitable story of all authors. For all other were fain to take their matter, as the fortune of the countries whereof they wrote fell out: But this man being excellent in wit, learning, and experience, hath chosen the special acts of the best persons, of the famousest nations of the world." (*North*).

English History is always with us, but only in the earliest years is it studied alone. It is not, as we know, possible always to get the ideal book, so we use the best we can find and supplement with historical essays of literary value. Literature is hardly a distinct subject, so closely is it associated with history, whether general or English; and whether it be contemporary or merely illustrative; and it is astonishing how much sound learning children acquire when the thought of an age is made to synchronise with its political and social developments. A point which I should like to bring before the reader is the peculiar part which poetry plays in making us aware of this thought of the ages, including our own. Every age, every epoch, has its poetic aspect, its quintessence, as it were, and happy the people who have a Shakespeare, a Dante, a Milton, a Burns, to gather up and preserve its meaning as a world possession.

Let me repeat that what is called 'composition' is an inevitable consequence of this free yet exact use of books and requires no special attention until the pupil is old enough to take naturally a critical interest in the use of words. Civics takes place as a separate subject, but it is so closely bound up with literature and history on the one hand and with ethics, or, what we call every-day morals, on the other, that the division of subjects is only nominal.

275   We have considered in a previous chapter* what we do for children as inhabitants of a world ordered by natural law. Here we have a contention with some teachers of science who maintain that a child can only learn what he discovers for himself *de novo*. The theory is plausible, but the practice is disappointingly narrow and inexpensive. The teacher has got his knowledge through books; why then are they taboo for the children? Probably the reason is that text-books of science are dessicated to the last degree, so the teacher hopes to make up for their dryness by familiar talk about the Hydra, for example, as a creature capable of close friendships, about the sea anemone as a 'Granny' of enormous longevity; that is, the interest of the subject

* Chapter X.

is made to depend upon side issues. The French scientists know better; they perceive that as there is an essence of history which is poetry so there is an essence of science to be expressed in exquisite prose. We have a few books of this character in English and we use them in the P.U.S. in conjunction with field work and drawing—a great promoter of enthusiasm for nature.

I have already shown* what we do, for example, in the way of affording children familiar acquaintance with great music and great pictures. An eminent art-dealer in London paid us a pretty compliment when he said,—"Lord help the children!" were our work to come to an end; and he had reason for he had just sold to P.U.S. children thousands of little exquisite reproductions of certain pictures by Velasqeuz which were the study of the term; no wonder that a man who loves art and believes in it should feel that something worth while was being done. In drawing, the scholars work very freely in colour from natural figures and objects and draw scenes visualised in the term's reading. We do not teach drawing as a means of self-expression; the scholars express, not themselves, but what they can see and what they conceive.

I have already gone into the teaching of languages; the habit of fixed attention and ready narration which the P.U.S. pupils acquire should be of value in this branch of work, and I believe a new era is opening for us and we English will at last become linguists. At the House of Education the

276

* Chapter X.

students narrate in French,*—more readily and copiously than they do in English,— the courses of lectures in French history and literature which form part of their work. In German and Italian they are able to read a scene in a play and 'tell' the scene in character, or a short passage from a narrative. We rather emphasise Italian, the language is so beautiful and the literature so rich, and I should like to suggest that schools should do the same. Latin and Greek we learn in the usual ways, but we apply the method of narration to the former.

I must commend any further study of the *rationale* of our syllabus to the reader's own kind consideration; he will perceive that we have a principle of correlation in things essential, but no fatiguing practice of it in detail. But to one more statement, a very daring one, I beg for favourable attention. The common theory and practice of education are on trial. It is idle to 'develop the faculties' if there be no faculties, but only *mind*, which, like Wordsworth's cloud, moves altogether when it moves at all. Therefore, those subjects whose *raison d'être* is to develop this and the other faculty are practically out of court and we must seek another basis for education. Subjects of instruction which would be valuable if reason, judgment, imagination, had to be 'developed' become as meretricious, as much 'accomplishments,' as those early Victorian accomplishments over which we make merry. Education must be in touch with

---

* See Chapter X.

life. We must learn what we *desire to know*. Nobody talks to his friend about 'stinks,' about the niceties of Greek accents, nor, unless the two be mathematicians, about surds. But, when Jupiter is regnant, how good to tell and to learn! What a welcome companion is he who can distinguish between songs that differ in the vespers of the birds! How grateful the company of the reader of history who brings forward parallels to episodes in the great War! We are apt to work for one thing in the hope that we shall get another and a very different thing; we don't. If we work for public examinations, the questions in which must be of a narrow academic cast, we get a narrow, accurate, somewhat sterile type of mind. We reap as we have sown.

The future of England depends largely upon Secondary schools; let the Heads of these lay out a liberal field of study and astonishingly fair things will grow in that garden of mind in which we are invited to sow the seeds of all knowledge. My bold proposal is that the Heads of Secondary Schools from the least to the greatest should adopt a scheme of work following the lines I have indicated, *faute de mieux*, that of the Parents' Union School, and that they should do this for the nation's sake. Mr. Masefield remarks,—

> "There can be no great art without great fable. Great art can only exist where great men brood intensely on something upon which all men brood a little. Without a popular body of fable there can be no unselfish art in

any country. Shakespeare's art was selfish till he turned to the great tales in the four most popular books of his time, Holinshed, North's Plutarch, Cinthio and De Belleforest. Since the newspaper became powerful, topic has supplanted fable and subject comes to the artist untrimmed and unlit by the vitality of many minds."

It is this vitality of many minds that we aim at securing and entreat educational workers and thinkers to join in forming a common body of thought which shall make England great in art no doubt, and also great in life. 278 This is the way to make great men and not by petty efforts to form character in this direction or in that. Let us take it to ourselves that great character comes out of great thoughts, and that great thought must be initiated by great thinkers; then we shall have a definite aim in education. Thinking and not doing is the source of character.

(Here followed a set of examination answers in each form. Space forbids their inclusion but specimen sets can be seen at the P.N.E.U. Office.)

Chapter 3

The Scope of Continuation Schools

A hundred years ago, about the close of the Napole- onic wars, there was such another stirring among the dry bones as we are aware of to-day. All the world knew then, as now, that war was the outcome of the wrong thinking of ignorance, and that education was the nostrum for minds diseased.

Prussia led the way; not the children but the young people were the immediate concern of Statesmen, and, guided by the philosophy of Fichte, and organised under the statesmanship of Stein, that noble league of youth, the Tugendbund, came into being. Prussia was miserably impoverished, but her concern was not with the arts which should make her rich; her young people looked to philosophic principles for precept and to history for example, and, it was well with the land.

Not only in Prussia but throughout western Europe there was a more or less active intellectual renaissance, but, whether because the times were not ripe or the peoples were not worthy, the high ideals of the early days of the century were superseded by the utilitarian motive.

When the 'Continuation School' movement revived, envy of the commercial and manufacturing successes of England actuated the new effort; and already in 1829 a Bavarian statesman had announced that if you would have the fruit you must sow the seed, that is, manufacturing success is to be had only at the cost of technical education.

280   We all know the result in the great Munich schools where first-rate organisation and admirable teaching have produced an appreciable effect upon German industries. But the best German minds have long been aware that "an education which has powerful economic interests behind it is apt to become too narrowly utilitarian in motive and to lose that ideal element which gives all education its chief power over character." As Mr. Lecky has said concerning morals, "the Utilitarian theory is profoundly immoral."

The occasion brought forth the man; we know how in 1900 Dr. Kirschensteiner chanced to see the announcement of a prize offered for an essay on the best way of training youth. He wrote the essay, was crowned by the Academy of his country, and that essay in pamphlet form has influenced opinion and directed action throughout the west: Professors Dewey and Stanley Hall in the United States, Dr. Armstrong and Sir Philip Magnus at home, are among its leading exponents.

And what was the note of this new gospel of education?

Practically that same note which had proceeded from England, France, Switzerland, a century earlier: a utilitarian education should be universal and compulsory; child and adolescent should be "saturated with the spirit of service, provided with the instruments of effective self-direction." Behold, Utopia at hand! every young person fitted, body and soul, for the uses of society; as for his own uses, what he should be in and for himself—why, what matter?

It is not that the eminent educationalists I have referred to would willingly sacrifice the individual youth to society; on the contrary they would raise him, give him place and power, give him opportunity; place his feet on the rungs of that ladder we used to hear about; but we have all been misled by mistaken views as to the function of education. We have believed that knowledge may be derived from sensation, that what we have seen with our eyes and our hands have handled affords us the nutriment our souls demand. No doubt a boy uses his mind to some purpose when he makes, for example, an ingenious model; and, seeing mind at work, we run away with the notion that food and work are synonymous terms; for the body they may be so in a certain sense, for work brings pay and pay buys food, but no such indirect transaction is possible to mind; a mind perpetually at heavy work is a sort of intellectual navvy, whose food must be proportioned to his labour. Our great statesmen, Gladstone, Lord Salisbury and others, knew this, and their wide and deep reading in other matters than politics should not occasion surprise.

281

The War has forced new ideas upon us; we begin, for instance, to realise the avidity of the *adult* mind for instruction; it was startling to read of 1,500 soldier candidates for twenty vacant places in a certain class. We begin to see that mind, the mind of all sorts and conditions of men, requires its rations, wholesome and regularly served. As things are we shall have to see to it that everybody gets fed; but our hope is that henceforth we shall bring up our young people with self-sustaining minds, as well as self-sustaining bodies, by a due ordering of the process of education. We hope so to awaken and direct mind hunger that every man's mind will look after itself.

What is the proper food of mind, has already been discussed but we may assume that education should make our boys and girls rich towards God (we remember the fool of the parable who failed because he was *not* "rich towards God"), rich towards society and rich towards themselves. I will not press my point by urging the moral bankruptcy which has been exposed to us during recent years as co-existent with, if not caused by, utilitarian education; for the catastrophe has been accelerated by the sort of moral madness of which we too have had our seasons in the past,—witness our *Barnaby Rudge* and *Peveril of the Peak* episodes; we have indeed been carried off our feet by a fallacious notion once and again, but our national insanity has on each occasion been short-lived because our education hitherto has not taught us to believe a lie.

We are not worse than others, and if we think well of

ourselves as a nation, why, national pride and personal modesty do not go ill together; in peace-time we have bitter things to say of our British working-man, but all the same he compares favourably with the somewhat sardonic Latin, the sullen Teuton, whom we all know. And the better man does the better work. We have heard much of German efficiency, and perhaps the German excels in little matters like doors that shut, blinds that draw, springs that act, things of domestic utility important in a country with a more extreme climate than ours; but these are little matters and perhaps our failing is, not to do our best except on big occasions; give us a big job or a big war and we show our mettle.

But probably in all our considerable industries we excel. German women will purr over the material of our dresses with "Ach, englisches Tuch!" Well dressed men are English tailored in English cloths. We buy, or bought, things "made in Germany" because they were cheap, but the most costly and most desired goods in German shops are advertised as "englisch."

This is a point to be borne in mind in considering the education of adolescents. We are given to depreciating ourselves and each other, but in fact we have no lee-way to make up; as both a manufacturing and commercial nation we are well in the van and are without inducement to sell the people's birthright for a mess of pottage.

Before I come to the point I desire to make, let us consider whether the problem of Continuation Schools has been attacked anywhere more successfully than in those countries of Middle Europe. Some of them, Germany especially, have done all that is to be done in response to the cry for efficiency with its resultant big returns and high wages; but from the beginning of the Continuation School movement in, say, 1806, the four north-western countries have worked towards different ends. In Denmark they have, not Continuation Schools, but People's High Schools, a pleasanter name for possibly a pleasanter thing.

Denmark, like Germany, was, as we know, devastated by the Napoleonic wars, but had been vitalised by the liberation of its serfs in 1788, and this prepared the ground for Grundtvig, that poet, historian and enthusiast, who became the "Father of the People's High Schools."

"Where there is most life, there is the victory," said he, and the immediate way to an access of life he saw in "A Danish High School accessible to young people all over the land," a school which should inspire "admiration for what is great, love for what is beautiful, faithfulness and affection, peace and unity, innocent cheerfulness, pleasure and mirth." Observe, there is no word of 'efficiency' in this poet's dream, but he did assure Charles VIII that with such a school, "a well of healing in the land," he might afford to smile at the newspapers, whether they chose to praise or blame The King gave heed, begged for a further development of his plans than was afforded in the original pamphlet, and by 1845 the schools he had dreamed of began to be.

We cannot follow the development of these Danish People's Schools, but in 1903-4 their pupils numbered

over three thousand men and rather more women, and
wise men cherished the hope that "the new Danish school   284
for youth is to have the good fortune to blend all classes of
the people into one."

All of these High Schools bear the mark of the genius
of their "Father"—whose pupils have known how to sum
up his teaching in three sayings,—"Spirit is might; Spirit
reveals itself in spirit; Spirit works only in freedom." We
are able to trace the source of these sayings, and indeed this
movement seems to have been from the first profoundly
Christian—Christian in no narrow sense, but sharing the
wide liberality of that *Allegoria filosofica della Religione
Cattolica* conceived by the 'Angelic Doctor' and pictured by
Simone Memmi on the walls of the Spanish chapel in Santa
Maria Novella (Florence): the several teachers commemo-
rated were themselves illustrious pagans but not therefore
the less under Divine teaching. Here, it seems to me, is
an educational *credo* worth reviving in these utilitarian
days, and some such creed seems to have been Grundtvig's,
though probably independently conceived. His great hope
is that "above all, some acquaintance with popular literature,
especially with the poetry and history of one's own country,
will create a brand new world of readers all over the land."

I cannot go into the question of the Agricultural Schools
of which it is said that "the Danish Agricultural School
is the child of the Danish Folkshöjskole, and must, like
this, have Christian faith and national life for its basis." In
the careless days before the War we could all testify to the

excellence of Danish butter, but did we consider the "resolution and capacity" with which Danish peasants passed over
from the making of poor butter in their various small hold-
ings to the "manufacture in co-operative dairies of butter
of an almost uniform fineness"? This, too, says an eminent
Swedish Professor, is due to the High Schools, for, said he,
"Just as the enrichment of the soil gives the best conditions
285   for the seeds sown in it, so a well-grounded humanistic
training provides the surest basis for business capacity, and
not the least so in the case of the coming farmers."* These
are weighty words deserving our consideration at a moment
when we, too, are on the eve of a new departure.

The three neighbouring countries watched the experiments in Denmark with keen interest, and almost
simultaneously People's High Schools sprang up in all four.

These northern High Schools, necessarily winter schools,
were not open at the time of my visit, but two or three
things casually observed might, I think, be traced to their
influence. For instance, Copenhagen itself, as compared
with Munich, strikes one as a city with a soul. At the Hague,
again, I saw an artisan in his working clothes shewing pictures in one of the galleries to his boy of seven who looked
earnestly and listened eagerly. The young people in the
great Delft porcelain works shewed traces of culture and
gentleness in countenance and manner. But nothing struck

---

* cf. *Continuation Schools*, ed. by Sir Michael Sadler, and
published by the Manchester University, 1908, to which the
writer is greatly indebted.

me more than what I saw in the general shop of an out of the way village in Sweden; the villagers were peasants and the one shop sold cabbages and herrings, cheese and calico; but across the small-paned window was a shelf closely packed with volumes in paper covers which had not had time to get dusty; of course I could not read all the titles, but among them were translations from French, German and English. I noticed slim volumes of Scott, Dickens, Thackeray, Ruskin, Carlyle and the last thing out One felt assured that the village was in 'kingdom come,' that of a long winter's evening, in any home, one read aloud whilst the rest worked, that there was much to talk about when friends met and lovers walked. (How sad, by the way, to read that 'Tommy,' whom we all love and revere, is quick 286 to form friendships but that these do not progress for the friends have nothing to talk about.) Think of little plays got up, of public readings given by the villagers themselves; might such things be with us, the lure of the town would cease to draw our village men and maids, for the village that can offer a happy community life, sustained by the people themselves, is able to hold its people.

Our upper and middle classes, professional and other, are singularly stable folk, and they are so, not because of their material but of their intellectual well-being; in this sense only they are most of them the 'Haves' as compared with the 'Have-nots.' The reason is not far to seek. Are there not agitators abroad whose business it is to sow seeds of discontent in the gaping minds of the multitude? The full mind passes on, but that which is empty seizes on *any* new notion with avidity, and is hardly to be blamed for doing so; a hungry mind takes what it can get, and the baker is apt to be lenient about prosecuting the starving man who steals a loaf. I do not hesitate to say that the constantly recurring misery of our age, 'Labour Unrest,' is to be laid at the door, not of the working man, but of the nation which has not troubled itself to consider the natural hunger of mind and the manner of meat such hunger demands.

I have tried to establish that the Kultur offered by the Munich type of Continuation School has had no good effect upon morals or manners and no conspicuously good effect upon manufactures.

That England is under no necessity to follow Germany's lead in this matter for Germany allows our superiority by paying a high price for our goods.

That Denmark and the neighbouring states, on the contrary, excel in those things in which we fall short.

That the People's High Schools of Denmark are worthier of our imitation than the Continuation Schools of Germany.

That they are so because character and conduct, intelligence and initiative, are the outcome of a humanistic education in which the knowledge of God is put first.

But we cannot take educational prescriptions designed for another patient; the Grundtvig Schools are for students ranging from eighteen to twenty-five, not for the more difficult ages from fourteen to eighteen. Again, these

People's High Schools are residential. In countries so largely agricultural it is possible for a great part of the young adult population to spend the five winter months year by year at one of these People's High Schools. Their case and ours do not go on all fours. Our problem is the young adolescent in a country largely manufacturing.

Now, we have received our cloth, and not in ungenerous measure. How shall we cut our coat, that is, how shall we spend those seven or eight hours a week in which "Education" is to do her part for the young citizen? If we take the easiest way, we shall let the boy do what he is doing for the rest of the week,—work for his employer, whether directly, by way of increased output, or indirectly, by way of increased skill. This would be a betrayal. No employer wishes to take with one hand what he gives with the other; besides, what employer doubts the ability of his staff to train his young employees? Again, the technique of any employment takes but little time to understand. It is the practice that is of value, and such practice is—work. Continuation Schools should not exist for technical instruction; they are established definitely for the sort of education of which such instruction forms no part; and will not the evening hours be free as they are at present for technical classes, gymnastic clubs, and various forms of recreative exercise?

This particular gift of *time* must be dedicated to things 288 of the mind if we believe that mind too requires its rations and that to use the mind is by no means the same thing as to feed it.

With the best will in the world to give boys and girls something on which to chew the cud, real mind-stuff for digestion and assimilation, we find that the flood-gates, are opened; an ocean of things good to know overwhelms us and we have—eight hours a week! We seize on that blessed word compromise and see two possibilities: we are in a hurry to make good citizens. Now, good citizens must have sound opinions about law, duty, work, wages, what not; so we pour opinions into the young people from the lips of lecturer or teacher, his opinions, which they are intended to take as theirs. In the next place there is so much to be learned that a selection must needs be made; the teacher makes this selection and the young people are "poured into like a bucket," which, says Carlyle, "is not exhilarating to any soul." Some ground is covered; teachers and Education Authorities are satisfied; and if, when the time comes, the young people leave school discontented and uneasy, if their work bore them and their leisure bore them, if their pleasures are mean and meagre, and if they become men and women rather eager than otherwise for the excitement of a strike, that is because the Continuation, as the Elementary, School will have failed to find them.

This is the real educational difficulty in schools for all classes, for pupils of all ages,—the enormous field of knowledge which it is necessary to cover in order to live with intelligence and moral insight. Know one thing well and you have the power to apprehend many things is the academic solution, which has not worked altogether badly, but it cannot be stretched to fit our present occasion,—the "Enlightenment of the Masses." What we may call the 'academic' doctrine assumes that mind like body is capable of development in various directions by means of due exercise. Profounder educational thought, however, reveals mind to us as of enormous capacity, self-active, present in everyone and making but one demand—its proper pabulum. Feed mind duly and its activities take care of themselves. As the well-fed workman is fit for all his labours, so the duly nourished mind knows, thinks, feels, judges with general righteousness. The good man and magnanimous citizen is he who has been fed with food convenient for him. 289

Such a view of education naturally includes religion, not only "for his God doth instruct him and doth teach him," but because we may take knowledge roughly as of three sorts,—knowledge of God, to be got first-hand through the sacred writings, knowledge of man, to be arrived at through history, poetry, tale; through the customs of cities and nations, civics; through the laws of self-government, morals. One other great branch of knowledge remains. Every youth should know some thing of the flowers of the field, the birds of the air, the stars in their courses, the innumerable phenomena that come under general observation; he should have some knowledge of physics, though chemistry perhaps should be reserved for those who have a vocation that way.

Here are we on the verge of that new life for our country which we all purpose, faced with infinite possibilities on either hand,—the vast range of knowledge and the vast educability of mind. Another certainty presents itself, that we have not time for short cuts: the training of muscle and sense, however necessary, does not nourish mind; and, on the other hand, the verbiage of a lecturer is not assimilated. There is no education but self-education and only as the young student works with his own mind is anything effected.

But we are not without hope. An astounding field has been opened to us; thousands of children in Council Schools are doing incredible things with freedom and joy. They have taken in hand their own education and are greedy of knowledge for its own sake, knowledge in the three great fields that I have indicated.

The fact is that a great discovery has been vouchsafed to us, greater, I think, as concerns education, than any since the invention of the first alphabet. Let us again refer to Coleridge* on the origin of great discoveries. Coleridge gives no qualification to the minds which receive these great ideas, they are not described as great minds, but, he says, they are "previously prepared to receive them," that is, the great ideas. If the reader will forgive me for saying so I think my mind has been so prepared—by extraordinary incapacity in one direction, the direction, roughly, of academic attainments, and by some degree of capacity in other directions, and it has been gradually borne in upon me that this incapacity and this capacity are pretty general,

---

* Page 106 [original pagination].

and perhaps afford a key to the problem of education. A further preparation came to me in unusual opportunities for testing and understanding the minds of children and young people. I am anxious to bring this idea of a discovery before the reader because our methods are so simple and obvious that people are inclined to take them up at random and say that extensive reading is a "good idea which we have all tried more or less" and that free narration "is a good plan in which there is nothing new." It is true that we all read and that narration is as natural as breathing, its value depending solely upon what is narrated. What we have perhaps failed to discover hitherto is the immense hunger for knowledge (curiosity) existing in everyone and the immeasurable power of attention with which everyone is endowed: that everyone likes knowledge best in a literary form: that the knowledge should be exceedingly various concerning many things on which the mind of man reflects;   291 but that knowledge is acquired only by what we may call "the *act of knowing*," which is both encouraged and tested by narration, and which further requires the later test and record afforded by examinations. This is nothing new, you will say, and possibly no natural law in action appears extraordinarily new; we take flying already as a matter of course; but though there is nothing surprising in the action of natural laws, the results are exceedingly surprising, and to that test we willingly submit these methods.

"All is not for all" was the sad conclusion of that Danish patriot and prophet. No doubt Grundtvig thought of the impassable barriers presented by a poor and mean vocabulary and a field of thought without literary background. So "all is not for all" he said, even as a prophet of our own proclaims that a worthy education is only for the *élite*. Books are not for the people, was Grundtvig's conclusion; wherefore those young Danes were lectured to by men of enthusiasm who had their country's literature and history at their fingers' ends and could convey the temper of their own minds. A great deal was effected, but minds nourished at the lips of a teacher have not the stability of those which seek their own meat.

But what if all *were* for all, if the great hope of Comenius—"All knowledge for all men"—were in process of taking shape? This is what we have established in many thousands of cases, even in those of dull and backward children, that any person can understand any book of the right calibre (a question to be determined mainly by the age of the young reader); that the book must be in literary form; that children and young persons require no elucidation of what they read; that their attention does not flag while so engaged; that they master a few pages at a single reading so thoroughly that they can 'tell it back' at the time or months later whether it be the *Pilgrim's Progress* or one of Bacon's Essays or Shakespeare's plays; that they throw individuality into this telling back so that no two tell quite the same tale; that they learn incidentally to write and speak with vigour and style and usually to spell well. Now this art of telling back is *Education* and is very enriching. We all practise it, we go over in our minds the points of a conversation, a lecture, a sermon, an article, and we are so made that only those ideas and arguments which we go over are we able to retain. Desultory reading or hearing is entertaining and refreshing, but is only educative here and there as our attention is strongly arrested. Further, we not only retain but realise, understand, what we thus go over. Each incident stands out, every phrase acquires new force, each link in the argument is riveted, in fact we have performed THE ACT OF KNOWING, and that which we have read, or heard, becomes a part of ourselves, it is assimilated after the due rejection of waste matter. Like those famous men of old we have found out "knowledge meet for the people" and to our surprise it is the best knowledge conveyed in the best form that they demand. Is it possible that hitherto we have all been like those other teachers of the past who were chidden because they had taken away the key of knowledge, not entering in themselves and hindering those who would enter in?

To-day we are in this position. We realise that there is an act of knowing to be performed; that no one can know without this act, that it must be self-performed, that it is as agreeable and natural to the average child or man as singing is to the song thrush, that "to know" is indeed a natural function. Yet we hear of the *incuria* which prevails in most schools, while there before us are the young consumed with the desire to know, can we but find out what they want to know and how they require to be taught.

Humanistic education, whether in English or Latin, 293

affects conduct powerfully; knowledge of this sort is very welcome to children and young persons; a good deal of ground may be covered because a single reading of a passage suffices; this sort of humanistic work has been tried with good effect; and if our Continuation Schools are to be of value they must afford an education on some such lines.

The Parents' Union School, originally organized* for the benefit of children educated at home, is worked by means of programmes followed by examination papers sent out term by term. When the same work, if not the whole of it, was taken up by Council Schools,† the advantage of such an organisation was apparent, especially in that it afforded a common curriculum for children of all classes. By using this curriculum we were enabled to see that the slum child in a poor school compares quite favourably with the child of clever or opulent parents who had given heed to his education.

Now one of our national difficulties is the fact that we have no common basis of thought or ground for reflection. No doubt, by pretty copious reading, links of common interests might be established, and the schoolroom might do at least as much for the general life as does the cricket-pitch. The scheme works practically without a hitch in Council Schools; this is the sort of work that the highest class in these Schools, (in Standard VII), are doing with great success and very great delight. They read English, French and General History (three or four volumes), two or three

* 1890.
† 1913.

books dealing with citizenship and morals from various points of view; Literature, contemporary with the history read (several works); natural history, physical geography and science (three or four books); Scripture (chiefly the Bible). Every term brings a new programme of work, the continuation usually of books already in reading. Children in Secondary Schools and in families remain for one year in Form IV and that work seems adapted to the status of Continuation Schools for the first year or two. After that the more advanced programme (Forms V and VI) might be used in the same way. This work would appeal to young people as being unlike the ordinary school grind, and as giving them opportunity for consecutive speaking and essay writing.

There is probably no better test of a liberal education than the number of names a person is able to use accurately and familiarly as occasion requires. We all recollect a character of Miss Austen's who had no opinion to offer as to whether the Bermudas should be described as the West Indies or not, because she had never called them anything in her life!

Now, here is an alphabetical (uncorrected) list taken from the examination papers of a girl of thirteen, containing 213 proper names, all of them used accurately, easily and with interest.

Amaziah, Ariel, Ayrshire, Arcot, America, Austrian Army, Artemidorus, Antium, Aufidius, Auditors, Apotheosis, Altai Mts., Assouan, Africa, Atbara, Annulosa,

Arachnoida, Armadillo, Albumen, Abdomen, Auricles, Angle, Arc.

Burns (Robert), Bastille, Bombay, Bengal, Burke, Black Hole of Calcutta, British Museum, Benevolence, Basalt, Butterfly, Beetles, Blood-vessels, Berber, Blue Nile Baghdad, Burne Jones.

Cowper, Calcutta, Clive, Canada, Colonel Luttrel, Cleopatra, Candace, Coriolanus, Cassowary, Cormorants, Curlews, Cranes, Calyptra, Cotton grass, Chalk, Conglomerate, Crustacea, Cheiroptera, Carnivora, Chyle, Centre of Circle, China Proper, Canton, Cairo, Cheops, Circe.

'Dick Primrose,' "Deserted Village," Dupleix, Demotic characters, Ducks, Despotic Government, Doctor Livingstone, Deposits, Delta, Diaphragm, Duodenum.

England, East India Company, Economical Reform, Europe, Emperor of Austria, Empress of Russia, Emu, Eastern Turkestan, Egypt.

295   France, Frederick the Great, Frederick William of Prussia, Flightless birds, First Cataract, Foraminifera.

Gadarenes, Gizeh, Great Commoner, George III, General Warrants, Governor General, Grace and Free-will, Greek language, Generosity, Gulls, Granite, Grubs, Gastric juice, Globules.

Huldah, Highlands of Scotland, Herodotus, Hieroglyphics, Herons, Hoang-ho, Hedgehog, Hydrochloric Acid, Hydrocarbons, Heart.

Isaiah, India, Influence of light.

Josiah, Judah, Jehosaphat, Jerusalem, Jonas, Jonah, Jesuits, Jansenists, Japan.

Künersdorf, Kuen Lun Mts., Kioto, Karnac, Khartum, Kolcheng, Kalabari.

Lord North, "Lords in Waiting" of Love, Land birds, Lamellae, Luxor, Lake Ngami, Loanda, Lake Nyassa.

Manasseh, Mongolia, Manchuria, Madras, Mahrattas, Member of Parliament, Middlesex, Methodists, Mississippi Company, Maria Theresa, Mummies, Microscopic Shells, Membrane.

Nagasaki, Nile, Nitrogenous food.

'Olivia Primrose,' Ostriches.

Pharisees, 'Primrose (Mrs.),' Philosophers Plassey, Pitt, Prime Minister, Pragmatic Sanction, Prague, Peace of Hubertusburg, Pity, Puffins, Penguins, Plovers, Pelicans, Plants, Polytrichum formosum, Peristom, Porphyric, Puddingstone, Pepsin, Peptone, Pancreas, Pulmonary artery, Pamir Plateau, Prairies, Pyramid, Portuguese West Africa.

Quilemane.

Rome, Rossbach, Rosetta Stone, Rhea, Rodentia.

Sea of Galilee, 'Sophia Primrose,' Surajah Dowlah, Seven Years' War, Silesia, Saxony, Secretary, Storks, Sandpipers, Seedlings.

"The Task," Treaty of Dresden, Tullus, Trade Unions, Trustees, Treasurer, Tropical countries.

Ulysses, Ungulata.

Volcanic eruptions, Vermes, Vertebrate, Villi,

Ventricles, Vernae Cavae, Vicar of Wakefield, Volscians, Vice President.

Wallace, Walpole, War of Independence, Wilkes, Whitfield, Wesley, War of the Austrian Succession, Water birds, Wady Halfa.

Yang-tse-kiang.

Zonga, Zambesi, Zorndorff.

296   This is 'Secondary' work, but supposing the young people of a Continuation School, who could not read all the books on the programmes, got some degree of intimacy, some association, with, say, one hundred such names in a term, we might believe that they were receiving a liberal education. This is the sort of work we hope to see done in Continuation Schools by pupils from fourteen to sixteen. The young people of the future between sixteen and eighteen should be prepared to work in Forms V and VI.

It is not the best children that answer the examination questions; the general rule is that everybody takes every question. I have touched only on the more humanistic subjects as whatever is done in Mathematics, for instance, the Head of the Continuation School will no doubt arrange; and indeed so much has been done in the Elementary School already that probably the keeping of fictitious account books would be a sufficient exercise for young people who show some mathematical talent.

No cost whatever is attached to the adoption and continued working of this method* except the cost of books

---

* In Elementary and Continuation Schools.

and of these, young wage-earners would no doubt buy their own, so that by degrees each would form his little library of books that he has read, understands and knows his way about. I should like to quote a few sentences from Professor Eucken on the education of the people:—

> "By education of the people it must not for a moment be supposed that we mean a special kind of education. We do not refer to a condensed preparation of our spiritual and intellectual possessions, suitable for the needs and interests of the great masses; we are not thinking of a diluted concoction of the real draught of education which we are so kind and condescending as to dispense to the majority. No! . . . there is only one education common to us all." "We can all unite in the construction of a spiritual world over against that of petty human routine. Thus there is, in truth, a possibility of a truly human education, and therefore of a true education of the people."

The Jena Professor sees clearly enough the task before us all; but he sees, or sets forth, no possible way of accomplishing it, nor is there any other way than that which we have set forth that can afford this sort of liberal education; the electric telegraph was not discovered twice over.

After all our protests we are in our way utilitarian for no other study is so remunerative as that of the 'humanities.' Let me draw the reader's attention to one point. Instability, unrest, among our wage-earners is the serious danger threatening our social life. Now it is said that nothing can act but where it is and the class which acts steadily where it is, at some outpost of empire, on a home estate, in Parliament, where you will, is the class educated at Public Schools, that is, men brought up on the 'humanities.' Strong language will be used about the deadness and decadence of these men although they do much of our national work. Their defects are obvious and manifold, but still, as I say, the public work that is done is, for the most part, done by men whom no one could describe as progressive. Is there not some confusion of ideas about this fetish of progress? Do we not confound progress with movement, action, assuming that where these are there is necessarily advance? Whereas much of our activity is like the waves of the sea, going always and arriving never. What we desire is the still progress of growth that comes of root striking downwards and fruit urging upwards. And this progress in character and conduct is not attained through conditions of environment or influence but only through the growth of ideas, received with conscious intellectual effort.

It will be possible to have only a little of this strong meat in Continuation Schools, but a little goes a long way, how far, our Public School men illustrate; for a careful analysis will bring us to the conclusion that not Latin and Greek, Games, Athletics, or environment, but the 'humanities' in English alone will bring forth the stability and efficiency which we desire to see in all classes of society.

I have said that we have after all a generous allowance of cloth from which to cut our garment, seven or eight hours

298

a week. In that time we may get in, page for page, book for book, as full a complement of the 'humanities,' poetry, history, essay, tragedy, comedy, philosophy, between the ages of fourteen and eighteen, as our public men have imbibed at their schools. To be sure these do it in the classic tongues while for those there is only plain English; but however duly we magnify Greek literature we cannot honestly say that that of England is second to any the world has yet seen. We can give to the people the thought of the best minds and we can secure on their part the conscious intellectual effort, the act of knowing, which bears fruit in capability, character and conduct. We cannot offer to the people the grace of scholarship in the allotted time, but no doubt earnest souls will find a way to get this surpassing excellence also; if there be profit in 'grinding at Grammar' that they must forego, too, but the inspiration and delight of entering into an intellectual world full of associations, this they should have, a well of healing and fountain of delight.

Now a common ground of thought is inestimable in what may be called its cohesive value; and what we desire to afford to the nation at large is such another background of thought, sketched in like that of the Public School man from the books men and women have read at school, books which made them intimate with Pitt and Fox, 'Dick Swiveller,' 'Mrs. Quickly,' with daffodils and clouds and nightingales as the poets have seen them, with a thousand promiscuous and seemingly purposeless scenes and sayings which somehow combine to serve the purpose of a 299 background throwing the thoughts and incidents of to-day into clear relief. For this reason we, like the Public Schools, all read the same books, with such an intensive single reading that for the rest of the lives of these young people phrases or allusions they come across will kindle in their eyes that 'light which never was on sea or land.' We may hope that Public Schools will presently add this modicum of English to their classical studies; then the candidate for election will have something to appeal to other than the desire to better himself, which is supposed to dominate every man. By the way, is the paucity of literary or historical allusions, not in Latin, to be heard in the House due to the fact that the audience cannot be counted upon to rise to a reference not included in the well-known school books? If so, we shall change all that; once the *masses* read, the *classes* must read, too, and the Peace will be signalised by a new bond of intellectual life in common.

"There is no more dreadful sight," says Goethe, "than ignorance in action," and is not this the sight that is at the present time dismaying us all? Demos is king to-day, and who may dispute his right? But let us all give him the chance to become that philosopher-king who according to an ancient dream was to be the fit ruler, or rulers, of the people. The hopeful sign is that Demos himself perceives his lack, and clamours for the humanistic education in which he sees his salvation.

Chapter 4

*The Basis of National Strength**

A LIBERAL EDUCATION FROM A NATIONAL STANDPOINT

I

KNOWLEDGE

We have from time to time given some atten- 300 tion to the failure of our attempts to educate "The Average Boy," and it may be useful to look into one or two fundamental principles upon which this question and others seem to me to depend. For if our conceptions of education are heterogeneous and incoherent, naturally, we shall have a tangle of examination schemes evolved to test our ill-conceived work.

Educationally, we are in a bad way. We were told some

---

* The Author owes to the Editor of *The Times* permission to reprint the chapters under this heading written in 1912; as also the happy titles of the several chapters and the general title.

time ago, in *Across the Bridges*, of the rapid deterioration of the bright intelligent responsive schoolboy who has passed through the sixth and seventh standards. Why? we ask. Industrial unrest often reveals virtue, even heroism of a sort, in the working man, but a lamentable want of knowledge—lack of education; he appears to have little insight, imagination, or power of reflection. The tendency in his class is that "dangerous tendency which we must all do our best to resist" indicated by Mr. Burns at a public meeting some few years ago; "the spirit of the horde," he said, "is being developed; and whether it is in exhibitions, sports, or legislation, the individual is becoming less and less important and the mob more and more so." And again, "the tendency of the present day in all modern movements is for great crowds to be brought together to see other people play; and that is extending not only to play, but to other fields of life." Could the industrial movement of to-day be better diagnosed? Again we ask, Why? As for those young men from Public Schools who fail in the Dominions, enough has been said about them; but those other Public School men who succeed in a measure at outposts of the Empire because of the virtue that is in them, do they not fail sometimes in an equal measure for lack of the insight, imagination, intelligence, which come of knowledge? As for the people who stay at home, "educated" men and women, I write as an old woman who remembers how in the sixties and seventies "countenance" was much talked of; "an intelligent countenance," "a fine countenance," "a noble countenance," were matters of daily comment. The word has dropped out of use; is it because the thing signified has dropped out of existence? Countenance is a manifestation of thought, feeling, intelligence; and it is none of these, but stolid indifference combined with physical well-being, that we read in many faces to-day.

If we have these grounds for discontent, education is no doubt the culprit at the bar, though there never was, I suppose, a more heroic and devoted body of teachers at work. They get for themselves the greater blessing of those who give; but the children suffer, poor little souls; "poured into like a bucket," they receive without stint, and little comes of it. There is no lack of zeal on the part of the teaching profession, but there is a tendency amongst us to depreciate knowledge and to depreciate our scholars. Now, knowledge is the material of education, as flour is the material of bread; there are substitutes for knowledge, no doubt, 302 as there are for flour. Before the era of free meals I heard of a little girl in East London whose mother gave her a penny, to buy dinner for herself and her little sister, when the two set out for school. The child confided to her teacher that a ha'porth of aniseed drops "stays your stomach" more than a halfpenny bun. Now, our schools are worked more or less upon aniseed drops—marks, prizes, scholarships, blue ribbons, all of which "stay the stomach" of the boy who does not get the knowledge that he needs. That is the point. He needs knowledge as much as he needs bread and milk; his appetite for knowledge is as healthy as his appetite for his dinner; and an abundant regular supply at short intervals of various knowledge is a constitutional necessity for the growing youth as well as for the curious child; and yet we stay his hunger pangs upon "aniseed drops."

We do worse. We say, "What is the good of knowledge? Give a boy professional instruction, whether he is to be a barrister or a bricklayer, and strike out from his curriculum Greek or geography, or whatever is not of utilitarian value. Teach him to play the game and handle the ropes of his calling, and you have done the best for him." Now, here is a most mischievous fallacy, an assertion that a child is to be brought up for the uses of society only and not for his own uses. Here we get the answer to the repeated question that suggested itself in a survey of our educational condition. We launch children upon too arid and confined a life. Now personal delight, joy in living, is a chief object of education; Socrates conceived that knowledge is for pleasure, in the sense, not that knowledge is one source, but is the source of pleasure.

It is for their own sakes that children should get knowledge. The power to take a generous view of men and their motives, to see where the greatness of a given character lies, to have one's judgment of present events illustrated and corrected by historic and literary parallels, to have, indeed, the power of comprehensive judgment—these are admirable assets within the power of every one according to the measure of his mind; and these are not the only gains which knowledge affords. The person who can live upon his own intellectual resources and never know a dull hour (though anxious and sad hours will come) is indeed enviable in these days of intellectual inanition, when we depend upon spectacular entertainments *pour passer le temps*.

If knowledge means so much to us, "What is knowledge?" the reader asks. We can give only a negative answer. Knowledge is not instruction, information, scholarship, a well-stored memory. It is passed, like the light of a torch, from mind to mind, and the flame can be kindled at original minds only. Thought, we know, breeds thought; it is as vital thought touches our minds that our ideas are vitalized, and out of our ideas comes our conduct of life. The case for reform hardly needs demonstration, but now we begin to see the way of reform. The direct and immediate impact of great minds upon his own mind is necessary to the education of a child. Most of us can get into touch with original minds chiefly through books; and if we want to know how far a school provides intellectual sustenance for its scholars, we may ask to see the list of books in reading during the current term. If the list be short, the scholar will not get enough mind-stuff; if the books are not various, his will not be an all-round development; if they are not original, but compiled at second hand, he will find no material in them for his intellectual growth. Again, if they are too easy and too direct, if they tell him straight away what he is to think, he will read, but he will not appropriate. Just as a man has to eat a good dinner in order that his physical energies may be stimulated to select and secrete that small portion which

304 is vital to him, so must the intellectual energies be stimulated to extract what the individual needs by a generous supply, and also by a way of presentation that is not obvious. We have the highest authority for the indirect method of teaching proper to literature, and especially to poetry. The parables of Christ remain dark sayings; but what is there more precious in the world's store of knowledge?

How injurious then is our habit of depreciating children; we water their books down and drain them of literary flavour, because we wrongly suppose that children cannot understand what we understand ourselves; what is worse, we explain and we question. A few pedagogic maxims should help us, such as, "Do not explain" "Do not question," "Let one reading of a passage suffice," "Require the pupil to relate the passage he has read." The child must read to know; his teacher's business is to see that he knows. All the acts of generalization, analysis, comparison, judgment, and so on, the mind performs for itself in the act of knowing. If we doubt this, we have only to try the effect of putting ourselves to sleep by relating silently and carefully, say, a chapter of Jane Austen or a chapter of the Bible, read once before going to bed. The degree of insight, the visualization, that comes with this sort of mental exercise is surprising.

As I have said, a child in his seventh year will relate *The Pilgrim's Progress*, chapter by chapter, though he cannot read it, and some half-dozen other books of the best we can find for him. In his eighth or ninth year he works happily with a dozen books at a time, books of history, adventures, travels, poems. From his tenth to his twelfth year he reads considerable books of English and French history, seriously written, Shakespeare's historical plays. North's *Plutarch's Lives*, and a dozen other worthy books. As he goes up the school, his reading becomes wider and more difficult, but every one knows the reading proper at the ages of fifteen, seventeen, eighteen. The right books are given, but not enough of them. The reading dietary is too meagre for the making of a full man. A score of first-rate books should appear in the school curriculum term by term. The point that I insist upon, however, is that from his sixth year the child should be an "educated child" for his age, should love his lesson books, and enjoy a terminal examination on the books he has read. Children brought up largely on books compare favourably with those educated on a few books and many lectures; they have generous enthusiasms, keen sympathies, a wide outlook and sound judgment, because they are treated from the first as beings of "large discourse looking before and after." They are persons of leisure too, with time for hobbies, because their work is easily done in the hours of morning school.

It is not necessary to speak of modern languages and mathematics, field work in natural history, handiwork, etc. Schools are pretty much agreed about the treatment of these subjects. As for Latin and Greek, the teaching of these and the possibility of getting in any work beyond these is a crucial question; but I think it is open to Public Schoolmasters to discover that, given boys who have read

305

and thought, and who have maintained the habit of almost perfect attention that a child begins with, the necessary amount of work in the Classics may be done in a much shorter time, and that the mind of the pupil is the more alert because it is engaged in handling various subjects.

Perhaps, too, some enlightened Headmaster may come to distinguish between scholarship and knowledge—a distinction which practical men, like Napoleon, for example, have known how to draw. Probably there never was a life on which the 'humanities' exercised a more powerful influence; rarely has there been such an example of the power of the informed mind to conquer the world. Napoleon is the final answer to the contention that a knowledge of books has no practical value, for there was, perhaps, no incident in his career that was not suggested, inspired, illustrated by some historical precedent, some literary apophthegm. He was, as we know, no scholar, but he read diligently, even in the midst of absorbing affairs, Homer, the Bible, the Koran, poetry, history, Plutarch.

Nations grow great upon books as truly as do individuals. We know how that heroic young Queen, Louisa of Prussia, perceived that the downfall of her country was not due to Napoleon alone, but also to national ignorance, and that if Prussia were to rise it must be through the study of history. So she set herself to work at the history of modern Europe during that sojourn at Memel, when she knew poverty as a peasant woman knows it. The disciples of Kant founded a league of virtue to arouse Prussian students to the duty of patriotism; Fichte knew how to issue a trumpet call; the nation became a nation of students, and the son of Queen Louisa established the German Empire! Alas, that an age should have come when the 'humanities' were proscribed on German soil—and humanity followed them into exile! A noble view of education was as righteousness exalting a nation; but, alas, we all know what universal havoc and disaster have proceeded from the debased and materialised theory of education promulgated at Munich.

The Danes, again, as we all know, owe their rise out of illiteracy to the Napoleonic impulse. After we had seized their battleships, by way of clipping the claws of Bonaparte, they set to work to make themselves the first farmers in Europe; this they have done in and through their schools and their continuation schools, where they get, not technical instruction, but a pretty wide course in history and literature. As for the Japanese revolution of some fifty years ago, history has little to show of a finer quality; and this, again, was the work of a literary people.

If we would not be left behind by the East and the West we must, as other nations have done, "add to our virtue, knowledge"; and we are still competent, as some of these are not, to mount from the bottom rung of the Apostolic educational ladder. It rests with us to add to our faith, virtue, and to our virtue, knowledge. It is an unheard of thing that the youth of a great nation should grow up without those ideals, slow enough in maturing, which are to be gathered for the most part from wide and wisely directed reading.

II

LETTERS, KNOWLEDGE AND VIRTUE

The following fragments of a valuable letter illustrate the contention of the foregoing chapter:—

"There is one thing, however, one note of regret, and that is that one paragraph, that on classical education, was not more expanded. I am satisfied that your central view covers the whole truth; and I am going to give you a small individual experience illustrating this fact—viz., that an early education in the great books of our own language, read, with enjoyment, by children and appropriately given to them from year to year, is the true groundwork of later expansion. Here is the story:—My three daughters were suckled on Walter Scott and Shakespeare. Later, about the ages of from ten to twelve, off their own, they took up Plutarch's Lives, Bunyan, Defoe, and in the same period they refused to learn arithmetic and geography, the former on the ground of its monotony, and the latter, because, although they loved it, they held that the existing system of teaching geography was 'rotten,' and that geography ought to be learnt by going to the places. I knew better than to remonstrate. I meekly suggested that perhaps they would substitute something else in their curriculum, and they said at once, in an obviously prepared sentence, 'That's just it, we want to learn Latin and harmony.' Now here comes *your* point (in that lamentably abbreviated paragraph):—

'Given boys (or girls) who have read and thought, 308
and who have maintained the habit of almost perfect
attention that a child begins with, the necessary amount
of work in the classics may be done in a much shorter
time, and the mind of the pupil is the more alert because
it is engaged in handling various subjects.'

Six months later these girls knew more Latin than I
learnt in six years under distinguished scholars with very
eminent names. They could sling passages from Horace
appropriately; they knew the first two Eclogues and half
the Aeneid by heart; they regarded Cicero's Letters to
Atticus as a 'penny post' affair, and were quite unduly
familiar with the private life of Seneca. But all this did
not interfere with their painting or their horsemanship,
and better authorities on cricket and the Turf I don't
happen to know. That is the illustrative episode. The
point, in my mind, is that an early education from great
books with the large ideas and the large virtues is the
only true foundation of knowledge—the knowledge
worth having."

This interesting letter brings us straight to a question
which I thought had been pretty fully threshed out; and
I tackle it with diffidence, only because an outsider may
see aspects overlooked by experts. The gist of the charges
brought against Public Schools is,—Classics take up so
much time that there is no opportunity for *Litterae Hu-
maniores* in any other form. It is easy to say,—Gain time

by giving up Greek; but, in the first place, Public Schools, with our old Universities in sequence, are our educational achievement. Other efforts are experimental, but this one thing we know—that men are turned out from this course who are practically unmatched for quality, culture, and power; even the average B.A. shows up better than his compeers, and a degree in Arts signifies more than one in any other faculty.

We return thus to my original contention—that letters, primarily, are the content of knowledge; that if Wellington ever said how Waterloo was won, it was not on the playing-fields only, but in the class-rooms of Eton; that Caesar, Thucydides, *Prometheus Bound*, have won more battles than we know on fields civil and military. A little strong meat goes a long way, and even the average Public School boy turns out a capable man. But, alas, if capable, he is also ignorant; he does not know the history and literature of his own country or any other. He has not realised that knowledge is, not a store, but rather a state that a person remains within or drops out of. His degree taken, he shuts his books, reads the newspapers a little, perhaps a magazine or two, but otherwise occupies himself with the interests of sports, games, shows, or his employment. What is to be done, we wonder vaguely, to secure to this average boy some tincture of knowledge and some taste for knowledge? The expedient of dropping Greek to make room for other things recurs; but on reflection we say, "No"; for culture begins with the knowledge that everything has been known and everything has been perfectly said these two thousand years ago and more. This knowledge, slowly drummed into a youth, should keep him from swelled head, from joining in the "We are the people" cry of the blatant patriot; and there is no better way of knowing a people than to know something of their own words in their own speech.

It is well, by the way, that we should remember that we have as a nation an enormous loss to make good; time was, and not so long ago, when rich and poor were intimately familiar with one of the three great classical literatures. Men's thoughts were coloured, their speech moulded, their conduct more or less governed, by the pastoral idylls called "Genesis," the impassioned poetry of Isaiah, the divine philosophy of John, the rhetoric of Paul—all, writings, like the rest of the Bible, in what Matthew Arnold calls "the grand manner." Here is the well of English undefiled from which men have drawn the best that our literature holds, as well as their philosophy of life, their philosophy of history, and that principal knowledge we are practising to do without— 310 the knowledge of God. And we wonder that the governing classes should forget how to rule as those who serve; and that the working man, brought up on "Readers" in lieu of a great literature, should act with the obstinate recklessness proper to ignorance.

But to return to the main issue. How shall we instruct the ignorance and yet retain the classical culture of the average Public School boy? I should like to suggest, again, with diffidence, that he, like his more brilliant compeer, is driven through a mill the outpour of which should be scholarship. Now, scholarship is an exquisite distinction which it would be ill for us as a nation to miss; but if all the men in an assemblage were decorated, who would care to wear an order? Some things are precious for their rarity, and to put a school in the running for this goal is as absurd as the ambition of the little boy who meant to be a Knight of the Garter when he grew up. The thing is not to be done; some men are born to be scholars, as the shape of their heads testifies. The rest of us take pleasure in their decoration, but are not envious, for scholarship is not the best thing, and does not necessarily imply that vital touch of mind upon mind out of which is got knowledge. As for erudition, we may leave that out of count, it is hardly even an aim at the present time. The geniuses, as one to some thousands, say, of our best, do not trouble themselves much about the regimen we offer—classics or modern languages, or what not; an idle tale, a puppet show, the meanest flower that blows, is enough for them. Anyway, they take care of themselves, and we come back to the average boy.

He must learn his Greek and Latin, but there is an easier way; the girls mentioned in the letter I cite had hit upon it. That favourite girl pupil of Vittorino's who spoke and wrote Greek with "remarkable purity" at twelve, having, so to speak, done with Latin at an earlier age—she, we may be sure, had not been through the grammar school grind. Nor had any of the learned ladies of the Italian and the French Renaissance, the list of whose accomplishments leaves us

311

breathless. While still children, we know how early they married, their knowledge of the classics was copious (and not too wholesome), they knew two or three modern languages, could treat the wounded, nurse the sick, prepare simples, govern great households, ride to chase, yes, and kill too! and do exquisite embroidery. Our own women of the Tudor times appear likewise to have been "infinitely informed" and to have carried their learning gaily; Maria Theresa, by no means a learned lady, could make speeches and converse with her Magyar nobles in Latin, and they could respond, neither knowing the native speech of the other. If these things were true of girls and women, how much more was expected of boys and men!

Are we persons of less intelligence, or how did they do it all? *Every preparatory school knows how.* Perhaps few boys enter Public Schools who could not pass "Responsions," that is, who are not, as far as Greek goes, ready for Oxford. I once heard a Headmaster say:—

> "A boy does as much Latin now by the age of twelve as he will ever need for examination purposes, and he spends the next eight years in doing over again and again the same work! A clever boy of twelve could easily pass Responsions."

A headmaster in Newfoundland mentions in his school report for 1905 a boy who "began Greek in October and passed the Oxford Responsions in January."

There is a leakage somewhere, and there is overlapping, and both are due to the examinations upon which scholarships are awarded. Something must be done, because Public Schools, with all their splendid records, are 312 not effective in the sense that they turn out the average boy a good all-round man. For better or for worse, who knows? the Democracy is coming in like a flood, and our old foundations will be tossed about in the welter unless we make haste to strengthen our weak places. Might not a commission—consisting of two or three headmasters, as many preparatory school masters, University "Dons," and public men (once public school boys and now the fathers of such boys) look into the question and devise examination tests which shall safeguard Letters, ancient and modern, without putting too high a premium upon scholarship?

Once the hands of schoolmasters were united, they would no doubt devise means by which our friend, the average boy, would get such a knowledge of the classics as should open life-long resources to him. Like the 'Baron of Bradwardine' he would go about with a pocket Livy (as he would say, "Titus Livius,") to be read, not laboured at a few lines at a time: *The Seven against Thebes, Iphigenia in Aulis,* the few tragedies left to us by the great dramatists would form part of the familiar background of his thoughts. He would know somewhat of the best that has been written in Greek and Latin, whether through printed translations or through the text itself rendered in the sort of running translation which some masters know how to give. *Pari passu*, he would do his share of gerund-grind, and construe the two or three books of his present limited acquaintance. But his limitations would be recognised, and he would not be required to turn out Greek and Latin verse.

Meantime his master will require him to know pretty intimately a hundred worthy books in addition to the great novels—to be read in class periods, in vacation, and in leisure time—his knowledge of each to be tested by a single bit of oral description or written work in verse or prose. "Ground he at Grammar," sums up every successful school boy's record as it did that of the dead "Grammarian"; but the ten or twelve years of school life should yield more than this.

313

I say nothing now about the teaching of science, for which most schools provide, except that for our generation, science seems to me to be the way of intellectual advance. All the same, the necessity incumbent upon us at the moment is to inculcate a knowledge of *Letters*. Men and their motives, the historical sequence of events, principles for the conduct of life, in fact, practical philosophy, is what the emergencies of the times require us to possess, and to be able to communicate. These things are not to be arrived at by any short cut of economics, eugenics, and the like, but are the gathered harvests of many seasons' sowing of poetry, literature, history. The nation is in sore need of wise men, and these must be made out of educated boys.

III

KNOWLEDGE, REASON, AND REBELLION

We have been very busy about education these sixty years or more—diligently digging, pruning, watering; but there is something amiss with our tree of knowledge; its fruits, both good and evil, are of a mean, crabbed sort, with so little to choose between them that superior persons find it hard to determine which is which. To examine the individual apples would be a long process, but let me take one at a venture: is it not true that a conviction of irresponsibility characterises our generation?

If this be true, seeing that we all think as we have been brought up to think, our education is at fault. Faulty education is to blame if private property be recklessly injured in broad day, if working men do vital injury to their country thinking to serve their caste, if there be people who love to have it so, as long as their own interests are immune. The melancholy fact is that the people who do damage to private property, to public interests, and to that more delicate asset of a nation, public opinion, are all by way of being educated in their several degrees. All of them can write and speak clearly, think logically if not sincerely, and exhibit a certain practical ability. It is true that the War has changed much and has brought us a temporary salvation, but education must secure to us our gains or the last state of the nation may be worse than the first.

No doubt we are better and not worse than our forefathers; and, where we err, it is through ignorance. "Through ignorance ye did it," was said of the worst crime that men have done; and that appalling offence was wrought for no worse reason than because it is the habit of more or less lettered ignorance to follow specious arguments to logical conclusions. The sapient East knows all about it. Lady Lugard tells us how "the Copts have a saying that 'in the beginning when God created things He added to everything its second.' 'I go to Syria,' said Reason; 'I go with you,' said Rebellion." We need not follow the other pairs that went forth, but still Reason is apt to be accompanied by Rebellion when it sets out in search of a logical issue.

For it is a fatal error to think that reason can take the place of knowledge, that reason is infallible, that reasonable conclusions are of necessity right conclusions. Reason is a man's servant, not his master; and behaves like a good and faithful servant—a sort of 'Caleb Balderstone,' ready to lie royally in his master's behoof—and bring logical demonstration of any premiss which the will chooses to entertain. But the will is the man, the will chooses; and the man must *know*, if the will is to make just and discriminating decisions. This is what Shakespeare, as great a philosopher as a poet, set himself to teach us, line upon line, precept upon precept. His 'Leontes,' 'Othello,' 'Lear,' 'Prospero,' 'Brutus,' 315 preach on the one text—that a man's reason brings certain infallible proofs of any notions he has wilfully chosen to take up. There is no escape for us, no short cut; art is long, especially the art of living.

In the days when the working man represented only

the unit of his family he picked up enough knowledge to go on with at church and chapel, by scrutinizing his neighbour's doings, in the village parliament, held at pump or "public," from the weekly news-sheet. But we have changed all that: bodies of working men have learned by means of union to act with a momentum which may be paralysing or propelling *according to whether the men have or have not knowledge*. Without knowledge, Reason carries a man into the wilderness and Rebellion joins company. The man is not to be blamed: it is a glorious thing to perceive your mind, your reasoning power, acting of its own accord as it were and producing argument after argument in support of any initial notion; how is a man to be persuaded, when he wakes up to this tremendous power he has of involuntary reasoning, that his conclusions are not necessarily right, but rather that he who reasons without knowledge is like a child playing with edged tools? Following his reason, he acquires this and the other sort of freedom; but is it not written:—

> "Nor yet
> (Grave this upon thy heart!) if spiritual things
> Be lost through apathy, or scorn, or fear,
> Shalt thou thy humbler franchises support.
> However hardly won or justly dear."

If, then, the manners and the destinies of men are shaped by knowledge, it may be well to inquire further into the nature of that evasive entity. Matthew Arnold helps us by offering a threefold classification which appeals to common sense—knowledge of God, knowledge of men, and knowl- 316 edge of the natural world; or, as we should say, Divinity, the Humanities, and Science. But I think we may go further and say that Letters, if not (as I said before) the main content of knowledge, constitute anyway the container-—the wrought salver, the exquisite vase, even the alabaster box to hold the ointment.

If a man cannot think without words, if he who thinks with words will certainly express his thoughts, what of the monosyllabic habit that is falling upon men of all classes? The chatter of many women and some men does not count, for thought is the last thing it is meant to express. The Greeks believed that a training in the use and power of words was the chief part of education, recognising that if the thought fathers the word, so does the word in turn father the thought. They concerned themselves with no language, ancient or modern, save their own, but of that they acquired a consummate appreciation. With the words came the great thoughts, expressed in whatever way the emergencies of the State called for—in wise laws, victorious battles, glorious temples, sculpture, drama. For great thoughts anticipate great works; and these come only to a people conversant with the great thoughts that have been written and said. In what strength did the youngest and greatest of our Premiers bring about the "revival of England"? He was fortified by illimitable reading, by a present sense of a thousand impossibilities that had been brought to pass—of a thousand things so wisely said that wise action was a necessary outcome. To say that we as a nation are suffering from our contemptuous depreciation of knowledge is to say that we scorn Letters, the proper vehicle of *all* knowledge.

Let us glance at the three departments of knowledge to see in regard to which of the three we are most in error. Some of us are content with such knowledge of Divinity as is to be picked up from the weekly sermon heard in church, but even with the qualification of a degree in Arts I wonder do our divines lift us as much as they might into that serener region where words fitly spoken beget thoughts of peace and holy purpose? That worship is the main end of our Church services is a sublime ideal, but, "The Way, without which there is no going, the Truth, without which there is no knowing, the Life, without which there is no living," must needs be set before us in "words that burn," and we wait for preachers like those of a bygone day, "Whose pulpit thunders shook a nation's soul."

It is possible that the Church may err in keeping us underfed upon that knowledge which is life, but she does not send us away empty. We get some little share, too, of literature, poetry, history: a phrase, a line, lights up a day for us; to read of Charles Fox's having said, "Poetry's everything," of that black conqueror of the Soudan who said, "Without learning life would have neither pleasure nor savour"—these things do us good, we cannot tell why.

But there is a region of apparent sterility in our

intellectual life. Science says of literature, "I'll none of it," and science is the preoccupation of our age. Whatever we study must be divested to the bone, and the principle of life goes with the flesh we strip away: history expires in the process, poetry cannot come to birth, religion faints; we sit down to the dry bones of science and say, Here is knowledge, all the knowledge there is to know. "I think that is very wonderful," a little girl wrote in an examination paper after trying to explain why a leaf is green. That little girl had found the principle—admiration, wonder—which makes science vital, and without wonder her highest value is, not spiritual, but utilitarian. A man might as well collect matchboxes, like those charming people in one of Anatole France's novels, as search for diatoma, unless the wonder of the world be ever fresh before his eyes. In the eighteenth century science was alive, quick with emotion, and therefore it found expression in literature. Still, a Lister, a Pasteur, moves us, and we feel that in one department of science, anyway, men stirred by the passion of humanity ("letters" at the fountain head?) are doing monumental work.

But for the most part science as she is taught leaves us cold; the utility of scientific discoveries does not appeal to the best that is in us, though it makes a pretty urgent and general appeal to our lower avidities. But the fault is not in science—that mode of revelation which is granted to our generation, may we reverently say?—but in our presentation of it by means of facts and figures and demonstrations that mean no more to the general audience than the point demonstrated, never showing the wonder and magnificent reach of the law unfolded. The Hebrew poet who taught us that "Breadcorn is bruised . . . because his God doth instruct him and doth teach him," glorified life. Coleridge has revealed the innermost secret, whether of science or literature: speaking on the genesis of an idea, he says, "When the idea of Nature (presented to chosen minds by a Higher Power than Nature herself)," etc. The man who would write for us about the true inwardness of wireless telegraphy, say, how truly it was a discovery, a revealing of that which was there and had been there all along, might make our hearts burn within us. No doubt there are many scientific men who are also men of letters, and some scientific books as inspiring as great poems—but science is waiting for its literature; and, though we cannot live in shameful ignorance and must get what we can out of the sources open to us, science as it is too commonly taught tends to leave us crude in thought and hard and narrow in judgment.

319   We are told that in times of great upheaval it profits not to cast blame on this or that section of the community; that we are all to blame even for the offences of individuals; and we partly believe it because our fathers have told us; thus did the prophets humble themselves before God, and bemoaned each his exceeding great sin in the sin of his people. We, too, are meek under chastisements, but we are vague and, to that extent, insincere. Perhaps our duty is to give serious thought to the problems of our national life; then we may come to realise that man does not live by

bread alone; we may perceive that "bread" (or cake!) is our sole and final offer to all persons of all classes; that we are losing our sense of any values excepting money values; that our young men no longer see visions, and are attracted to a career in proportion as "there's money in it." Nothing can come out of nothing, and, if we bring up the children of the nation on sordid hopes and low ambitions, need we be surprised that every man plays for his own hand?

We recognise now and then, when the shoe pinches, that the nation is in the threes of a revolution, but do we take trouble to find out the cause of "industrial unrest" and the correct attitude of the public towards that unrest? The revolution which is in progress may, it seems to me, develop on either of two lines: the men may get those "humbler franchises" they covet, but at the loss of "spiritual things"—such as the character for fair play, straight dealing, and loyalty to contract, which we like to think of as distinctively English. But what about the warning that these "humbler franchises" will be likewise lost? Trade unionism is no new thing; centuries ago and for centuries, as we know, England and Europe were under the dominion of those states within the State—the Trades Guilds. At this distance of time we can afford to admire these for the spiritual things to which they held fast; their religious organisation, the thorough training they afforded to their apprentices, and the obligation 320 every member of a guild was under to use just weights and measures and to turn out first rate work of whatever kind. But, notwithstanding these moral safeguards, the tyranny of the guilds became insupportable, and they disappeared into the limbo of things no longer serviceable. Could any dream of Socialism, again, offer more perfect conditions than did the Russian village communes? But these too established a tyranny which was felt to be more oppressive than serfdom itself: the *Mir* disappeared, lost in that Gehenna which engulfed the guilds.

Wordsworth's prophetic lines should instruct us. "However hardly won or justly dear" those humbler franchises for which men are standing out in their tens of thousands with unanimity, courage, devotion to a cause justified by their REASON, they will not be able to support those same franchises if spiritual things, the real things of life, be lost in gaining them. Therefore we may predict that the present movement may well issue in worse things but will not issue in the triumph of either trade unionism or syndicalism.

Here is our opportunity. We blame the workmen for their irresponsible action, for what seems to us the reckless way in which the poorest are impoverished and multitudes of workers are compelled to unwilling idleness. But those of us who are neither miners nor owners may not allow ourselves irresponsible thought or speech, and we may contribute our quota towards appeasement. It is within everybody's province to influence public opinion, if it be only the opinion of two or three; we may raise the whole question to a higher plane, the plane of those spiritual things—duty, responsibility, brotherly love (towards all men)—which make the final appeal. We could not, and we need not try to, obstruct the revolution of which we are vaguely conscious, but we may help to make it a turn of the wheel which shall bring us out of the darkness of a Simplon Tunnel into the light and glory of a Lombard plain. We may, respecting the claims of working men, perceive that they demand too little, and that the things they demand are not those which matter. Even the shock of a revolution is not too high a price for an experience which should convince us that knowledge is the basis of a nation's strength.

321

IV

NEW AND OLD CONCEPTIONS OF KNOWLEDGE

I have so far advanced that "knowledge" is undefined and probably indefinable; that it is a state out of which persons may pass and into which they may return, but never a store upon which they may draw; that knowledge-hunger is as universal as bread-hunger; that our best provision for conveying knowledge is marvellously successful with the best men, but rather futile with the second best; that persons whose education has not enriched them with knowledge store up information (statistics and other facts), upon which they use their reasoning powers; that the attempt to reason without knowledge is disastrous; and that, during the present distress, England is, for various economical reasons, in a condition of intellectual inanition consequent upon a failure in her food supply, in this case the supply of food proper for the mind. I have glanced at Knowledge under the three headings suggested by one who speaks with authority, and have contended that, even if the knowledge be divisible, the vehicle by which it is carried is one and indivisible, and that it is generally impossible for the mind to receive knowledge except through the channel of letters.

But the mediaeval mind had, as we know, a more satisfactory conception of knowledge than we have arrived at. Knowledge is for us a thing of shreds and patches, knowledge of this and of that, with yawning gaps between.

The scholastic mediaeval mind, probably working on the scattered hints which the Scriptures offer, worked out a sublime *Filosofica della Religione Cattolica*, pictured, for example, in the great fresco painted by Simone Memmi and Taddeo Gaddi (which Ruskin has taught us to know), and implied in "The Adoration of the Lamb" painted by the two Van Eycks. In the first picture we get a Pentecostal Descent, first, upon the cardinal virtues and the Christian graces, then, upon prophets and apostles, and below these upon the seven Liberal Arts represented each by its captain figure, Cicero, Aristotle, Zoroaster, etc., none of them Christian, not one of them a Hebrew. Here we get the magnificent idea that all knowledge (undebased) comes from above and is conveyed to minds which are, as Coleridge says, previously prepared to receive it; and, further, that it comes to a mind so prepared, without question as to whether it be the mind of pagan or Christian; a truly liberal catholic idea, it seems to me, corresponding marvellously with the facts of life. As sublime and even more explicit is the Promethean fable which informed the Greek mind. With the sense of a sudden plunge we come down to our own random and ineffectual notions, and are tempted to cry with Wordsworth,—

> "Great God! I'd rather be
> A Pagan suckled in a creed outworn,"

and know that a God had brought gifts of knowledge to men at awful cost, than to sit serene in the vague belief that knowledge arrives in incoherent particles, no one knows how and no one knows whence; or that it is self-generated in a man here and there who gets out of himself new insight into the motions of mind and heart, a new perception of the laws of life, the hint of a new amelioration in the condition of men.

Because the notion that we entertain of knowledge as being heterogeneous lies at the root of our heterogeneous theories of education, it may be as well to quote a passage from Ruskin's description of that picture in the chapel of the Church of Santa Maria Novella to which I have referred:

> "On this side and the opposite side of the Chapel are represented by Simon Memmi's hand, the teaching power of the Spirit of God and the saving power of the Christ of God in the world according to the understanding of Florence in his time.
>
> "We will take the side of intellect first. Beneath the

pouring forth of the Holy Spirit in the point of the arch beneath are the three Evangelical Virtues. Without these, says Florence, you can have no science. Without Love, Faith and Hope—no intelligence. Under these are the four Cardinal Virtues ... Temperance, Prudence, Justice, Fortitude. Under these are the great Prophets and Apostles. .... Under the line of Prophets, as powers summoned by their voices are the mythic figures of the seven theological or spiritual and the seven geological or natural sciences; and under the feet of each of them the figure of its Captain-teacher to the world." (*Mornings in Florence.*)

That is, the Florentines of the Middle Ages believed in "the teaching power of the Spirit of God," believed not only that the seven Liberal Arts were fully under the direct outpouring of the Holy Ghost, but that every fruitful idea, every original conception, be it in geometry, or grammar, or music, was directly derived from a Divine source.

Whether we receive it or not, and the Scriptures abundantly support such a theory regarding the occurrence of knowledge, we cannot fail to perceive that here we have a harmonious and ennobling scheme of education and philosophy. It is a pity that the exigencies of his immediate work prevented Ruskin from inquiring further into the origin, the final source, of knowledge, but we may continue the inquiry for ourselves. In "the teaching power of the Spirit of God" we have a pregnant and inspiring phrase. Supposing that we accept this mediaeval philosophy tentatively for present relief, what would be our gains?

First, the enormous relief afforded by a sense of unity of purpose, of progressive evolution, in the education of the race. It induces great ease of mind to think that knowledge is dealt out to us according to our preparedness and according to our needs; that God whispers in the ear of the man who is ready in order that he may be the vehicle to carry the new knowledge to the rest of us. "God has a few of us whom He whispers in the ear," 'Abt Vogler' is made to say; and another poet causes his Explorer to cry:—

"God chose me for His whisper, and I've found it, and
     it's yours!"

Next, that knowledge, in this light, is no longer sacred and secular, great and trivial, practical and theoretical. All knowledge, dealt out to us in such portions as we are ready for, is sacred; knowledge is, perhaps, a beautiful whole, a great unity, embracing God and man and the universe, but having many parts which are not comparable with one another in the sense of less or more, because all are necessary and each has its functions. Next, we perceive that knowledge and the mind of man are to each other as are air and the lungs. The mind lives by means of knowledge; stagnates, faints, perishes, deprived of this necessary atmosphere.

That, it is not for a man to choose, "I will learn this or that, the rest is not my concern"; still less is it for parent or schoolmaster to limit a child to less than he can get at of the whole field of knowledge; for, in the domain of mind at least as much as in that of morals or religion, man is under a Divine Master; he has to know as he has to eat.

That, there is not one period of life, our school days, in which we sit down to regular meals of intellectual diet, but that we must eat every day in order to live every day.

That, knowledge and what is known as "learning" are not to be confounded; learning may still be an available store when it is not knowledge; but by knowledge one grows, becomes more of a person, and that is all that there is to show for it. We sometimes wonder at the simplicity and modesty of persons whose knowledge is matter of repute; but they are not hiding their light; they are not aware of any unusual possessions; they have nothing to show but themselves, but we feel the force of their personalities. Now, forceful personalities, persons of weight and integrity, of decision and sound judgment, are what the country is most in need of; and, if we propose to bring such persons up for the public service, the gradual inception of knowledge is one condition amongst others.

There are various delightfully "new" educational systems in favour, in all of which a grain of knowledge is presented in a gallon of warm diluent. We have the theory that it does not matter what a child learns, but only how he learns it; which is as sound as, It does not matter what a child eats, but only how he eats it, therefore feed him on sawdust! Then, we have Rousseau's primitive man theory, that a child must get all his knowledge through his own senses and by his own wits, as if there were no knowledge waiting to be passed on by the small torch-bearer; and there is the theory which obtained in Catholic England, exemplified in more than one of the Waverley Novels, in the sports purveyed for her tenantry by 'Lady Margaret Bellenden,' for example. Those men and maidens had been trained as children to be "supple, active, healthy, with senses alert, ready for dance and song, with an eye and ear ready for the beautiful, intelligent, happy, capable." (I quote from a valuable letter in *The Times*). What with our morris-dances, pageants, living pictures, miracle plays, and so on, we are reviving the Stuart educational ideals, and no doubt we do well to aim at increasing the general joy. But our age requires more of us; in the sort of self-activity and self-expression implied in these and in half a dozen other educational theories, knowledge plays no part, and the city *gamin* exhibits in perfection every quality of gaiety, alert intelligence, delight in shows, which we set ourselves to cultivate.

"With all thy getting, get understanding," is the message for our needs, and understanding is, in one sense, the conscious act of the mind in apprehending knowledge, which is in fact relative, and does not exist for any person until that person's mind acts upon the intellectual matter presented to it. "Why will ye not understand?" is the repeated and poignant question of the Gospels.

That is what ails us as a nation, we do not understand; not ignorant persons only, but educated men and women, employ fallacious arguments, offer prejudices for principles, and platitudes for ideas. If it be argued that these failures are due less to ignorance than to insincerity, I should reply that insincerity is an outcome of ignorance; the darkened intelligence cannot see clearly. "The day is unto them that know," but knowledge is by no means the facile acquirement of those who, according to Ruskin, "cram to pass and not to know."

I would not be understood as passing strictures upon the vast and excellent educational work nearly all teachers are doing; it is impossible to go into an Elementary School without being impressed by the competence of the teachers and the intelligence of the children; I have already paid a worthless tribute to Public Schools, and should like here to add a word of affectionate and hearty appreciation of the High School girl as I know her, thoughtful and well educated—a person quite undeserving of the slings and 327   arrows of outrageous criticism too freely aimed at her. As for our new Universities, they remove the stigma under which many of us have suffered in presence of the numerous centres of intellectual life which add dignity and grace to continental cities. The new Universities are full of promise for the land.

We have, no doubt, arrived at a good starting place, but we may not consider that the journey is accomplished. I need not repeat the charges to which we have laid ourselves open because of our ignorance, but I shall endeavour to take a closer survey of the field of education as regarded from the standpoint of knowledge and the innate affinities existing in the mind with that knowledge which is proper for it. For the present the need is that "abstract knowledge" should present itself to practical persons as the crying demand of the nation; the "mandate," let us say, pronounced by certain general failures to understand the science of relations, and that other neglected form of knowledge, "the science of the proportion of things."

V

EDUCATION AND THE FULLNESS OF LIFE

"I must live my life!" said the notorious bandit who before the War terrorized Paris; and we have heard the sort of cant often, even before *The Doll's House* gave to "self-expression" the dignity of a cult; nevertheless, the brigand Bonnot has done an ill turn to society, for a misguiding theory neatly put is more dangerous than an ill-example.

We are tired of the man who claims to live his life at the general expense, of the girl who will live hers to her family's annoyance or distress; but there really is a great opportunity open to the nation which will set itself to consider what the life of a man should be and will give each individual a chance to live his life.

We are doing something; we are trying to open the book of nature to children by the proper key—knowledge, 328 acquaintance by look and name, if not more, with bird and flower and tree; we see, too, that the magic of poetry makes knowledge vital, and children and grown-ups quote a verse which shall add blackness to the ashbud, tender wonder to that "flower in the crannied wall," a thrill to the song of the lark. As for the numerous field clubs of the northern towns, the members of which, weavers, miners, artisans, reveal themselves as accomplished botanists, birdmen, geologists, their Saturday rambles mean not only "life," but splendid joy. It is to be hoped that the opportunities afforded in the schools will prepare women to take more part in these excursions; at present the work done is too thorough for their endurance and for their slight attainments.

In another direction we are doing well; we are so made that every dynamic relation, be it leap-frog or high-flying, which we establish with Mother Earth, is a cause of joy; we begin to see this and are encouraging swimming, dancing, hockey, and so on, all instruments of present joy and permanent health. Again, we know that the human hand is a wonderful and exquisite instrument to be used in a hundred movements exacting delicacy, direction and force; every such movement is a cause of joy as it leads to the pleasure of execution and the triumph of success. We begin to understand this and make some efforts to train the young in the deft handling of tools and the practice of handicrafts. Some day, perhaps, we shall see apprenticeship to trades revived, and good and beautiful work enforced. In so far, we are laying ourselves out to secure that each shall "live his life"; and that, not at his neighbour's expense; because, so wonderful is the economy of the world that when a man really lives his life he benefits his neighbour as well as himself; we all thrive in the well-being of each. We are perceiving, too, that a human being is endowed with an ear attuned to harmony and melody, with a voice 329 from which music may issue, hands whose delicate action may draw forth sounds in enthralling sequence. With the ancient Greeks, we begin to realise that music is a necessary part of education. So, too, of pictorial art; at last we understand that every one can draw, and that, because to draw is delightful, every one should be taught how; that every one delights in pictures, and that education is concerned to teach him what pictures to delight in.

A person may sing and dance, enjoy music and natural beauty, sketch what he sees, have satisfaction in his own good craftsmanship, labour with his hands at honest work, perceiving that work is better than wages; may live his life in various directions, the more the merrier. A certain pleasant play of the intellect attends the doing of all these things; his mind is agreeably exercised; he thinks upon what he is doing, often with excitement, sometimes with enthusiasm. He says, "I must live my life," and he lives it in as many of these ways as are open to him; no other life is impoverished to supply his fullness, but, on the contrary, the sum of general joy in well-being is increased both through sympathy and by imitation.

This is the sort of ideal that is obtaining in our schools and in the public mind, so that the next generation bid fair to be provided with many ways of living their lives, ways which do not encroach upon the lives of others. Here is the contribution of our generation to the science of education, and it is not an unworthy one; we perceive that a person is to be brought up in the first place for his own uses, and after that for the uses of society; but, as a matter of fact, the person who "lives his life" most completely is also of most service to others because he contains within him provision for many serviceable activities which are employed in living his life; and, besides, there is a negative advantage to the community in the fact that the man is able to live on his own resources.

330   But a man is not made up only of eyes to see, a heart to enjoy, limbs delightful in the using, hands satisfied with perfect execution: life in all these kinds is open more or less to all but the idly depraved. But what of man's eager, hungry, restless, insatiable mind? True, we teach him the mechanical art of reading while he is at school, but we do not teach him to read; he has little power of attention, a poor vocabulary, little habit of conceiving any life but his own; to add to the gate-money at a football match is his notion of adventure and diversion.

We are, in fact, only taking count of the purlieus of that vast domain which pertains to every man in right of his human nature. We neglect mind. We need not consider brain; a duly nourished and duly exercised mind takes care of its physical organ provided that organ also receives its proper material nourishment. But our fault, our exceeding great fault, is that we keep our own minds and the

minds of our children shamefully underfed. The mind is a
spiritual octopus, reaching out limbs in every direction to
draw in enormous rations of that which under the action
of the mind itself becomes knowledge. Nothing can stale
its infinite variety; the heavens and the earth, the past, the
present, and future, things great and things minute, nations
and men, the universe, all are within the scope of the human
intelligence. But there would appear to be, as we have seen,
an unsuspected unwritten law concerning the nature of the
"material" which is converted into knowledge during the
act of apprehension. The idea of the *Logos* did not come
by chance to the later Greeks; "The Word" is not a mean-
ingless title applied to the second Person of the Trinity; it
is not without significance that every utterance which fell
from Him is marked by exquisite literary fitness; (a child's
comment on a hymn that was read to her was, "that is not
poetry; Jesus would have said it *much* better"); in rendering
an account of His august commission Christ said:—"I have
given unto them *the words* which Thou gavest me"; and one
disciple voiced the rest when he said, "Thou hast *the words*
of eternal life." The Greeks knew better than we that words
are more than things, more than events; with all primitive
peoples rhetoric appears to have been a power; the grand
old sayings which we have scorned as inventions are coming
to their own again, because, what modern is capable of such
inventions? Men move the world, but the motives which
move men are conveyed by words. Now, a person is limited
by the number of things he is able to call by their names,

qualify by appropriate epithets; this is no mere pedantic ruling, it belongs to that unfathomable mystery we call human nature; and the modern notion of education, with its shibboleth of "things not words," is intrinsically demoralizing. The human intelligence demands letters, literature, with a more than bread-hunger. It is almost within living memory how the newly emancipated American negroes fell upon books as the famished Israelites fell upon food in the deserted camp of Sennacherib.

Only as he has been and is nourished upon books is a man able to "live his life." A great deal of mechanical labour is necessarily performed in solitude; the miner, the farm-labourer, cannot think all the time of the block he is hewing, the furrow he is ploughing; how good that he should be figuring to himself the trial scene in the *Heart of Midlothian*, the "high-jinks" in *Guy Mannering*, that his imagination should be playing with 'Ann Page' or 'Mrs. Quickly,' or that his labour goes the better "because his secret soul a holy strain repeats." People, working people, do these things. Many a one can say out of a rich experience, "My mind to me a kingdom is"; many a one cries with Browning's 'Paracelsus,' "God! Thou art mind! Unto the master-mind, Mind should be precious. Spare my mind alone!" We know how "*Have mynde*" appears on the tiles paving the choir of St. Cross; but "*mynde*," like body, must have its meat.

Faith has grown feeble in these days, hope faints in our heavy ways, but charity waxes strong; we would make all men millionaires if we could, or, at any rate, take from the millionaires to give to the multitude. No doubt some beneficent and venturous Robin Hood of a minister will arise (has arisen?) to take steps in that direction; but when all has been done in the way of social amelioration we shall not have enabled men to "live their lives" unless we have given them a literary education of such sort that they choose to continue in the pleasant places of the mind. "That is all very well in theory," some one objects, "but look at the Masses, are they able to receive Letters? When they talk it is in journalese, and anything in the nature of a book must be watered down and padded to suit their comprehension." But is it not true that working men talk in "journalese" because it is only the newspapers that do them the grace to meet them frankly on their own level? Neither school education nor life has put books in their way, and their adoption of the only literary speech that offers but proves a natural aptitude for Letters. One cannot always avoid appeal to the authority one knows to be final, and I will not apologise for citing the fact at which no doubt we have all wondered that Christ should expose the profoundest philosophy to the multitude, the "Many," whom even Socrates contemns.

May I quote, with apologies to the writer, a letter signed "A Working Man," written in answer to one of mine which was honoured by being reprinted in *The Times Weekly Edition*? (It is good, by the way, that such a journal should be in the hands of working men). My correspondent "thanks Heaven that there are still a few persons left in this country who regard education as somewhat different from a means of *keeping a shop*." We may all thank Heaven that there are working men who value knowledge for its own sake and hate to have it presented to them as a means of getting on.

The fact is, Letters make a universal appeal because they respond to certain innate affinities: young Tennysons, De Quinceys, and the like, are, as we all know, inordinate readers, but these are capable of foraging on their own account; it is for the average, the dull, and the backward boy I would lay urgent claim to a literary education; the minds of such as these respond to this and to no other appeal, and they turn out perfectly intelligent persons, open to knowledge by many avenues. For working men whose intelligence is in excess of their education, Letters are the accessible vehicle of knowledge; having learned the elements of reading, writing, and summing, it is unnecessary to trouble them with any other "beggarly elements"; their natural intelligence and mature minds make them capable of dealing with difficulties as they occur; and for further elucidation every working men's club should have an encyclopaedia. Some men naturally take to learning, and will struggle manfully with their Latin grammar, and Cicero, their Euclid and trigonometry. Happy they! But the general conclusion remains, that for men and women of all ages, all classes, and all complexions of mind, Letters are an imperative and daily requirement to satisfy that universal mind-hunger, the neglect of which gives rise to emotional disturbances, and, as a consequence, to evils that dismay us.

VI

KNOWLEDGE IN LITERARY FORM

I have so far urged that knowledge is necessary to men, and that, in the initial stages, it must be conveyed through a literary medium, whether it be knowledge of physics or of Letters, because there would seem to be some inherent quality in mind which prepares it to respond to this form of appeal and no other. I say in the initial stages, because possibly, when the mind becomes conversant with knowledge of a given type, it unconsciously translates the driest formulae into living speech; perhaps it is for some such reason that mathematics seem to fall outside this rule of literary presentation; mathematics, like music, is a speech in itself, a speech irrefragibly logical, of exquisite clarity, meeting the requirements of mind.

To consider Letters as the staple of education is no new thing; nor is the suggestion new that to turn a young person into a library is to educate him. But here we are brought to a stand; the mind demands method, orderly presentation, as inevitably as it demands knowledge; and it may be that our educational misadventures are due to the fact that we have allowed ourselves to take up any haphazard ordering that is recommended with sufficient pertinacity.

But no one can live without a philosophy which points out the order, means and end of effort, intellectual or other; to fail in discovering this is to fall into melancholia, or more active madness: so we go about picking up a maxim here, a motto there, an idea elsewhere, and make a patchwork of the whole which we call our principles; beggarly fragments enough we piece together to cover our nakedness and a hundred phrases which one may hear any day betray lives founded upon an ignoble philosophy. No doubt people are better than their words, better than their own thoughts; we speak of ourselves as "finite beings," but is there any limit to the generosity and nobility of almost any person? The hastily spoken "It is the rule at sea," that distressed us a while ago, what a vista does it disclose of chivalric tenderness, entire self-sacrifice! Human nature has not failed; what has failed us is philosophy, and that applied philosophy which is called education. Philosophy, all the philosophies, old and new, land us on the horns of a dilemma; either we do well by ourselves and seek our own perfection of nature or condition, or we do well by others to our own loss or deterioration. If there is a mean, philosophy does not declare it.

There are things of which we have desperate need: we want a new scale of values: I suppose we all felt when, in those days before the War, we read how several millionaires went down in the "Titanic" disaster, not only that their millions did not matter, but that they did not matter to them; that possibly they felt themselves well quit of an incessant fatigue. We want more life: there is not life enough for our living; we have no great engrossing interests; we hasten from one engagement to another and glance furtively at the clock to see how time, life, is getting on; we triumph if a week seems to have passed quickly; who knows but that the approach of an inevitable end might find us glad to get it all over? We want hope: we busy ourselves excitedly about some object of desire, but the pleasure we get is in effort, not in attainment; and we read, before the War, of the number of suicides among Continental schoolboys, for instance, with secret understanding; what is there to live for? We want to be governed: servants like to receive their "orders"; soldiers and schoolboys enjoy discipline; there is satisfaction in stringent Court etiquette; the fact of being "under orders" adds dignity to character. When we revolt it is only that we may transfer our allegiance. We want a new start: we are sick of ourselves and of knowing in advance how we shall behave and how we shall feel on all occasions; the change we half-unconsciously desire is to other aims, other ways of looking at things. We feel that we are more than there is room for; other conditions might give us room; we don't know; any way, we are uneasy. These are two or three of the secret matters that oppress us, and we are in need of a philosophy which shall deal with such things of the spirit. We believe we should be able to rise to its demands, however exigeant, for the failure is not in us or in human nature so much as in our limited knowledge of conditions.

The cry of decadence is dispiriting, but is it well-founded? The beautiful little gowns that have come down as heirlooms would not fit the "divinely tall" daughters of many a house where they are treasured. We have become frank, truthful, kind; our conscientiousness and our charity are morbid; we cannot rest in our beds for a disproportionate anxiety for the well-being of everybody; we even exceed the generous hazard, that, peradventure for a good man one might be found to die; almost any man will risk his life for the perishing without question of good or bad; and we expect no less from firemen, doctors, life-boatmen, parsons, the general public. And what a comment on the splendid magnanimity of men does the War afford!

An annoying inquiry concerning risks at sea almost resulted in a ruling that no one should let himself be saved so long as others were in danger; it is preposterous, but is what human nature expects of itself. No, we are not decadent on the whole, and our uneasiness is perhaps caused by growing pains. We may be poor things, but we are ready to break forth into singing should the chance open to us of a full life of passionate devotion. Now, all our exigeant demands are met by words written in a Book, and by the manifestations of a Person; and we are waiting for a Christianity such as the world has not yet known. Hitherto, Christ has existed for our uses; but what if a time were coming when we, also, should taste the "orientall fragrancie" of, "My Master!" So it shall be when the shout of a King is among us, and are there not premonitions? But these things come not by prayer and fasting, by good works and self-denial, alone; there is something prior to all these upon which our Master insists with distressful urgency, "Why will ye not know? Why will ye not understand?"

My excuse for touching upon our most intimate concerns is that this matter, too, belongs to the domain of

337

Letters; if we propose to seek knowledge we must proceed in an orderly way, recognising that the principal knowledge is of most importance; the present writer writes and the reader reads, because we are all moved by the spirit of our time; these things are our secret preoccupation, for we have come out of a long alienation as persons "wearied with trifles," and are ready and anxious for a new age. We know the way, and we know where to find our rule of the road; but we must bring a new zeal and a new method to our studies; we may no longer dip here and there or read a perfunctory chapter with a view to find some word of counsel or comfort for our use. We are engaged in the study of, in noting the development of, that consummate philosophy which meets every occasion of our lives, all demands of the intellect, every uneasiness of the soul.

The arrogance which pronounces judgment upon the written "Word" upon so slight an acquaintance as would hardly enable us to cover a sheet or two of paper with sayings of the Master, which confines the Divine teaching to the great Sermon, of which we are able to rehearse some half-dozen sentences, is as absurd as it is blameworthy. Let us give at least as profound attention to the teaching of Christ as the disciples of Plato, say, gave to his words of wisdom. Let us observe, notebook in hand, the orderly and progressive sequence, the penetrating quality, the irresistible appeal, the unique content of the Divine teaching; (for this purpose it might be well to use some 338 one of the approximately chronological arrangements of the Gospel History in the words of the text). Let us read, not for our profiting, though that will come, but for love of that knowledge which is better than thousands of gold and silver. By and by we perceive that this knowledge is the chief thing in life; the meaning of Christ's saying, "Behold, I make all things new," dawns upon us; we get new ideas as to the relative worth of things; new vigour, new joy, new hope are ours.

If we believe that knowledge is the principal thing, that knowledge is tri-partite, and that the fundamental knowledge is the knowledge of God, we shall bring up our children as students of Divinity and shall pursue our own life-long studies in the same school. Then we shall find that the weekly sermons for which we are prepared are as bread to the hungry; and we shall perhaps understand how enormous is the demand we make upon the clergy for living, original thought. It is only as we are initiated that science and "Nature" come to our aid in this chief pursuit; then, they "their great Original proclaim"; but while we are ignorant of the principal knowledge they remain dumb. Literature and history have always great matters to speak of or suggest, because they deal with states or phases of moral government and moral anarchy, and tacitly indicate to us the sole key to all this unintelligible world; and literature not only reveals to us the deepest things of the human spirit, but it is profitable also "for example of life and instruction in manners."

We are at the parting of the ways; our latest educational authority, one who knows and loves little children, would away with all tales and histories that appeal to the imagination; let children learn by means of things, is her mandate; and the charm and tenderness with which it is delivered may well blind us to its desolating character. We recognise Rousseau, of course, and his *Emile*, that self-sufficient person who should know nothing of the past, should see no visions, allow no authority. But human nature in children is stronger than the eighteenth century philosopher and the theories which he continues to inform. Whoever has told a fairy tale to a child has been made aware of that natural appetency for letters to which it is our business to minister. Are we not able to believe that words are more than meat, and, so believing, shall we not rise up and insist that children shall have a liberal diet of the spirit? Rousseau, in spite of false analogies, fallacious arguments, was able to summon fashionable mothers and men of the world throughout Europe to the great task of education, because his eloquence convinced them that this was their assigned work and a work capable of achievement; and we who perhaps see with clearer eyes should do well to cherish this legacy—the conviction that the education of the succeeding generation is the chief business of every age.

Nevertheless, though we are ourselves emerging from the slough of materialism, we are willing to plunge children into its heavy ways through the agency of a "practical" and "useful" education; but children have their rights, and among these is the freedom of the city of mind. Let them use things, know things, learn through things, by all means;

339

but the more they know Letters the better they will be able, with due instruction, to handle things. I do not hesitate to say that the whole of a child's instruction should be conveyed through the best literary medium available. His history books should be written with the lucidity, concentration, personal conviction, directness, and admirable simplicity which characterizes a work of literary calibre. So should his geography books; the so-called scientific method of teaching geography now in vogue is calculated to place a child in a somewhat priggish relation to Mother Earth; it is impossible, too, that the human intelligence should assimilate the sentences one meets with in many books for children, but the memory retains them and the child is put in the false attitude of one who offers pseudo-knowledge. Most of the geography books, for example, require to be translated into terms of literature before they can be apprehended. Great confidence is placed in diagrammatic and pictorial representation, and it is true that children enjoy diagrams and understand them as they enjoy and understand puzzles; but there is apt to be in their minds a great gulf between the diagram and the fact it illustrates. We trust much to pictures, lantern slides, cinematograph displays; but without labour there is no profit, and probably the pictures which remain with us are those which we have first conceived through the medium of words; pictures may help us to correct our notions, but the imagination does not work upon a visual presentation; we lay the phrases of a description on our palette and make our own pictures;

(works of art belong to another category). We recollect how Dr. Arnold was uneasy until he got details enough to form a mental picture of a place new to him. So it is with children and all persons of original mind: a map to put the place in position, and then, all about it, is what we want.

Readings in literature, whether of prose or poetry, should generally illustrate the historical period studied; but selections should be avoided; children should read the whole book or the whole poem to which they are introduced. Here we are confronted by a serious difficulty. Plato, we know, determined that the poets in his "Republic" should be well looked after lest they should write matter to corrupt the morals of youth; aware of what happened in Europe when the flood-gates of knowledge were opened, Erasmus was anxiously solicitous on this score, and it is a little surprising to find that here, Rossetti was on the side of the angels. Will the publishers who, since Friedrich Perthes 341 discovered their educational mission, have done so much for the world, help us in this matter also? They must excise with a most sparing hand, always under the guidance of a jealous scholar; but what an ease of conscience it would be to teachers if they could throw open the world of books to their scholars without fear of the mental and moral smudge left by a single prurient passage! Many, too, who have taken out their freedom in the republic of letters would be well content to keep complete library editions in costly bindings in their proper place, while handy volumes in daily use might be left about without uneasiness.

The Old Testament itself after such a (very guarded) process would be more available for the reading of children; and few persons would feel that Shakespeare's plays suffered from the removal of obscenities here and there. In this regard we cherish a too superstitious piety. In another matter, let that great "remedial thinker," Dr. Arnold, advise us:—"Adjust your proposed amount of reading to your time and inclination; but whether that amount be large or small let it be varied in its kind and widely varied. If I have a confident opinion on any one point connected with the improvement of the human mind it is on this." Here we get support for a varied and liberal curriculum; and, as a matter of fact, we find that the pupil who studies a number of subjects knows them as well as he who studies a few knows those few.

Children should read books, not about books and about authors; this sort of reading may be left for the spare hours of the dilettante. Their reading should be carefully ordered, for the most part in historical sequence; they should read to know, whether it be *Robinson Crusoe* or Huxley's *Physiography*; their knowledge should be tested, not by questions, but by the oral (and occasionally the written) reproduction of a passage after one reading; all further processes that we concern ourselves about in teaching, the mind performs for itself; and, lastly, this sort of reading should be the chief business in the class room.

We are at a crucial moment in the history of English education. John Bull is ruminating. He says, "I have laboured at the higher education of women; let them back to the cooking-pot and distaff and learn the science(!) of domestic economy. I have tried for these forty years to educate the children of the people. What is the result? Strikes and swelled head! Let them have 'prentice schools and learn what will be their business in life!" John Bull is wrong. In so far as we have failed it is that we have offered the pedantry, the mere verbiage, of knowledge in lieu of knowledge itself; and it is time for all who do not hold knowledge in contempt to be up and doing; there is time yet to save England and to make of her a greater nation, more worthy of her opportunities. But the country of our love will not stand still; if we let the people sink into the mire of a material education our doom is sealed; eyes now living will see us take even a third-rate place among the nations, for it is knowledge that exalteth a nation, because out of duly-ordered knowledge proceedeth righteousness and prosperity ensueth.

"Think clear, feel deep, bear fruit well," says our once familiar mentor, Matthew Arnold, and his monition exactly meets our needs.

2023 note: originally published as "Supplementary" and not "Book III," the following section has been adjusted to match Miss Mason's handwritten notes of her vision for this edition and its terminology. See the Foreword by Art Middlekauff for further details.

Book 3

Chapter 1

Too Wide a Mesh

The wide world dreaming on things to come" is concentrating on a luminous figure of education which it beholds, dimly, emerging from a cloudy horizon. This gracious presence is to change the world, to give to all men wider possibilities, other thoughts, aims: but, alas, this Education which is to be open to all promises no more on a nearer view than to make Opportunity universal—that is, in spiritual things, he may take who has the power and he may keep who can.

The net is cast wide no doubt and brings in a mighty haul but the meshes are so wide that it will only retain big fishes. Now this is the history of education since the world was and is no new thing. The medieval schools of castle or abbey, the Renaissance schools, the very schools of China, have all been conducted upon this plan. Education is for him who wants it and can take it but is no universal boon like the air we breathe or the sunshine we revel in.

459

We are a little sorry for the effect of this limitation upon the 'working classes': only a small percentage of the children of these are 'big' enough to be retained in the examination net which, to do it justice, explores all waters. A few of the pass men may do big things and fill big posts, but for the rest, a large percentage is, in practice, illiterate except for the spelling out of a local 'rag' for football and parish news.

But is the mischief confined to what we call the 'working classes'? Is it not a fact that in most schools the full force of instruction is turned on upon a few boys who are likely to distinguish themselves? While for the rest of the school teaching is duly given no doubt but the boys find they may take it or leave it as the humour takes them.

We were all fascinated a while ago by the story of a pair of charming 'Twins'; these went through the usual preparatory school education and then passed on to a great Public School where they remained until they were nineteen; that is, they had ten or twelve good years among most excellent opportunities. As they were attractive boys we may take it that their masters were not at any rate unwilling to teach them. Their record should have been quite a good one, and, though it is the fashion to sneer a little at Public Schools, we know that these have turned out and do turn out the best and most intellectual men the country has occasion for. Therefore what happened in the case of these 'Twins' does not cast any reflection upon Public Schools but solely upon the system of the Big Mesh. Here are some of the things we read in that delightful biography:—

"While in hospital after a smash at polo R— wrote to
F—:—'I enjoyed it immensely. What lucky people we
are taking an interest in so many things!'"

Surely here was material for a schoolmaster to work upon!
Again, we read:—

"They never ceased to wonder at the magnificence of the
world and they carried a divine innocence into soldiering
and travel and sport and business and, not least,—into
the shadows of the Great War."

And this 'wonder' of theirs was the note that marked them
at school. Again, what material for their instructors!

"But," we read, "at X— they showed little interest in
books and, later, were wont to lament to each other that
'They had left school wholly uneducated.'" (The italics are
ours.)

Their kindly biographer and dear friend goes on to say:— 345

"But they learnt other things,—the gift of leadership, for
instance, and the power of getting alongside all varieties
of human nature."

But was not this nature rather than nurture, school nurture at any rate, for these gifts seem to have been a family

inheritance? Born in 1880, they left school in 1899, when there follows a delightful record for the one brother of successful and adventurous sport while—

> "R— was soon absorbed in the city . . . and beginning to lament his want of education." "F—, while in Egypt was greatly impressed by Lord Cromer and writes to R—, 'he is quite the biggest man we have! . . . to hear him talk is worth hearing.'"

The two brothers correspond constantly and R— takes the part of mentor to his brother. He advises him to learn *The Times* leaders by heart to improve his style,—"because they are very good English." Again,—

> "I will send you out next mail a very good book, *Science and Education*, by Professor Huxley which I have marked in several places, the sort of book you can read over again." R— "had discovered that he was very badly educated and was determined to remedy this defect:—'It don't matter. . . . I do believe not having learned at X— so long as one does so now.'"

See the fine loyalty of the young man; his failures were not to be put down to his school!

If the schools take credit for any one thing it is that they show their pupils 'how to learn'; but do they? We are told that R— set to work at a queer assortment of books and writes to F—:—

"Anyone can improve his memory: the best way is by learning by heart—no matter what—and then when you think you know it, say it or write it. . . . After two or three days you are sure to forget it again and then instead of looking at the book 'strain your mind' and try to remember it. Above all things always keep your mind employed. One great man (I forget which) used to see a number on a door, say 69, and tried to remember all that had happened in the years ending in 69. Or, see a horse and remember how many you have seen that day. . . . Asquith always learns things by heart, he never wastes a minute; as soon as he has nothing to do he picks up some book. He reads till 1-30 every night. When driving to the Temple next morning he thinks over what he has read. Result: he has a marvellous memory and knows everything."

346

Think of the Herculean labours the poor fellow set for both himself and his brother! They ran an intellectual race across a ploughed field after heavy rain and the marvel is that they made way at all. Yet these two brothers had sufficient intellectual zeal to have made them great men as Ambassadors, Governors of Dominions, Statesmen, what not; whereas so far as things of the mind go, they spent their days in a hopeless struggle, alert for any indication which might help them to make up lee-way, and all because, according to their own confession, they 'had learned nothing at school.' Here are further indications of R—'s labours in the field of knowledge:—

"I am reading Rosebery's *Napoleon* and will send it to you. What a wonder he was! Never spent a moment of his life without learning something. . . . I enclose an essay from Bacon's book. Learn it by heart if you can. I have and think it a clinker. . . . I have also finished *Life of Macaulay*. I have always wondered how our great politicians and literary chaps live. . . . I also send you a Shakespeare. I learnt Antony's harangue to the Romans after Caesar's death; I am also trying to learn a little about electricity and railroad organization, so have my time filled up. *Pickwick Papers* I also send to you. I have always avoided this sort of books but Dickens' works are miles funnier than the rotten novels one sees. . . . I have learnt one thing by my reading and my conversation with Professors,—*you and I go at a subject all wrong*." (Italics ours.)

These letters are pathetic documents and, that they are reassuring also, let us be thankful. They do go to prove that the desire of knowledge is inextinguishable whatever schools do or leave undone; but have these nothing to answer for when a pursuit which should yield ever recurring refreshment becomes dogged labour over heavy roads with little pleasure in progress?

Here, again, is another evidence of the limitations attending an utter absence of education. A cultivated sense of humour is a great factor in a joyous life, but these young men are without it. Perhaps the youth addicted to sports usually fails to appreciate delicate nonsense; sports are too strenuous to admit of a subtler, more airy kind of play and we read:—

> "R— heard Mr. Balfour and Lord Reay praising *Alice in Wonderland*. Deeply impressed he bought the book as soon as he returned to London and read it earnestly. To his horror he saw no sense in it. Then it struck him that it might be meant as nonsense and he had another try, when he concluded that it was rather funny but he remained disappointed."

We need not follow the career of these interesting men further. Both fell early before they were forty. Their fine qualities and their personal fascination remained with them to the end, as did also, alas, their invincible ignorance. They laboured indefatigably, but, as R— remarked,—"You and I go at a subject all wrong!"

The schools must tell us why men who attained mediocre successes and the personal favour due to charming manners and sweet natures were yet somewhat depressed and disappointed on account of the ignorance which they made blind and futile efforts to correct; but they never got so far as to learn that knowledge is delightful *because one likes it*; and that no effort at self-education can do anything until one has found out this supreme delightfulness of knowledge.

It must be noted that this failure of a great school to fulfil its purpose occurred twenty years ago, and that no

348   educational body has made more well-considered and enlightened advances than have the Headmasters of the great Public Schools. Probably that delightful group of Eton boys in *Coningsby* has always been and is to-day typical; there is a certain knightly character in the fine bearing and intelligent countenances of the Head Boys one comes across there which speaks well for their intellectual activity. The question is whether more might not be done with the average boy.

The function of the schools is no doubt to feed their scholars on knowledge until they have created in them a healthy appetite which they will go on satisfying for themselves day by day throughout life. We must give up the farce of teaching young people how to learn, which is just as felicitous a labour and just as necessary as to teach a child the motions of eating without offering him food; and studies which are pursued with a view to improve the mind must in future take a back seat.

The multitudinous things that every person wants to know must be made accessible in the schoolroom, not by diagrams, digests, and abstract principles; but boys and girls, like 'Kit's little brother,' must learn 'what oysters is' by supping on oysters. There is absolutely no avenue to knowledge but knowledge itself, and the schools must begin, not by qualifying the mind to deal with knowledge, but by affording all the best books containing all the sorts of knowledge which these 'Twins,' like everyone else, wanted to know. We have to face two difficulties. We do not believe in children as intellectual persons nor in knowledge as requisite and necessary for intellectual life. It is a pity that education is conducted *in camera* save for the examination lists which shew how the best pupils in a school have acquitted themselves, the half-dozen or dozen best in a big school. Finely conscientious as teachers are they can hardly fail to give undue importance to their group of candidates for examination and a school of four or five hundred stands or falls by a dozen head boys.

[See note under Table of Contents for (*a*) the large number of children's answers, and (*b*) Book IV of which only Chapter 1 appears in this volume].

Chapter 2

Two Educational Ideals
A paper written for the P.N.E.U. Conference, 1910, and revised 1922. Printed in *The Parents' Review*, 1928, pp. 1-19

"Return to us again;
And give us manners, virtue, freedom, power."

We are all willing to admit that *education should   1
be a training for wise citizenship.* I propose to
examine two current ideals of education, one
of them summarised in that great and sonorous saying of
Milton's which claims as the end of education that the
pupil should be enabled "to perform justly, skilfully and
magnanimously, all the offices both public and private of
peace and war."

It takes several generations for an idea to exhaust itself
and most of us who have theories of education derive them
consciously or unconsciously from Rousseau; his enormous influence appears to me to be due partly to the air of

omniscience with which he prescribes for all the occasions of a child's life, and partly to the aptness of the moment at which his oracle was delivered. He was the *avant courier* of revolutionary thought; he preached liberty in an age of tyranny, due self-regard in an age of undue subjection, and the right of children to share in all the noble conceptions in the air. No wonder he had an enthusiastic audience! But he is for all time; what gratitude do we all owe to the genius who set courtly mothers to the nursing of their own babies, who told every father that "to the human race he owes men; to society, men fitted for society; to the state, citizens;" adding, that the father who brings children into the world has not only the duty of supporting them but of educating them *himself*. How wise! we say, and we are right.

How sensible, we add, when we are told that children should be early accustomed to darkness or they will scream in the dark. But when the sage tells us that food and sleep should not be regular, because regularity forms habit and habit adds a new want to those of nature; and, again, that "the only habit a child should be allowed to form is to contract no habits whatever,"—we pause, recognizing that habits are inevitable if they be only habits of irregularity and disorder!

The fortunate connection between a child's restless, and often mischievous, activity and his powerlessness is indicated, and we are reminded of the danger of letting children think that those about them are instruments for their use. "In this way they become disagreeable, tyrannical, imperious, perverse, unruly. . . . Power to control others awakens and gratifies self-love, and habit makes it strong." From this wise perception he deduces certain maxims, to the effect, (1) that we must leave the children freedom in the use of the little strength that they have; (2) that it is our duty to supply what they lack whether in intelligence or in physical strength; (3) that we must give them only the help they need and "yield nothing to their whims"; (4) the fourth maxim is especially interesting as it contains the first protest in *Émile* against "opinion"—"we must watch the children so that we may judge which of their desires are natural and which of them spring from opinion."

All this has passed into the fabric of our thought about education. So too, have such axioms as that "if children were not so often threatened or caressed, they would be less timid or less stubborn." And this about toys,—"A little twig with its own leaves and fruit, a poppy-head in which the seeds can be heard rattling, a stick of licquorice he can suck and chew, will amuse a child as well as splendid baubles, and will not accustom him to luxury from his very birth." How wise, too, is this,—"Even as in his swaddling clothes the child hears his nurse's babble, he hears in class the verbiage of his teacher"; and Rousseau points out how our injudicious haste to make children speak, issues in their learning slowly, and speaking indistinctly, and, what is worse, in their giving their own meaning to the words they use, which is different from ours. In this way he accounts for the precocious sayings of children.

In the second book of *Émile*, Rousseau carries the boy from his fifth year to his twelfth. He tells us how he stops the habit of crying and cures the boy of self-pity by taking no notice of his distress, because "to suffer is the first and most necessary thing for him to learn." This is illuminating; but—we pause when we read—"He should depend, not obey; he should demand not command." Is this, indeed, we ask, the whole duty of a child, or is not, rather, the power of willing obedience the best gift we can confer on him? But here are words of wisdom,—

"If he believes you weak, he will soon be stubborn,"

and,

"if the body be too much at ease, the moral nature becomes too much corrupted." "The child who has only to wish in order to obtain his wish thinks himself the owner of the universe." "At his age, incapable of reasoning, all reasons given seem to him only pretexts." "Nature has made children to be loved and helped, has she made them to be obeyed and feared?"

When we come to the following, we question gravely,—"Since with years of reason civil bondage begins, why anticipate it by slavery at home?" This "civil bondage" is that obedience to law and custom which civilization demands. We, who believe in the duty of forming habits, prefer that the child should grow up with the habits of a civilized being to ease his way in life; knowing that such habits make for freedom, and that to be without them leaves child or man a bond-servant to a thousand trivial considerations.

Jean Jacques protests against Locke's maxim, that we ought not to command children but reason with them, because "if children understood how to reason, they would not need to be educated." "I would rather require a child ten years old to be five feet high than to be judicious." Here we hold with Rousseau, but not because we think a child incapable of reasoning—his extremely logical mind is often confusing to his elders—but because we believe that he should be brought up in that attitude of "proud submission and dignified obedience," to use Burke's noble phrase, which will become him hereafter as a citizen. It is because we would give children the habit of chivalrous obedience that we do not allow them to "wrangle and rebel." But how right Rousseau is in thinking that when we give our reasons to children and suppose we have convinced them by arguments, we have often to fall back upon "motives of avarice, or of fear, or of vanity, while the children pretend to be convinced by reason."

We come now and then upon puzzling utterances,—"with children, use force; with men, reason," we are told; and are aghast until we recollect that that idol of the market-place which the author definitely sets himself to overthrow is—authority. We may "never, absolutely never, command them to do a thing, whatever it may be." One wonders in what fashion the poor child would grow up who had never, absolutely never, experienced the repose of simple obedience. As it is, this revolutionary theory of Rousseau's is working havoc with our nerves; the child who has not learned the finality of *must* becomes the restless prey of "chance desires." Here, however, is a word to be pondered.

> "It is marvellous that in undertaking to educate a child, no other means of guiding him should have been devised than emulation, jealousy, envy, vanity, vile fear, all of them poisons most dangerous."

We cannot read unmoved; we no longer employ "vile fear," but what have we to say for the other four? So long as we have a system of education based upon marks, places, prizes, scholarships, we count a child virtuous in proportion as he is moved by emulation, envy, vanity, greed. When Tom has "got up two" in his class and tells you that Ned Somers has "gone down four," your boy is losing in moral value more than he appears to be gaining in intellectual alertness.

Here is a passage from Émile in precise contradiction to our fundamental doctrine that,—a child is born a person:—

> "Do not give your pupil any sort of lesson verbally: he ought to receive none except from experience. Inflict upon him no kind of punishment, for he does not know

what being in fault means; never oblige him to ask pardon, for he does not know what it is to offend you. His actions being without moral quality, he can do nothing which is morally bad, or which deserves either punishment or reproof."

And, again,

"they (children) should not use the mind at all until it has all its faculties . . . the earliest education ought to be purely negative."

"Dead as a door-nail!" has been said of the "faculties": no doubt they are dead, but a theory dies hard; and Rousseau's elaborate scheme for the development of the intellectual attributes presupposes that the several "faculties" are in water-tight compartments; else, how could any one of them, reason, imagination, or what not, make an independent start, as if one arm, or one ear took to growing by itself! We allow that all the members of the body are one body—fed by one food, wearied by one work, refreshed by one sleep, vitalized upon one air, but still we cling to the notion that the "faculties" are many and that each requires the separate consideration of the teacher; truly, a fond thing and vainly imagined!

But this "faculty" theory is as mischievous as it is mistaken; holding it, we undervalue children; we do not say that they are "wanting"; but we assume it; and talk down to them, dilute their intellectual diet, hold over their moral responsibilities, play fast and loose with them as beings who are not fully accountable and therefore whom we need not consider seriously. This radical error vitiates the whole of Rousseau's theory; Émile, all through his pupilship, is incapable alike of intellectual comprehension and of moral perception. His master would give him the idea of property, and this is the preamble:—

> "Our first natural movements have reference to our own preservation and well-being. Thus our first idea of justice is not as due from us, but *to* us. One error in the education of to-day is, that by speaking to children first of their duties and never of their rights, we commence at the wrong end, and tell them of what they cannot understand, and what cannot interest them."

And this, when every nurse knows that the baby gives and takes with quite equal readiness, because there is no first-developed and no second-developed "faculty" in question. We have a charming tale of the boy planting beans and the gardener digging them up, and justifying himself because he has already appropriated the plot: all to teach the boy, what he knows already, that what is another's is not his, and what is his is not another's. But in this story we get a worse example of the depreciation of children to which this kind of glass-house culture leads; for the gardener had been carefully instructed to show himself a churl, to play a part, for the edification of Émile, who is to believe that gardener and tutor are behaving naturally.

Always, exquisite little traps, moral and intellectual, are set for the boy, and always, he falls into them, taking fair play for granted, never supposing, for example, that he has been led into the forest in order that he may lose himself and find his way home by means of his compass: no, he is to believe that his tutor is lost also and has no idea what to do next until the happy thought of the compass presents itself.

The conjuror, too, who delivers a homily showing that his tricks are his property and that for Émile to try them is to do him an injury,—well, it is all very pretty, but it has been carefully got up, a little play enacted in several scenes, which the boy is to take in good part as a real occurrence.

Most of us know how quickly children see through plots of the kind and how entirely they disapprove of them: and they are right; the child is taken at a disadvantage; he is as one of the audience called up on the stage to play with an actor who has got up his part. And this, from a philosopher who, on every other page of this treatise on "natural" education, instructs us that the truth, the whole truth, and nothing but the truth, must be employed in the education of Émile!

We get another example of ingenious imbecility in that race to the big stone, whoever got there first, tutor or boy, to find a slice of cake. And no doubt the tutor played his part well, lost in the running and acted his disappointment when the cake fell to another. It is a nursery trick, but we do not approve of it in the nursery. Cakes, sweetmeats, the licquorice stick we have already heard of, are the lawful rewards for which Émile is to contend because—greediness is natural to children! We must read Rousseau *cum grano*, because a man cannot put into a book more than he is, whether morally or intellectually. We remember, no doubt, that Goldsmith "wrote like an angel and talked like poor Poll," but then he wrote like an angel because he was a little like an angel, and talked like poor Poll because that circle of wits bullied him. Rousseau was sensuous, and the incitements he offered were cakes and lollipops; he was markedly wanting in moral integrity, and we find that his delightful scheme is full of tricky expedients. But Rousseau was a poetic genius with the gift of seeing into the heart of things; and, as long as education remains the concern of most men and women, we shall continue to follow his lead; but because there is much dross with the gold, we must discriminate and eliminate.

The execrable heresy, that, it does not matter what a child knows but only *how he learns it*, is another by-product of the faculty-theory, an expression of the notion that it is we who make persons, not God Almighty; or at any rate, that it rests with us to fill in a vague sketch. Therefore, says Rousseau, "a child ought to receive no lessons except from experience." Therefore, "children are incapable of judging, really have no memory."

7   I fear we fail as much as did Rousseau to realize the consequences of a contempt of knowledge. This is how

it works: The child has not yet developed such and such faculties, may not develop all until he is a man; therefore, our appeal shall be to the "faculty" we know he has; he shall learn about nothing but what he can see with his eyes, handle with his hands; his own experience shall be his teacher; as for the wealth of knowledge the world has acquired, what is that to him or us? Our business is to develop his "faculties" and, by and by, he will use them as he pleases. So we labour to convince the young scholar that he hates knowledge, that books are not for him, that he can only learn from *things*, and must begin upon them as if he were a young savage to whom the minds of other men brought no gains. And all this, because we suppose our business is to teach a child to *think*, and to think in a certain order—that in which his "faculties" are developed! As a result, the education we give is *sterile*—no other word characterizes it justly. Races and ages have their periods of temptation as well as individual men; and we are in the wilderness—being tempted to make bread; nor have we yet learned to reply to the tempter,—"Man shall not live by bread alone," but by "Words," by all those words of insight and knowledge which we believe have come down to us since time began, and continue to come as we are able to receive them. And observe, this knowledge is vital: men shall live by it, and without it they shall not live. Because we minimise the knowledge we give in our schools, our pupils leave us intellectually devitalized. "Pity the children, another 'Subject' is forced upon them!" is the cry of our newspapers. "Happy children, another way of joy is opened to them!" is what we may live to read!

But we are not without excuse; we have all gone wrong in the train of Rousseau; we have been taught to think that knowledge does not matter, that sharpened faculties are our concern; that, given these, the person will get all the knowledge he wants hereafter; which may easily be, for if he has not been nourished on knowledge as a child he never acquires the appetite. It was not for nothing that the two sorts of life and the two sorts of nutriment were brought before us in that wilderness scene: are we not able to understand a parable? Can we not comprehend that as the body is able to deal with its meat, without interference from us, so spirit (including, I suppose, mind, heart, soul, whatever is not body), is able to deal with the knowledge laid before it, without impertinent interference? The "faculties," if there be faculties, are not our business; and our concern with knowledge is not that we may *know*, but that we may be nourished and grow; for it is as possible to secrete knowledge as to secrete proteids, unhealthily.

Rousseau maintains that children cannot learn geometry because they rarely retain ideas and still more rarely the relation of one idea to another, and this, though not a century before, Blaise Pascal, a boy of twelve, had built up a science of geometry all his own! As has been well said, Mathematics, like Music, take little account of age. For the same reason, he repudiates the study of languages for children, because "the child cannot grasp ideas." But how true is this of the study of Geography.

"In any study, words that represent things are nothing
without the ideas of the things they represent. We, however, limit children to these signs, without ever being
able to make them understand the things represented.
We think we are teaching a child the description of the
earth, when he is merely learning maps. We teach him
the names of cities, countries, rivers; he has no idea that
they exist anywhere but on the map we use in pointing
them out to him."

A child must begin by learning to know the country
about him, to make and follow a plan of his father's garden,
for example, and here, as in so much else, all that is best
in modern teaching is derived from Rousseau. What can
be better than the way he takes the boy out to watch the
sunrise, and later, the sunset, and sees to it that he observes
for himself without instruction that sunrise and sunset
take place at opposite points of the heavens—so, the sun
has travelled!

"A spherical top, turning on its point, shall represent the
heavens revolving on their axis; the two extremities of
the top are the two poles. The child will be interested
in knowing one of them, which I will show him near
the tail of Ursa Minor. . . . We have seen the sun rise at
mid-summer; we will also watch its rising at Christmas
or some other fine day in winter. . . . 'How queer that
is! the sun does not rise where it used to rise! Here are
our old landmarks, and now it is rising over yonder . . .'

While the child, studying the sphere, is transported into the heavens, bring him back to the measurement of the earth and show him first his own home."

Equally sound is Émile's introduction to Physics.

"When lying at full length in the bath, raise the arm horizontally out of the water, and you feel it burdened by a great weight: air is therefore heavy. Put air in equilibrium with other bodies, and you can measure its weight. From these observations were constructed the barometer, the siphon, the air-gun, and the air-pump. All the laws of statics and hydrostatics were discovered by experiments as simple as these. I would not have my pupil study them in a laboratory of experimental physics. I dislike the array of machines and instruments. The parade of science is fatal to science itself. All those machines frighten the child; or else their singular forms divide and distract the attention he ought to give to their effects."

Here, is a lesson which we should take to heart to-day, writing in letters of gold upon every school house: "the *parade* of science is fatal to science itself."

Here, again, are words of wisdom:

"All ideas of manhood that a child can understand give us opportunities of teaching him; but of those he cannot understand he should remain in entire ignorance."

Could there be more delicate counsel on a delicate subject which tempts some of us to rush in all too rashly?

The teaching of History is condemned with more consistency than wisdom.

> "A more ridiculous method obliges children to study history, supposed to be within their comprehension because it is only a collection of facts. . . . Do we imagine that the true understanding of events can be separated from that of their causes and effect? and that the historic and the moral are so far asunder that the one can be understood without the other?"

Of course, Émile is necessarily without imagination and judgment, and cannot study history intelligently. But we, who believe that a child is a person, do not presuppose these intellectual *lacunae*; and we find children full of eager interest in the subject and very capable of just reflection; fit from an early age, in fact, to derive ideas of worthy citizenship from Plutarch's Lives, and to bring their reading of history to bear upon what is going on to-day.

Perhaps, Rousseau has said the last word as to the cultivation of the Senses.

> "To exercise the senses is not merely to use them, but to learn how to judge correctly by means of them; we may say, to learn how to feel. For we cannot feel, or hear, or see, otherwise than as we have been taught." After

commending every sort of muscular activity, he adds: "Use, then, not only your bodily strength, but all the senses which direct it. Make as much of each as possible, and verify the impressions of one by those of another. Measure, count, weigh, and compare. Use no strength till after you have calculated the resistance it will meet. . . . If the boy wishes to carry a burden exactly as heavy as his strength will bear, without the test of first lifting it, must he not estimate its weight by the eye?"

As regards an open-air life, physical exercise and physical training, we are still far from realizing this eighteenth century ideal. For Rousseau's young savage living *en plein air* was the *rule*, living under shelter the *exception*, an ideal for us to struggle towards. And so attractive are this open-air life, the apparent self-dependence, these seemingly casual studies pursued by inductive processes, that we must moderate our enthusiasm by allowing the Master himself to expose the system of subtle and absolute tyranny, which, in the name of liberty, he imposes on Émile:

"Let your pupil suppose himself master, while you are really master. No subjection is so perfect as that which retains the appearance of liberty; for thus the will is itself made captive. Is not the helpless, unknowing child at your mercy? Do you not, so far as he is concerned, control everything around him? Have you not power to influence him as you please? Are not his work, his play, his pain, in your hands, whether he knows it or not? Doubtless he ought to do only what he pleases; but your choice ought to control his wishes. He ought to take no step that you have not directed; he ought not to open his lips without your knowing what he is about to say."

We perceive that the Jesuit schools had left their mark on Rousseau's thought; it is not thus that Englishmen are made; but are we doing nothing towards establishing a *tutorial hierarchy*? It is not only that parents still feel they have the power (and the right) to influence their child as they please, but when he goes to school do we teachers not endeavour to keep his mind in our hands, to pose before him as fountains of all knowledge, and to deny him immediate access to the great minds which should affect him through the books they have written?

I have tried to give a sketch of Rousseau's educational scheme, desultory, after the manner of Émile, and necessarily very inadequate. But let us consider the *Result* in the Master's own words, and contemplate Émile at fifteen:

"Émile understands only the natural and purely physical sciences. He does not even know the name of history, or the meaning of metaphysics and ethics. He knows the essential relations between man and man. He does not readily generalise or conceive of abstractions. . . . He makes no attempt to learn the nature of things, but only such of their relations as concern himself. He estimates external things only by their relation to him; but this estimate is exact and *positive*, and in it, fancies and conventionalities have no share. *He values most those things that are most useful to him; and never deviating from this standard, is not influenced by general opinion.*"

(I have italicized certain phrases to bring out more strongly points of resemblance between Émile and our own school-boys and girls).

"Émile is industrious, temperate, patient, and full of courage. His imagination, never aroused, does not exaggerate dangers. He feels few discomforts, and can bear pain with fortitude, because he has never learned to contend with fate. . . . In a word, Émile has every virtue which *affects himself. . . . He considers himself independently of others*, and is satisfied when others do not think of him at all. *He exacts nothing from others and never thinks of owing anything to them.* He is alone in human society, and *depends solely upon himself. . . .* He has sound constitution, active limbs, a fair, unprejudiced mind, a heart free and without passions. Self-love, the first and most natural of all, has scarcely manifested itself at all."

11

We have him here with us in England in the twentieth century and know him well. He is an attractive person, but aloof; perhaps the more attractive because he is aloof, and because he is healthy, well-grown, vigorous; "a nice boy," we say, and we are glad that he is not a "bookworm." The only thing to be urged against the education that turns him out is—that he remains what he is now. As a man he is still aloof—from pictures and books, from social movements, from the making of history, from civic affairs. Sport rouses him for he believes it will make him "fit." His country may be in the throes of a political crisis and he asks: "How's the cricket?" It is not that he is a bad fellow or consciously selfish, but his imagination is dormant. Comprehensive ideas do not appeal to him though he is apt enough for partisan strife; and as we have learned to our delight and gratitude he is faithful unto death to country and cause. But a great war is a costly instrument to bring out the best that is in a man; it rests with us to try if education may not serve the same purpose.

When he comes to choose a career, he asks (or rather asked), Does it offer a snug berth? Not that he cares much for money, but, for a certain manner of living, and neither wife nor vocation tempts him from this individualistic standpoint. They might be worse, these young people whom we are educating, but somehow their point of view is wrong, and Milton shows us how: their standpoint is purely individualistic; his, purely altruistic. Milton with a mind formed upon classical ideals perceives that a man must be brought up for the uses, and for all the uses, his city or his country may have for him—for uses public and private—in peace and war.

To earn his living is not a chief end of man, but to fill

his place as a citizen, with a comprehensive outlook upon all the offices, public and private of a citizen and a patriot. Therefore, he is not to be brought up to one thing, whether to grind the points of pins or add up figures on a stool. He must understand, think worthy thoughts of, every part of a citizen's life and duty, so that he shall not only fulfil his own share, but shall bring just and magnanimous thoughts to bear on other men's offices as well as his own, and shall have skill and judgment, not only for his own but for the general use. For, see what it would be to the State to have citizens of this magnanimous type: "Tammany"—could not grow up in such a State, nor professionalism in games, nor payment for every office of honour held for the public good.

Rousseau claims that he is showing his pupil a path of knowledge, long, endless and tedious to follow; "I am showing him how to take the first steps so that he may know the beginning, but allow him to go on farther." Émile certainly has the advantage of our young people in that he knows "the natural and purely physical sciences;" but we are making headway in that respect and may yet do well when we come to realize the force of Rousseau's axiom that "the parade of science is fatal to science itself." Like Émile, our boys and girls hardly know the name of history or the meaning of metaphysics and ethics. How then can they perform justly the offices to which they are called as men and women, citizens and patriots? We are almost without general conceptions as to what is required by justice towards the persons, characters, opinions and interests of the persons with whom we come into contact. We say damaging things recklessly, we misrepresent opinions, falsify statements, wink at public jobbing, allow unhindered play to malice and envy in our thoughts and speech. If all this came of what used to be called "original sin," and was not to be helped or hindered, there would be little use in discussing the matter. My contention is, that these social faults, exhibited in private life and public offices, are the result of an education faulty in theory. Of course, there will always be base and malicious persons, but it is against well-meaning and kindly folk (including ourselves) that these railing accusations may with justice be brought. We mean well enough and have our own loyalties and generosities, but, like Émile, we have not been taught ethics, nor do we know "the meaning of metaphysics" in any sense that would help us to understand the interaction of thought and feeling in other minds. Like Émile, again, "we know nothing of the moral relations between man and man." How is it possible for such an one as our system of education turns out to deal justly in all his relations, public and private? It will be urged that Rousseau undertakes only to lead his pupil into a path of knowledge which should prove endless; he will learn this delicate justice and respect for the feelings of others as he grows older: but that is the whole contention. 13 People go on as they begin because they are not imperfect, partially-developed, defective beings during the time of their education, but are persons, with, in their degree, all the powers of a person and all the duties of a person. If boys and girls are taught on narrow individualistic lines, if they learn just what will pay in an examination and be of service to them in after life, they will get the habit of considering what will "pay" and will not learn to think sympathetically and therefore justly.

But Milton would have the pupil taught to perform his various offices "skilfully." Here, I think, the sort of "Robinson Crusoe" life that Émile was to lead should help a man to be skilful for his own uses at any rate; and we are giving a good deal of attention to this line of education. We are offering all sorts of hand and eye training, and are opening out splendid fields for practice, whether as School Cadets, Scouts, or what not. This is first-rate work, the more so because Milton's third essential, "magnanimity," is taken into account. Here, however, is our great failure: we not only fail to be magnanimous as a generation but we do not realize what a great quality this is. If we want the right man or woman for any office, public or private, we need not look for experience, cleverness, organising power, knowledge of detail, in the candidate. What we want is Magnanimity, a certain largeness of mind and wideness of outlook, which will see the bearing of one thing upon another, the relation of every part to the whole, and of the whole to the whole of human society. Magnanimity is the perfect fruit of character, the outcome of a wide knowledge of men and affairs, past and present, upon which insight and imagination have been brought to bear. It is the finest result of education, and Émile, who does not know what history means, can have none of it. If we would have our boys and girls look at life with "larger, other eyes," we must see to it that they are saturated with history, poetry, all that literature which recognises that the proper study of mankind is man, man in particular, ethics, metaphysics, poetry, (by the way, Émile never seems to have heard of poetry!) and men in general,—civics, economics, history, above all, history, without too much care to point the moral or adorn the tale. It is as examples, parallels, warnings, strike himself, and not as they are pointed out to him, that history begins to be of service to the boy and he begins to perceive that his country is of more consequence than himself, and that it is a better thing to help in the general progress than to advance himself.

14

Isaac Walton tells us of that most admirable mother, Mrs. Herbert (the mother of the saintly George)—

> "In this time of her widowhood, she being desirous to give Edward, her eldest son, such advantages of learning and other education as might suit his birth and fortune, and thereby make him more fit for the service of his country, did," etc. Let us note, the end towards which this mother deliberately educated her son was, "the service of his country."

In proportion as our outlook becomes altruistic rather than individualistic—and that is the development to be expected of a Christian people—we shall, no doubt, arrive at Machiavelli's science of politics, that is, we shall compare that which happens under our own eyes with that which in similar circumstances occurred in the past, here or elsewhere. By means of such comparison we may succeed in understanding what we should do, since "men are always the same and have the same passions, and when circumstances are identical, the same causes lead to the same effects and therefore the same facts ought to suggest the same" (or opposite) "rules of conduct." "I have heard," says Machiavelli, "that history is the teacher of our actions and especially of our rulers; the world has always been inhabited by men with the same passions as our own, and there have always been rulers and ruled, and good subjects and bad subjects, and those who rebel and are punished." There is good in things evil, would men observingly distil it out, and the Florentine's science of statesmanship may yet unfold itself under those moral and religious sanctions he would away with.

I am inclined to think that the doctrine, that a child is born a person, that every child is a person, should make for magnanimity. We shall perceive that we are no such great people after all, that the very great amelioration in the conditions of life which we must recognize is due rather to the spread of Christian principles than to the inventions and discoveries about which we are a little puffed up. Was not that smith of ancient chronicle, who according to the mediaevalists, perceived, conceived, or as we would say, invented, *Music*—from the ring of the hammer on the anvil at least as great an inventor as any we have produced? We are suffering from megalomania, the symptoms of swelled head appearing in one class of persons in reference to their country, and in another class in reference to the age they live in, this wonderful twentieth century:—

"We throw out acclamations of self-thanking,   15
    self-admiring,
With, for every mile run faster, 'Oh, the wondrous,
    wondrous Age!'"

E. B. B.

But a knowledge of history should cure all that, and we should be inclined, with Machiavelli, to look to history for the solution of many a problem.

Consider Plutarch's narrative of how Numa Pompilius was made king. We need not ask how much is Numa and how much is Plutarch, but the young person who has ruminated quietly and after his or her own fashion, between, say, the ages of eight and eighteen, upon matters of this kind, has some definite conception of the meaning of citizenship; and, as every child is a person, open to the fine impulses proper to a person, the outcome of such reading must needs be profitable, alike to the nation and the individual. We must be on our guard as to the sort of history books we give our scholars. It is rather the custom to make the study of history entertaining by depreciating all that has gone before our own wonderful times; and truly wonderful they are; but we must remember that so long as there have been persons in the world, there have been persons of heroic mould and magnanimous spirit, and a cavalier way of treating history is an indication of both ignorance and bad taste.

If magnanimity is the essential quality of a good citizen, and, further, if magnanimity is a gradual and unconscious development of mind and character upon great thoughts and great studies, we are able to understand why the *Humanities* have been the staple of education during a good many ages of the world's history. Perhaps both the matter and method of these studies require a good deal of overhauling; perhaps, our young people must read not only a few books in a "dead" language, even though these be incomparably good, but must have a wide range of reading both in literature and history, for the most part in the mother tongue. But, allowing for due and necessary changes, it must always remain true that the *Humanities* should form the staple of the education of the child.

The *Danger* to which I referred arises from our good intentions and our zeal in following what seems to us a forward movement. All that which is considered educational progress to-day is founded upon Rousseau; we are content that our boys and girls should know "nothing of the moral relations between man and man"; that "the boy," to quote Rousseau, "should estimate external things only by their relation to him"; and that he should "consider himself independently of others." This is the consummation of what

Rousseau calls natural and what we call scientific education. That scientific education in due measure is a good and necessary development no one will deny. To live under the dominance of, and in relation to, innumerable natural laws of whose workings we are ignorant, would be to revert to a condition of brutish ignorance and superstition. Never again can Science be excluded from our curriculum.

But a new idea is presenting itself; our sons and daughters must be brought up to be good citizens; and to play their part, not merely as individuals but as members profitable to the community, they must be *humane*. Now, science does not belong to the humanities. It is entirely *unhumane*, because it is concerned with matters which are of accidental rather than of essential importance to men. No doubt science is a good schoolmaster and produces very fine individual virtues, but not of a kind directly serviceable and sympathetic to the community. We are, I know, inclined to protest and to say that doctors are the most humane class of men among us; certainly they are, but not because they are scientific men but because they are past masters in the humanities, learned at first-hand *in the school of life*. On the whole, young men decline the professions; they do not take Orders nor enter the Services; curates are not to be had for love or money, and both Woolwich and Sandhurst sometimes have been reduced to the necessity of allowing men to enter without due qualifications. The young men do not care for these careers because they can "do themselves" better. They are fine, rather splendid fellows, but their concern is about themselves, and this, not through any natural depravity, but through the temper of their education, for even in schools where there is little enough science taught, the general spirit is scientific or practical.

To sum up:—Rousseau is the inspirer of modern progressive education.

We must avail ourselves of the scientific spirit of the age in our educational work.

But the scientific spirit is not humane, and if we wish to train good citizens we must see to it that the *Humanities* are widely studied in our schools.

17   We must not allow ourselves to be handicapped by Rousseau's doctrine of faculties progressively developed.

If we believe that children are *Persons*, we are inexcusable if we do not supply them with liberal knowledge of all those things which affect persons.

We must discriminate wisely; a person is equally a person whether he walks on foot or uses a motor-car or an aeroplane; therefore we are not free to regard advance in such matters as these as essential to human progress.

It is necessary, then, that we exercise judgment in selecting such aliment of knowledge for our children as shall cause them to grow into efficient citizens.

Milton promises generously. Could anything be more inviting than this?

> "I shall straight conduct you to a hillside, where I will
> point you out the right path of a virtuous and noble

education; laborious indeed at the first ascent, but else so smooth, so green, so full of goodly prospect and melodious sounds on every side, that the harp of Orpheus was not more charming. I doubt not but ye shall have more ado to drive our dullest and laziest youth, our stocks and stubs from the infinite desire of such a happy nurture, than we have now to haul and drag our choicest and hopefullest wits to that feast of sow-thistles and brambles which is commonly set before them as all the food and entertainment of the tenderest and most docile age. I call, therefore, a complete and generous education, that which fits a man to perform, justly, skilfully, and magnanimously all the offices, both private and public, of peace and war."

But it is rather in the spirit than in the letter of his further indications that we find help towards Milton's ideal of a "complete and generous education." We may agree with him that, "we do amiss to spend seven or eight years merely in scraping together so much miserable Latin and Greek as might be learned otherwise easily and delightfully in one year," but we have certainly not yet discovered how to do the work easily and delightfully in one year. The point upon which some of us are inclined to argue with Milton is that young people are capable of carrying on a great many more studies contemporaneously with delight and profit than we exact of them: and this larger scheme of studies may be covered in a very much shorter schoolday than is usually allowed, if the habit of perfect attention is required from the first, a habit which is to be acquired easily by children who are accustomed to use the best books for themselves and have not to listen to what Rousseau calls "the *verbiage*" of the teacher.

It is well that we should be reminded in these too tolerant days of what Milton held to be *the end* of learning—not the chief end, or an important end—but *the* end.

18   "The end, then, of learning is, to repair the ruins of our first parents by regaining to know God aright, and out of that knowledge to love him, to imitate him, to be like him, as we may the nearest by possessing our souls of true virtue, which, being united to the heavenly grace of faith, makes up the highest perfection."

The Nemesis which has come upon us for our careless neglect of this 'end' is a curious example of how incalculable may be the consequences of a more or less casual neglect. We have ceased to think it our most important concern to teach religion to children, and, as a corollary, we have withdrawn one of the three or four great literatures of the world from the knowledge of the people,—a literature including just laws, pure ethics, sublime poetry, history as instructive as, and no more mythical than any history of any nation, biography, epistles of wonderful power and charm, and the great epic of the world written in the four Gospels.

Time was when the children of working-men had as

perfect a phrase by phrase and line by line familiarity with a very large part of this great literature as a good "Grecian" has with his Aeschylus and Plato. Then we had character as a people; then we made for ourselves a great name among the nations; then we were, there is reason to believe, the magnanimous citizens to whom a Shakespeare could appeal. But we have changed all that; it is not that we do not give careful and conscientious religious instruction, but rather perhaps that we are in a transition stage when we no longer feel that it is legitimate, in face of the great access of knowledge with which the world is endowed, to educate in our Public Schools upon the Classics only, and, in our elementary schools, upon Bible literature only; and we have not yet found out a perfect way, nor exactly what to substitute for the curricula followed through many generations.

But we need not be discouraged. Those who listen to the myriad voices of the hour will hear the cry arising from many an unexpected quarter—"My soul is athirst for the living God!" The young people are beginning to discover for themselves that they want the Bible; and when they do so we shall have to give it to them: perhaps the day will come when we shall not consider John Stuart Mill and Herbert Spencer the best guides to propose to those young people overseas to whom we offer the benefits of a western education. I have come across no sign of the times more interesting than the movement which is going on among what in America are called "College Men." It appears that in one University after another men have quite spontaneously

19

formed themselves into groups for the definite study of the Scriptures—not of books about the Bible, but the Bible itself; not in obedience to any Church or sect or revivalist movement, but merely with the desire to search the Scriptures, do several thousands of these young men devote some part of their leisure to a study which, there, as here, is out of their ordinary curriculum. This seems to me one indication of a great impulse which is moving Christian peoples in various manners towards that "end" of education which Milton recognized; and for this and other reasons, it is not amiss to close the consideration of these *Two Ideals of Education* with the noble invocation of Wordsworth:—

"Milton, thou shouldst be living at this hour:
England hath need of thee: she is a fen
Of stagnant waters; altar, sword and pen,
Fireside, the heroic wealth of hall and bower,
Have forfeited their ancient English dower
Of inward happiness. We are selfish men;
Oh, raise us up, return to us again;
And give us manners, virtue, freedom, power;
Thy soul was like a Star, and dwelt apart:
Thou hadst a voice whose sound was like the sea
Pure as the naked heavens, majestic, free,
So didst thou travel on life's common way,
In cheerful godliness: and yet thy heart
The lowliest duties on herself did lay."

Appendix

SOME IMPRESSIONS OF
THE AMBLESIDE METHOD

I.

BY THE HEADMASTER OF A COUNCIL SCHOOL.*

The scheme has been in operation in the school for over two years, and the change in interest is most marked. From Form I. onwards pupils feel that the school is a joy and a delight. There is a surprising keenness in the work, and the boys have become very alert. The characters in the books are clothed with such a reality as to make them a part of the life of the children. The battle between the Greeks and Trojans has been fought over again with sticks made from orange boxes, the boys agreeing among themselves who should be Hector, Agamemnon and Ulysses. The home-life has become awakened by new and strange names. At first parents thought that someone at school was qualifying for a place in an asylum. Now they are interested in the narrations of their children and find somewhere among the disused things of the home that there are copies of Scott or Dickens which belonged to their great-grandfathers. These now occupy an honourable place and are daily read.

---

* With acknowledgements to the Editor of the *Nineteenth Century and After*.

This new interest is revealed in the quality, quantity and sentence-construction of written composition. While there still remains the spelling difficulty, children now see the need for words and their correct spelling. During the last two years spelling has much improved, and the vocabulary of the average child has greatly increased. The quality of the composition has become vastly higher. In fact when comparisons are made with the work of children of the same age two years ago, the change is hardly credible. The following written exercises show what has been done after a year's work with the methods. They are given as written. A boy, age 7.

> *St. Alban.*—One day a man fled to Alban's house and he asked Alban to hide him as quickly as he could. 'What evil have you done? said Alban. 'No evil,' said he, 'but I am a Christian.' The next day Alban was talking to Amphibalus when a servant came and said the soldiers were at the gate. Then Amphibalus said 'Amen.' 'Do not be afraid,' said Alban, 'my servants will take you through a secret passage. Take off your cape.' Amphibalus did as he was told. Then Alban put on the cape and waited for the Romans. When the Romans saw who he was they took him to the Governor.

A boy, age 8.

> *Coronation of Arthur.*—Then with her two sons came Bellicent and King Leodogran asked if she knew about

Arthur. She said 'O king, I will tell thee,' and she began her story of the coronation. As Arthur sat on the throne and the knights knelt to be knighted, he gave them such strict laws that some had pale faces, others had flushed faces. The sword was put down in front of him. He looked at it and on one side it said 'Take me,' on the other it said 'Cast me away,' and Arthur's face was sad; but Merlin said 'Take it, the time to cast it away is long.' So Arthur took it. Beside the throne was Merlin, and near him was the Lady of the Lake, who was clothed in white samite, while incense curled about her. She lived down in the deep, and whatever storms were upon the water she was calm, and she could walk on the water like our Lord. They heard the sound of holy hymns from out of the deep. Coming from a window behind the throne, which had upon it the Crucifixion, were three coloured rays, flame, vert, and azure, which showed three queens. They were tall and stood in silence ready to help him at his need.

A boy, age 9.

Scrooge.—While Scrooge was sitting in front of the fire taking his gruel he glanced at the tiles on which were pictures of the scriptures. But instead of seeing the real pictures he saw Marley's face. He got up and after walking up and down the room several times said 'Humbug.' He looked at a big bell which began to ring, and so did every bell in the house. They all stopped at once. Then he heard a clanking noise over the wine casks. He then remembered that ghosts pulled chains and began to feel rather frightened. All at once the cellar door flew open with a booming sound. Then it came into Scrooge's room and stood in front of him. Scrooge said, 'What do you want with me?' 'Much,' said the ghost. The ghost was transparent, so that Scrooge could see the two buttons on the back of his coat. He wore the same tights, the same waistcoat, and the same everything. Scrooge said 'Can you sit down?' The ghost said 'I can,' and did so.

Boy, age 12.

Excalibur.—'Excalibur' was the name of King Arthur's sword. He found it one fine summer's day when walking by a lake. An arm rose up from out the bosom of the lake clothed in white samite, mystic, wonderful. He rowed across and took it and wore it like a king.

The hilt was set in with diamonds of extraordinary value, costly pearls, and myriads of topaz-lights and jacinth work of the subtlest jewellery. Arthur gazed so long that both his eyes were dazzled with the bright lights. On one side were the words 'Take me,' and on the other 'Cast me away.' He did not know what to do, but Merlin, the old magician, said 'The time to cast is far away from now,' so Arthur kept it and used it well.

The scene next comes to where the king is lying

smitten thro' the helm in a ruined chapel, a broken chancel with a broken cross. The king is very sick, and thinks his wound has taken cold and that he will die before help comes.

The time had come to throw the sword away.

King Arthur said to Sir Bedivere, 'Take my brand Excalibur, which was my pride, and throw it into the middle mere, watch what thou see'st and lightly bring me word.'

Sir Bedivere went. He paused and looked at the sword and thought it would be better to leave 'Excalibur' concealed there among the many knotted water-flags that grew beside the mere. So lightly Sir Bedivere went to the king.

The king drawing thicker breath said 'What hast thou seen, or what hast heard?' And answer made the bold Sir Bedivere, 'I heard the ripple washing in the reeds, and the wild water lapping on the crag.' 'Ah! unknightly traitor-hearted, Authority forgets a dying king, go again I bid thee.' Sir Bedivere went a second time counting the dewy pebbles as he went. Again as he took the sword its richness overpowered him, and he hid it a second time. Would it not be better to keep the sword that it might be put in some great monarch's treasure-house and be shown at a joust of arms by some old man saying 'This is King Arthur's sword Excalibur wrought by the lonely Maiden of the Lake, nine years she wrought it sitting in the deeps upon the hidden bases of the hills.' So back he went to the king. 'Hast thou performed my command? what has thou seen, or what hast heard?' To this the traitor-hearted Bedivere replied 'I heard the long ripple washing on the crag, and the wild water lapping in the reeds.' King Arthur mad with rage said 'Go again, and if thou spare to fling Excalibur a third time, I will arise and slay thee with mine own hand, for a man may fail in duty twice and yet the third time may prosper, Get thee hence.'

Down the rocks and ridges leapt Sir Bedivere, leaping among the bulrush beds, he clutched the sword, and strongly wheeled and threw it. The great brand made lightnings in the splendour of the moon, and ere it dipped the surface an arm rose up clothed in white samite, mystic, wonderful, and brandished it three times and drew it under. And lightly went Sir Bedivere to the king. 'Ah,' said the king, 'I see by thine eyes what thou hast done, tell me what thou hast seen, or what hast heard.' Sir Bedivere told his story, and at the king's request carried him to the edge of the mere.

There is the greatest hope of the changes which will follow from these methods. The self-activity of the child finds an outlet in 'doing things' for himself; the learning by the scholars and not the teaching by the teachers gives confidence and self-reliance; the interest in the doings of men and women will act as a sure antidote against boredom and listlessness; the training to see a motive in action will lead to the weighing of newspaper talk and the deeds of men. A child leaving school with such a mass of experience will be loath to take his opinions from second-hand sources. The cultivation of an appreciation for pictures, music and poetry will give a distinct tone to the afterlife. The proper use of books and the reading habit will fit a child, either to continue a higher education or to become an intelligent and skilful craftsman. This liberal education has its foundation in the religious, moral and spiritual ideas of the great minds of the past and present. The child is an individual waiting for the real experiences of life; the State is an aggregation of individuals each of whom gives something to the qualities of that State, and every British-born child comes into the world with potentialities which should make for the welfare of the British Empire. To transform these possibilities into real qualities is the first and last duty of all who have the care of the future citizens of our glorious Empire. As the individual helps to give character to the State, so education prepares the individual to fulfil the obligations of service, humanity and religion.

II.

BY THE HEADMASTER OF ANOTHER COUNCIL SCHOOL.

Yes. Our children have had oral lessons and voyages imaginary, and contour lessons, and worse still commercial geography, and date books, and pleasant extracts in reading books that you could read in three months, and whose thoroughfares you traversed backwards or forwards for the remaining nine months till you were bored stiff.

But you say, What is this extra reading that Miss Mason gives? Let me give you a list of what my kiddies in smoke-grimed Leeds have read in the Autumn term.

We read a section of Arnold Forster's English History, the contemporary section of French History, roughly speaking, from the Napoleonic Wars to the beginning of the Crimean War. We read some of *The Antiquary* of Scott, the 2nd Canto of Byron's *Childe Harold, The Ancient Mariner, The Lay of the Last Minstrel*, selections from Burns, Goldsmith, Wordsworth, Cowper and Shelley. We learned something of the Painters,—Turner, Gainsborough, Romney and others, and contemplated copies of their works. We looked upon the history of our country, not only on the political and social side, but also saw it as it was reflected in the painters and writers of the time. We watched the unfolding flower and growing seed in the Nature Books of Stopes and saw it actually in the growing plant. We read the delightful nature stories of Bees, etc., in *The Fairyland of Science*.

9   We turned to the unchanging East and saw, as through a glass darkly, the land of the Pharaohs, portrayed in the Book of the British Museum, marched and fought again with Alexander in the pages of Plutarch, learned to know the meaning and purpose of our own lives in Miss Mason's book, *Ourselves*, began to grasp the faith and trust that underlies all true citizenship in Arnold Forster's *Laws of Every*

Day Life, and last, but not least, wandered in the Forest of Arden in the company of Rosalind, Orlando, Touchstone, the melancholy Jacques, under the guidance of one William Shakespeare. . . .

But there are certain things we did find out. First, as I have already hinted, a limiting of our view as to the value of the oral lesson, an enhancing as to the value of letting the child come face to face with the best writers on a subject. Second, the discovery that the pupil had greater powers of mind than we (optimists always) had given him credit for, that the child thought not specially in single words, but more frequently in whole blocks, that the quicker children had almost uncanny powers of "sensing" a passage, that they took a whole picture in a sort of stride and passed on.

We found that ideas were being garnered and vocabularies were enlarging. We found that pupils were discovering harmonies between ideas really similar, belonging to different circumstances, and better still, collision between one kind of experience and another—that hard but most certain way of knowledge—that mental upset between different analyses, to be harmonized by some truth deeper still, that was waiting for the seeker before peace could again reign.

Then comes the question: Did the children attend? Now, there is the secret of the method. All the lessons call for what Professor James calls exteriorization. The Professor says somewhere: "If a man have knowledge and cannot exteriorize it, then he really hasn't got it." A somewhat Hibernian remark, but true. Therefore each lesson calls for exteriorization and this helps towards concentration in the hearer. Two ways of exteriorization come to mind:—

1. The written. Twenty minutes reading and ten composition (and you get more in that ten than you used to get in the thirty in the old composition lesson).
2. Oral. Narration of the meaning of the part read, and here you get a rapid improvement in the pupil's power of expressing himself as well as in verbal memory. One boy (gifted with verbal memory), after hearing the soliloquy, The Seven Ages of Man, read once, stood out and gave it very nearly verbatim. It was very remarkable.

10

It is something if by this scheme one has been enabled to let in the light and air of a gentler and cleaner life and open pathways of joy along roads otherwise choked or barred by ignorance or upbringing, or worse.

"Let knowledge grow from more to more,
But chiefly reverence in us dwell."

III.

BY A DIRECTOR OF EDUCATION.

Miss Mason's aim is to educate a child to fulfil all the duties of a citizen, to comprehend and appreciate what is great and good, and to form character in conformity with the principles of religion and morality. The child is looked upon as a living, active, enquiring being, rather than a blank sheet of paper. All the potentialities of greatness are present, and the object of education is to transform these into realities.

Nature Study occupies an important place in the method, and offers unlimited material for observation, comparison and contrast. Men, books and things are the educational *media*. I need not elaborate this. The methods are fully dealt with in the P.N.E.U. pamphlets, and in *Home Education* and *School Education*, by Miss Mason.

The more practical aims seem to us to be:—

1. To help the child to carry forward youthful ardour and a desire for knowledge.
2. To maintain a keen interest all through school life, as a preparation for larger and wider interests.
3. To foster habits of concentration, continuous effort and self-reliance.
4. To enable the child to talk and write naturally and easily on what has been read or observed.
5. To cultivate a love for and sympathy with what is finest in both nature and the arts.

In order to touch the child at many points, a wide curriculum is provided. From the beginning good literature is read to the children, and narration by the scholars follows each reading. Food for thought is thus given and a vocabulary supplied for the expression of ideas. When narration becomes easy and free, the child is ready for written composition. An excellent preparation is thus given for individual study in higher Forms. When individual study begins, the reproduction is mostly written. Here there is no suggestive questioning by the teacher nor can there be any shirking by the pupils. Each member of a class must reveal himself. At first the reproduction closely follows the book, which is natural; later the work becomes more original and individual. The study of an author provides ample materials for exercises in composition. Nature study is first taken from real things. The child sees and handles while the teacher guides and suggests. The teacher next reads a description from a standard work, and in most cases this is amplified by the pupils reading from a well written primer or text book. Thus the child seems to be able at a much earlier stage than usual to fit together his own philosophy of nature and life. History and Geography are approached through well written books read to the children in sections, and reproduced by them orally. Citizenship is based on Plutarch's *Lives*, an admirable preparation for the study of *The Rights and Duties of a Citizen* and the *Laws of Everyday Life*, by Arnold Forster. To develop some appreciation of Art, six pictures are studied each term, and in the higher forms this is linked with the drawing lessons. A well-known artist friend of mine is of opinion that all this is wrong, but his story is too long to tell you here. Music has a place in the curriculum, and with older pupils some attempts are made to cultivate musical appreciation by playing selections from some great master after a simple talk on the life and aspirations of the composer. On the principles of my artist friend this also should be all wrong. Handwork takes an important place. The scenes depicted in various books are used for original expression work in drawing. In the higher forms, Elementary Science affords many opportunities for the making of simple apparatus, and the school garden forms an important adjunct to the work of each programme. Both boys and girls take some Hygiene and Physiology in Form IV. . . .

When these difficulties had been understood and grappled with, both teachers and scholars took on a new alertness. . . .

We find that the careful selection of books in each subject makes the work more definite. The subject matter is ready to hand and the function of the teacher is to read it to the pupils in a natural, sympathetic and realistic way. The teacher becomes a medium conveying the thoughts expressed in the printed page. There is no explanation before reading; children are given an opportunity to interpret ideas for themselves. When uncommon words occur, they are written on the black-board before the reading begins. If any point has not been understood the explanations are given. We find marked improvements in all the phases of school life. The power of attention is much stronger. Children discuss with each other persons, scenes and incidents read to them, a practice which overflows into the homes. The older members of a family tell the younger ones about their new knowledge. Powers of general observation have improved. Conversational readiness becomes a characteristic. A quarter of a century of these methods with all the children of England and the strong silent Englishman should be a rare bird! Written exercises show a marked advance on previous work. . . .

We have noted that children obviously make far greater efforts than before. Learning seems to have become easy, although the pace is decidedly quicker. Greater demands are made upon the resources and watchfulness of the teacher. . . .

The books chosen for general reading are thoroughly appreciated and enjoyed. Children enter into the spirit of the books and display a real insight into motives; humour is enjoyed; pathos brings tears and treachery, indignation and disgust. So great is the interest in these books that children frequently purchase books for their own use. Copies have been purchased, varying in number from fifty to one hundred in a school of, *David Copperfield, Old Curiosity Shop, Christmas Carol, King Lear, Twelfth Night, Coriolanus, As You Like It,* Tennyson's *Poems, Pilgrim's Progress.* So begin private libraries!

IV.

BY ANOTHER SCHOOLMASTER.

When we were teaching classes in the mass we had little opportunity, but now with our classes working privately in small sections, we can help a backward reader, discuss the portion of a book which any child is studying, and in many ways exert our influence on the children who require it. I place this advantage as one of the great ones of P.N.E.U. methods—personal contact with the individual. 13

I should like now to say a few words concerning the advantages which have accrued from eighteen months' usage of P.N.E.U. methods. Many, I won't say all, for that would be an ideal almost too much to expect, but many children have cultivated a taste for good literature and surely, if a child has learnt to appreciate the value of good books, the teaching has not been in vain. I have known children choose copies of some of the books as presents from parents, etc. I have known them borrow the books from school to make up lost ground. I have observed the interest shown in the P.U.S. lessons, and these are signs of what I have just stated. The children have secured greater freedom of expression. Compositions are less hackneyed and the quality has improved in such a manner as to be almost incredible without actually seeing the books. Term examinations prove that the knowledge gained is not here to-day and gone to-morrow. The field of information is very comprehensive as a perusal of the study books will show.

V.

BY A SCHOOLMISTRESS.

Examination weeks.—We took the Examination Tests as far as we had gone in the work. All the girls turned up in fine form and we scarcely had an absentee that week. I have known of girls attending well before a School Treat or a Concert came off—but of girls attending a whole week for an examination I had never heard—or thought possible. However it is quite true.

The tests were worked and the girls did as well as they possibly could. I never realised that there was so much in the girls, and the papers show that what was really in came out. I was quite surprised at the results, though many a girl went through a heart searching performance to answer the questions. It did them a world of good; they found out that if they had been inattentive or absent, it was no good—they simply could not work the papers and so lost marks and their position in class. It was quite a study to the elder girls. It was a hard week, but the girls really liked the examination.

Of all the work this term we found the History—from Arnold Forster's *History of England*—the most difficult. This scheme requires in the teachers an absolute enthusiasm for the work, and they must have in some form or other a love of books.

14   I should now like to summarise what appear to me the chief advantages of the scheme. First—from the teacher's view.

The work is so interesting that teachers, young and old, love to be in school amongst their work. The young teacher learns and gains knowledge as she teaches, and it is a heaven-sent boon to a teacher who has been many years teaching "Drudgery," and we have all felt the latter at times.

No single lesson is monotonous. Something fresh in every lesson.

Children are more at ease with their teacher, and are not afraid to speak out. It brings out all the individuality in the child and the teacher.

The teachers say that they would not like to go back to the old scheme for all the world; they are heart and soul in love with the new work.

From the child's point of view:—

Children learn to study by themselves.

They hear and read the very best carefully chosen books, and children who read from the very best books must express their thoughts in good English.

They are kept interested, and their enthusiasm in school is unbounded.

Their lives are full of joy, the joy of learning (and the little ones love to learn), the joy of coming to school, the joy of real living.

They enter school with love and leave it with regret on going to work—not like the boy who watched the clock all the morning, and when the teacher asked him if he had to go on an important errand, said, "No sir," but when 12 o'clock struck he jumped up and said with a glad ring in his voice, "I'm off, I am fourteen years of age to-day," and rushed out of the school. What a tragedy lay in those few words!

VI.

BY ANOTHER SCHOOLMISTRESS.

Most briefly speaking, it may be summed up in the words that the actual attention rather than memory is brought into play. Now this is done through the medium of narration and composition. A passage or passages from some good book, a whole story, even, is read to the children, and they either narrate what they have heard on the conclusion of the reading, or write a composition on it. This is a very different thing from learning by heart. Whereas memorizing can become a purely mechanical repetition of words till they have been imprinted on the brain, and involving no actual understanding of the meaning thereof, narration, or the writing out of a subject, which has been but once read to the children, must call for close attention on their part.

Speaking of our customary method of education at an educational meeting, Dr. Napier said that in spite of the improvements in teaching, apparatus and text-books, the boys who left school to-day were little superior to those of thirty or forty years ago. Too much attention was given to teaching: too little to making the children learn: and the sloppiness of natural opinion was greatly encouraged by the lack of intellectual discipline and training. If children were taught to learn, to think and to suffer in order to get knowledge, then when they grew up they would appreciate the value of forming opinions and the solemn necessity of having no opinions till they knew the facts.

But to return to the scheme we are now considering.

It might be suggested at the outset that this narrating or writing of a subject after one reading is too difficult for children. It has now been proved by those who have tried the method that it is not so. Also the fact must always be borne in mind that a little difficulty stimulates, and we ought no more to hesitate in giving intellectual food to children after they have passed the first stages of babyhood, than we would hesitate to give meat to a growing child. . . .

Many books must be used and a great deal of reading done, and as there is so much to read time only allows it to be read once.

Besides the permanent books, different Classical Plays and Poems every three months, also some good standard novel and various other books are used. Reproductions of six pictures by some famous artist are used each term, these only cost 2s. the set and are of the greatest educational value.

Reading Miss Mason's scheme in conjunction with a mental review of one's own childhood, one realizes almost instinctively its practical worth. One knows so well the lasting impression, or memory rather, of any story which one has either heard or read, and repeated to some younger brother or sister, a totally different memory from that obtained by mere learning by heart from the written page, which, as already said, can often be nothing but a parrot-like repetition, with no real understanding of the matter in hand.

Of course, by Miss Mason's method, word for word repetition is frequently obtained, but it is not mechanical learning; it is a gradual training of the mind to a quick understanding, and, *through* the understanding, to the memorizing of the subject.

Those who have ever themselves attempted to memorize a sermon or lecture in order to repeat it to some friend, will easily understand and appreciate the method Miss Mason suggests. They will know how, from at first being able to repeat nothing but the salient facts, gradually the memory will learn to assimilate not only the salient facts but also the details, and even the very words in which they were embodied. The sermon or lecture is, in fact, reconstructed in the mind, at first merely in part, eventually as a complete whole. Ordinary listening would never have obtained this result. It was obtained through the stimulus of the prospective narration.

Now, it is very certain that if children are taught to concentrate, or to have their attention attractively caught, their actual powers of memory are, as a whole, considerably greater than those of an older person. . . .

We have found it to be a scheme which educates in the best sense of the word. By it the child is encouraged to work out his own line of thought, instead of following—or not following—one particular line worked out by the teacher in order to arrive at a certain fact or idea. The child does more work, while the teacher does less; and surely this is of the very essence of education, the end towards which education should be directed. The scheme gives scope for originality, and therefore each child's nature becomes, in a measure, the natural result of its own originality. Hitherto there has been little real chance of calling forth the latent individuality of the children. It was impossible that it should be so, when the set portions of work, whatever practical use they might be in themselves, were merely perfectly learned and memorized. It was almost impossible to judge how much the child had really understood, how much the child *had made its own*, how much it had actually stored up in the treasure house of the brain.

There is no question but that, when children have been taught really to appreciate good literature, they still retain their taste for it on leaving school.

Good literature and good language are practically synonymous terms. Through the reading, and, above all, the narrating of good literature, the children's vocabulary is greatly enlarged. Naturally a number of the words are entirely new and unfamiliar to them, but then so were all words unfamiliar in their infancy; it simply means adding to the store they already possess, and it is surprising how soon they begin to use these new and complex words, at first only when narrating, but later in their compositions, and even in their own conversations.

The powers of reasoning are greatly developed by this method. The mind, having plenty to feed upon, grows in intellect and activity. Questions are looked at from many points of view, and a clearer and broader outlook on life is the result. . . .

The scheme places the best, and the best only, before the

children, whose thoughts and ideas, being turned always towards the light, grow in intelligence as naturally as a plant grows towards the sun. They become more intellectual, and the whole tone of the school is gradually raised. We have noticed this fact particularly among our children after six months' training.

Recently one of the clergy made especial comment on the reasoning and intellectual powers of the elder girls. Having given them a lesson on the Sermon on the Mount, dealing with its deeper aspects, he was exceedingly surprised and pleased to find how thoroughly the girls had grasped his instruction and reasoned out the underlying and deeper meaning. He felt fully convinced that this development of their reasoning powers was the result of the new method of training which we had been adopting during the last six months.

In every case we find the interest of the children aroused, and they are invariably on the alert. This is particularly noticeable in the youngest children, those of six, seven and eight years of age. . . .

Other books which they thoroughly enjoy are, "The Age of Fable" by Thomas Bullfinch, and "Stories from Troy and Greece" by Andrew Lang; but perhaps the favourite of all is "Bleak House." Possibly this is on account of the evident pleasure in comparing and contrasting the different persons in the novel. They are undoubtedly quick in discovering the characteristics of each, in recognizing and

being attracted by what is noble and good, and in promptly 18
denouncing all meanness and hypocrisy.

Of course this is exactly what we teachers want. If our
girls will only be drawn to make heroes and heroines of the
right kind of fiction people, they will naturally be led to a
desire to imitate them, and they will, as naturally, learn to
despise the meaner characters. They will, in fact, half unconsciously make friends of the best fiction people,—not
forgetting also those who have lived in fact,—and these
mind-friendships will imperceptibly lead them on towards
the goal of true womanhood.

Attendance.—The attendance has undoubtedly improved, for although quite good before it is much better in
this way, the elder girls very seldom stay away at odd times
to help in different ways; they are evidently keen to be at
school and "where there is a will there is a way."

VII.
(i)

*From the Report on the P.N.E.U. Experiment in Gloucestershire.
By H. W. Household. (Secretary for Education, Gloucestershire.)*

It was in November, 1916, that Miss Mason's method and
its achievements first became known to us. By the following
March five Schools in the County had embarked upon the
course.

By 1918 twenty-six schools were working under the scheme. To each of these Schools a circular letter was addressed.

County Education Office,
Shire Hall, Gloucester,
4th January, 1919.

Dear Sir (or Madam),

Now that Miss Mason's Scheme has been working for some time in more than a score of Schools, I am anxious to be able to tell the Education Committee what measure of success is attending it. Owing to the War conditions I have not been able to visit the Schools as I should have liked to do, but even if I had visited them I should not have felt able—nor should I have been the proper person—to estimate the results of the Scheme.

You and your staff, and perhaps some of your children, can do it with much surer touch; and I should be very grateful if each School would let me have reports and memoranda from any of those who are teaching or are being taught, who feel that they have anything that they would like to say, no matter how trifling it may seem. I shall make it my business to digest the heap of material which I hope will flow in upon me, and in return I may be able to give back something to the Schools.

Needless to say, I want to know just what you are all

really thinking. If you do not accept Miss Mason's aims, or like her methods, or approve her choice of books, I should like to know it. If you are in complete sympathy then I should like to have illustrations of the results that are being attained.

19

In the December number of the "Parents' Review," there is a most suggestive article on Education and Kultur by E.K.—initials behind which is no doubt concealed the name of Miss Kitching, Miss Mason's friend and Secretary—which will point lines of thought and help to weigh up achievement.

I hope that nobody will make a burden of what I ask. Much or little, I shall be grateful for what you send. It may be that in some cases the moment has not come for saying anything. It will come later. Where it has come there will be things to say, and those are the things that I should like to hear.

In any report that I may frame on your material it would probably be the general wish that individual Schools should remain anonymous.

I am, yours truly,

(signed) H. W. Household,

Secretary.

The admirable reports which have been sent in are too long to be printed in full. In summarising their contents it has seemed best to take in sequence the various points brought out by the many writers, and to illustrate the argument by extracts. The extracts have sometimes been shortened by the omission (always indicated) of a few words or sentences, but nothing material has been left out in any passage quoted. The compiler has studied to present every point of view and line of argument with fairness.

Perhaps it was rather early to ask for such reports. The Schools had been working under almost every possible disadvantage. Many were understaffed; the influenza epidemic had played havoc with the attendance and the work; books came late from the publishers, and in many cases did not come at all. There was much to discourage, and little to hearten, save the cheering light which at times shone through the clouds of difficulty from the far horizon, where a new sun was rising with promise of a cloudless noon. Eleven of the Schools have marked its rising, and await with a sure confidence the vision of its meridian glory. The teachers of three, "lost leaders" of whom better things were hoped, have fallen by the way, stumbling on rocks of their own imagining, and have sought leave to go back again to the old familiar darkness. They have gone. They could not see the light, and said stoutly it was not there. Three have not felt able to send in any report but their success can hardly be doubted. Of the rest most have beheld elusive gleams, and press forward bravely and hopefully, though not without mistake and trials and disappointments.

20   The difficulties encountered are real. That they are often a result of misunderstanding, and so self-created, rather

adds to than diminishes their power to obstruct. Let us look at them through the eyes of those who have found them sometimes very dragons in their path.

Some—among them one of the fallen—feared the terminal examinations. They remembered the annual nightmare of their early teaching days, and said that examinations must lead to cramming. They would not believe that these examinations do not; that revision is not attempted; that the fulness of the syllabus makes it, and is intended to make it, quite impossible; that (greatest of all joys) it is found to be unnecessary. "The old idea of constant revision is rendered impossible," says the Head Master of N. "If I interpret Miss Mason correctly (and he does) she discountenances this repetition as unnecessary and harmful, and certainly I have long since discovered that time spent in going over, again and again, work already done is generally wearisome and unprofitable."

Some lack confidence in the children whom they teach. "The Scheme," they say "was never intended for the child in the Elementary School. It was intended for children working at home."

Or, as another, an assistant, writes, "The Scheme would be a most excellent one if used in Secondary Schools, or in Institutions, where the aim is to turn out *students*, thoroughly well-learned in the things of ancient days. . . . Practically all our pupils have to become *workers* at an early age. . . . It is folly to waste the short and precious school-days in so much book learning, when the child's chief need is a practical knowledge of how to meet the difficulties of everyday life. Students are seldom practical people, and the British Empire of the future needs workers rather than bookworms."

Alas! alas! that any teacher should so write. Must not the workers be thinkers too? Must they not learn the great lessons of the ages—the experience of the past with its successes and its failures, the wisdom of the wise and the folly of the foolish—if they are to steer the ship of state by safe ways to the harbour of well-being and contentment, and not end disastrously upon the rocks?

The British Museum and Plutarch's *Lives*, says another, "are difficult for younger children. The scenes and lives of people that approach more nearly to their own time would seem to be of a more practical value.... The average person knows nothing of these people and can be expected to care little about unearthing the dim and distant past."

The same note occurs in other reports. Sometimes it sounds more harshly still. "It is utterly immaterial to me," says one, "what the Babylonians wore, or what the Assyrians built. . . . History should deal chiefly with the past century." Shall we not think with pity of what those who write thus have themselves missed somewhere in the days of their youth? Imagination—the gracious influence that does all the gilding of our life, and is also the very source of the great conceptions that lead to material success and social well-being—imagination in them has atrophied and come to nought.

"The study of Plutarch's *Lives*," says another, "seems suitable only for riper minds. If the Lives as a whole were studied the scholars might get an idea of the foundation of the Roman and Grecian Empires." But he has missed the whole purpose of the study, which is by no means to give them "an idea of the foundation of the Roman and Grecian Empires," but something very different. Old Montaigne* shall tell him what it is.

"He (the teacher) shall by the help of Histories inform himself of the worthiest minds that were in the best ages. It is a frivolous study if a man list, but of invaluable worth to such as can make use of it. . . . What profit shall he not reap touching this point, reading the lives of our Plutarch? Always conditioned the master bethink himself whereto his charge tendeth, and that he imprint not so much in his scholar's mind the date of the ruin of Carthage, as the manners of Hannibal and Scipio, nor so much where Marcellus died, as because he was unworthy of his devoir he died there; that he teach him not so much to know Histories, as to judge of them. . . . To some kind of men it is a mere grammatical study, but to others a perfect anatomy of Philosophy, by means whereof the secretes part of our nature is searched into."

It is all plain enough to those whose eyes are open. Let us hear another teacher, the Head Master of Q. There is no disguising that the children find Plutarch difficult, but

---

* *Of the Institution and Education of Children*. Essays, Book I., chap. xxv.

22 they are meant to find him difficult. The joy comes when the difficulties are mastered, and they are being mastered at Q.

"Among the subjects new to teachers and scholars," we are told, "the study of 'Citizenship' through Plutarch's *Lives* seems to have presented difficulty. In some instances this is due to the difficult sentences of the translation. . . . This difficulty has been overcome to a certain extent by greater acquaintance with the style of the writing; but more so, however, by a recognition of two things. First, that to explain the meaning of the words destroys interest in the story and annoys the child. Second, that in many instances it is unnecessary. Although a child's dictionary knowledge of the meaning of words is lacking, it does not follow that the meaning of a sentence or paragraph is unknown to him. . . . Neither is the correct employment of the words beyond him in writing or narrating.

"The further example of this power to grasp the meaning of a writer without being able to define the words in detail, was afforded by 'The Talisman.' In two forms the teachers set out with the purpose of taking it chapter by chapter, dwelling on the explanation of the meaning of words. The result was disappointing. Mechanical progress was slow and laboured. Interest in the *story* was killed. Written tests showed little grasp of the story, and in spite of such careful digging in the sentences the gold remained hidden. I suggested letting the children read silently—testing by narration—and then written tests; and then only in those parts where the incident and description were likely to appeal. Only such explanation was given as was asked for by the children, or which was likely to bring into greater clearness some necessary point. The results were much better. The children imagined the characters and pictured the incidents for themselves. The Third Crusade, its incidents and actors, became something more than a chapter in Arnold Forster's History. Written tests showed that the author had been followed, and in reproducing his story the children reproduced his words."

"The children very much appreciated the story of Romulus and Remus," says an uncertified assistant in the same School, "and seem to have set out with the determination to enjoy the life story of Lycurgus. It is in this book—Plutarch's *Lives*—and the History of Rome which are the subjects of interesting compositions." For this young teacher (she is only 21) has found that "Narration has greatly improved their English. The children have a larger vocabulary. They have a clearer way of expressing themselves, and are not afraid of speaking in front of the other scholars. . . . Then again there are so many subjects for Compositions and the Compositions have certainly improved; they are not as scrappy as they used to be. The subjects of their essays are more interesting."

The Head Master of N. remarks that "the benefits on the whole are undeniable, and in some individual instances quite surprising. We have found that some boys, who formerly were inattentive and forgetful, have become interested, industrious and intelligent in their outlook. I would give first place to the increased interest taken by the classes in their lessons. To secure this and its consequent attention is an achievement, and the best proof of the mental training afforded."

"It is wonderful," says the Head Mistress of C., "how the expression in written work has improved, and what quantities will be written . . . and what an amount of information is gathered and remembered, and long remembered too."

There is the answer to that examination bogey. Let the teachers and the children lay it. There is no need of other words than theirs.

An Assistant who teaches the eight-year-olds in M. writes, "Miss Mason's Scheme is at present one of great surprises. We did not take any examination at the end of the Summer Term, and many sighs were uttered and great dread felt when we heard we were taking the Christmas Examination. The feelings of utter helplessness and chaos grew worse as the dreaded Monday morning came. There was no relief when the questions came, many of which were on the first lessons of the term. The teacher stood before the class and gave out the first examination, a history question on the very first story told in the last week of August.

"For a moment or two there was a blank. Then one by one the children pulled themselves together, and gathered up from the backs of their memories with most wonderful results. Hardly a tiny detail was missing by the time they had finished. After the first plunge the teacher breathed, and each examination was waited for with greater and greater serenity."

The teacher of the seven-year-olds in the same school says:—"Several times during the term I felt very doubtful of the success of the Scheme, as often the work seemed far beyond the capacity of the children, but the examination proved that my doubts were groundless. They attacked the examination well, and one of the most striking results was the way the children corrected their own English when they knew I was writing down their exact answers."

"We did not think that they could do it" is the note of many reports.

The children themselves like the examinations. "In spite of all the drawbacks of the last term the children would have been keenly disappointed if the examination had not been held," writes the Head Master of G. In some schools it was noted that the attendance was exceptionally good during the examination week. Nobody would willingly miss the papers.

Marking examination papers in large numbers is a trying task, but "marking the papers written by the scholars this term was exceedingly interesting work," says an Assistant in W., whose class must number nearly fifty children. But let us go back to the doubtful ones again. Their hesitations and objections are really very useful and may enable us to help them. Their identity is hidden and the pen, like the surgeon's knife, may have a kindly purpose, when by probing it brings harmful growths to light.

"I think that a far better selection of reading books might be made," says one of those who have abandoned the scheme; "Children of 12 and 13 do not enjoy a Scott or a Shakespeare. They find them too difficult." Let us see what others have to say of Scott and Shakespeare.

"*The Talisman* is very hard-worded, but it is ever so interesting," says a girl of twelve in M.

Shakespeare has proved himself a triumphant and wholly glorious success in many of the Schools. "we were sorry the play of *King John* did not come in time for us to be able to read it—we simply enjoyed *Macbeth*," says another girl of twelve in M.

"There always seems joy when Shakespeare is announced," says the Head Mistress of C., and she adds that "many girls have bought a complete copy of Shakespeare's Works."

The writer has himself seen and felt the joy of the children in acting some of the great scenes from the plays, scenes which in one case that he recalls (it was at D.) they had not touched for more than three months. By their own desire they had harked back to the work of the previous term. Of course to get this spirit and this success needs good teaching. In beginning this Scheme in a school," writes the Head Mistress of A., "the teacher must live in her class. She must pass in and out among the girls while they are reading and see that nothing is passed over that is not understood; read the context with the child, take the hard word out, and the child will herself find out the meaning of it by seeing its use in the sentence. I find now that there is no need to go to the girls, they come out to me." Elsewhere she says, "I find Miss Mason's scheme just what we needed. The variety of subjects, which are so cleverly arranged that they blend into one whole, charms the children. They love to read and they love to be read to. . . . I find too that the children are beginning to appreciate language. I was reading to them one day one of the old Norse legends; the whole class of over thirty girls was wrapped in attention, when one of them remarked in a pause in the reading, 'Isn't that like poetry?'"

An Uncertificated Assistant in G. who takes Form IA. Says "The work is undoubtedly extremely interesting both for teacher and for scholar. It adds an entirely new outlook to the average child in the Elementary School. . . . It makes even small children realise that there are thousands of good books which they had never heard of, and it makes them wish that they could read them. . . .

"The improvement in the children's vocabulary is already marked, and quite little children are slowly acquiring the habit of distinguishing between synonyms because they are so constantly hearing the correct words applied in the different meanings. They also use these words for themselves when writing down their stories and lessons. They are beginning to appreciate beauty of prose and verse. The memory is strengthened considerably."

The Head Master of the same School refers to the influence of the Scheme upon the tone of the School (which is always high). "During the nine months Miss Mason's Scheme has been worked," he says "there is an added delightful stimulus, which I had hardly thought possible among children who already loved their work."

Perhaps then we may dismiss the objection of one of the faint-hearted that "the books are written in a language far above that which the vocabulary of the children will allow them to read with moderate comfort," remarking only that
26 the aim must always be ahead of the achievement, and that the ability of the children to enjoy and profit by the books is far greater than he thinks. The Assistant Mistress, who teaches form IB., in M., puts the first point quite plainly. "The choice of books for Standard I. is good," she says, "they are sufficiently beyond the children to be of real educational value." And where some of the books are felt to be difficult (perhaps too difficult) it is recognized that "when the lower forms have had more practice in the working of the Scheme, no doubt our older forms will be able to grasp these. We cannot expect our girls to grasp the Scheme in its entirety at once." It should be added that the Head Mistress of C., who writes thus, is delighted with the results that have been achieved.

Some teachers do not understand the value of the delightful books on Natural History, and think that they either supplant the natural study of Nature or leave no time for it. The children know better. Child after child writes to say how much they have enjoyed reading about the stars. That shows what the books are doing. The unbeliever who writes, "More would surely be gained by watching the development of frog spawn to tadpole and frog, than from reading so many pages from a book on the subject at a season when the spawn cannot be obtained," may really take heart. The child will look for the frog spawn, if that has caught his interest, when the time comes round—mercifully not as a member of a class under direction, but as a happy, curious, little soul following up by himself many a quest inspired by the delightful pages. We do not, need not, cannot read about every thing just (and only just) at the moment when it reveals itself. The appeal made to the children by the study of *Plant Life*, *The Fairyland of Science*, *Life and Her Children*, *The Sciences*, and other books, the interest which they excite and the activity of mind which they set up, are noticed by several teachers.

A valuable appreciation of the method and its results was received from the Head Master of Q., who has already been quoted at some length. The following passages are interesting and suggestive.

"The subjects seem to be many; yet nearly one half, comprising considerably more than half the bulk of work set in the programmes, is but one subject—Reading.

"Every educated person is indebted for the best part of his powers to Reading. From the very outset of his educational adventures a child is being trained in the use of this power to read for pleasure and information. Incidentally the attitude of us teachers towards the subject is corrected. The technique of reading had the chief place; and while the reading lesson offered the opportunity to secure clearness of speech, yet that achievement is of less

value to the individual than his power to read with purpose. In spite of the appearance on our time-tables of so
many reading lessons, whatever fluency and accuracy of
vocal interpretation we secured was not accompanied by
the more important mental interpretation. . . . Under the
scheme Reading throughout has improved, as it is bound
to do. And the child in narrating gives better modulation
of voice than was ever before secured when it was sought
for as a thing apart. . . .

"It is clear that the intellectual interest of the child is
aroused, and that teacher and pupils alike have greater pleasure in their common task. It is a common task. Both are
engaged in a study of the same subject from the same books.
The teacher is no longer to be regarded as the fountain of
all knowledge. . . . The spirit of self-help is engendered. The
habit of doing for oneself is required from the beginning;
and it is evident that if a child is educated on these lines
from the age of seven to fourteen it will have the habit of
mind which will enable it to achieve rich results in the
informative period of its development from fourteen years
onward.

"This power of self-preparation is already noticeable, and,
naturally, in a greater degree in Form IV. And when Continuation Schools are established, such children, trained
in this way, should be able to pass into these schools and
derive the greatest possible amount of benefit from their
continued training.

"A further hope! When children have gone from

Elementary to Secondary Schools, it has been observed that they have not readily adjusted themselves to new conditions. This is due, no doubt, in great part to the fact that they are unable to study when left to themselves. The habit of relying on the teacher is strong with them, and when required to delve for themselves they are unable to do so. Although provided with the tools of the student, they know not how to use them. The hope is that this reproach on elementary training will be removed.

"Among those results which are clearly due P.U.S. methods is the increased power of concentration; and I think Miss Mason's claim that narration secures concentration may be Conceded. Written tests show this. When a lesson was tested by what the books on 'School Methods' called 'rapid, vigorous questioning,' the written tests, even when immediately following, were disappointing. Narration shows the grasp a child has of its reading, and at the same time strengthens its grasp. Its confidence in its possession is confirmed, so that it is not afraid to write or speak afterwards for fear of being wrong. It knows how much it has at its command. . . . 28

"There appear to me to be two errors into which we may fall in connection with narration. The first lies in the preparation. This preparation is done either by the teacher reading the selected part, or by the child reading it—aloud or silently. Assuming the teacher's reading to be good, that method seems to give better results. Modulation, emphasis, gesture, even attitude of body, help in interpretation. The child's mind can concentrate on what is read. The mechanical difficulty of reading is removed, and there is no break in the flow of thought. But the object is to train in the habit of purposeful reading. To do that with hope of success, there should be an increasing amount of silent preparation, not only as the scholar progresses from form to form, but also from term to term in its forms. . . .

"The second danger springs from the fear in the teacher's mind that the prescribed amount of work will not be done each term. This fear tempts one to overdo the personal method of reading, and to rely too much on the best children. Those with weaker powers of understanding do not receive chances (of narrating) in sufficient number either to develop greater powers or to give them confidence and encouragement. More than that, if not continually called upon to take a share, equivalent to their powers, in narrating, the lazy habit of mind, springing from and fostered by reliance on other minds, will grow with them. . . .

"Composition, oral and written, is undoubtedly improved. Narration secures better oral composition, and the improvement in the written work follows. . . . The children write at greater length, and acquaintance with good models is seen in the fuller language and better construction. . . . Finally, the interest in reading is greater. Children borrow the books for evening reading.* In two cases the parent (mother) wished to read, and it may be so in other instances, without a definite request for their use being made. The

29

---

* Note.—Several teachers comment on this new borrowing of books.

'atmosphere' surrounding the work of the school is differ- ent. It is freer; and the freer conditions are not felt by the staff only. Whatever may be the ultimate judgment on the methods and work of the P.U.S., none of us would go back within the narrower limits of the old system with anything but an ill grace."

The Head Master of R. has sent some interesting notes. "The most pleasing of all," he says, "has been the eagerness among the older scholars to narrate, a thing I could never get them to do previously, and, greatly to my astonishment, scholars I thought to be almost hopeless are in many cases the most exact and fluent narrators. Because of the oral work the scholars have enlarged their vocabularies, can ex- press their ideas more exactly, and exercise a greater amount of intelligence in answering problems and questions based upon the work studied.

"The work under Miss Mason's Scheme is going to cause our scholars to think clearly and reason logically. When they leave school they are going to read for themselves, think for themselves, and act for themselves. In this way they will make intelligent citizens. The greatest benefit which I think the scheme will confer upon our pupils is this: they will read sufficient (and will read it intelligently) to make them want to read more, and next to character the greatest benefit a school can confer on a scholar, is to make that scholar love good books, and give him the power to read those books intelligently. The school of the past has not done this. Some children have loved books in spite of the drudgery of school readers, but whilst most children could read fluently, few understood and could retain the subject matter.

"On one point only in the scheme," says the same master, "am I a little fearful. . . . In the summer term the book set for Standard V. children, 10-13 years of age, was Lytton's *Harold*. This book fitted in beautifully with the period of history set for study (1066-1189) but few children enjoyed it because, except for about three places, it was not really interesting to the majority of the class. Children generally learn to break the shell of the nut to get to the kernel, very slowly. To read dozens of pages of description tires them. They want to get on with the story. I want to get my scholars not only to read books but to love them." Well, his doubt is put on record. The experience of others will be his too. The younger children as they come up the school *will* love these books. Skill and devotion such as his are not going to fail.

30   "The children do much more work for themselves," says the Head Mistress of C. An uncertificated Assistant in her school who takes form IB. has also written a most useful report. "Interest," she says, "grows more and more as each term commences. . . . There is scarcely a child who cannot narrate some of the lesson, though at first it is given in rather a disjointed and disconnected way, which in time gives place in most cases to a very complete story.

"Their spelling too, has greatly improved. Whereas in years gone by nothing much was expected of Standards I. and II., now quite difficult words are accurately written.

"The children also have lost much of their old shyness when talking to strangers.

"The written work has improved wonderfully. The little girls have plenty to write about now and are not at a loss as to what to say; rather the reverse, they have to stop because the time is up. . . .

"For their Nature Study we read *The Wood I Know* and Mrs. Fisher's *Eyes and No Eyes* series, *Birds of the Air*, *Insect Life* and *Plant Life in Field and Garden*. It is wonderful how the children have brightened up and really observe. They come for this lesson now eager to tell what they have noticed on their way to and from school, or when out for a walk, and most of them are anxious for information about something or other they have discovered during the week. . . .

"*The Child's Garden of Verse* the girls have become quite familiar with and know many of the poems by heart. The fact that many of the children now possess a copy of their own, having chosen it for a Christmas present, speaks for itself.

"Pictures I think all children naturally love, but in these there is fascination in bringing out the detail. The little ones constantly bring pictures which have a connection with those studied as well as with their other lessons.

"Naturally the 'Book of Fairy Tales' is the favourite. I really believe every child would rather forego a half holiday than lose the tale. They are allowed in turn to take home a spare copy. No child ever forgets it when it is her turn for the book, it is carried home with great rejoicings."

This teacher has certainly gone to the very heart of the subject.

31 "Picture Study," says the Head Master of H., who on some points still has doubts, "is most acceptable. It is rare to see a picture without a child studying it during playtimes and before and after School. We find that the children *do* notice detail; they do exercise their powers of imagination; and the *do* attempt sound, logical reasoning." He thinks that Shakespeare and Scott are too difficult for Standards III. And IV., and "Interesting and valuable though it is (he doubts) the practicability of including so many branches or aspects of Nature Study. The sun has risen above the horizon, but it is not yet high noon. The fuller light will come, but he is a sound and cautious teacher, and he will not say that he sees when he does not.

In the mining district there are difficulties. "Many of the children," says the Head Mistress of Z., "come from homes where the Forest dialect is more often spoken than English. These need a rather liberal and repeated explanation of un-usual words or phrases.... Necessarily our progress is slow."

The Head Master of Y. has the same difficulty. "The parents, brothers and sisters," he says, "although not illit-erate, possess but a dreadfully limited vocabulary; indeed most of their conversation is carried on in the Forest ver-nacular, which does not lend itself in the least to poetic expression, or pretty flights of imagination, neither does it assist in the interpretation of even comparatively easy English. Our children cannot comprehend the meaning of any but the simplest words. Consequently we have to paraphrase liberally ... which does not appear to coincide with Miss Mason's ideas. When the stories are thus simplified . . . they are thoroughly enjoyed, and as a rule very well memorised. . . .

"Picture Study is producing good results in training the observation."

This is all to the good, but he still has doubts. "There appears," he says, "to be little that is really new in the Scheme," which means that the sun has not yet broken through the clouds, and he thinks that "the usual disabilities under which elementary teachers work—larger classes, extreme diversities of intellect, and the apathetic attitude of many of the parents towards education," demand a larger allowance.

One must not be afraid of crudeness or of many blunders in the first efforts at written expression. "The chief objection some teachers seem to have about the method," says the Head Mistress of B., "is that the child's work is not perfect, they like to see a little done and done perfectly, and thus they would sacrifice everything for accuracy and show. . . . I feel convinced that no teacher will welcome the method until she is satisfied to accept imperfect work (but the child's best) and be content to get gradual improvement."

This is quite true of course, and we have here the error which is especially characteristic of the elementary School, with its numbing experience of "payment by results." Like most errors it is a weed of luxuriant growth, very difficult to eradicate when once established. "The Suggestions for the consideration of Teachers," issued by the Board of

Education, still battle with it. "The teaching of composition, like that of any other subject," says Paragraph 25, "consists, not in shielding a child from every danger of mistake, but in enabling him gradually to correct his errors for himself."

One delightful consequence of the method still remains to be noticed. "It is surprising," says the teacher of Form IB., in M., "how the children will link up one subject with another, and it is usually a sensible connection. . . . The children have done it before, but it seems to me that by Miss Mason's Scheme they are helped more efficiently." The teacher of Form III. In the same School also brings out this feature. "The girls," she says, "are certainly learning to connect and apply the information which they get from the books, and have at times expressed surprise that one book throws light on the subject matter of a different book. Here are the beginnings of an appreciation of wide reading which broadens one's outlook on life."

"Their curiosity and interest is always aroused when they read in one book a name or a fact which is connected with something which they have read in another book, and as the books chosen deal with the same period in history, this often happens," is how the teacher of Form IIA. in Q. puts the same fact, which, of course has provoked comment in several other schools.

The joy of recognition is great. The supply of books in the Elementary School is usually so meagre that it is almost unknown to the children. Under its thrilling stimulating influence the mind grows fast.

Some of us had guessed perhaps what the children think of the books we usually give them. Let a girl of twelve in M. tell us what she thinks of the new and the old.

"They (the new books) are the most interesting books," 33 she says, "I have ever read in school. Ever so many grown-up people would like the chance of having these books to read." It has been said, with justice, that "it is not well to teach our democracy to read unless we also teach it to think."

We may succeed in teaching it to read on the worse than parsimonious allowance of half-a-crown per child per year for books, but we shall certainly never teach it to think for the money. By our niggardliness we make it impossible really to educate. "At last," says the teacher of Form III. in M —"At last we have what we have always wanted—books and more books." Of course they cost money. The Scheme cannot be worked cheaply. Perhaps one day the Board of Education may think fit to investigate the expenditure upon books, and fix some minimum sum per child below which it shall not fall. But the books must be chosen wisely or much of their value is lost. Miss Mason does for the teachers what very many teachers are as yet unable to do for themselves. Her method is simple like most great methods, but simple as it is we have all missed it, every syllabus-maker of us. Learned and unlearned must share the same reproach. . . .

The teaching tradition was founded when there were no printed books. It dates from the days of manuscripts, and it was powerfully reinforced a hundred years ago by the great pioneers of elementary education, who could afford no books, or next to none, for their large classes. Even within the memory of many men and women, who are still teaching, three books a year (little text-books of poor quality), were the meagre allowance of the child in the elementary school. The teacher had to talk; there was no other way. With great skill the Training College equipped him for the task. It is proud of what it did, and so is he. And they are rightly proud; but they ought not to have had to do it, and now that it no longer need be done, now that books can be provided (they cost more, of course, than the elementary school, even in these days, has been used to spend) there should be an end of "chalk and talk."

The popular estimate of the teacher has been very irritating, but it has not been wholly unjust. In the general eye he is an autocrat, slightly severe, rather inclined to repress inconvenient initiative, to set one pace which all must keep. His foible is omniscience; his word is law. Children (and, very often adults) must listen to him with respect and above all in silence. It is for him to fill the stage; they are but the crowd. That, with just a touch of caricature, describes, not unfairly, what the long tradition of oral teaching has made him. Miss Mason's teachers leave the stage to the child and the book. They are but the prompters in the wings. They speak when they are need. It is the child who is all-important. Joyfully (and there is a new joy in their faces) they serve him, and by serving learn the last secret of their art.

(ii)

In a previous article* the leading principles that underlie Miss Mason's methods were set forth; for the most part in her own words. The passages quoted were taken from one of her most recent pamphlets, "A Liberal Education in Secondary Schools." Nothing could be clearer or more suggestive than they are. But difficulties arise when the first attempt is made to apply new principles to working conditions, and few teachers who were not already familiar with Miss Mason's work would find it possible to adopt her methods without further explanation. There are quite a number of difficulties, some real, some imaginary, that have to be faced and overcome. Fortunately, if one is faithful to Miss Mason's principles, they are soon overcome. The writer has had many opportunities of seeing and hearing what they are. He is only an administrator now, but once he was a teacher, and his fellow teachers of to-day are kind to him and tell him many things, that without their help he would never learn. Some part of what he has learnt from them about the working of Miss Mason's methods he will try to pass on to others.

At the outset there was some uneasiness about the examination that comes at the end of every term. The record of examinations in the primary school is not a good one. Those who remember what they once were, want no more. Examinations they say, must lead to cramming.

---

* printed elsewhere

These examinations, however, do not. They cannot if the method is followed faithfully. The child reads the book once ("a second reading," you will remember, "would be fatal"), narrates what he has read in whole or part on the instant, and again in an examination paper months later.

35   No revision is attempted: it is unnecessary, and the syllabus is so full that there is no time for it. So cramming is impossible. "But," some will say, "my children could never work an examination paper under such conditions." Let them try.

The children themselves like the examinations. They always like doing difficult things that they discover to be within their power. Even the seven-year olds take their share, dictating their answers for the most part, either to their teacher or to some older scholar who has been sent in to help.

The same papers are worked all over the world by children in schools of many types, from many kinds of homes. There is a bond between all these children, a very real bond that works for good. Children born and bred under the most diverse conditions have common interests, the interests that arise from common studies, common tastes. They are reading the same books, learning the same poetry, acting the same plays, studying the same pictures. When they meet in after-life, the tiresome class barriers that only exist where there are no common interests, will vanish. Those who have been Miss Mason's children will be able to talk to one another about all that they have in common, as boys or girls, who have been through any other famous school.

"Reading the same books!" says someone. "How can that be? Surely we can choose our own books?" No, Miss Mason chooses them. If she did not, the examination would be impossible, the essential interweaving of the subjects would be imperilled, the bond of union between all the schools and all the children would be dissolved. There comes down each term a printed programme for each class, with its lists of books and the amounts to be read. Those programmes are the fruit of a life's study. They have been carefully worked out, and experimented with. Each item has its relation to the rest. They are the suggestions which a great teacher offers her fellows. However strange it may seem, they are welcomed. After all we are not so unaccustomed to having books prescribed for our use. Are there not syllabuses and examinations well known to all of us, that at one time or another, as pupil or teacher, we have followed without protest, though perhaps protest would not have been wholly undeserved? Let us take heart.

It is not possible to print in full a programme for a term, but let us glance at some of the books which Form II. A and B (Standards IV. and III.) used during the autumn term.

For English History they were reading Arnold Forster's *History of England*, pp. 326-396 (1547-1603). The contemporary French History was being studied in Mrs. Creighton's *First History of France*, pp. 157-189. At the same time the class were reading *A Midsummer Night's Dream*, and Scott's *Kenilworth*, and were learning Macaulay's *Armada*. The two histories, of course, are always in the programme: the other books change term by term to suit the period that is being studied.

For Geography they were reading Book III., pp. 83-122, of *The Ambleside Geography Books* (chapters on some of the English counties), and some books of travel, adventure, and sea-warfare. For Natural History, *The Sciences*, by E. S. Holden, pp. 149-182; *The Changing Year*, by F. M. Haines, August to December, and *Life and Her Children*, by Arabella Buckley, pp. 261-301, were being used.

Some first lessons in Citizenship were being learned from Plutarch's *Lives*, *Solon* being the life studied. If Form II. B was working separately it was using Mrs. Beesly's *Stories from the History of Rome*, pp. 33-61 instead.

For Picture Study a characteristic, and with the children, a favourite subject, little reproductions of six pictures by Israels and Mauve were being used. This term they have Van Dyck.

But we cannot follow the programme further. Enough has been given to serve for illustration; enough to provoke a score of questions. Let us deal with a few of them.

Does every child have all of these books? Not all. Some, e.g., Plutarch's *Lives* and *The Changing Year*, are intended to be read aloud to the children by the teacher. Most of the others are intended for the children's use, but even a generous education committee will hardly be able to provide them all. *The History of France*, therefore, will probably be read aloud by the teacher, and very likely *The Sciences* as well. Arnold Forster costs 8s. 6d. a copy, and probably at first you will have to do with one book between two children, and make the books serve Form III. as well. There are ways of managing, and the teacher who wishes to adopt the method will not be left unaided.

"These books," it will be said, "are very hard, much too hard for the children of a village school." Experience has proved that they are not. They seem hard at first, though not even then impossibly hard, to children who were not introduced to the method at the beginning; to a child who began in the lowest form they offer no difficulty but what it will face with confidence. Arnold Forster, of course, is not easy reading; and in a junior school, which has been following the method for four or five terms, the writer was told a few weeks ago that the staff thought that it would be better for Standard III. (the top class) to drop the work of Form II. B, and be content with that of Form I. A. While they all loved Shakespeare (for, unspoiled by notes, no other writer is so universally enjoyed), Arnold Forster was thought to be beyond them. It is useless to ask for too much, so he assented; and then, to his secret joy, the two class teachers began to wonder whether after all the change would be wise, for A and B and C and D would be so disappointed. They were interested, and had been asking to be allowed to take the books home. Think of it! Boys in Standard III. wanted to read Arnold Forster's history at home! That is one little illustration of what the method does.

Plutarch and Scott are both of them difficult for children of nine and ten, but much of the difficulty is really created by teachers who have not quite grasped the secret of the method, and who forget how they themselves began to read. We did not as children check at each hard word, each passage that was obscure to us, in our *Treasure Island*. We read on, content to get the story. And as we read book after book we gained power and mastered the difficulties unconsciously. It was very seldom that we paused to ask for help.

We *will* interfere too much, forgetting Miss Mason's warning, and making of ourselves an unnecessary "bridge between the pupil and the real teacher, the man who has written the book." Another student of Miss Mason's methods gives us the result of her experience. "In the schools," she says, where the teachers do not explain and interpret, but let the knowledge make its own appeal, the children prove their natural capacity to understand."

Let us have faith in them. Our troubles generally arise because we forget what Miss Mason has told us. The full development of the power of narration calls, of course, for skill and judgment on the part of the teacher. One needs to see a good teacher take a lesson. The first attempts are humble, but the amount that is read before narration follows soon rises from a sentence to a paragraph, a page, or with the older children, considerably more. With large classes every child cannot narrate at each lesson but all are ready to narrate. Many will contribute points that the narrators omit, and help to build up the story. Some children are extraordinarily exact narrators, reproducing the writer's very words in many passages. But it is no mere parrot memory that is brought into play, for both the knowledge and the vocabulary become the child's own. They are, as it were, fused in his mind. They are at his command, and reappear at the most unlikely times.

The effect upon the composition of all this reading of good books followed by narration is nothing short of startling. The quantity that even children in Standard III. will write is beyond belief. Equally beyond belief are the wealth of language, the feeling for style and rhythm, the reasoned sense of order ("What next?"), the kindling imagination, the love of literature, the beginnings of a perception of what wide reading means.

Of course this looks like the exaggeration of an enthusiast possessed by a new idea. To such a charge the writer can only reply, as he has replied before, "Go and see." He believes that many of the children of ten to twelve years of age in primary schools that are following the method, are racing ahead of their fellows in secondary schools who come from favoured homes. No one can say of them what is so often said of the children from the primary school, that they come up to the secondary school unable to study when left to themselves.

iii.

THE AMBLESIDE METHOD AND SECONDARY EDUCATION.[*]

By H. W. Household.

The writer has already upon several occasions directed attention to the remarkable results that are being obtained in a number of public elementary schools, which are following the programmes and employing the methods of Miss Charlotte Mason. Much interest is being taken in the work which those schools are doing. They receive many enquiries and many visits. Naturally, however, a still greater interest attaches to the source from which the methods and their inspiration are derived—the Secondary Training College and the Practising School conducted by Miss Mason herself at the House of Education at Ambleside. The writer has on two occasions spent some delightful days there as Miss Mason's guest. He has watched the work done by the students and the children, and he would like to put on record something of what he saw.

Two of the lessons that he saw were of great interest, and, so it seemed to him, of much significance to all who are concerned with secondary education. The first was a French lesson.[†]

39

---

[*] By kind permission of the Editor of "The Journal of Education and School World."

[†] See Chapter X of *An Essay Towards a Philosophy of Education: Languages.*

The second lesson, a short lesson sandwiched between others as a demonstration for the visitor's benefit, was given by a student to Form V. in the Practising School, girls whose ages range from sixteen to seventeen and a half. The form was reading Browning's "A Death in the Desert." The forty lines beginning, "Go back, far, farther, to the birth of things," were read straight through by the girls in turn, the rest following in their books; and again, without pause or hesitation after the one reading, narration began, and the girls in turn took up the paraphrase of the difficult lines in well chosen language, and with a precision that bore witness to their close attention, and to their thorough understanding of what had been read.

In every class it was the same. The oral narration and the written composition, and "reports" of lessons, were of extraordinary excellence. There had been interest, there had been close concentration, and the result was power, mastery.

Two other features in the methods compel the attention of those who are familiar with the work of the public schools and of the public secondary schools. The first is that interest, attention, and concentration are secured, and all the extraordinary results that flow from them are obtained, "without mark, prize place, praise, or blame." The second feature is equally arresting and suggestive. There is no evening preparation, and by the whole of that amount the hours are shortened. There is no revision for examination, and the time spent over revision in other schools is saved. The examination at the end of each term is as searching as one could wish, but what is read once and then narrated is known, and no revision is required.

In the elementary schools interest, attention, concentration are as easily obtained; there is the same power, the same mastery. The writer could produce many exercise books and examination papers in literature, history, and geography which, for their facility of expression, their range of vocabulary, and their wealth of ideas, would bear comparison with similar books and papers in any secondary school.*

VIII.

(i)

COURAGE IN EDUCATION.[†] (1917).

By Mrs. Clement Parsons.

At a recent Meeting of the British Association Sir Arthur Evans, in his Presidential Address, deplored the fact that present-day education fails to interest either children or their parents, and the Bishop of Carlisle, in the November number of this Review, charged national education with the double shortcoming of failure to interest children and inability to spiritualise them. 'Multitudes of children hate school,' wrote the Bishop, and 'Every child has a soul...and

---

* There are at present (1924) 170 Council Schools in Gloucestershire working on this Method.
† Reprinted by kind permission of the Editor of *The Nineteenth Century*

on the nation's soul in the long run depends the nation's destiny. Our education has partially forgotten this fact.'

In some elementary schools in the North of England an experiment is being made the working of which is so wonderful that the present writer, one among seventy pilgrims attracted during the last two years to the pioneer school of the group, cannot choose but tell what is being done there.

The experiment arose out of the discontent of one Headmistress with elementary education on the usual lines. In her own words:

> I am extremely dissatisfied with the results obtained when I consider all the time and trouble taken; all the energy and thought expended on our work. There is too much work done by the teacher—too little by the child. The children's memories are not good, and the reason they do not remember things seems to be because of a lack of *living* interest. Their power of expression is weak, and their vocabularies are poor. The children are getting their information too much in tabloid form, in spite of illustrations, pictures, etc., hence this mental indigestion and arrested mental development.

For these reasons this Headmistress obtained permission to substitute another method, one which, though new in elementary schools, has been in force for twenty-five years in private schools that work under 'The Parents' Union School,' the creation of a now veteran educator,

Charlotte M. Mason, of Ambleside. The method proceeds from a philosophy, or call it a point of view with regard to children, which may be thus summarised:

41　　A child is a person. Not a machine, embryo, jug to be poured into, 'average child,' or numeral in a school census but a person.

Being a person, with the aptitudes of one, a child possesses, among the rest, appetite for knowledge, and knowledge nourishes his mind as food his body.

He best assimilates knowledge that includes an appeal to imagination. Therefore—and also because literature forms taste—the best books should be his principal lesson-books.

A child loves to retell at length what has interested him. When telling it he does not only memorise but puts in an additional something of himself that demonstrates assimilation.

Out of these four basic simplicities has been evolved the method of teaching I will describe in its newest embodiment.

The outside environment, a mining village of the West Riding, the tram terminus of a great town, is distinctly unsympathetic. It consists of a black-gray, expressionless street of bare cottages in barren gardens, the only colour enamel advertisements of black lead and soaps nailed to walls. Nothing else visible but slate shingles, gray stone, and, near the school, where the village ends, the road, between black hedges, murkily sloping to the moor. The weather, on this winter day, shares the Brontë character. It is a morning of low sky, cold wind, penetrating, disheartening rain. A few women with shawls over their heads move about, raucous-voiced. Some of the mothers are temporary workers, and where there can be no home midday meal the children bring bread and butter to school and get their cocoa heated on the school stove.

In such a setting, narrow and earth-bound, what fostering, one might well ask, is possible for idealism, for the subtle thing that's spirit, for the quality of Admiration by which, said Wordsworth, men live? If inside the schoolhouse one were to find mechanical education, over-strained teachers hammering at incurious scholars, a Procrustes' bed to which every child is stretched or shortened, and other defects on account of which the critics in the Press arraign elementary schools, then woe betide the collective soul of the rising generation in this Yorkshire village, typical of many villages!

In the usual Council School class-room, glass-screened from its neighbor rooms and brightened by pictures and flowers, an assistant teacher stood reading to a class of forty girls, their average age seven. She read two pages—a traveller's account of African parrots—reading slowly, reading into the children, letting them feel how interesting she, the reader, found the book, but never pausing to interpolate any word of explanation or definition. The children sat, engrossed in what was being read, and, moreover, aware that at the end of this, the one and only reading of it, some of them would be required to narrate. As soon as the reading ended, up rose a forest of small arms. One girl was called forward.

She faced the class and quite without self-consciousness
gave what to a visitor seemed an astonishing narration of
what she had heard, astonishing in its consecutiveness, in
the ease with which she had made the adult vocabulary her
own, and in the good intonation copied from the teacher's.
She proved to be by no means the show child. Others, one
after another, came forward with the same quiet confidence either to take up the tale where a predecessor had
been told to stop or to supply details earlier narrators had
missed. The general level of narration was most impressive,
and so were the alertness of the children, their delight in
any lively touch of description. And the enthusiasm is for
knowledge for its own sake; there are no marks, no places,
no prizes, no external rewards whatever in the school. One
might have imagined the scholars were teaching the teacher,
so busy and free were they, so unobtrusive she. It is only in
the younger classes that the children are read to instead of
reading for themselves. The reading habit, the power of
self-sustained attention took time to form, but the result
in mental development has proved time and trouble well
expended. The mistress said that the power of quiet reading,
weak at first, had so strengthened term by term that she
could not have imagined beforehand the present capacity
to master a subject and get the better of a difficulty.

In the next room geography was being crisply and ar-
restingly read to a Standard II class, and, while this was
going on—so whole-hearted is the concentration the new
method induces—another class that had to share the room

was studying with absorbed eyes (each girl privately at her own desk) postcard photographs of a picture by Pieter de Hooch, on which one of the weekly Picture Talks was shortly to be held.

The geography lesson turned on Japan, and after it the teacher showed a pair of chopsticks and asked the children if they could remember anything about chopsticks in the lesson of a week earlier. The children positively clamoured to get a hearing. 43

'We are in a little verandah,' began an unkempt child, clearly not from a good home, in a grimy pinafore—it was a surprise to hear 'verandah' from her lips—'a closed up verandah. We have to do the best we can to eat our meal up with chopsticks. When we do get it in our mouths it feels like leather. Yosoji [this fluently said] who is in the background looks at us and he laughs a little bit.'

Another child carries on. 'The little maid begins to giggle and Yosoji has to give a little giggle too. And the water in the bath was red-hot and the Japanese are fond of getting into it when it was hot.'

The head teacher entered, and asked if anyone could tell the story of Perseus. It had been read aloud six weeks before from Andrew Lang's *Tales of Troy and Greece*. The children's ardour over Perseus and the telling of his story must have been due, no doubt, to the magic of a noble tale over unspoilt minds. 'You must only tell me a very little bit,' warned the mistress, but already eighteen or twenty children were contributing incidents and names, and to the visitor there was something uncanny—or should one say divine?—in hearing their lively, ready utterance of such words as Zeus, the Temple of Apol-l-o, Danaë, the god-dess, Acrisius, Polydectes, words they had only heard once in class, and that six weeks earlier. The great truth that interest carries attention and that where attention has been absolute memory does not fail, because the committal to memory has been a vital, not mechanical, process, was here strikingly illustrated. Interest is to knowledge what flavour is to food. The moment interest fails during a lesson, attention, the mother of memory, slackens. Children always and only remember what has truly interested them. Once thoroughly interested in a subject and keen to know more about it, almost every child will welcome effort, as babies love hard crusts.

No child can keep the bow bent for long, so the reading must be brief. Ten minutes are long enough for the young beginner, but the length of time naturally depends on age, stage of training, and the difficulty of the matter.

The next class consisted of girls of average age eleven who sat silently reading *Macbeth* in Blackie's Plain-Text Shakespeare (6d. a volume), one copy between two. The book difficulty in this education by books is, indeed, the apparent obstacle in the way of its wide adoption in Council Schools, but, seeing that in this pioneer school £20 has provided a sufficiency of books for a year for a hundred and sixty children, the difficulty is not too serious. In the case of the dearer books, such as *Our Island Story* (10s. 6d.), the expense is, even in private schools, a consideration, but is met by the fact that a book of this type covers two or three years. The scrapping of 'specially prepared' books, summaries, abridgements, school Readers, leaves each child the possessor of a little library of living books.

To return to the *Macbeth* students. Three girls were asked to read aloud the page they were studying, the scene between the Doctor and the Gentlewoman with Lady Macbeth. They came to the front with self-possession, and, with a little pacing to and fro on the part of Lady Macbeth, they read the scene in a spell-bound way that even to a hardened playgoer was nothing less than thrilling, and, in view of the readers' parentage and home surroundings, infinitely touching. One had been disposed to think, These are selected children, these are the aristocrats, but it was not so. The child who read Lady Macbeth, giving the difficult words, 'Come, come, come, come,' their full weight and just betraying her Northern vowels in 'blood,' is the eldest of ten children of a soldier whose wife has only the Army allowances.

Afterwards, the books were closed, and the class was asked to 'Write what you think led the Doctor to come to this conclusion about the illness of Lady Macbeth: "I think, but dare not speak."' Here is a paper, taken up at random and very little different from any other. It was written by a girl of twelve.

In a small ante-room a doctor and gentlewoman were talking of Lady Macbeth.

The doctor was trying to persuade the gentlewoman

to tell him what Lady Macbeth had said any time as she was walking in her sleep, for it was an accustomed thing for her to do so.

While they were thus talking about her, she came walking very slowly into the ante-room with a taper which was lit in her hand.

With the other hand she was rubbing the hand that held the taper, and all the time was talking of different things.

Some were about spots of blood on her hand, and about Duncan having a lot of blood in him, and yet all the time she was in a fast sleep. At last she went to bed not knowing she had been up.

When she had gone the doctor said 'I think, but dare not speak.'

He must have thought that Lady Macbeth had killed Duncan, but dare not say so for many reasons.

First, because Macbeth, who was now king, could have him hanged.

Another reason was he had not sufficient proof that it was true.

So he bid the gentlewoman good-night, saying 'This is beyond my practice,' and the gentlewoman replied 'I would not have a heart in my bosom like hers for all the world. Good-night, good doctor,' and there they separated, not saying a word to anyone about what they had heard or thought.

Such narrations show what incalculable educative power this teaching by literature, i.e., letting literature make its undimmed appeal, has over children. Something provocative, something quickening has passed from the soul of Shakespeare to their souls that would never reach them were they 'taught' 'Is this a dagger?' and other dislocated extracts in the ordinary way, and through it they gain foundations for all manner of discernments. One could see the responsive glow spring to their eyes—the eyes of these miners' children in their uncouth village.

The new method trusts the children and gives their self-activity full play. The narrations about Lady Macbeth were not memory work but genuinely intellectual, the interaction of the characters thought out and assimilated. As to whether the assimilation of a great imaginative scene from Shakespeare is suitable school work for a miner's child, one must reply in the words of a Labour leader who said recently 'The question is not what a working man's child should learn but what any man's child should learn.' The man in the street is certainly the worse for having but one adjective wherewith to express himself, and the fact comments significantly on the education that reared him. 'He learned nothing great' said Stubbs of Henry the Third. To learn what is great—this alone constitutes a liberal education,* and a liberal education is the essential basis of

---

* Cf. 'Education should aim at giving a child a philosophy, and philosophy simply means the contemplation of the important things in life' (*A Dominie Dismissed*, by A. S.

vocational education for the children of our democracy who to-morrow must take part in the rebuilding ahead. The more a child learns great things the more of a person, intelligent, magnanimous, sober-minded, does he become.

Round the school-room walls were pinned original illustrations of *Macbeth* in coloured chalks by the children. One girl, perhaps doubting her power to deal with protagonists, had chosen to illustrate the line

A sailor's wife had chestnuts in her lap.

Take care of the reading, let that be plenteous, varied, and first-rate, and spelling and grammar will to a large extent take care of themselves. Composition is no longer an isolated subject: it develops unconsciously by narration, written or spoken.

'The knowledge of God is the principal knowledge,' wrote Charlotte Mason in 1886 in her first book, *Home Education*, 'therefore the Bible lesson is the chief lesson.' The object of Bible teaching by the Ambleside method is to get children to know the very words of the Bible. Narrative portions of the Old Testament and the Gospel story are read to the 1st Form, and the children are asked to narrate them. How much they catch of the spirit and literary flavour is shown by the following, dictated by a girl of nine in the terminal examination.

46

Neill)—a great saying.

'Tell the story of Jairus' daughter':—

Jairus came to Jesus and said: 'Master, my daughter is very ill, please make her better.' And then another man came and said: 'Don't trouble Jesus, because your daughter is dead.' But Jesus went with Jairus, and when He got to the place where Jairus lived everybody was weeping, and He said: 'Weep not, for your daughter is not dead, but sleepeth'; and they mocked Him and said 'Of course she is dead.' And He went into the room and left everybody else outside, and said to the daughter, 'Arise,' and she arose, and He said to the mother and father, 'Give her something to eat that you may see that she is really alive.'

The teacher prepares the lesson very studiously beforehand with set books chosen for helpfulness in suggestion and in the treatment of difficulties. A teacher spoke of one of the children to whom, coming home from church, some grown-up said, concerning the preacher, 'What a dreadful man not to believe the world was made in six days when the Bible tells us it was!' To which the boy of seven replied 'After all, it does not matter if God did it in six days or thousands of years. I think it would be more wonderful to take a long time over it.'

Since children naturally enjoy Bible stories in their own clear-cut language, the teacher does not talk a great deal. A new passage will probably have to be connected with the last lesson, and an Oriental custom, such as the wailing for Jairus' daughter, explained. The children may be helped to form pictures in their minds, such as that of five thousand men, beside women and children, sitting down in ranks where there was much grass in the place.

The times we are living through do everything to justify the great stress the founder of the Parents' Union School has always laid on Bible teaching. The men in the trenches 47 have found they 'want God'; the children at school, men and women of to-morrow, want God too. No other book exists through which they can so vividly learn the nearness of God, the meaning of right, the law of consequence, as the Old Testament. It is the most powerful of lesson-books but it needs intelligent handling as every powerful instrument does. New Testament teaching is on a different plane. There, the pervading idea is not the distant scene, the *ancien régime*, but a Person to adore and serve. This idea is the centre of Parents' Union education, but it is impossible here to dwell adequately on the hope and promise of its radiating idealism.

By history we learn just judgments, the art of living, and the love of people and nations, therefore history is given a leading place among subjects. To it in the elder classes (not yet reached in elementary schools) are added civic morals and economics through the study of such books as *The Citizen and the State* by J. St. Loe Strachey and *The Laws of Everyday Life* by H. O. Arnold-Forster. Plutarch's *Julius Caesar* (1s.), recently substituted for the ordinary primer in a little mountain school in Wales, has completely vivified its history classes. Life speaks to life.

In the Yorkshire school a passage from *Modern Painters* on lichen and mosses was written without comment on the board. The children read it heedfully, the board was turned away, and they wrote what they could. A half-timer of twelve remembered the statement that to the humble work of the forerunners, lichen and moss, the 'cedar kissing the blue sky' owes its existence. Perhaps she thought 'blue' too everyday a word for the poetic prose she had been reading, for she wrote 'the azure sky.' To a visitor it seemed mighty pretty that a child, looking as she looked, should have put in from her inner vocabulary 'azure.' She was a stickler for exactitude, all the same, and at the end of her narration added, as postscript, 'By saying the cedar kisses the sky it means that it is so tall that it looks as if it is nearly touching the sky.' There was no parroting here, but the child's mind self-expressive, supple, and moving in a genuinely intellectual element.

These children take into their homes something of what goes on in the school. When a child was ill her classmates went and told her what they had read in the various books on the morning she was away. Some of the children asked for their books as Christmas presents.* Next to the first great cause of slum housing most of the slovenliness and brutality that exist come ignorance of resources for good occupation of leisure, and that comes of ignorance that life

48

---

* Since this article has been in print twenty-five scholars out of a class of forty in another of these schools bought copies of *Twelfth Night*, as their mothers wanted to read it, and in one home the father, mother, and children read it through in four evenings, each taking a part.

is of the spirit, not of the flesh. It is a matter of supreme moment that the rising generation should be given definite preparation for the occupation of leisure by the initiation of varied interests.

Education by Things stands beside Education by Books in order that children shall know and love nature and real-ise the happiness of handicrafts. Nothing could be better in these directions than the original designs, cardboard models, embroidered overalls, and nature drawings that caught one's eye in the Yorkshire school. Material for the nature drawings is week by week supplied, for that treeless, flowerless country, by unseen schoolmates in more favoured districts. There is no forgetfulness of mechanical and utility subjects, but in these less reform is needed since they are, generally speaking, well taught everywhere to-day.

It may perhaps be permitted an unprejudiced listener to record that as regarded a similar lesson on Richard the Second, heard, first, in one of the Yorkshire elementary schools, and, afterwards, in a 'Parents' Union' class in a private house in London where the pupils belonged, em-phatically, to the governing class, the comparison was by no means unfavourable to the rough miners' children and the little half-timers. One somehow felt the latter were hungrier and had more zest for food. The impression given supported the contention that no difference should be made in the food offered, whether the pupil be rich or poor, 'elementary,' 'private,' or 'public.'

But in both places the outstanding fact was the

self-activity of the children, the absence of wandering glances, listless faces, sleepy minds, the immunity from class boredom, that bugbear of stereotyped teaching where, while the teacher teaches even to hoarseness, the scholars become daily more hostile or more impervious to learning. Here, the scholars learn, they are not 'taught,' and the memory one carries away is not of a 'teacher' asking questions to elicit what has been taken in, but of children asking questions to satisfy their desire to know. Once, in the Mayfair class, when the teacher was called downstairs, 49 three beginners, who could scarcely read, somehow read for themselves and on her return begged to narrate. All this struck a visitor as a wonderful contrast to those classes often met with in all manner of schools wherein little more is expected of the children than to listen to a beautiful oral lesson and contribute 'Yes' and 'No' and a few other passive monosyllables to the questions asked. *No profit grows, where is no pleasure ta'en*, said the wisest of mankind. *Studies serve for delight*, said the next wisest. The new method illustrates these profound dicta.

Children have a passion for having their education placed in their own hands. Knowledge is just *food*, and a child's mind craves food to its taste and can assimilate it, and the greater variety it deals with the sounder and stronger is its development. Mental power is like bodily power in having no relation to class. The only differences are between individuals.

Though I was not able, for lack of time, to hear a Picture

Talk in the mining village, I should like to describe one I heard a week ago in a Parents' Union school in London, average age nine. The teacher put up an octavo photograph of de Hooch's *The Courtyard of a Dutch House* in the National Gallery. 'When the War is over we shall go to see this picture in its beautiful colours,' she began. She gave a few facts about de Hooch, helped by a *Chart of Mediaeval and Modern Painters* (Lamley and Co., 6d.) pinned to the blackboard. A second copy of the photograph was handed round and each child was asked to write down one noticeable thing in it, 'something out of the way,' said the teacher, as though it were a game. One by one, the children read out:

'A broom on the floor bound with white.'

'There is a door through the wall—a sort of hatchway.'

'Some letters on the wall opposite.'

Teacher: 'Could you find some better words than "wall," John?'

John: 'Above the arch.'

'There are steps leading up to the wall.'

'Beside the open door there is Pieter de Hooch's name on a little stone. It is P. D. H. a.d. 1653.'

'Right at the back the bricks are put in the same way as on the arch in the front.'

'There is a box with rubbish in.'

'The cobbles are quite smooth.'

'The little roses growing.'

'Flowers in the foreground.'

Teacher: 'What do we mean by a vista?'

'When we can see through a door and see down a   50
passage and see through another door.'

Teacher: 'Why does the other lady look so much
darker?'

'Because she is in the shadow of the door.'

'Because she is further away.'

Teacher: 'Because she is in what we call the middle
distance. Now I am going to ask you to draw the lady.
She is about seven heads high—that is about the height
of a woman.'

She draws on her board, and, as she draws, says:

'Her head is all in shadow and a bit of her kerchief.
What I put in white on the board you will remember
to put in black with your pencil. Dutch ladies nearly
all wear these little jackets, don't they? And the lady
herself throws a shadow. Her shadow goes half-way up
the wall. The light just catches her on the shoulder. The
light catches her down the edge of her frock. If you walk
along a dark passage the light just shows on each side of
your skirt. Have you noticed that effect? The Dutch lady
is smiling to the child. Always patient and kind and not
"Oh, what a bother you are!" When the Dutch came to
England with William of Orange they could teach the
English how to keep their back yards nice and tidy and
how to make a broom out of almost nothing.

'What other pictures of Pieter de Hooch have you seen this term?'

'A Terior with Woman and Boy.'

'What's that, Joyce, a Terior?'

'I mean Interior with Woman and Boy—and the arched doorway and the almond tree outside in the street opposite the house.'

This lesson and these children are undoubtedly alive, and it is a thrilling thought that the same training is going on in the ugly, hopeless-looking mining village and in other Council schools in various parts of England where the same method is being adopted. In the mining village six reproductions each of Millet, Watts, Corot, Meissonier, Raphael, Memling, and Dürer have been studied during the last two years. 'My scholars take a surprising interest,' reports the Head of the school, 'in the pictures and life stories of the artists.' Children who have had even a little of this training can never in after years feel so blankly at sea as working people do to-day who without preparation drift into the galleries of which they are, after all, part owners. Without previous preparation even a conducted visit to a museum or gallery is apt to degenerate into a melancholy farce of yawns and flippancies. These children, on the other hand, will have relationships already formed with pictures, and a habit of looking for their decorative and human details. If, after the War, art and manufacturing industry must draw closer together for the sake of the nation's prosperity, these foundations of sympathy with art may count as no mean part of the elementary outfit, regarded from the standard of livelihood. And since the larger hope of education is fulness of life these picture talks may rank as one of the most liberalising, as they are certainly one of the favourite, lessons in the whole curriculum. 51

'I think I could understand, Mummy, if you did not explain *quite* so much,' said the harried little girl. In the schools where the teachers do not explain and interpret but let knowledge make its own appeal the children prove their natural capacity to understand. The teachers, on their side, seem singularly fresh and unstaled. They are saved the endless correction of exercise books and the 'getting up' of lessons, and they, equally with the scholars, live on great ideas. A number of elementary assistant teachers who have tested the new experiment wrote down their opinions. Among them:

> 'The strain on teacher's voice is much less than when lessons are oral.'
> 'It is much more interesting to children to receive knowledge first hand from a good authority.'
> 'Work is set definitely on books used.'
> 'Written work shows improvement in spelling and matter. There is not any padding in the composition.'
> 'A training for the child to consult a book for itself.'

Lady Bell, in her thought-rousing *At the Works*, stated that during a year in Middlesbrough only 4½ people out of every 100 took out a book from their very good Free Library.

The ironworkers, she reported, had no formed acquaintances in literature, and therefore did not know what to ask for. The Parents' Union has entered the elementary school to try to modify for the adults of to-morrow so regrettable a state of things. Popular Educators with their Self-Help Smiles ideals are not what are wanted for our children in village and city. Success may be desirable and a livelihood is necessary, but it is not because we have received guidance concerning these things from Shakespeare and Dickens and Lamb and Carlyle and Stevenson that we laud their glorious names. The themes of literature are beauty, and ethics, 'and love, and man's unconquerable mind,' and on these humanities must be based that liberal education which is the right and needful food of every child of the nation.

(ii)

STUDIES ARE FOR DELIGHT.[*]
By Willingham F. Rawnsley.
PART II.[†]

52   Now perhaps the reader can see the governing principle of this method by which the absolute attention of the whole class is secured. It consists in the fact, which all the children recognize, that the passages which they listen to *will only be read once*. They are eager to hear and delighted to be chosen

---

[*] I cannot illustrate the working of this method in elementary schools better than by quoting (with his kind permission) passages from 'Studies are for Delight,' an article written after a little tour among the Schools in Gloucestershire.
[†] Part I. set forth these principles and methods very fully.

as narrators, and proud of success in that capacity; and they know that unless they give the closest attention they will have no chance, but will be left out of the game. This makes them serious and eager listeners; and the habit once formed is not forgotten, but attends them with increasingly good results all through their school career. Henceforth, interest in their work being awakened, they take a real pleasure in it; and the more they hear and read the more they desire to read. This desire being established, all the rest follows easily, and the children teach themselves and work hard at doing it; for Miss Mason's contention is that children should teach themselves by reading to themselves, and that *they must labour* and not have the work done for them. Books and more books, and all of the best are what is needed and these are supplied in plenty, and a fresh list is made out in advance for each term, most if not all of which are read and assimilated as the test examinations show, the teacher setting all this going in each class, helping with any necessary explanations and illustrations, and keeping lazy ones up to the mark; always at hand to help or explain or draw attention to points they might miss but never pumping facts into the pupils, only encouraging them to feed their own minds on the good literature provided. The teacher also tests the value of the books for educative purposes.

One thing more. This method depends greatly on the teacher who must have enthusiasm and sympathy as well as endless patience, and, what officials so often lack, imagination. This is a thing which happily the child *does* possess, and it is increased by the reading of the classic mythology and the fairy tales in which they all take such delight. Madame Montessori refuses to allow that the child has imagination and she will have nothing to do with fairy tales which, next to dolls, are the great delight of English children, but seem to be unknown in Italy. The method also brings out a hitherto unsuspected intellectual power in children from the poorest homes, only waiting its opportunity to expand, and that opportunity Miss Mason offers by a plentiful supply of the right books.

53

***

Such then is the "education by the humanities," i.e., through the Masterpieces of English Literature, and it is not only intellectual power that the children gain but as one of the ablest of the Head Teachers in a Gloucestershire School well says "books have a tremendous influence on *character*, and to bring children up amongst good books is an education in itself."

It is an education too not only intellectual of the mind, but also moral, of the will, which governs in the world of morals, and further by means of well-selected books on various subjects many doors are opened to the children leading by pleasant paths to knowledge of birds and flowers and the nature of the earth and wonders of the starry heavens; and by the pictures they study and by the classic stories and modern fairy tales their emotions are stirred, and the realms of art and beauty opened to them. All this and not less than this is aimed at and certainly attained in considerable measure, whilst the life of the teacher is made easier and more joyful, to match the delights of the children in helping themselves to knowledge and power.

This is no vain dream, but an assured reality; and is it not a great gain that during their early years children should have a really deep draught of that joy in work which is alas lacking in industrial life? There is no other method of education that even pretends to do this; and, given the right kind of teacher, on which so much depends, it all comes back to books and these we have to ask the Education Authorities to supply. They are more expensive than the little manuals and selections, for we only wish to have whole works so as to study the authors, or at least some of their chief writings, as wholes and not in snippets. The study of literature without some knowledge of the Author is rather futile, and the children themselves see and take an interest in the connection of Plays, Novels and History: as one boy expressed it "our history fitted in with our plays and the plays fitted in with the novels," e.g., "the Talisman" made the history of Richard I. more vivid, "Long Will" (by F. Converse) illustrated Richard II., and Shakespeare's "King John" and "Henry V." made the chapters in Arnold Forster's "History of England" full of reality. In some schools the children by weekly payments have bought for their own, copies of the plays and of the Waverly Novels to take home, and have read them through several times, 23 boys in one school bought "The Talisman." Well-selected Books in Natural History are found to be very attractive. Some of Plutarch's "Lives" are read with great interest and there is hardly any play of Shakespeare's which cannot hold the child's attention and help in his self-education. And though these books cost more than the Little Manuals and reading books issued to the schools by the Education Boards, they last over several years, and of the most expensive only one copy is needed which is read aloud by the teacher, also the books which one set of children have done with can be taken up by the next lot for they are not thumbed to pieces in three or four years: so they are not in the end much more expensive than those at present supplied, and are they not well worth it?

Some of you would think that some of the books are too difficult for the children to understand. Well, it is not necessary that they should on first reading understand every sentence, but they don't mind that, and they do get the drift of the work and come to realise the full meaning after a time of a bit which at first was hard, and occasional bits which they passed over do not interfere with their interest in or understanding of the story as a whole. Thus books become the children's delight and schooltime a pleasure and education a reality.

I append some of the answers to examination questions made by children in the Gloucestershire Schools.

Children of eight usually dictate their answers, but this little fellow in the —— School, writes his own: the handwriting is quite clear and the stops are right, but the spelling of the proper name has been a difficulty.

Question: Tell how Patroclus went to battle and was slain.

"Patroclus went to Achilles and said "Will you lend me
your armour"? Achilles said yes, then Patroclus started
off. Patroclus rode swiftly down the hill, when the Trojans saw him they began to run away thinking it was
Achilles. The two horses of Achilles were called "the
children of the West Wind." Proclus climbed up the
walls of Troy thrice, but Hector saw him, so he told his
charioteer to fling a big stone at him, but Proclus went
to fling a bit stone at Hector which missed him but the
stone hit the charioteer. Then Hector drew his spear
and sent it clean through the body of Proctius. Then
Proctoctolus fell to the ground. Then Prococlus was
carried to the ladies who washed him. Achilles wept over
the body and ordered a gold cup to lay Proctcoclus on.
Afterwards he held sports, wrestling, racing and chariot
racing. Ulysses was wrestling and racing."

55

This same boy of 8 having read the "Pilgrim's Progress"
tells how Christian got out of the Slough of Despond.

"Christian was on his way with Pliable to the wicket gate
until they fell into some mud. Christian had a burden
on his back. They began to sink lower and lower, at last
they began to struggle and Pliable got out of the mud,
so he ran away home leaving Christian their. Then a man
named Help came along and said "Didn't you see the
steps"? Christian said "I fell in." Then Help said give me
your hand, so he pulled Christian out and then Christian
started for the wicket gate."

This eight year old then writes a long account of a voyage round North Britain showing that he knows his geography well, for which he gets full marks; and in History he gives a short account of the sailing of the Mayflower and the founding of Plymouth.

He is not too young to take an intelligent interest in a picture by Carpaccio which he describes. He also draws a diagram showing the poles and the Equator, taking care to inform us that the axis and the Equator are not real lines but imaginary. His Natural History paper answers he dictates; and this is how he describes the arum.

> "The wild arum is not a perfect flower. It only has stamens and pistil, no petals. It grows in the hedges and we sometimes call it the cuckoo-pint or Ladies' finger. If a bee or other insect came along he would think it would be a nice place to lay its eggs, but when he gets there he finds it is hard, then he crawls downwards till he comes to the little hairs which he passes and through which he can't get back out. He is flying about the stamens and getting covered with dust then the sweet juice comes and then the hairs die and he is able to get out, the little stamens turn into red berries for the winter and are very poisonous."

It will be noticed that in common with most of our poets who generally speak of the singing bird as "she," though it is only the male who sings, our little friend gets the sex wrong and speaks all through of the little worker be as 'he.'

I will now give a specimen of the work of a ten year old who has done so well that she has won a "Free Place" in a Girls' High School. She is asked to give the life history of a Butterfly.

"The first form of the butterfly is the egg and the mother leaves the eggs in a place where when hatched they will have plenty of food when they are hatched; the next form is a grub. It crawls about on the cabbage leaves until it becomes so big that it has to rest for a time. When it has rested awhile it goes on eating greedily. It then climbs up to a mossy branch of a tree and makes a hillock; it then rests its two back legs in this hillock and splits its skin. The next skin grows hard, into a chrysilis and it sometimes stays like this all the winter. By and by this hard skin gets so thin and transparent that you can see the form of the butterfly inside. In the warm weather the nerves begin to send messages to the limbs to move about. It then begins to appear, and begins to move slowly and surely about. When it gets stronger it flies away to a flower or plant and most likely into a field to find a mate. It has very pretty wings but they have a lot of pollen on them and if you touch it much, it all comes off."

I have only selected some of the answers of the younger children, but I will give one specimen of the work of a boy of 13. It is called a Picture Study and the children were asked to describe the St. George by Carpaccio, so the boy writes as follows:

"This picture of St. George and the Dragon is a very horrible one it shows many skulls. The fight is taking place near the sea and the ground must have been very marshy. The Dragon is rushing at St. George and St. George is rushing at him: where they are fighting is the Dragon's Den. The head of the dragon is somewhat after the same as a bagger (badger) because its mouth is open and is showing its teeth just like a bagger. With all these skulls and parts of the bodies of men who have tried to slay the Dragon but have been unsuccessful we should think that St. George would have been trembling with fear, but he looks determined to overcome the dragon for the sake of Una, who is watching the combat afar off. In the background there is in the distance, a big castle and rocks with a lighthouse on the top. There is also on the sea a ship gliding through an archway and another on the side. The tail of the dragon is curled round a tree. This picture of St. George and the dragon was painted by Carpaccio."

The boy who wrote this is one of a pair of brothers who were, by the mistress of the little school to which they properly belonged, found to be somewhat unmanageable. Their father was serving in the army and the mother had to be out at work, so the home could do nothing for the boys. One, when he first came to a larger school, seemed to have no ideas at all and no interest in his work, but in spite of the handicap of his home and previous school life,

Miss Mason's method has appealed to him and the change in him is spoken of by his present teacher as little short of miraculous, and the result, in quite a short time, is that he has got the offer of a good situation and will, without doubt, go ahead and make his way.

The humanizing power of this teaching "by the humanities" shows itself not only in the way it appeals to and gets grip on children who have not responded to other methods, but even those children who are called "backward" and are distinctly deficient in power and intelligence have, after a term in which they have been slowly getting hold of the 57 meanings of things, been found to be able to take a pleasure in their lessons and eventually to put on a bright look and to take their part in narrating with the rest of the class. I have seen one instance of this and heard of several others. One girl I saw used to go about with her mouth open and a silly look on her face, and dull eyes, but after nine months she was looking alert and like other children, and this was brought about by seeing all round her the delight manifested by the others in their daily work. Happily the teachers in these schools do not try to cut all children to one pattern or to thrust information down their throats, but allow time and environment to produce effects slow but sure.

But to get back to the children's work. These examination papers are not set for the purpose of placing the writers in examination order but just to test them and make out whether they have assimilated what they have read in the term.

A girl of 10, amongst other very well written answers sends up the following in a literature paper. Being asked to "write a short résumé of the play 'Samson Agonistes' quoting any lines that interested you. What do you know of the author's early life?" she writes:

"Samson is a captive by the Philistines, and has his eyes put out. He has to work very hard, and, when he goes out he has chains on him. His friends come to see him, and among them is Manoah, his father. Manoah tries to comfort him by saying he will ransom him. Presently an officer comes in and asks Samson to let him see how great his strength is, and will he go with him. For the Philistines are going to offer a sacrifice to their god Dragon, for putting Samson into their hands. Samson went with the officer and leaves his friends to talk together. While they are talking they hear a great noise, and they know it is the Philistines cheering when they see Samson. After a short time they hear a crash, and a messenger comes running out. He tells them that Samson has pulled down the pillars in Gaza, and all the lords in the gallery fell down on him, and killed him. Manoah is very sad. John Milton was the author of Samson Agonistes. He was born on a bleak day in December. When he was quite young he went to school and also had a tutor. But he was not content with this, but used to stay up at night till eleven or twelve o'clock doing lessons. When he was older he went to Cambridge University. When he was grown up he went away for a month and when he came back he brought a wife with him. He went out a bachelor and came back a married man. His wife was a Royalist and he was a Puritan. After two or three days of feasting Mary (for that was her name) was left with her husband. But John did not have any more feasting and Mary did not like it. One day she asked her husband if she could have a month's holiday with her mother. John consented and Mary went. But a month passed and she did not return. Milton said he would never love her again and he would not have her at his house. He set to work harder than before. He had pupils and they thought him a strict master. The puritans were winning in the war and Mary, her brothers and sisters and her parents were turned out of their house. Mary's mother told her to go back to her husband but she was afraid. It was decided that Milton's friends and Mary's friends should meet and decide whether Mary should go back with Milton. One days John went to see a friend of his whom he visited often. He was waiting for him when the door was opened and who should come in but Mary. She fell down on her knees and asked for forgiveness. So Milton let her, and her family, her father and his pupils stay with him. But one day Mary died and left him with three motherless girls, the eldest of whom was only six. John was very sad and wrote a poem about her."

58

Pretty good for 10 years old!

In the next specimen a boy in Form III., aged 11, sends up a beautifully written set of answers in his Citizenship and Geography papers, with an account of Admiral Lord Nelson which shows how interesting biographies of great men are to school boys.

In the Citizenship Paper he is asked: "What is meant by (*a*) the Cabinet? (*b*) A Cabinet Minister? What are the duties of the Cabinet?" He writes as follows.

> "The Cabinet is a number of men who are elected from the winning party in Parliament. The leader of this party is acknowledged the Prime Minister. At present the Coalition is the Cabinet. The Cabinet is the link that joins the Government of the Country to the Parliament. The members each have a separate duty to perform. Each minister is appointed head of a department and he is responsible for its actions. The Chancellor of the Exchequer is head of the money affairs. The Home Office, the Admiralty, and the Food Office are all presided over by a Cabinet Minister. The duty of the Cabinet is to see to the affairs of the State. The army, navy, etc., are kept up by the Cabinet. The King takes his personal advice from the chief ministers. They have the power to "impeach" any minister."

Finally I add a page or two from a paper by a child of 13 on General History which seems to me to be something far above the work ever obtained in any but these schools

I have been describing, and to show how the reading of good literature and the acquaintance with the History of the Greeks open up avenues of undreamed interest which take hold of the imagination of these alert young minds in a truly surprising matter.

GENERAL HISTORY. FORM IV.
Give some account of the "picture gallery" we have in the Greek vases in the British Museum.

"On these vases were painted pictures of the life of the Hellenes or Greeks. On one is a picture of a baby reaching for a toy or crawling on the floor. This shows that the Greek children had toys as we have now. The painting of a Greek boy offering his toys to the gods, is on another vase. It shows the love borne by the boys to the beloved treasures of their childhood. One is offering his beloved "bounding ball." On other vases are pictures of maidens dancing, or making dresses called 'Chitons' which were very plain but beautiful. On the lid of a Grecian lady's toilet box is the picture of a wedding scene, in which the bride and bridegroom, attended by the usual crowd of spectators, are going home from the temple. On one vase is a picture of a typical Grecian feast. The youths are seen playing 'Cottobos' the name meaning sound of a successful hit. The 'Cottobos' is a construction resembling a modern lamp standard with a large saucer-shaped bowl half way down. At the top is a little

59

figure and poised upon that is a smaller bowl. The object of the game is to throw the dregs of wine on to the top bowl, so unbalancing it to make it fall with a clang on the lower bowl. On another set of vases are the physical exercises done by Grecian youths. One is seen throwing quoits and another throwing a seemingly heavy weight. Two youths engaged in a wrestling match struggle near the weight thrower. On the back of the most of these vases is a picture of Athene with sword, shield, and sometimes spear in her hands. Lastly, a beautiful, yet sad set of pictures are painted on the vases. The funeral and burial services of heroes of Greece. They shew the mourning and reverence with which the heroes were laid to rest. On one particular vase in this set is the supposed ferryman Charon bearing in his ferry-boat the souls of the dead over the river Styx; to rest evermore. To finish is a picture of a hero in the sports taking his prize, a vase of olive oil for his merit."

The language alone used in these specimen answers, and especially in the last, shows how immensely the children have profited by their reading both in grasp of their subjects and in language and style of expression; and surely the introduction of this method of instruction into elementary schools, this "education by the humanities" is just what "labour" stands most in need of.

For this education the first requirement is books and books of the right kind. "*Recorded language*," Sir E. Ray

Lankester* tells us, "preserved and handed on from generation to generation, is an ever-increasing gigantic inheritance.
... It is clear that knowledge of that which is, and primarily
knowledge of the Great Record must be the most important
factor in the future progress of Mankind."

---

* Nature, August 12th, 1920.

Acknowledgments

SPECIAL THANKS TO THE FOLLOWING PEOPLE:

- Terri Shown, without whose courage and connections this project would not have happened; Sharie Schnell for design consultation and encouragement; and Jenny Erb for showing up with the light at the end of the tunnel.
- JacQueline Roe, who helps keep Smidgen Press moving forward, and Janelle Mills who did the same for this project's transcription and proofreading.
- Faye Morrissey at The Armitt for being a liaison and helping sort out images/artefacts.
- Deani Van Pelt of the Charlotte Mason Institute, for helping dial in this project and providing both her first edition *Philosophy* and a hard copy of "Some Impressions."
- Art Middlekauff of Charlotte Mason Poetry (CMP), for accepting an eleventh-hour request

about permissions; thanks, too, to the CMP transcription team for their assistance with the "Two Educational Ideals" text.

- Carroll Smith, John Thorley, and Jack Beckman for insight into Miss Mason's circle of cocatalysts.

- The Smidgen Press Ambassador team, newsletter subscribers, and our connections online who kept checking in and sending feedback; some of you may never know the dark moments that a casual comment helped pull one of us through. Thank you.

- And to the families of our small-but-growing team at Smidgen Press. None of us could do this without you. We love you dearly.

598

We hope you have enjoyed this book.

Smidgen Press is a boutique publishing house that specializes in bringing classic books back into print. We aim to honor heritage texts (and their authors) while providing trustworthy perspectives, beautiful books, and accessible digital editions to today's readers.

**Your reviews help other readers
find us when you mention Smidgen Press.**
*We always appreciate social media tags:
@SmidgenPress.*

» Stay in touch: **SmidgenPress.com/newsletter**
» Request a book: **SmidgenPress.com/requests**
» Email our team: **hello@SmidgenPress.com**

You can also request to join our Ambassador team and get first news of all our releases and sales! That application is at SmidgenPress.com/ambassadors.

About the Charlotte Mason Institute

Charlotte Mason envisioned a relational education in a living environment filled with books, experiences, nature, and ideas, where the child is viewed as a person and the educator as one who cooperates with God.

The Charlotte Mason Institute aims to bring this kind of education to all students and teachers in every setting. We believe that children are born whole persons, with appetites for knowledge and strong powers of mind.

To this end, we integrate our scholarly research of Mason's original writings, curriculum, and other publications with current research on educational practice and child development and implement appropriate changes as new connections and discoveries are made.

The Charlotte Mason Institute began as an annual gathering of thoughtful school and home educators who desired to learn more about the theory and practice of Charlotte Mason's ideas for education. These annual gatherings remain our signature event.

Through the years we have also grown to gather educators around our curriculum, Alveary, a full curriculum (grades 1-12), which is used by thousands of students in homes and classrooms across North America and beyond. We also provide courses and certifications to give educators confidence in teaching with Mason's philosophy and publish resources to support educators worldwide. Visit cminst.org to learn more.

About Charlotte Mason Poetry

Charlotte Mason Poetry is a blog and podcast dedicated to promoting an authentic interpretation of Charlotte Mason's life work. Our international team of volunteers discover, research, transcribe, and interpret documents by Charlotte Mason and her early followers to make them easily accessible to a new generation.

Learn more about this labor of love at
CharlotteMasonPoetry.org.

Also available from Smidgen Press

The Fortunes of Philippa (Angela Brazil). A young girl must leave her ambassador father and the South American country she loves, and go to English boarding school. Described as the original boarding school author, Brazil paved the way for today's popular fictional schools, like the Harry Potter series. Smidgen Press, 2021.

Frankenstein (Mary W. Shelley). An all-new edition of the Gothic classic, with artwork never before published in the same edition as Mary Shelley's own introduction. Smidgen Press, 2021.

Mr. Hermit Miser and the Neighborly Pumpkin (Christine Noble Govan, illus. Anne Merriman Peck). Can a pumpkin vine bring together a grumpy group of neighbors? Children's picture book, Smidgen Press, 2022.

The Prisoner of Zenda (Anthony Hope). A doppelganger stand-in story: an English guest must pretend he's the Ruritanian king, so the true king's kidnapper won't win the crown ... and the girl. Smidgen Press, 2020.

The Real Fairy Folk (Louise Jamison). In the spirit of *Alice in Wonderland,* a young girl learns the secret of listening to the creatures around her. Filled with over 100 illustrations, 40+ new to this edition. Smidgen Press, 2022.

The Story of the Other Wise Man (Henry van Dyke). A wise man seeks to cross the desert, then looks until the end of his life for the foretold Messiah. This 8x10 full-color edition preserves the 8 color plates painted by illustrator J.R. Flanagan with over 40 other line art drawings throughout. Smidgen Press, 2021.

The Voyagers (Padraic Colum). Short stories, beginning with Plato's description of Atlantis, to Irish and Norse legends, and through the Age of Exploration. Smidgen Press, 2022.

Made in United States
North Haven, CT
14 February 2025

65855769R00383